Published by

7/22, Ansari Road, Darya Ganj, New Delhi-110002
Phones : +91-11-40775252, 40775214, 23273880, 23275880
Fax: +91-11-23285873
Web: www.atlanticbooks.com
E-mail: orders@atlanticbooks.com

Disclaimer

- The author and the publisher have taken every effort to the maximum of their skill, expertise and knowledge to provide correct material in the book. Even then if some mistakes persist in the content of the book, the publisher does not take responsibility for the same. The publisher shall have no liability to any person or entity with respect to any loss or damage caused, or alleged to have been caused directly or indirectly, by the information contained in this book.
- The author has fully tried to follow the copyright law. However, if any work is found to be similar, it is unintentional and the same should not be used as defamatory or to file legal suit against the author.
- If the readers find any mistakes, we shall be grateful to them for pointing out those to us so that these can be corrected in the next edition.
- All disputes are subject to the jurisdiction of Delhi courts only.

Printed & bound in India by Atlantic Print Services

Four Modern European Plays

Reflection and Discussion

Ghosts, The Good Woman of Setzuan, Waiting for Godot, Rhinoceros

C.G. Shyamala

ATLANTIC
PUBLISHERS & DISTRIBUTORS (P) LTD

Acknowledgements

The present book is the outcome of study and analyses of intricacies and nuances of dramatic art; however, the contribution of academicians and institutes needs to be acknowledged. I thank UGC-CEC for accepting my proposal for the Massive Open Online Course (MOOC) on Modern European Drama. This book will be a resource not only for students and academicians interested in drama but also in academic circles where drama is a part of the syllabus.

I recognise all Professors who whole-heartedly assented to examine and evaluate the work during every stage of its development. I thank Dr. Betsy Paul for the Foreword to this book after reading the entire work within a short span of time. Atlantic Publishers and Distributors Pvt. Ltd., New Delhi, deserves appreciation for the prompt response to get the book published.

My family owes my gratitude for supporting me in this endeavour. Dear God, without your Blessings, this work would not have materialised. I am indebted to you for your Grace that has helped me withstand several hurdles throughout my journey.

C.G. Shyamala

Foreword

David Mamet, the American playwright, calls theatre as "the place where people go to hear the truth." The truth of the theatre permeates into the spectators' soul and recreates them. This is why theatre is so relevant to humankind. Every generation has to look at its theatre anew and hear its truth. And, in the contemporary world of coexisting pluralities, to get a grasp of the different facets of available truth, it is essential to know theatre in all its variations, in its multiple locations. And, such theatres, if they are to be fully comprehended, do need scholarly interpretations and introductions to their contexts. Dr. C.G. Shyamala's book, *Four Modern European Plays: Reflection and Discussion,* serves this purpose of aiding the spectators to travel easily through the unfamiliar trajectory of alien cultures.

This book is remarkable in that it not only analyses individual plays, but also brings to life the age itself in its explication of the plays. And, it does not stop there, but goes on to bring alive the locality of the play, its nation, and its particular theoretical frame. Thus, though it is based on the undergraduate syllabus prepared by UGC-CEC for MOOC on modern European drama, this is not a mere exam oriented guide, but a handy reference book for both students and teachers. Its exhaustive explanations on the origin and development of drama contextualizing the four prescribed plays is noteworthy and is bound to be of great help to both scholars, teachers, and even the general public interested in modern European theatre.

The book starts with an introduction to drama as such, giving an apt entry to the domain of theatre, and slowly and easily leads the reader to world theatre. It is from there that the reader is introduced to European theatre and modern European plays. Before the in-depth analyses of each play, a detailed definition of its genre and its political and historical context make the understanding of the ensuing discussions very candid.

The referential nature of the book is further enhanced by the inclusion of a scholarly glossary explaining unfamiliar terms in simple phrases. Moreover, though the book contains exhaustive material in itself, it allows the readers to go beyond it by pointing to further avenues of knowledge accumulation through a long list of books for further reference and through web links to related sites.

Moreover, Dr. Shyamala's profound knowledge, sharp understanding, and comprehensive outlook make the reading of each analysis a delight. On a personal note, I too am deeply appreciative of Dr. Shyamala's hard work, sincerity, and absolute dedication to her profession which alone could bring about the materialization of such a book.

The book, I am sure, is a worthy addition to contemporary scholarship on European theatre and I recommend it as a ready reference to anyone who is interested in the topic.

Dr. Betsy Paul C.
HoD & Associate Professor of English,
St. Aloysius College, Elthuruth,
Thrissur, Kerala, India.

Introduction

Literature primarily evolves from the desire to narrate a story, to arrange words to suit a specific purpose, and to relate the narrative with a lived experience. Genres of literature that include prose, poetry, drama, fiction, and short stories are the product of the imaginative faculty that speak of the unique human capability of invention. The fundamental objective of literature is to entertain anybody with profound and delightful expressions. The creative writer employs his artistic skill, churns out reflections, and creates a masterpiece in art, and the reader or the audience ponders over thoughts behind the creation, frames opinions as well as relishes the ingenuity of the artist.

Dramatic art occupies a distinctive position in literature because its impact is immediately realised by the audience through its performance in front of them. During the performance of a play on a stage, drama depicts life experiences realistically. The characters interact with the audience and the enactment invites opinions and criticism from the audience. Drama is, therefore, realised in performance and as described by Robert Di Yanni, it is a "staged art" (quoted in Dukore, 867). As a literary art form, drama possesses the innate capacity to reflect, impersonate, re-create, and re-enact life on stage. The enactment is the characters' roles on stage, and drama is apprehended as an act of communication where there is constant interaction with incidents in life.

The enactment turns out to be an imitative impulse that expresses itself at three levels. First, as dramatic performances, where characters or the cast crew realise the identities that they have feigned to adopt their parts and assume various roles, personalities, and instances. Second, drama is employed to elaborate a dramatic composition that uses language and pantomime for stage presentations. Written compositions that may not be enacted are also categorised as drama and they are as much enjoyed when read as others are performed. Third, since drama is a literary art, it is a branch of literature that primarily incorporates character, dialogue, and stage-direction apart from other paraphernalia.

Drama has been defined by several scholars from the East and the West. Aristotle considers drama as an imitation of action and relates it to *mimesis*, which is a natural and instinctive process in human beings. Bertolt Brecht employs drama as a tool to expose the society and its circumstances, and initiate social and political vicissitudes. Martin Esslin elucidates the following definitions of drama:

1. Drama could be inferred as a display of the play instinct as in children who play the roles of mother and father.
2. Drama is something to be seen and it is organised as something to be seen.
3. Drama is a kind of enacted fiction, an art form, which is based on mimetic action.
4. Drama, in the arts is the most refined and elegant expression of thought, closest to the truth that is reality.
5. Drama is the most tangible art form that can recreate human condition and individual association.

George Bernard Shaw sees drama as a medium to express his discontentment with existing conditions in the society and the need for amelioration becomes pertinent. Barring the reformative zeal, drama also functions to portray human consciousness. The move from the periphery to the inner-core of human interactions and impulses unearths covert implications, patterns, or designs within the matrix of human predicaments, interactions, and involvements.

The origin of drama in other non-European countries is intimately related to religion and culture, and later manifests itself as the depiction of contemporaneity in expression. To mention about drama from the Eastern part of the world, i.e., from India, Bharata's *Natyashastra* is the foremost treatise on drama that includes dance, music, and spectacle. Dramas from other prominent Eastern countries such as China and Japan are connected with traditional forms of representation.

Drama is not just a representation of facts, events, episodes, or stories, but the depiction of human responses to changing circumstances. The candid and vivid expressions staged or written elicit responses from every conscious spectator or reader to comment, criticise, evaluate, associate, or oppose the range of emotions or facts presented without compromising the pleasure aspect or disputing the need to entertain.

Over years, the roles of the author, the reader, here the dramatist and the director have undergone ramifications that highlight the dynamism of this art form. Experimentation in techniques, range of themes, style of depiction, stage properties, and the function of dramatic art have significantly transformed the stage. The influence of media, especially films, has encroached upon audience; yet, several theatre companies have survived and stage artists have received critical acclaim.

At this juncture, it would be apposite to mention the scope and relevance of this book. The chapters in this book are e-materials prepared by me for the Massive Open Online Course (MOOC) on Modern European Drama at the Under-Graduate level as the Course Co-ordinator and Principal Investigator run under the aegis of UGC-CEC on SWAYAM platform in 2021. The book elaborately discusses four Modern European plays —*Ghosts*, *The Good Woman of Setzuan*, *Waiting for Godot* and *Rhinoceros,* mentioned in the syllabus for the development of MOOCs.

A comprehensive compilation, the chapters trace the origin and characteristic facets of drama and moves on to expatiate the contribution of dramatists from all over the world. The trajectory drawn provides a wide over-view of elements of drama, the implicit theories of drama formulated by dramatists, and elaborate discussion of four modern European plays. The intention of the author is to familiarise readers with the features of drama that are influenced by social, political, and economic upheavals at specific periods in the history of the world and associate changes with the creativity of the artist, here the dramatist.

Discussions in this endeavour delineate specific attributes of each play that have immensely influenced the literary arena at different phases of the development of dramatic art. The contributions of Henrik Ibsen, Bertolt Brecht, Samuel Beckett, and Eugene Ionesco revolutionised theatre to the extent that their influences reverberated the world for a significant period.

Postmodern drama owes its diversity of themes, marvellous or ludicrous stage properties, felicity of expression, and the artful use of artistic devices to these four dramatists that ushered a fresh look at drama and its artistic features by either denouncing earlier modes of presentation or announcing a novel mode of dramatic performance.

For the benefit of the academia and theatre enthusiasts, the book traces the evolution of drama, progresses to provide a comprehensive view of drama across continents, and provides in-depth analyses of the four plays under discussion. It is hoped that this attempt would encourage readers to comprehend nuances of drama and offer its unique perspectives.

References

Brockett, Oscar G. *The Essential Theatre*. Holt, Rinehart, and Winston, 1980.

Crown, Brian. *Studying Drama*. Longman, 1983.

Dukore, B.F. *Dramatic Theory and Criticism: Greeks to Grotowski*. Holt, Rinehart, and Winston, 1974.

Esslin, Martin. *An Anatomy of Drama*. Hill and Wang, 1976.

Scholes, R., and C.H. Klaus. *Elements of Drama*. Oxford UP, 1971.

Contents

Chapter 1

Introduction to Drama

The Origin of Drama

Scholars of literature and historians believe that roots of drama stem from primitive societies that used role-play to teach codes and behaviours of each society as a part of a strategy to survive. The knowledge of skills needed to hunt using appropriate weapons, and an awareness of rules stipulated for warfare are crucial to emerge as successful warriors or hunters. The re-enactment of hunts undertaken by a group of hunters among primitive groups dressed in animal hides probably gave rise to the first actors who used animal skin as costume to imitate an action and relate the story of their adventure to an audience, the non-hunters (Kramme 2).

Later, diverse methods could have been planned by the tribes to act out a successful hunt before the kill and this could have led to the use of magic to protect them from hidden dangers before they carried out the actual hunt. This repeated "magical theatre" (Kramme 2) performance, as mentioned could have been made a practice, a ritual and the chosen one, the spiritual leader among the tribe, who is the shaman mediated religious celebrations of the particular tribe. The oral repetition to teach basic concepts of customs in relation to nature could have transmitted mythical or historical stories in order to preserve race-memory of the tribe. Since the tribes remain in close contact with nature, change of seasons, cycles of the moon and the other natural phenomena are looked up with religious fervour and reverence. Ceremonies are conducted, performances, staged and sacrifices are made in veneration of unexplainable aspects of nature to appease it and escape its wrath.

Religion and theatre are intertwined and performances have become inevitable in religious observances. Questions of life, death, and the after-life have led to the belief in a power that necessitates societal rituals. In order to vouchsafe alleviation of negativity and ominous predictions, impersonation or disguise to act out ceremonies to placate gods have been carried out. Since then, civilisations have carried down this process of enactment over years to usher newer connotations with respect to changing conditions of the people over periods of time. Traditions and oral practices have assumed wider implications that relate to several customs that have been transmitted to successive generations in several societies.

Mere dramatic performances of rituals and impersonation of characters cannot suffice a theatrical presentation for the presence of the audience is important. Theatre entails a separate audience of spectators and the performance is considered entertainment. However, since the sixteenth century, the terms 'theatre' and 'drama' have been used synonymously to roughly denote the representation or enactment of a story by actors in front of an audience to serve as recreation. Drama is derived from the Greek word *dran*, which means "to do" or "to perform," which is closely related to the Greek word *drainein* that denotes "to be ready to do" and implies readiness to perform an action on stage (*The Shorter* 743).

The word theatre is derived from the Greek word *theatron*, which denotes a place to view and the space to enact dramatic performances. Actors and spectators involved have acted out myths, legends, and folklores to portray social conflicts, dilemmas, and struggles of the times. The theatre is also used as a tool for issuing social and political propagandas, presenting religious rituals and educating the masses.

It is generally believed that the art of drama in a Western form of literature is grounded in Greek literature. Some scholars attribute the origin of drama to Egypt where a theatrical performance carved on a stone tablet, probably four thousand years old recounts how a three-day pageant that that depicted actual battles, processions on boats and elaborate ceremonies, which narrated murder, dismemberment and resurrection of God Osiris was arranged and performed by Ikhernofret of Abydos. Music and dance associated with death and rejuvenation is represented in Egyptian hieroglyphs from around 2500 BCE and recorded by the Greek scholar Herodotus (c. 484-425/413 BCE). It is presumed that in China, around 5400 BCE, rituals and worship to the accompaniment of music and dance were enjoyed by Emperors. Written classical Chinese poetic drama is recorded from 700s BCE only. In ancient India, dances were linked with rituals and seasons.

Greek Drama: Beginnings

Early Greek drama is associated with celebration and performances as a part of festivals and celebrations for sowing and harvesting of crops to commemorate God Dionysus the Greek God of wine, winemaking, grape cultivation, fertility, ritual madness, theatre, and religious ecstasy who dies and is reborn every year. It is believed that to honour his death, a group of fifty men would dance around an altar on which a goat would later be sacrificed. He may have been worshiped as early as 1500-1100 BC by the Mycenean Greeks. His Roman name is Bacchus.

In his play *Acharnians* (425 BC), *Aristophanes* (450 BC-388 BC) ridicules the way in which God Dionysus is worshipped. As a prayer is recited, a family, which occupies a higher status in the society walks in procession and the daughter, a maiden carries the sacrifice for God. A slave carries a phallus and the father sings an indecorous song, while the wife watches from the roof of the house. At times, the procession would be held in tandem with the symbolic wedding of the wife of a prominent citizen of the state to the temple of Dionysus, who is represented as a long-bearded elderly man with two pint-sized horns on his forehead that mark his vitality; however, this later came to be associated with adultery. The crown made of ivy and the budding *thyrsus*, which is a ritual staff of narthex or fennel twisted and wound with ivy and vine leaves and covered with a pine cone indicates that God Dionysius is unaffected by change of seasons.

Virgins lead the procession of God Dionysius and Bacchantes, in the attire as satyrs (the goat-like deities) in goatskins or in garments with wine stains on them and faces smudged with dregs of wine accompany them closely. A few of the Bacchantes wear death masks and grave clothes to embody the dead. The goat-singers chant the tragic or ritualistic goat-songs called *tragos*, from which genre, tragedy would later arise. Dithyrambic songs and dances are presented at the temple and alongside, and young men known as *komos*, after participating in the procession on chariots would sing witty and bawdy songs called *comedies* and take part in comic phallic sport events.

Dionysus is believed to be the friend of Icarias, the King of Icara. The tyrant Pisistratus who ruled the city of Dionysus in 6th century BC is supposed to have organised a series of public festivals and one of these the "City of Dionysia" in honour of the God Dionysus is marked by music, song, dance, and poetry. Thespis (580-520 BC) of Icara left the audience dumbstruck when he leaped into a wooden cart and recited poetry as if he was the character whose lines were being read. He is accorded the first actor for his solo performance in verse without the chorus and the term *thespian* has been assigned to actors since then.

The dramatic contests, a part of the festival would extend up to five or six days. On the last three days, different playwrights would present four plays each on consecutive days. The first three plays are tragedies that form a trilogy that are related by theme, myth, or characters. The fourth, the satyr play is a lewd burlesque that is insignificant. Playwrights would contest fiercely to win the laurel wreath at the competition.

The beginning of Greek drama is found in a kind of ritual choral hymn, called a *dithyramb*, performed by men and boys in honour of God Dionysus. The narrative songs in the dithyramb verse by a single person, and later performed by a group called the chorus initiated dramatic art. As the Greek society developed and became more composite, the dithyramb began to lose its religious function and was replaced by a certain form of storytelling. Initially, characters were not assigned specific voices, but a second voice was introduced that paved the way for a song narrative that later came to be known as the dialogue.

Early Greek and Roman Plays

Greek Drama

The Greeks used complex stage devices to make the plays as effective as possible. Performances took place in the open on the sides of a hill surrounding a circular area called the *orchestra,* where the chorus danced. Wooden seats which were later replaced by stones were built to accommodate around 17000 spectators. A small area, the *skene* was built at the rear of the acting area where the actors changed masks and costumes. The *skene* was later built with stone and painted according to the scene to be depicted. The God-walk was situated on the roof of the *skene* where the actors depicting gods delivered their speeches.

A hoist that resembled a crane, the *machina* was mobile enough to enable actors to appear as if they were flying and lower them from the roof of the *skene.* The character that appeared at the *machina* was usually represented as the God from Mount Olympus who came down to earth to intervene in the play and resolve conflicts. The use of this feature is known as *deus ex machina*, translated as God from the machine. This term is used even in contemporary times to indicate the use of an artificial plot device in a play to resolve issues.

The actors were limited in number and a tragic actor distinguished himself by wearing masks, padded costumes and thick-soled, high-heeled laced shoes called "buskins" or "cothurnus". In contrast, the comic actor wore light-weight, low shoes called "socks". Masks prevented actors from changing expression, hence actors' expressions remained consistent throughout the performance. Since the portion allotted to the speaking place was insignificant, the depiction of elaborate scenes and magnificent stage pictures was improbable. Similarly, the distance of actors from spectators made it impossible to dramatise detailed gestures. The language employed in dramas was rhetorical and not colloquial or conversational. The presence of the chorus with its solemn dancing and singing imparted a lyrical and theatrical quality to the performances on the stage.

The chorus that played an immense role in the early Greek plays functioned primarily to elaborate the situation, make the audience aware of happenings and comment on established norms to engage with tactors. However, the role of the chorus was taken over by actors in later plays. Some modern plays that employ the chorus are the tragic play *Antigone* (1944) by the French dramatist John Anouilh (1910-87), the stage manager in the metatheatrical three-act play *Our Town* (1938) by the American playwright Thornton Wilder (1897-1975) and El Gallo in the musical theatre *The Fantasticks* (1960) with music by the American composer Harvey Schmidt and lyrics by the American lyricist Tom Jones.

The Greek theatre projected clashes between destiny and human ambition. The Greek tragedies elucidated the futility of human efforts to challenge fate. Aeschylus (525-456 BC), Sophocles (496-406 BC) and Euripides (485-406 BC) were the greatest writers of Greek tragedy who wrote in the 4th and 5th centuries BC. Aeschylus contributed around ninety plays out of which only seven have been preserved. He is referred by many critics as the father of tragedy. Aeschylus is noted for his majestic language and unique style of presentation. His only surviving Greek trilogy, *The Oresteia* (5th century BC) is the story of the murder of Agamemnon, the revenge taken by his children and the punishment and subsequent acquittal of his son. The play involves the murder of Agamemnon by Clytemnestra, the murder of Clytemnestra by Orestes, the trial of Orestes, the end of the curse on the House of Atreus and the pacification of the Erinyes.

Sophocles is recognised for his well-crafted plays, brilliant plot-structure and majestic language that together beautify and unify his works. His belief in the divine qualities that human beings possess allowing them to struggle against fate brings about an amazing balance between the intervention of Gods in affairs of men and man's struggle against fate portrayed in his plays, and hence his characters emerge the strongest ever to walk on the stage in the effort to put up with the trials and tribulations of life. His *Oedipus Rex* (429 BC) stands as one of the most powerful and exceptional examples of dramatic irony that Aristotle described it as the ideal tragedy. *Antigone* (~441 BC), a great tragedy written by Sophocles describes the efforts of Antigone to bury her brother Polynices who is denied a proper burial by their uncle Creon for murdering Eteocles, their sibling. She is left to die in a cave for disobeying Creon and only when his world crumbles, does Creon realise the futility of pride and punishment that are against laws of Gods.

Euripides depicts the imbroglios in people's lives as a result of the cataclysms that arise in human relationships, and his plays succinctly reveal pathos, sorrow, and compassion of human ties and familial bonds. Of the 92 plays written by him, 17 tragedies and one satyr play subsist. *The Trojan Women*, first presented at the City Dionysia of 415 BC and the two other unconnected tragedies *Alexandros* and *Palamedes*, and the comedic satyr play *Sisyphos* are lost to antiquity. *Medea* (431 BC) is the tragedy of a woman who seeks revenge on her husband to the extent of killing her sons in order to grieve him. *Medea* and *Antigone* are unparalleled poignant depictions of women in literature.

Classical Greek comedy is divided into three periods—old, middle, and new. The exceptional Greek author of the comedy of the old period is Aristophanes whose 11 out of the 40 plays are preserved. An accomplished satirist and social critic, he mocked the leaders of Athens and their gods. Three of his best known plays are *The Frogs* (405 BC), a written contest between Aeschylus and Euripides in Hades, judged by Dionysus himself; *The Clouds* (423 BC), a travesty on Socrates and Greek education; and *Lysistrata* (411 BC), a derisive indictment on war. His first nine plays, known for wild comic fantasy are labelled Old Comedy. His last two plays are categorised as Middle Comedy for their quiet and coherent nature.

Antiphanes (408 to 334 BCE), the comic poet of Athens wrote during the middle period. His plays concentrate on myths that do not feature persons of national importance and professional expertise. Other plays by him focus on intrigues of individual lives. Menander (342/41-290 BC), the most influential of the new period wrote the notable comedies *Dyskolos* (317-316 BC) and *Samia* (315 BC), and among hundred scripts he had written only one of the scripts, *Dyskolos* survives. His comedies are centred on amorous manoeuvers of young lovers and though he is not an accomplished writer, he greatly influenced the Roman comedy writers Plautus and Terence, who later motivated the English writers of the Middle Ages.

Roman Drama

While most Roman plays were adaptations of the Greek ones, comic representations of daily life were interspersed with comedy and the development of plot or character was neglected. The Roman playwright of the Old Latin period Plautus (254-184 BC) and the Roman African playwright Terence (195/185-159? BC) were the two prominent writers of Roman comedy. There weren't any permanent theatres and a temporary stage was erected when a presentation was required. It was only after two hundred years that amphitheatres, large circular arenas surrounded by tiers of seats were built. During the beginning of the 1st century AD, Seneca (4 BC-AD 65) the Roman Stoic philosopher, statesman, and dramatist emerged one of the prominent writers of tragedy. Ten plays are endorsed to Seneca and he is popular for the plays *Medea* (50 BC), *Phaedra* (~54 AD), *Thyestes, Oedipus*, and *Agamemnon* (1 AD), that serve as the impetus for the type of drama known as Revenge Tragedy, starting with Thomas Kyd's *The Spanish Tragedy* and extending into the Jacobean era.

Drama in Medieval Europe

There were no permanent theatres in England and a partial manuscript of the Western European liturgical drama of the 10th century is the only evidence of performance in the Middle Ages. The liturgical drama was performed by monks on Easter. These plays were in the form of a question-and-answer song in Latin and the performers were primarily priests and choir boys, but nuns were allowed to participate only after a brief period. The Saint plays or Miracle plays and Mystery plays became popular forms of drama of the church. While the Saint plays focussed on legends of saints, the Mystery plays were based on biblical history. Some Mystery plays originating from the towns such as Chester, York, and Coventry still subsist and are regularly performed. The Passion Play, which directs to the last week of Christ's life is a celebrated liturgical drama performed for the Easter service. The Passion Play is still performed in Europe at Oberammergau, Germany by citizens of the Bavarian village, where it was first performed in 1634 and is being recreated every ten years since 1760.

The early Saint plays and Mystery plays were performed in churches on raised platforms called mansions that represented biblical settings such as Heaven, Hell, and the Sea of Galilee. When these dramas gained popularity, the performances were shifted to the town square where mansions were built in a straight line. Evidences prove that players went around several places to depict lives of saints and the life of Christ using these temporary and movable settings.

Theatre on the Streets

By the late 14th century, craft guilds were formed by groups of players and they overtook the presentation of plays in England. The performances by guilds were held during the festival of Corpus Christi, which had been officially inaugurated in AD 1311. While most of the members of guilds were associated with the church, they were secular in nature and actors spoke in English so that all people could understand religious depictions. Liturgical plays were presented by guilds on pageant wagons, the stages on wheels. These wagons comprised of two levels, the upper level, which was the platform stage and the lower one, the dressing room. Each guild had its pageant wagon decorated depending on the play to be enacted in the cycle, which was a series of short plays that illustrated the conscientious description of the creation of the world by God until Doomsday. Performances staged included those of Adam and Even in the Garden of Eden, Moses receiving the Ten Commandments or the resurrection of Christ.

Secular Dramas, Morality Plays and Moral Interludes

Secular dramas called folk dramas developed simultaneously with liturgical productions. Folk plays were popular performances conducted outdoors during planting and harvest times and on Christmas. Apart from innumerable lively, humorous and commonplace incidents staged by the folk group, the most important performance is Robin Hood plays (c. 1300) with the hero robbing the rich and passing on the booty to the poor.

Morality plays replaced folk dramas in the 15th century. They were didactic in nature and preached differences between moral values and sin in the context of religion. These plays were peculiar in that they were allegorical representations that employed symbolic characters that corresponded to abstract personae. Poverty, Knowledge, Ignorance, Austerity, Pride, Honesty, Truth, Vices and Virtues, the Seven Deadly Sins, the Good and the Evil surfaced as characters that debated and struggled against each other so that the audience recognised and differentiated one form the other, chastised themselves and led a fruitful life. *Everyman* is the only Morality play that is still being performed.

Since ecclesiastics disapproved Morality plays of the conventional liturgical drama, these plays were replaced by the Moral Interludes in the early 16th century. The Moral Interludes were shorter in length than the traditional Morality plays and they incorporated several humorous characters and incidents. John Heywood's (1497-1580) farcical interlude *The Four P's* (1520-22) is quite popular. A Pardoner, a Pedlar, a Palmer and a [Pothecary] are the characters in the play that engage in humorous conversation. The other interlude by Heywood is *The Play of the Weather* (1533). Later, the secular dramatists, under the patronage of the nobility formed the initial acting companies. Several varieties of drama such as the chronicle plays, productions based on historical events, masques and inventive displays were written and performed under the influence of patrons and some of the presentations even lionised the nobility.

Conclusion

The origin and evolution of drama in the earlier phase is a mere act of imitation in the primitive form during prehistoric times with the only evidences being rudiments of engravings. The growth and development of civilisations necessitated several modes of expression of thoughts and emotions. In tune with changes in nature, the early societies discovered drama or enactments to communicate, celebrate and pay obeisance to their deities. The Greek drama began initially with festivities for God Dionysius that included songs, spectacles, dance, and dialogues of a particular nature. Thespis is recognised the first actor and with his performance, a novel mode of expression arose. To the view of thousands of spectators, dramatists in Greece staged their plays in the amphitheatre and included various dramatic devices to enhance artistic and win accolades.

Aeschylus, Sophocles and Euripides, Aristophanes, Antiphanes and Menander to name a few later prominent Greek dramatists influenced the Roman writers Terence and Plautus with their tragedies and comedies that had profound influence on the European stage. Beginning with the Miracle and Mystery plays by the Church, in Latin, the English drama gradually became secular and dealt with moral issues, principles to be followed in life and social commitments to be made, using English as the medium of instruction. Under patrons, the English drama opened new vistas for exposition, commentary and commendation.

Glossary

strategy	: scheme, plan or tactic
stipulated	: specified or required
fervour	: zeal or enthusiasm
intertwined	: linked or connected
connotation	: implication or inference
dilemma	: predicament or quandary
propaganda	: publicity
attribute	: feature or trait
rejuvenation	: rebirth or revival
phallus	: image or representation of the male sexual organ
Bacchantes (Roman)	: a priest or priestess or a follower of God Bacchus
pintsized	: tiny or minute
indecorous	: undignified or impolite
in tandem with	: happening at the same time
lewd	: vulgar or bawdy
burlesque	: parody or imitation
dismemberment	: mutilation or maiming

resurrection : rebirth or restoration
amorous : passionate or loving
lionise : glorify or praise

References

Abrams, M.H. and Geoffrey Galt Harpham. *A Glossary of Literary Terms*. 11th ed. Cengage Learning, 2015.

Albert, Edward. *History of English Literature*. 5th ed. Oxford UP, 1979.

Kramme, Michael. *Theatre through the Ages*. Mark Twain Media Inc. Publishers, 1996.

Prasad, B. *A Background to the Study of English Literature*. Macmillan, 2009.

Ridgeway, William. *The Origin of Tragedy: With Special Reference to the Greek Tragedians*. Blom, 1966.

The Shorter Oxford English Dictionary. 6th ed., vol. 1. Oxford UP, 2007.

Webster, T.B.L. *The Greek Chorus*. Methuen, 1970.

Wise, Jennifer. *Dionysus Writes*. Cornell, 1998.

https://www.britannica.com/art/dramatic-literature/Drama-in-Western-cultures

https://www.ancient.eu/Greek_Theatre/

https://www.britannica.com/art/Western-theatre/Ancient-Greece

http://www.ancientathens.org/

http://elibrary.bsu.az/books_400/N_159.pdf

https://theodora.com/encyclopedia/d/drama.html

Chapter 2

Nuances of Dramatic Art and Theatrical Performances

Introduction

Drama is the confluence of several facets that relate to and contribute to the advancement and expansion of the genre to adapt to the demands of contemporary times. The major elements of drama are categorised into three important groups, namely the literary, technical, and performance. While plot, character, script, setting, monologue and dialogue relate to the literary factor, the scenery, costumes, sound, music and makeup constitute technical elements. Acting, speaking, and non-verbal expressions are characterised as components of performance. Each constituent undergoes modifications in accordance with socio-economic and political conditions, cultural changes, religious beliefs and the response of the audience of the particular epoch. Essential elements of drama specifically discussed in this chapter are setting, plot, character, structure, style, theme, audience, and dialogue. The other parameters would be examined in the course of chapters.

Components of Drama

Setting

The setting of the drama provides adequate information about the play and its connotations, changes in the deportment of characters and predicts their actions. This denotes that a suitable environment is created by the dramatist to inform about the context in which the main action of the story is situated. Since the dramatist works in a restricted space with minimal equipment, settings on the stage have to be arranged in ways that would enable the audience to experience the play completely. Time, place, and the social environment taken together account for the dramatic action that sets the drama in motion. The setting provides the atmosphere to the background of the play. The use of lighting, props, and scenery supplement the performance of the play and the dramatic text is a verbal input into the description of the setting of the play.

The plays of the early twentieth century by Henrik Ibsen, George Bernard Shaw, and Anton Chekov are realistic in nature and hence they require elaborate stage properties for their lively enactment in a realistic environment. In contrast, the plays of later twentieth century of Samuel Beckett and Harold Pinter among the other Absurd dramatists do not require extensive stage arrangements because they overtly flout the conventions of drama. Time is an important factor and many contemporary plays that make use of non-realistic settings discard time and place. Tom Stoppard's play *Rosencrantz and Guildenstern are Dead* (1966) and *Top Girls* (1982) by Caryl Churchill are developed in a background that sets time apart. Bertolt Brecht's *Mother Courage* (1939) and Churchill's *Top Girls* use myths in relation to society. In these dramas, the stage is built to effect the desired response from the audience, which is quite challenging.

Plot

A plot in drama designates the plan, scheme or arrangement of events. The plot accounts for the integrity, unity, and coherence of the play to enable the audience to comprehend the events in the play and associate the incidents in a logical manner. Incidents and characters are organised so as to induce curiosity and suspense in the spectators and enable them to delineate the specifics of characterisation that are related to the plot. Aristotle, in his *Poetics* (335 BC) remarks that the plot is the "soul of tragedy". Dramatic plot, according to Aristotle comprises exposition, conflict, rising action and climax followed by a falling action and resolution. A plot involves a conflict that could be external, between the major character and the others in the play or internal that takes place in the mind of the protagonist or it could include both. Aristotle mentions that the plot must be well-constructed with a definite beginning, middle, and an end and its action must be cohesive. Aristotle divides plots into two—the simple and the complex ones. A simple plot is one in which the action is simple and continuous and the change of fortune of the character takes place without the reversal of the situation and recognition. In a complex plot, conversely, the change of fortune of the character is associated with a reversal of the situation or recognition or by both.

Aristotle identifies two types of plots—the unified plot and the episodic plot. The unified plot is the conventional form that based on causality where one event causes another to happen. The play starts from the beginning, moves on to the middle, where the incidents take place as a consequence of what happened initially and culminates when the conflicts are resolved in the end, which is definite. The removal of any one incident would affect the organic structure or coherence of the play. In contrast, the episodic plot is devoid of the causal relationship between the incidents and the removal of any aspect of the plot would not disturb the unity of the play. Though Aristotle disapproved the episodic plot, modern dramatists resort to this strategy.

The subplot or underplot is a secondary line of action in a drama that usually contrasts with or reinforces the main plot. In the modern Absurd plays, the plot remains static without any appreciable development. In some plays of the later twentieth century, plots are circular in the sense that the play ends where it has begun as in Samuel Beckett's *Waiting for Godot* or begins where it ended as in Beckett's *Endgame*. Contemporary drama usually rejects a clearly demarcated plot and prefers the disjointed and fragmentary one.

Character

Characters are indispensable to drama. Each character in a play is distinct in every aspect of physical, social, economic background and role in the play. The plot of the play centers around the character and the dramatic action of the play is led by the characters. The process of developing a character is called characterisation. The character is revealed through the dialogue and through actions of the actor. In Greek drama, the best actor in the lead role is called the protagonist and the deuteragonist supports the hero throughout the narrative. The antagonist is the rival who sets forth the conflict in the play.

In *Aspects of the Novel* (1927), E.M. Forster classifies characters into flat and round depending on the pattern of their behaviour. A flat character is built around a single idea or quality that remains unchanged over the course of the narrative. Benvolio, in Shakespeare's *Romeo and Juliet* is a flat character who remains composed and balanced in temperament and strives to maintain peace between the discordant families. Queen Gertrude, in Shakespeare's *Hamlet* is a weak character who fails to recognise Hamlet's animosity for Claudius. She is an example of a flat character that is unaware of Claudius' intrigues to usurp his brother's throne and machinations to trap her in marriage. Hamlet, on the other hand, is a round character, mysterious, enigmatic, reserved, contemplative, but prone to procrastination, which is his tragic flaw. A round character is complex and capable of growth and change in the course of the narrative.

A foil is a character that exhibits similar traits or opposite ones to a greater or lesser degree than the main character. A confidant (male) is someone in whom the central character confides in, and reveals his thoughts, emotions, and intentions, which could be caught only by the audience, and in the process unfolds his or her personality. For instance, Horatio is the confidant of Hamlet in Shakespeare's *Hamlet* (feminine-confidante).

Stock characters that frequently appear in plays are differentiated from the other characters by their flatness. So, they are parodied, criticised and considered clichéd depictions. Stock characters are the buffoon, bawdy soldiers, a hag, the miserly father, a mad scientist, an outlaw, a superhero and so on. A raisonneur is a character who functions as the spokesperson of the playwright and conveys certain truths underlined in the plot to the audience, which is similar to the chorus in ancient Greek drama. The Fool in Shakespeare's *King Lear* is the perfect example of a raisonneur who speaks with clarity and reason to make Lear recognise and realise his mistakes.

Structure

The dramatic structure refers to the organisation of events that includes the selection and order of scenes in a play. Aristotle, in *Poetics*, mentions that the plot must be well-structured and organic with a proper beginning, middle, and an end. He mentions: "A whole is what has a beginning and middle and end". The plot must be complete in the sense that it should be logical and incidents should be so perfectly bound together by the plot that each action would indelibly lead to the other. The Roman classicist critic Horace (65 BC-8 BC) proposes the five-act structure for a play in his *Ars Poetica* (19 BC) and claims that the length of a play should neither be too short nor exceed five acts.

In 1863, the German playwright Gustav Freytag advocated the five-act dramatic structure named Freytag's Pyramid that is constructed on:

(i) Exposition (introduction part or the initial incident)
(ii) Rising action (rise or growth of action that leads to the crisis)
(iii) Climax (the crisis)
(iv) Falling action (return or fall or resolution) and
(v) Catastrophe (denouement, resolution, or revelation) (Chandler 100).

Modern and postmodern plays deviate from this model and the dramatist experiments with the structure of the play.

Dramas of the twentieth-century plays are classified as climactic, episodic, and circular. The plays are said to be climactic in structure if the action takes place in a short period of time, has a fewer number of characters, scenes, and events, and a tightly-constructed plot without any loosely knit elements that would fit comfortably into the label of a well-made play; standing examples are plays of Henrik Ibsen, August Strindberg, and Arthur Miller.

Plays with the episodic structure consist of numerous episodes that extend over longer periods of time and take place in different locales. Episodic drama abounds in characters and includes parallel plots and subplots that grow in tandem with the main plot. Shorter scenes often intervene longer ones and the comic and the serious scenes surface in a particular pattern. Plays of Shakespeare and Christopher Marlowe are characterised episodic in structure.

The plays of the Theatre of the Absurd maintain a circular structure in the sense that they do not progress in a linear manner and the action fails to move forward in the play, thereby the play ends where it begins or vice-versa. Plays of Samuel Beckett, Eugene Ionesco and Harold Pinter fall into this category.

Style

Every playwright has a unique way of presentation of dialogues and treatment of stage devises and costumes. The specific period of time, nationality, affinity to a particular ideology and personal likes and dislikes account for divergent modes of presentation on stage beginning from Realism, Naturalism and moving on to Symbolism, Expressionism and so on. While the realistic style portrays a convincing imitation of real life situations and tries to create an illusion of reality on the stage with the use of language that seems to be as close as possible to real life, the naturalistic plays attempt to present a part of life in all its harsh reality and approach the actual situation more precisely than the realist.

The Symbolist movement that originated in France in the latter half of the 19th century, was interested in the spiritual realm of man's being, his dreams, fears, and fantasies. Drama picturised moods, suggestions, and evocations by deploying stylised language, dislocating time sequence, utilising masked characters, distorting stage sets and including special lights and sound effects. By the method of indirection, and the use of symbols from religious and arcane customs and rituals, dramatists imbued the stage with awe and wonder that shook the spectators. The Expressionistic style of drama, with its origin in Germany in the beginning of the 20th century, dwelt into man's subconscious existence through innovations in language, structure of the play, and theatrical effects.

Theme

Theme, the pivotal and unifying aspect of the plot is the predominant idea that a play conveys and relates to all major specifics of the story. It is usually implied, but gets revealed as the play progresses. Theme suggests the playwright's views expressed through the storyline, stated by a character or formed from the interplay of the plot, character, and dialogue. While ancient dramatists borrowed incidents from epics, myths, and histories as themes for their plays, later dramatists focused on social issues, complexities in human relationships, and the predicament of mankind to point out to a few.

Audience

Theatre infuses pleasure and provides aesthetic gratification that depends on the views of the audience. Aristotle believed that the enactment of a tragedy purged negative feelings. The audience of ancient Greek drama were extremely influential that they often interrupted the play by mocking the actors, yelling or throwing items if they disliked the performance. The Elizabethan spectators comprised of people from all classes of the society, so Shakespeare wrote his plays to entertain all the classes of people. While noblemen sat in boxes in playhouses, and ladies in galleries, the groundlings occupied the pit. The ordinary folk engaged in all forms of revelry even during the performance. The audience loved the supernatural element, spectacles and appreciated depictions of battles and murders.

Bertolt Brecht, through his concept of epic theatre visualised the contemplative audience that responded to the shattered illusions of reality on stage. The audience of contemporary theatre partakes of the extraordinary experiences as little effort is made to convey a particular message during a performance because the plot is absent and the theatre is open to interpretations. Moreover, Street and Ritualistic theaters engage the audience in performances.

Dialogue

Language in drama is expressed in the form of monologue, aside, soliloquy, and dialogues. Through dialogues, the nature of the character and the association with others are revealed. The drama progresses through the dialogue by providing necessary exposition of the past events, exposing complexities in relationship, and delving into the tensions and conflicts that are incorporated in the plot. Meaning may often be communicated through indirections. The unspoken thought or motivation underlying a dialogue is referred to as the subtext and considered the "inner essence" of drama by the Russian dramatist Konstantin Stanislavski.

Casual conversation is the most natural way in which speakers exchange their thoughts. However, a dialogue in a drama is a speech devised by the playwright for the characters that is specific within the canvas of the play. The dialogue exposes the dramatic situation and the relationship of the characters to each other, the attitudes, conflicts and their connections within the fictional world. A dialogue is more complex than a casual conversation because the entire presentation is not merely an interaction between the audience and the drama, but also a form of communication between the playwright and the audience. While the Symbolist and Expressionist theaters use symbols and special theatrical effects respectively, the Theatre of the Absurd explores the use of colours to experiment with non-standard forms of speech, stammer, hesitations, silences, pauses as newer forms of expressions.

Types of Drama

Tragedy

Representations that project serious actions that are catastrophic in the end for the protagonist is termed tragedy. Greek tragedy is one of the earliest forms of drama and Aristotle has outlined the characteristic features of the tragedy and the tragic hero in *Poetics*. The earliest known tragedies have been written by Aeschylus, Sophocles, Euripides, and the Roman dramatist Seneca. In English literature, the Elizabethan period witnessed the production of the finest works of English tragedy by dramatists Christopher Marlowe, William Shakespeare, and John Webster. The first English tragedy is *Gorboduc* (1562) written by the English playwrights Thomas Norton (1532-84) and Thomas Sackville (1536-1608). With the passage of time, considerable changes in the characteristics of tragedy have contributed to the expansion of this mode of presentation which shall be discussed in sections that follow.

Classical Greek Tragedy

Features

- The plot is chosen from Greek mythology, which is well known to all citizens so that they can easily follow the main storyline of the play.
- Characters wear padded costumes, heels and large masks to make themselves visible to the huge audience. There is no scope for any quick changes in disposition.
- Dialogue is rhetorical and not conversational in nature. Scenes of battles are narrated.
- The chorus is a group of men who wear masks and sing and dance and make comments on the moral, social, and religious attitudes of the age.
- The dramatist has to follow unities of time, place, and action.
- Aristotle defines tragedy as "the imitation of an action that is serious and also, as having magnitude, complete in itself...incorporating incidents arousing pity and fear, wherewith to accomplish the catharsis of such emotions." The tragic hero could be one who is of noble birth or high rank. He should be virtuous, but makes an error in judgement (*hamartia*), which is responsible for the reversal of his fortunes (*peripeteia*). This is accompanied by the moment when a crucial truth is discovered or some insight is gained by the protagonist (*anagnorisis*). The ultimate effect of the resolution of tragic drama on the audience is purgation of emotional tensions (*catharsis*). Tragedy, by arousing emotions in people, has a therapeutic effect as cleansing of emotions takes place.
- Aeschylus' *Oresteseia* trilogy; Euripides' *Medea*; and Sophocles' *Oedipus the King* (429 BC) are some of the best surviving Greek tragedies.

Senecan or Revenge Tragedy

The name is derived from the type of drama written and popularised by the Roman dramatist Seneca (4 BC-AD 65), whose plays are marked by bloodshed and the main theme is retribution with violence against reprobates. Senecan tragedies feature bloody revenge and the deployment of supernatural elements. Seneca's plays influenced Elizabethan tragedies and French Neoclassical tragedies.

Features

- Revenge is the predominant theme and a morally upright protagonist is pitted against scheming antagonists who are criminals.
- Oratorical and fervent speeches are made and Stichomythia, the precipitous exchange of dialogue that gives a sense of argument is employed.
- Murder, torture and other horrific incidents of violence are either reported or depicted by dumb show. Any form of disguise, murder, and supernatural interferences are inimitable to the progress of the drama.
- *The Spanish Tragedy* (1587) by Thomas Kyd (1558-94) is an apt example of the revenge tradition in English drama. The subject is murder and the hunt for revenge includes sensational incidents, suicide, play-within-the-play and a gruesome end with bloodshed on the stage. Christopher Marlowe's *The Jew of Malta* (1592) also belongs to this mode.
- William Shakespeare's *Titus Andronicus* (1590) and *Hamlet* (1603); and the horror plays by John Webster, *The Duchess of Malfi* and *The White Devil* (1612-13) are exemplars of this form.

Great Tragedies of William Shakespeare

Hamlet (1601), *Othello* (1603), *King Lear* (1605), and *Macbeth* (1606) are the Great Tragedies.

Features

- Protagonists are persons of high rank, but they move among persons of all classes of the society.
- Main characters suffer from a tragic flaw in their character that leads to their downfall. As Bradley

observes, "character is destiny". Hamlet's downfall is due to procrastination; Othello's, suspicion; King Lear's, excessive love for his daughters; and Macbeth's, vaulting ambition.

- Dialogues rendered by main characters are poetical, although it lapses to the colloquial and the familiar when dialogues are uttered by characters of lower rank.
- Unities of time and place are completely discarded and the unity of action rests on the ingenuity of the dramatist to interweave the action with the main plot and subplots.
- Violence and action predominate; the only exception is *Hamlet.*
- Comic relief, which is the inclusion of humorous scenes to relieve the intensity of tragic emotions and movements is included.

Neoclassical Tragedy

In the 16th century, Italian and French dramatists modified the ancient Greek and the Senecan models and established a form of Neoclassical tragedy that differed from earlier ones.

Features

- Chief characters are noblemen or persons of higher rank in the society.
- Importance is given to the relationship of the hero and the heroine.
- The chorus is replaced by the confidant who has little to do in the action of the play except listen to confessions of the protagonist and offer sympathy.
- The playwright exposes the daily life of individuals in an elevated and poetic language.
- French playwrights Pierre Corneille's *Medée* (1635) and *Le Cid* (1636); and Jean Racine's *Andro Maqaue* (1667) and *Phedre* (1677) are noted examples of Neoclassical tragedy.

Heroic Tragedy

Influenced by the French Neoclassical drama of Pierre Corneille, plays were written during the Restoration period. Sir William Davenant (1606-68) established this kind of drama in England. John Dryden (1631-1700) is regarded as the best exponent of this form.

Features

- The conflict between love on the one hand and duty on the other is the main subject of a heroic tragedy. Cataclysmic events such as war are depicted and they affect an entire nation. The theme of the heroic tragedy is of immense significance and the emotions presented are intense and gripping.
- The scale of the tragedy is usually set in exotic and faraway lands such as Mexico or India.
- The hero of this type of tragedy possesses great strength and moral virtues and the heroine is exceptionally beautiful and virtuous.
- These characters are torn between their passionate love and their duty towards the country or family.
- The language used is melodramatic and verbose.
- These tragedies are written in closed rhyming pairs of iambic pentameter lines. Due to its association with the heroic tragedy, this verse form is also known as heroic verse or heroic couplet.
- John Dryden's *The Conquest of Granada* (1670), *Love Triumphant* (1694), and *All for Love* (1677) are recognised examples of the heroic tragedy. George Villers, the Duke of Buckingham ridiculed the conventions of the heroic drama in his play *The Rehearsal* (1671).

Domestic Tragedy

This subgenre concentrates on the problems faced by the middle or lower class society. The English dramatist George Lillo's *The London Merchant* (1731) and the German poet and dramatist Christian Friedrich Hebbel's *Maria Magdalena* (1844) are examples of a domestic tragedy. The term "Domestic tragedy" is also used to describe the plays of the Norwegian playwright Henrik Ibsen.

Features

- Written in prose, plays are serious in tone and they depict realistic events.
- Devoid of triviality, concerns and everyday problems of middle or lower classes of the society are explicitly portrayed. Plays are centered around domestic matters, and personal grievances rather than issues of national and political importance or other grave issues that plague the society.
- Characters are common folks and problems outlined and explicated are commonplace. The audience is able to correlate personal experiences with the struggles of characters in dire circumstances.
- Characters' struggles kindle emotions of pity and sympathy.

Chronicle Plays

The defeat of the Spanish Armada in 1588 instilled greater nationalist feelings that propelled revisiting of history. Raphael Holinshed's *Chronicles of England*, in 1577 was referred to by English playwrights for producing dramas related to history. A chronicle refers to historical facts and a chronicle play deals with facts and incidents of historical and national importance rather than ordinary stories, legends, myths or fictitious events.

Features

- Either the life of a king or a person of national importance is the subject of the play.
- Both real and fictitious characters are featured. Minor episodes are invented by dramatists and enmeshed within the canvas of important events. Sometimes historical events are telescoped to suit the narrative.
- Common themes and storylines are related to ambition, responsibility towards the country, ascension to the throne, struggle for power and civil war.

- Christopher Marlowe's *Edward II* (1593), Shakespeare's *Richard III* (1591), and *Henry V* (1599) are history plays.

Masque

Masque, a form of courtly dramatic entertainment that originated in Italy, was popularised during the Stuart period and flourished in Europe in the 16th and 17th centuries.

Features

- The plot, usually taken from mythology was insignificant; however, it conveyed a message.
- Ladies and gentlemen of the courts of England were the principal characters that wore elaborate masks for the performance that involved a blend of poetry, music, song, and dance.
- Elaborate stage decorations and extravagant costumes were produced for each play and the entire production was spectacular.
- Masques were an inevitable part of banquets, celebrations and coronations. Aristocrats and the nobility were the regular spectators. The masque concluded with the removal of masks and the spectators danced with their partners amidst the audience.
- Ben Jonson wrote masques in the 17th century with stage design by the popular architect Inigo Jones. The noteworthy example of a masque in English is John Milton's *Comus* (1634).

Comedy

'Comedy' is derived from the Greek work *komos,* which means "carousal" or "merrymaking". There is nothing serious, disastrous or dangerous action and the story concludes on a propitious note for the principal characters. Comedies of the Greek dramatist Aristophanes are imbued with buffoonery, satire and social commentaries; antiphanes, poetry and menander, romantic intrigues of young lovers. The Roman writers Plautus and Terence wrote comedies that influenced the English writers of the Middle Ages. Nicholas Udall's *Ralph Royster Doyster* (1553) is considered the first English comedy. Comedy has evolved through times and subtypes of comedy are analysed henceforth.

Romantic Comedy

Romantic comedies are delightful plays that deal with frivolousness, follies, foibles, mix-up, arguments, and light-hearted misunderstandings between young lovers. Shakespeare's Romantic comedies, *A Midsummer Night's Dream* (1595/96); *As You Like It* (1599), and *Twelfth Night* (1601-02) are popular examples.

Features

- Young lovers are involved in entanglements and the progress of their love affair is marred by obstacles from parents, family feud, disagreements or unavoidable circumstances.
- Stock characters such as the witty fool, the drunkard, the beautiful heroine, the clever and cautious servant feature in these plays.
- The action of the play moves out to distant and unfamiliar locales like the Forest of Arden in *As You Like It*, the forest outside Athens in *A Midsummer Night's Dream*, and the land of Illyria in *Twelfth Night.*
- Cross-dressing and mistaken identities form a part of the plot in these plays. Dialogues are replete with wordplay, puns, and lewd jokes.

Tragicomedy

Both tragic and comic elements are harmoniously blended in a tragicomedy. It is discrete from a tragedy that comprises comic scenes and a comedy that includes tragic incidents. For instance, the Porter's scene in *Macbeth* and the Gravedigger's scene in *Hamlet* do not function to evoke laughter, on the contrary, they reinforce the intensity of the tragedy. On a similar note, a tragic background in *As You Like It* offers relief when glitches are resolved and tribulations are ultimately warded off. A tragicomedy partakes of both tragic as well as comic elements, but remains distinctive from both.

Features

- Mélanges of tragic and comic situations, character types, and plot provide the audience a view of both the dark and bright sides of life.
- The protagonist of a tragicomedy could face an imminent catastrophe, but the grievous situation is forestalled and the play ends on an exultant note.
- Characters of both the upper and the lower classes mingle and involve in the main plot. Some characters undergo some form of transformation towards the end of the play.
- Noteworthy examples are Shakespeare's *The Merchant of Venice* (1597) and *Winter's Tale* (1611); and Francis Beaumont and John Fletcher's *Philaster* (1610).

Comedy of Humours

The term 'humour' derives from the Latin *humor* (more properly *umor*), meaning "liquid". This type of comedy was popular in the late 16th and the early 17th centuries in England, and based on the medieval theory of humours. According to this theory, the body is believed to be constituted of four primary fluids or *humours*, namely blood, yellow bile, black bile, and phlegm. The proper balance of these fluids is essential for the maintenance of a healthy mind in a healthy body; however, an imbalance or excess of any one or other fluids would be marked by a specific kind of temperament as explained below:

Fluid	Personality	Characteristics
Blood	sanguine	kind, mirthful
Yellow bile	choleric	intolerant and irascible
Black bile	melancholic	gloomy, brooding and satiric
Phlegm	phlegmatic	weak, obstinate and spiteful

Features

- Major characters in these plays possess a predominant humour that makes them appear strange and peculiar. Avarice, cunningness, and dishonesty are some of the dominant traits of characters portrayed.

- Names of characters reveal their nature and attitude as Volpone, Wellbred, Corvino, Corbaccio, Knowall, and Brainworm to name a few.
- Examples of this drama include Ben Jonson's *Every Man in his Homour* (1598), *Every Man Out of his Humour* (1599), and *Volpone* (1606).

Comedy of Manners

This type of comedy was popular during the Restoration period. During the Puritanical rule, all theatres were closed down and little entertainment was offered; however, the Restoration brought with it unscrupulous behaviour coupled with the representation of licentiousness on stage and an excess of enjoyment, which probably is the outcome of the opening of theatres and the sudden spurt of freedom perfectly reflected and depicted in the *Comedy of Manners*.

Features

- This drama mainly features associations and intrigues of the upper middle-class ladies and gentlemen of England.
- The main plot is elaborate but superficial and scenes are constructed loosely. Stock characters such as envious husbands, flirtatious women, beaus, and libertines are involved in the sequence of main events in the play.
- Repartee, the form of dialogue, which is quick and witty and sometimes mildly insulting is used frequently.
- Immoral behaviour of the upper class is portrayed in obscene and licentious scenes. A bedroom scene with one or more characters hiding behind objects, curtains or screens as a part of scheming is inevitable.
- William Wycherley's *The Country Wife* (1675), William Congreve's *The Way of the World* (1700), Oliver Goldsmith's *She Stoops to Conquer* (1773), Richard Sheridan's *The School for Scandal* (1777), and Oscar Wilde's *The Importance of being Earnest* (1895) belong to this category.

Genteel Comedy

A subgenre of the *Comedy of Manners* that developed in the mid-18th century and popularised by the English essayist and playwright Joseph Addison (1672-1719), this comedy portrays the artificial style of 18th century drama.

Features

- These comedies accurately present affectations of the upper class who lived during and after the reign of Queen Anne. This comedy is characterised by artificiality and sentimentality and the amusement evolves from affectations of a shallow society.
- The tendency to moralise is evident and all forms of licentiousness are absolutely evaded.
- The finest example is the English playwright Colley Cibber's *The Careless Husband* (1704).

Sentimental Comedy

Principally, a reaction to the *Comedy of Manners* and popular in the mid-18th century, importance is given to misfortunes of ordinary men and women caught up in the quagmire of distressful situations that are ultimately overcome.

Features

- The aim of the dramatist is to compensate for drawbacks of the *Comedy of Manners*. The plays are didactic and rely upon the concept of poetic justice.
- These comedies portray a rather dismal and insipid view of life that is devoid of any form of amusement or happiness, but the favourable ending offers respite. The dramas lack wit or brilliance and nothing untoward happens nor do surprise events turn up.
- The hero is magnanimous and good-natured and the heroine is virtuous.
- Virtues of characters are portrayed more than vices. The distress of the middle classes is stressed and the sympathy of the audience is educed.

- Standing examples are Colley Cibber's *Loves Last Shift* (1696) and the Irish dramatists George Farquhar's *The Constant Couple* (1699) and Richard Steele's *The Conscious Lovers* (1722).

Closet Drama

A play that is meant only to be read and not staged is a Closet Drama. The German playwright Johann Wolfgang von Goethe's *Faust, Part I* (1908) and *Faust, Part II* (1832) were considered Closet dramas for some time, until they were staged. John Milton's *Samson Agonistes* (1671) and Percy Bysshe Shelley's *Prometheus Unbound* (1820) are Closet dramas.

Features

- As dramatists found the staging of plays in verse unprofitable, and they resorted to publishing their works than making efforts to staging them.
- Techniques of stage and properties are not given importance since these plays are intended for reading.
- Longer philosophical passages are more prominent and there is little action.

Farce

The Latin term *farsa* (farce) develops from *farcire*, which means "to stuff". Farce is a type of low comedy that includes burlesque and buffoonery and induces laughter not intended to censure the society. It was earlier used to describe the Interlude, the religious play in England.

Features

- A category of low comedy that uses slapstick and exaggeration. The plot, which is complex and intricate consists of preposterous situations and implausible and ludicrous actions. Instances of surprise events and sudden disclosures run through the course of the farce.
- Plot and situation are more significant than character and dialogue and the characters are often exaggerated caricatures that are not true to life.

- The English playwright Branden Thomas' *Charley's Aunt* (1892) is an example. Shakespeare's *A Midsummer Night's Dream* (1596) and *The Merry Wives of Windsor* (1597) comprise farcical elements. Christopher Marlowe has made use of farce in *Dr. Faustus* (1592) to provide comic relief.

Melodrama

Popular in the 19th century, an exaggerated tragedy is labelled melodrama. In modern usage, the term is associated with any form of writing that is sensational and consists of events that are unconvincing.

Features

- A melodramatic plot contains intrigue and themes are sensational. The actions depicted may be violent and gory.
- The protagonists suffer due to conspiracies of the antagonist; however, they emerge victorious due to their efforts, virtue or luck.
- Stereotypical characters pervade the stage and the morally upright and the evil characters are pitted against each other.
- The English playwright Edward Fitzball's *The Red Rover* (1829) and the Irish dramatist Dion Boucicault's *The Streets of London* (1864) are examples of melodrama.

Cup-and-Saucer Drama

This drama is set in a realistic environment against the domestic backdrop of an upper-class household. The action often takes place in the drawing room of a house and the screenplay incorporates serving tea. The English dramatist Thomas William Robertson's plays *Society* (1865) and *Caste* (1867) are examples of this drama.

Features

- These plays often portray serious contemporary issues such as class, conflicts, and social prejudice. The style of presentation is naturalistic and the stage settings and sustains are crafted as realistic as possible.

- There are no exaggerated or melodramatic speeches and real-life situations of characters are projected.

Problem Play

Popularly known as the comedy of ideas, the problem play presents issues that are confronted by the people in the society in an unconventional manner. The Norwegian dramatist Henrik Ibsen (1828-1906) perfected this form of drama and his play *The Doll's House* (1879) offers a critique of the lack of social opportunities for women. George Bernard Shaw's *Mrs. Warren's Profession* (1893) discusses the social issue of prostitution. Other problem plays include Ibsen's *Ghosts* and *Enemy of the People* (1882), and the English playwrights Harley Granville-Barker's *The Voysey Inheritance* (1905), and John Galsworthy's *Strife* (1909).

Features

- The plot revolves around contemporary social issues. The playwright's intention is to create awareness among the audience towards issues depicted.
- Characters typically represent conflicting points of view and characters often appear as spokespersons of the dramatist.
- The mode of presentation is realistic and the dramatist uses this mode of drama as a forum for discussions on social, political, and moral issues.
- A variation of the problem play is the discussion play where the playwright induces his characters to discuss social issues on stage in the form of a protracted debate rather than interweave the theme into the plot. An example is George Bernard Shaw's *Misalliance* (1910).

The Well-made Play

This play is constructed on a preset formula of a complex and artificial plot and ends with the resolution of issues and problems presented. The plays of French playwrights Eugéne Scribe (1791-1861) and Victorien Sardou (1831-1908), and the English dramatist Wilkie Collins are classified under this group.

Features

- The opening scene of the play presents a series of complications that is the outcome of incidents that have happened at an earlier time or in the past.
- The climax of the action is positioned at the end of the play.
- The plot includes a mystery that is revealed only to the audience. Suspense due to misunderstandings between characters, clandestine information, and mistaken identities are intimately tied to the plot. The twist in the plot arises due to numerous unforeseen incidents and the reversal of fortune is effected by the revelation of the unspecified information or matter.
- Techniques of the well-made play are employed by Henrik Ibsen in *A Doll's House* (1879) and Oscar Wilde in *The Importance of Being Earnest* (1895).

Expressionist Drama

Expressionism, an early 20th century movement though "not a well-defined movement" (Abrams 119), expressed its discontents with the artistic and literary expressions of realism both in theme and in style. The movement, in exposing the troubled emotional thoughts and experiences of the human mind by distorting and exaggerating principles of realistic presentations, succeeded in staging human types and the essential condition of mankind. Eminent precursors of this movement include the French poets Charles Baudelaire (1821-67) and Arthur Rimbaud (1854-91), the Russian novelist Fyodor Dostoevsky (1821-81), the German philosopher Friedrich Nietzsche (1844-1900) and August Strindberg (1849-1912), the Swedish dramatist.

Features

- The mode of presentation reflects thoughts of characters and the audience is exposed to a single thought process or attitude of the character. The speeches are short and movements on stage are artificial. Incoherent sentences and phrases and episodic renderings project the "oscillating emotional states" (Abrams 120).

- Characters are placed in situations in which, the outer world is distorted to project troubled states of mind of characters or the dramatist. Distorted sets, glaring lighting and bizarre costumes are used to expose the disturbed psyche.
- Strindberg's *A Dream Play* (1901), *To Damascus* (1898-1904) and *The Ghost Sonata* (1907) are some of the finest plays of this form. The German playwrights Oscar Kokoschka's *Murder, Hope of Women* (1909) and Walter Hasenclever's *The Sun* (1924); and the American plays *The Hairy Ape* (1922) by Eugune O'Neill and *The Adding Machine* (1923) by Elmer Rice are further examples of this class of drama.

Epic Theatre

This type of drama was founded by the German theatre-director Erwin Piscator (1893-1966) and popularised by the German dramatist Bertolt Brecht (1898-1956). The tag epic is used by Brecht to differentiate this particular style of writing from the conventional dramatic theatre. Brecht later referred to this theatre as dialectical theatre.

Features

- This theatre was a reaction against the characteristics of the well-made play, melodrama, Surrealism, and the Theatre of Cruelty. The naturalistic approach to drama was criticised by Brecht who believed this to be a form of escapism.
- This drama was involved in the exposition of political ideas. Brecht wanted his audience to observe the play and critically reflect on the plot through the 'alienation effect' that created a sense of detachment in the audience from the main action of the play. This would enhance the effectiveness of the play rather than advance mere empathy towards the characters. He used techniques such as flooding the entire theatre with bright lights, allowing his characters to directly interact with the audience and permitting actors to move sets to the obvious view of the audience.

- Features such as a narrator, slide projection, music, and placards were used.
- Brecht's *The Threepenny Opera* (1928) and *Mother Courage and Her Children* (1939) are dramas of this type.

Theatre of Cruelty

Coined by the French poet and playwright Antonin Artaud (1896-1948), the Theatre of Cruelty intends to shock the audience to unearth covert truths. His theory has given rise to a form of modern drama known as a happening, which could be defined as an action or a series of actions that primarily affect the senses. The portrayal does not necessitate a stage but it could be acted out in any public place with the active participation of the audience.

Features

- Discards stage setting and props.
- Actors perform and concomitantly serve as the audience.
- Bright lights, mime, sensational and horrific actions are employed.
- The French playwright Jean Genet (1910-86), the Polish theatre-director Jerzy Grotowski (1933-99), the English dramatist and Peter Brook (1925) were highly influenced by the ideas of Artaud.
- An adaption of Percy Bysshe Shelley's verse drama *The Cenci: A Tragedy in Five Acts* (1819) by Atraud is *Les Cenci* (1935), is based on the precepts of this theatre. Another prominent example is *Marat/Sade* (1963) by the German playwright Peter Weiss.

Absurd Drama

The Theatre of the Absurd that emerged in France during the 1950s is based on the formulations of Existentialism that proposes man to be an isolated creature that is forced to live in a meaningless world. The essential human condition is therefore absurd and man suffers from existential 'angst'. The Irish playwright Samuel Beckett, (1906-89), the Russian-born French dramatist Arthur Adamov (1908-70), the Romanian-French playwright Eugène Ionesco (1909-94), the French playwright Jean Genet (1910-86) and the British dramatist Harold Pinter (1930-2008) are some of the foremost exponents of this theatre. The term "theatre of the absurd" was coined by the Hungarian-born British dramatist and critic Martin Esslin in the book *Theatre of the Absurd* (1962).

Features

- The plot or story in the traditional sense is absent. There is no formal logic and conventional structure. The action in an absurd drama projects the predicament of man who struggles to exist in an incomprehensible world.
- Well-etched characters are absent and characters represent humanity in entirety that is aimless and incapable of rational thought and action.
- Dialogue is reduced to triteness, technological jargon and clichés. The futility of communication is expressed through the use of ellipses, long pauses, and silence. Slapstick comedy is one of the most important features of absurd drama.

Kitchen-Sink Drama

This drama is associated with the Angry Young Men movement in English literature in the 1950s. A group of British novelists and dramatists from the middle and working class backgrounds expressed their dissatisfaction with the detestable contemporary social, economic, and political conditions in drama to express their disillusionment and discontent at the failure of the Welfare State to come up to its assurances. The mood of anger, frustration, and resentment is reflected in theatre as 'kitchen-sink' is also expressed through art, novels, film, and television. The term 'kitchen-sink' also implies the burgeoning interest of contemporary artists on themes related to the recognisable aspects of domestic life.

Features

- Crises in lives of the lower and middle class youth that is educated but under duress due to deplorable living standards and working under menial conditions is depicted. The protagonist is typically an educated, intelligent, young man who criticises the discriminatory social conditions in England. The use of colloquial expressions effectively expresses their dissatisfaction at the appalling living conditions. Partisan attitudes of the political regime and rigid traditions and class systems are unflinchingly disparaged in the plays.

- Artificialities of the well-made play and the projection of the stereotypical working class in the plays are derided.
- The English playwrights John Osborne, in *Look Back in Anger* (1956), Bernard Kops, in *The Hamlet of Stepney Green* (1957), and Arnold Wesker, in *Chicken Soup with Barley* (1958) portray frustrations deftly.

Poor Theatre

This theatre is associated with Jerzy Grotowski (1933-99), the Polish theatre-director. Since it is experimental in nature, it is identified as 'laboratory theatre' and labelled 'Poor Theatre' because it does away with the intricate stage properties and expensive paraphernalia of a regular theatre.

Features

- The theatre does away with the traditional stage and performances take place in the open space.
- The effectiveness of this theatre entirely depends on the actor's voice, body movements and skill of presentation.
- Actors perform in and around the audience and the space between the performers and the audience is reduced.
- Minimal props are used and the costumes are plain. Instrumental music is replaced by the voice-effects of the characters.
- Ideas of Grotowski have paved the way for street plays known as third theatre. The Indian dramatist Badal Sircar's *Bhoma* (1975) and *Stale News* (1979) are written and performed according to the parameters of third theatre.

Bread and Puppet Theatre

Propounded by the dancer, sculptor and baker from Germany who migrated to the United States of America Peter Schumann (b. 1934) in 1963 in New York, this theatre is currently based in Vermont, in North-Eastern United States.

Features

- It is a form of a politically radical activist theatre that features enormous puppets that are almost 10 to 15 feet tall.
- The name is derived from the practice of sharing bread and sauce with the audience to create a sense of community and spread the fact that art is as indispensable to life as bread.
- This theatre has remained active through many demonstrations taken out throughout the United States since the 1960s and the campaigns especially with regard to the anti-war protest during the Vietnam war (1955-75) is commendable.
- Two praise-worthy shows of this ensemble include *Nativity* (1992) and *The Divine Reality Comedy*.

One-act Play

A drama in one act that could have shorter scenes is a One-act play. Mystery plays, Miracle plays, Morality plays and Interludes are short plays with a single theme. Absurd dramatists among other modern and postmodern dramatists have exploited one-act plays to meet their requirements.

Features

- It contains a specific plot, which is limited to a single episode or situation. The subject matter could be serious or comic. The dialogue, characters, and settings are specially designed for the situation to be presented.
- The number of characters is limited and the delineation of characters is related to the development of the plot.
- The climax is often the conclusion of the play. Some popular one-act plays are the Russian playwright

Anton Chekov's *A Marriage Proposal* (1890) and Samuel Beckett 's *Krapp's Last Tape* (1958). The Irish dramatists W.B. Yeats' *The Pot of Broth* (1902) and J.M. Synge's *Riders to the Sea* (1904) are the one-act plays that succinctly portray human man's struggle to survive amidst all odds.

Conclusion

Drama emerged as a form of enunciation to account for changes in the society that were responsible for analysing artistic innovativeness down the ages. Each category of drama diverged into multiple forms that spread across the globe to usher a probably different outlook on existing dramatic forms. Apart from the prominent dramatist, a host of other dramatists emerged that augmented the study of world literature. The ingenuity of each artist resulted in emergent forms of artistic creativity that compounded into variants and subcategories, unique and fascinating in their own ways. Theatre and drama, the exceptional twin forces etched figures in the minds of people that caught their sensibilities that stipulated profuse contributions of expressiveness in all possible frontiers.

The ability of a medium to interact with the masses to convey a message is the most effective way to infuse renewed interest in any field of enquiry. Drama and its branches spread across the globe in its varied forms to show how the appeal, distinctiveness and scope of the genre imparted a wider perspective of the world at large. Features and components of drama cannot be studied in isolation or the inherent components of each subcategory of drama highlight the multi-faceted propensity for innovation and entertainment. Using a blend of divergent methods of stagecraft, dialogue, settings and plot to lure the audience, drama emerged as one of the predominant modes of expression, demonstration, articulation and communication.

Glossary

confluence : convergence
facet : aspect or component
supplement : enhancement

effect	:	result in
machinations	:	scheming
animosity	:	hostility or loathing
intrigue	:	conspiracy
usurp	:	seize
procrastination	:	postponement
in tandem with	:	concurrently
infuse	:	permeate
revelry	:	merriment
cataclysmic	:	disastrous
devoid	:	without
propel	:	drive
precipitous	:	sudden
propitious	:	favourable
imbued	:	filled
foible	:	fault
mar	:	ruin
feud	:	quarrel
lewd	:	bawdy
tribulation	:	suffering
partakes of	:	shares
mélange	:	combination
forestall	:	prevent
Slapstick	:	It is the category of physical comedy discerned by humour, absurd situations, vigorous and violent actions. The comic persona, whose actions are unobstructed and perfectly timed should be adept at acrobatics, stunts and conjuring.
exultant	:	elated
avarice	:	greed
beau	:	lover
libertine	:	one who lacks morality, defies conventional religious beliefs and prefers free thinking.
insipid	:	dull

dismal : miserable
educe : extract or obtain
preposterous : outrageous or ridiculous
implausible : improbable
precursor : forerunner

References

Abrams, M.H. and Geoffrey, Galt Harpham. *A Glossary of Literary Terms*. 11th ed. Cengage Learning, 2015.

Brocket, Oscar G. *Theatre: An Introduction*. Holt, Rinehart and Winston, 1974.

Chandler, Daniel and Rod Munday. *Oxford Dictionary of Media and Communication*. Oxford UP, 2011.

Dukore, B.F. *Dramatic Theory and Criticism: Greek to Grotowsky*. Holt, Reinhart and Winston, 1974.

Elam, Keir. *The Semiotics of Theatre and Drama*. Routledge, 2009.

Gillespie Gerald Ernest Paul, editor. *Romantic Drama*. John Benjamins Publishing Company, 1994.

Scholes, R. and C.H. Klaus. *Elements of Drama*. Oxford UP, 1971.

Storm, William. *After Dionysus: A Theory of the Tragic*. Cornell UP, 1998.

https://www.britannica.com/art/Western-theatre/Theatre-of-the-20th-century-and-beyond

http://elibrary.bsu.az/books_400/N_159.pdf

https://www.encyclopedia.com/places/spain-portugal-italy-greece-and-balkans/greek-political-geography/drama

https://theodora.com/encyclopedia/d/drama.html

http://www.historyworld.net/timesearch/default.asp?conid=static_timeline&timelineid=769&page=1&keywords=Drama%20timeline

Chapter 3

World Drama: Diverse Expressions Characteristic of the Age

Introduction

Forms of expressions are not only noted for their novelty but also for unique ways of presentation. Drama has incorporated changing perceptions of dramatisation that have called in for newer techniques to cater to demands of the age. Drama from every part of the world, the East and the West have framed their distinctive combinations to enthrall the audience. Despite differences in origin, concept and theory, each type of drama has infused the spirit of the age and offered the setting to enunciate fresh domains of artistic communication.

Drama During the Renaissance

Renaissance that initially began in Italy and then spread to the other parts of Europe, and England, initiated a resurgence of the classics and art. Renaissance, which means "rebirth" stroked various art forms like painting, sculpture, music, and architecture. Drama, however, was rather slow to progress, and began its course with base imitations of the classical plays, and development if any can be attributed to the stage preparations, architectural patterns, coloured lighting and stage props. Opera, the drama accompanied by music was started by some scholars in Florence, Italy. To a single musical line sung with an instrument, the words of the song would be emphasised and the drama would be performed. England and France began their own operas that became quite popular throughout the seventeenth century. Since Opera originated Italy, the international language of the Opera still remains Italian.

Another popular form of drama that emerged during that time was Commedia dell'arte, "the comedy of profession". Comic improvisations with scenarios and the plots were staged before a performance. The actors would perform a comic action on stage, while the main plot called *lazzi*, continued. Speeches were memorised by the actors, and declarations of love, anger and hate as well as melodies, jests, proverbs, and comments were used when needed. The characters represented in this type of drama were principally of two social categories, the upper and the servant classes. Costumes and masks differentiated the characters; however, the upper-class characters such as the innamorati and the innamoratae, did not wear them.

The Renaissance in Other Parts of Europe

Spain developed the written drama with contributions from Miguel de Cervantes (1547-1616), Lope de Vega (1562-1635) and Pedro Calderón de la Barca (1600-81) contributing to the development of theatre. The character of Don Juan, a fictitious libertine originated from Spain. The Spanish dramatist Tirso de Molina shaped this character in his tragic drama *El burlador de Sevilla* (1630). France developed its theatre under the support of three major dramatists. Pierre Corneille (1606-84), the French tragedian's play *The Cid* gained immense fame. The other playwrights include Jean-Baptiste Poquelin, known by his stage name Molière (1622-73), whose plays *The Miser, The Misanthrope* and *The Imaginary Invalid* were staged several times, and Jean-Baptiste Racine's (1639-99) *Phaedra* was popular. The strolling players moved throughout several parts of Europe preforming in village squares and the castles and palaces of the noblemen and the royalty.

In England, the Renaissance probably from 1500-1600 reached the pinnacle of success with the dawn of the Elizabethan Age. Nicholas Udall's (1504-56) *Ralph Roister Doister,* the first English comedy in 1552 and the anonymous *Grammer Gurton's Needle* (1566) were produced. The first English tragedy *Gorboduc* was produced in 1561 by Thomas Norton and Thomas Sackville.

William Shakespeare (1564-1616), stands out in this period as the poet and playwright *par excellence*. Without any form of professional training or a "university wit" but elementary grammar education, Shakespeare reigned supreme, conquering the British stage and the hearts of the multitude, unparalleled and exceptionally. Versatile and ingenious, he surpassed the talents of Robert Greene who mocked Shakespeare's "shake-scene" of base forms. Shakespeare' wrote 38 plays that include his four great tragedies—*Hamlet* (1601), *Othello* (1603), *King Lear* (1605), and *Macbeth* (1606); the comedies, *A Midsummer Night's Dream* (1595/96) and *Twelfth Night* (1601-02)*;* the history plays, *Henry IV—Parts I and II* (1597/1612)*;* the so-called bitter comedies, *Measure for Measure* (1603)*, Troilus and Cressida* (1602)*, A Winter's Tale* (1623), *All's Well that Ends Well* (1623) and his last play *The Tempest* (1610-11), considered a tragicomedy.

The other significant playwrights and their plays are Christopher Marlowe's (1580-1634) *Tamburlaine the Great* (1587/88), *The Jew of Malta* (1589), and *Edward II* (1592); Thomas Kyd's (1558-94) Revenge Tragedy, *The Spanish Tragedy* (1587); Thomas Dekker's (1572-1632) *The Shoemakers Holiday* (1600); Thomas Heywood's (1575-1641) *A Woman Killed with Kindness* (1607); John Fletcher and Francis Beaumont's *The Maid's Tragedy (*1609); Francis Beaumont's (1585-1616) *The Knight of the Burning Pestle* (1613); Ben Jonson's (1572-1637) *Every Man in His Humour* (1598); *Volpone* (1605-1606), and *The Alchemist* (1610); and John Webster's (1578-25) *The Duchess of Malfi* (1612-13).

Elizabethan and Jacobean Theatre

Permanent Theatres

The secular plays that were performed in different locations around the country were regulated from performing and the 'strolling players' as they were nicknamed were restricted from moving around. James Burbage, a carpenter by profession and an actor was in-charge of The Lord Chamberlain's Men constructed the first English permanent theatre in 1576, which he named The Theatre. Soon other theatres such as The Curtain, The Fortune and The Swan were also built. By 1599, Burbage and his sons along with their company The Lord Chamberlain's Men had constructed the most celebrated theatre of all times The Globe on the south bank of the Thames. The first permanent theatres were open to the sky and Blackfriars theatre, under Burbage for the first time was enclosed, used artificial lighting, and introduced new effects into drama.

The Elizabethan Theatre and Playacting

The Globe, octagonal in structure, had the outer frame probably 30 meters in diameter with several tiers or seating enclosed by a roof of straw. The main stage was a platform, which projected out from one side of the outer construction into the central courtyard. Behind the stage was a room that served as the dressing room of the actors, the tiring house. The bedroom or inner rooms of the plays were acted out in the space called the study. The balcony on the second level of the acting area was the tarras behind which a curtain called an arras hung to conceal the chamber, which was often occupied by the stage musicians. Trapdoors on the floor of the stage were designed to depict underground, or graveyard scenes.

Above the stage, was a roof known as the heavens that protected the actors from the stage properties. Through a trapdoor in this roof, actors could descend on the trapeze as Gods. The sun, moon, stars were painted on the underside of the roof. At the back of the stage was a balcony, called the upper stage. Above the heavens was the scenery hut, which contained machinery to raise or lower the actors on stage.

Between the doors on the stage was an alcove known as the inner stage or discovery space, which would be curtained off but the actors could not be concealed from public view because there weren't any curtains around the stage to screen them. The depiction of scenery using props was minimal or absent and the playwright used to indicate to the audience of what they needed to imagine for each scene.

The area surrounding the stage was the pit, that revealed the sky for sunlight because there was no electricity at that time. A slope of the floor allowed rainwater to drain off. The groundlings had to pay a penny to stand in the pit, and the nobility occupied the seats in the gallery paying further charges. The most expensive seats were next to, above or on the stage.

Costumes were neither intricate nor factually perfect. Women were restricted to act out roles and all female roles were played by adolescent boys whose voices had not broken. The sound of a trumpet by a trumpeter in the tower above the scenery hut announced the beginning of a play and, a flag was flown on the tower on the day of the performance.

English Theatre during the Commonwealth Period

Between 1642 and 1660, England was under the leadership of Oliver Cromwell, a Puritan army officer who declared himself the Lord Protector of a unified Commonwealth of England, Scotland and Ireland in 1653. Since the Stuart royal family had gone into exile in Europe during this period, this phase is also known as the interregnum. The Puritans were hostile to the theatre as they felt that entertainment was sinful and in 1642, the parliament banned the staging of plays in London and for the next 18 years, English theatres remained closed.

The Restoration Period

In 1660, monarchy was restored and Charles Stuart, the son of King Charles I ascended the throne of England. This period is notable for the relaxations from the strict Puritan morality, but not without its own baggage of issues of licentiousness and immorality at the abrupt freedom attained. Theatre, sports and dancing were revived and the French influence on the English theatre was apparent with the French playwrights Pierre Corneille and Jean Racine setting the standards for Neoclassical tragedy. The Neoclassical standard for tragedy comprised of logical consistency of plot and the action, curtailed to a day's time and the events, at a specific location. Violent events could be depicted off stage and the dialogue, devoid of vulgarity was limited to the use of poetic phrases.

The two important companies of players, The Duke's Men, a company for younger performers led by William Davenant and The King's Company, the company for older or more experienced actors managed by Thomas Killigrew gained popularity. Theatre, for the first time in England got to have a proscenium arch and movable scenery at Lincoln's Inn Fields Theatre in 1661 and the initial performance was held in 1730. Thomas Killigrew, in 1662 founded the Drury Lane Theatre and displayed some of the most significant plays of Shakespeare, Beaumont and Fletcher. The principal actors were Thomas Betterton, Nell Gwynn, Elizabeth Barry, Anne Bracegirdle and Susanna Mountfort.

George Etheridge is known for the social Comedy of Manners, and William Wycherley portrayed the hypocrisy of the period in *The Country Wife* (1675). John Dryden's play *All for Love* (1678) is regarded one of the great Restoration masterpieces. Aphra Behn was the first professional woman dramatist, who wrote 18 plays, out of which some significant plays were topical satirical comedies that also exposed gender issues. *The Rover; or The Banish'd Cavaliers* (1677) and its sequel, *The Second Part of the Rover* (1681) were comedies of intrigue and regarded some of the best works on stage. George Farquhar's *The Recruiting Offer* (1706) and *The Beaux Stratagem* (1707); John Vanbrugh's *Relapse: Or Virtue in Danger* (1696) and *The Provoked Wife* (1697) were some of the successful plays of the period. William Congreve wrote his greatest play *The Way of the World* (1700).

The audience of this period comprised largely of members of the upper-class of London who came more to socialise than watch the happenings on stage. They were rude and passed uncouth comments during performances. Jeremy Collier's critical pamphlet *A Short View of the Immorality and Profaneness of the English Stage* denounced not only Congreve and Vanbrugh but also Shakespeare and many other Elizabethan playwrights.

English Theatre during the 18th Century

Innovations in theatre, from the size of the theatre to stage props underwent changes. The distance between the stage and the audience increased and the extent was further increased by placing the members of the orchestra in front of the stage in the area known as the 'orchestra pit'. Painted sceneries known as 'flats' depicted different scenes appropriately and the theatre was brightly lit on all sides using kerosene lamps and gas lamps. The structure of the theatre enhanced the stage effects and the efficiency of acoustics.

David Garrick took over the management of Drury Lane theatre and by mid-19th century, while the actor-managers had been replaced first by stage managers and later the directors. The Kemble family of actors and actresses, namely Roger Kemble and Sarah Ward and their descendants contributed to the spreading out of dramatic art and performances. The audience consisted of people of different classes whose peculiar mannerisms and behaviour were evident in their demeanour.

Richard Steele popularised Sentimental drama. Nicholas Rowe's *Tamerlane* (1702), *The Fair Penitent* (1703), and *The Tragedy of Jane Shore* (1714) were quite famous. John Gay wrote the most successful musical play of the period *The Beggar's Opera* (1722), which could be compared to the contemporary musical theatre. Colley Cibber's *Love's Last Shift; or, The Fool in Fashion* (1696), is generally considered the first Sentimental comedy, a form of drama that dominated the English stage for nearly a century and John Vanbrugh wrote the sequel *The Relapse, or, Virtue in Danger* (1696).

Later 18th Century Plays and Playwrights

Oliver Goldsmith wrote *The Good Natured Man* (1768) and the brilliant comedy *She Stoops to Conquer* (1773). Richard Brinsley Sheridan's first play *The Rivals* (1775), and the second, *The School for Scandal* (1977) are regarded as the best examples of the 18th century Comedy of Manners.

The Victorian Age

Significant advances in medicine, science and technology witnessed changes in population growth and occupation. Britain emerged as a major industrial power and a powerful global empire ruling over a quarter of the world's population. Class divisions were clearly defined and there existed sharp demarcations between the rich and the poor.

There was significant increase in mass popular entertainment and the theatrical genre called melodrama emerged. The first English melodrama, *A Tale of Mystery* (1802) written by Thomas Holcroft (1745-1809) was based on a French work *Coelina, ou l'enfant de mystère* (1800) by the French playwright Guilbert de Pixérécourt. Developed in France and Germany, the melodrama included an exaggerated plot with short scenes interspersed with music to appeal to emotions. Stereotypical characters were depicted with sensational incidents and the melodrama ended with the victory of the virtuous.

Codified gestures were used to convey certain emotions and the acting style was in the presentation mode with the actors facing out to the audience. Facial expressions and presentation of dialogue were presented in a rather exaggerated manner. Another convention of this genre was to have the actors 'freeze' on stage at certain moments of heightened emotions to create a dramatic montage.

The four major categories of melodrama that were prevalent mainly dealt with Gothic and supernatural narratives that incorporated supernatural elements, ghosts, vampires and grotesque themes; military and nautical stories that portrayed not only patriotism and bravery but also the horror and devastation caused by conflicts and war; domestic dramas, which dealt with serious moral issues such as adultery, illegitimate relationships, gambling and the battle between the sexes; and the sensational plays that were based on the lives of disreputable criminals and their horrendous crimes.

Theatre in the 19th Century, the Playwrights and Their Works

One of the greatest set designers of the 19th century theatre, Bruce 'Sensation' Smith of Drury Lane theatre created a miraculous wave in the theatre of the times with his fantastic theatrical innovations. Realistic and convincing scenic designs with the development of elaborate stage machinery contributed to theatrical spectacles, trapdoors and lifts, flying scenery and pyrotechnic effects. Water effects depicted shipwrecks, battles, fires, earthquakes and horse races. Stage lighting advanced to gas from oil in 1870, followed by limelight in 1837, and the electric light in the form of arch lamps from 1848 and finally to filament lamps in 1881. Smoke effects, coloured lights and flyers added to the scenic spectacle.

The English playwright Edward Fitzball (1792-1873) invented 'black projection' using light, set on a backstage track to project a shadow on to cotton gauze downstage so that the shadow of the object increased as the light moved further back from the object. His famous play *Jonathan Bradford: Or, the Murder at the Road-Side Inn: A Romance* (1827) used this technique. *The Innkeeper of Abbeville, or The Ostler and the Robber* (1820) a domestic crime melodrama; *The Floating Beacon; or, Norwegian Wreckers* (1824), a nautical melodrama; *Flying Dutchman; or the Phantom Ship: A Nautical Drama in Three Acts* (1826), a supernatural melodrama and, *Jonathan Bradford, or Murder at the Road-side Inn* (1833) that combined the elements of domestic and sensation drama. Douglas Jerrold (1803-57) produced two notable melodramas, *Fifteen Years of a Drunkard's Life* (1828), and *Black-eyed Susan; or All in the Downs* (1829), a nautical melodrama.

Naturalism and Realism: A Brief

Modern theatre, believed to have begun from the mid-19th century with the divergent philosophical propositions of realism and naturalism that replaced the Romantic movement initiated fresh vistas for theatrical nuances. Romanticism, which was significant in Europe from the late 18th century onwards focused on imagination, emotion, subjectivity, freedom to experiment in verse form and appreciation of nature and paved the way for a radical change in attitudes wherein objectivity, reason and scientific examination would explore the human condition. The wide-spread emphasis for political, social and economic reforms in the wake of advances in technology and the belief in science over religion in solving human problems were responsible for this transformation.

The rise of trade unions and the need for a pragmatic approach to resolve social and economic issues saw the working classes fighting for their rights and raising their concerns for better living conditions. For the first time in the history of

Europe, the issues faced by the common man had occupied the centre-stage of discussions among social and literary circles and Realism and Naturalism emerged as the natural outcome of these developments.

Realism, the artistic movement that began in the early 19th century depicted ordinary people in everyday situations in a realistic manner was propounded by the Norwegian playwright Henrik Ibsen, who is regarded as the father of modern realism. The three-dimensional characters he created and the situations he put them in were directly related to the lives of common man and the audience easily related to events on the stage.

Naturalism focussed on how technological and scientific developments had a direct bearing on the lives of ordinary citizens and the role of genetics that helped understand individual lives. Charles Darwin's *The Origin of Species* propounded that only the fittest of any natural species would survive to pass on its genetic material. In drama, the naturalistic bent of production addressed subjects in a scientific manner and the writer observed and studied human interaction, just as a scientist would work in a laboratory.

The elaborate explanation of Naturalism and Realism, their characteristics and the points of difference between the two movements would be detailed in the specific chapters on Henrik Ibsen and his dramatic technique.

Dramatists Who Contributed to Naturalism and Realism

The French dramatist and novelist Émile Zola (1840-1902), in the Preface to his novel *Thérèse Raquin* (1867) mentioned that within the ambit of the Naturalist movement, the writer's task was to dissever human nature and the environment with the irrefutable deftness of a scientist. Zola's stage adaptation of the novel served as a model for theatrical naturalism that influenced later French playwrights such as Henri Becque and Jean Jullien.

The French playwright Jean Jullien (1854-1919) proposed drama to be "a slice of life put on stage with art" after his play *The Serenade* (1887) was staged in the Théâtre Libre in Paris. He believed that the purpose of naturalistic theatre was to make the audience think during the performance and after the play ended.

The French actor, director and film critic André Antoine (1858-1943) founded the Théâtre Libre in 1887, which championed the new naturalistic style of drama and staged Zola's play *Thérèse Raquin* after the theatre group for which Zola previously worked had refused to do so. Henrik Ibsen's *Ghosts* (1881), which had been banned in most of Europe was staged in this theatre.

Henrik Ibsen (1828-1906), the Norwegian playwright who began writing epic-poetic dramas, moved on to write naturalistic plays, then turned to symbolic naturalism and ended writing absurdist surreal drama. Themes related to women's rights, sin, alienation and abandonment, abuse of power, corruption and sexual frustration were expressed creatively with greater insight into human nature in his plays. *The Feast at Solhaug* (1855), *The Pretenders* and *Brand* both in 1864 and *Peer Gynt* (1867) belong to the early phase of epic poetical dramas. *Pillars of Society* (1877), *A Doll's House* (1897), and *Ghosts* (1881) are the plays that fit into the naturalistic tradition. *The Lady from the Sea* (1888), *Hedda Gabler* (1890), and *The Master Builder* (1892) are the Symbolic naturalistic dramas and the Absurdist or Surrealist drama is *When We Dead Awaken* (1899).

August Strindberg (1848-1912), the Swedish dramatist wrote novels and short stories apart from the plays. In his preface to the play *Miss Julie* (1888), he used Darwin's evolutionary theory of the survival of the fittest to connote the replacement of the upper classes by the more forceful lower classes. His important plays are *The Father* (1887), *Miss Julie* (1888), and *The Bond* (1892) among the naturalistic plays and the symbolic drama *The Ghost Sonata* (1907).

George Bernard Shaw (1856-1950), the Anglo-Irish playwright, recognised as one of the greatest English playwrights won the Nobel Prize for Literature in 1925 and his extraordinary writing career that extended to almost sixty years explored a wide range of contemporary social and political issues that permeated the fabric of the society. A socialist and founder member of the

Fabian Society, Shaw vouchsafed social, political and economic reforms and denounced war and corruption.

In the essay "The Quintessence of Ibsenism", commissioned by the Fabian Society and published in 1891, Shaw discussed the importance of the plays of Ibsen and subsequently the English stage was used as the instrument of social reforms. His collection *Plays Pleasant and Unpleasant* (1898) dealt with serious social issues; although the pleasant works deployed comedy to convey a social point of view. *Widowers' Houses* (1892), *The Philanderer* and *Mrs. Warren's Profession* (1898), *The Man of Destiny* (1897), *Arms and the Man* (1894), *Candida* (1898) and *You Never Can Tell* (1897) are dramas that emphasised social injustice, corruption of all forms and the futility of war. *Caesar and Cleopatra* (1898) and *Pygmalion* (1893) are other works that made him the unparalleled doyen of drama during his times. With the combined effects of clarity of presentation, the use of wit, and the employment of elegant language that provoked laughter and appealed to the intelligence of his audience, the age granted him the status of the most prolific writer of England.

Naturalism has profoundly influenced modern theatrical development beginning from its origins in the mid-19th century until the present day. The intricacies of the movement affected the productions that were staged, acted and presented. The late works of Strindberg and Ibsen were experimental in nature and the effects of Expressionism surfaced in the beginning of the 20th century.

20th Century Drama

The 20th century, the seminal age that endorsed a profusion of artistic and technological advancements not only disseminated the seeds of improvisation but also garnered critical comments and assessments due to the mingling of art and science in dramatic performances. The Welsh Marxist theorist Raymond Williams (1921-88), in *Drama from Ibsen to Brecht* mentions that the drama of the 20th century is "a record of difficulty and struggle...from Ibsen to Brecht, [it is] one of the great periods of dramatic history, a major creative achievement of our own civilization which gives a continuing understanding, imagination and courage" (401). Theatrical forms developed and evolved but they neither obliterated the qualities or attributes of dramas of the earlier periods nor operated in isolation.

Realism and Naturalism had a tremendous influence on the dramas of the late 19th and the early 20th centuries. The concept of the well-made play, which originated in France seemed to have spread throughout Europe even in the dawn of Naturalism and Realism. The cornucopia of -isms that arose from the conglomeration of social, political, technological and economic changes necessitated appropriate and diverse artistic endeavours to project the inherent conflicts and contradictions that was characteristic of the age.

The Age of -isms

Symbolism in Theatre (1885-1910)

The Symbolist Movement that began in the late 19th century with the work of a group of French poets proliferated to the visual arts and theatre and reached its zenith between 1885 and 1910. The Symbolist Movement was a reaction against Naturalism and Realism and ushered the avant-garde in modern theatre through divergent styles of action and production. Playwrights and directors were profoundly influenced by the psychological examination of Sigmund Freud's *The Interpretations of Dreams* (1900). The elements of mysticism and spirituality pervaded the theatre and Realism suffered a setback.

The Symbolist plays focused on the revelation and depiction of the inner lives and intimate moments of the characters. Plays resorted to unconventional plot lines and the production techniques blended traditional and personal symbols, metaphorical language, poetry and music. The Belgian playwright and Symbolic dramatist Maurice Maeterlinck (1862-1949) believed that the theatre was a specter or a reflection or probably a projection of symbolic forms. His play *The Blind* (1890) incorporated the elements of symbolism.

Expressionism

The movement associated with 20th century art, which was the most influential in Germany rejected the idea that art was a mirror of reality. Expressionists advocated that the artist should confront the darkest aspects of reality through nightmarish visions of the world, and distort all the expressions of reality to create an emotional effect that would evoke moods and ideas. They admonished conformity and convention and rejected the precepts of the well-made play and stage realism, and instead depicted bizarre events and disjointed plots. Poetic or obscene language was used and the themes were closely associated with humanitarianism.

Anguished or imbalanced mental states were depicted using stage images, and exceedingly subjective dramatic action. The themes chosen opposed several unrestrained familial and societal norms and the characters were largely representative types with titles rather than names. One of the significant writers and practitioners of the Expressionistic technique was the German playwright Benjamin Franklin Wedekind (1864-1918) and his predominant works were *Pandora's Box* (1804); *Spring Awakening and the Lulu Plays* and *Earth Spirit*, both in 1895.

Surrealism

Andre Breton (1896-1966), the French poet and critic published *The Surrealist Manifesto* in 1924 that defined the Surrealist movement as one that conjoined the conscious and the unconscious experiences to construct an "absolute reality", the "surreal". Surrealism which means "dreamlike" or "real but not real" drew heavily on the theories of Sigmund Freud where imagination was fed by the unconscious mind and in this context, Breton defined a genius to be one who is able to accede this source of artistic creativity.

The French poet and playwright Alfred Jarry was one of the founders of the avant-garde and his works had a major influence on the development of the Surrealist and Absurdist movements in theatre. His works include the trilogy, *Ubu Roi*, which means *King Ubu* (1896); *Ubu Cocu*, translated as *Ubu Cuckolded* (1897) and *Ubu Enchaine* that is *Ubu Enchained* (1899). The plays were parodies of some of the tragic plays of Shakespeare and Sophocles' *Oedipus Rex*. These plays were staged using puppets, placards and masks while the acting style employed pantomime and burlesque. The central character King

Ubu, a grotesque or ludicrous character could be inferred as a metaphor for modern man.

The French dramatist and poet Antonin Artaud (1896-1948) formulated the Theatre of Cruelty and wrote manifestoes to elaborate his thoughts. By "cruelty" he meant "to constantly disturb the audiences' senses" in order to shock the spectators when they see the despicable condition of the world they live in, performed on stage. He firmly denounced the text of a dramatic presentation as it would destroy freedom on stage, and hence defeat the purpose of "cruelty". Gestures, sound, unusual scenery and lighting together formed a unique language that was superior to spoken words. Exchange of thoughts and feelings between the actor and audience took place on the mental or spiritual levels and in this sense the theatre became a critically challenging sensory event rather than a visually pleasurable literary experience.

Epic Theatre

The German playwright Bertolt Brecht (1898-1956) became one of the most prominent stage practitioners of the modern times with the inauguration of the Epic Theatre, which was based on Aristotle's principle of catharsis. Brecht claimed that his intention was not to entertain people but to make them think. Therefore, he structured his plays in an episodic manner, where the plots were intricate and numerous characters were involved. The action of the play often dealt with the history of a foreign land and the narrative directly informed the happenings on stage in association with stage machinations, music, back projections, signs and banners.

Brecht employed the *Verfremdungseffekt effect*, which is a German phrase that means "to make strange". By this alienation technique, Brecht desired to achieve a distancing effect so that the audience would intellectually interact with theatre and not emotionally relate to the characters and in turn enable the actors to directly address the audience. The notable epic plays were *The Threepenny Opera* (*Die Dreigroschenoper*) a "play with music" adapted from a translation by Elisabeth Hauptmann of John Gay's English ballad opera *The Beggar's Opera*; *Mother Courage and her Children* (1939), an anti-war play; *The Resistible Rise of Arturo Ui* (1941) subtitled "A Parable Play" about Hitler's rise to power and *The Caucasian Chalk Circle* (1943) derived from an original Chinese play *Circle of Chalk* by Li Quianfu.

Conclusion

Several modes of dramatic representations have played a crucial role in incorporating the conditions of the world that have forever changed the perceptions of the world. Beginning from the Renaissance to the modern theatre, innovative ideas have led to the burgeoning of theatres that have not only commented upon but also brought about a rapid change in the way the world at large, imaginary situations, characters and instances are presented in front of an audience. The changes mentioned have accounted for projecting the observable and the non-observable as well as the real and the material aspects of human life. Human tendencies through interaction with the world outside and the constant dialogue with the mind have contributed to a plethora of platforms that project both the levels of interaction.

The change from representations that gave importance to the dramatist rather than the audience was evident in the early periods of production; however, the later theatre ushered the move to break down the gap between the playwright and the audience. The actors on stage delved into lives of people as if they were real and brought about a novel look into the way in which themes could be projected. Modern drama encompassed Naturalism, Realism, Surrealism, and Expressionism that looked not only at the world outside but also into the inner turmoil of the human mind due to the perceptible changes.

Glossary

pyrotechnic : relating to fireworks

avant-garde : novel and experimental ideas and methods in art, music, or literature.

connote : imply

Fabian Society : Founded in 1884, this British organisation was committed to engage in parliamentary and reformist means to encourage the adoption of socialist and democratic policies by means of political reform rather than revolution or overthrow.

The Chalk Circle : Sometimes translated The Circle of Chalk by Li Qianfu, is a Yuan dynasty (1259-1368) Chinese classical zaju verse play and gong'an crime drama, in four acts with a prologue.

References

Bogart, Travis and William Oliver, editors. *Modern Drama: Essays in Criticism*. Oxford UP, 1971.

Gassner, John. *Masters of the Drama*. Dover, 1954.

Greenblatt, Stephen, editor. *The Norton Anthology of English Literature*. 10th ed., vol. 4. W.W. Norton and Company, 2018.

Jacquelin, Martin. *Voice in Modern Theatre*. Routledge, 1991.

Maria, Lilla Crisafulli, and Keir Elam, editors. *Women's Romantic Theatre and Drama: History, Agency, and Performativity*. Ashgate, 2010.

Styan, J.L. *Modern Drama in Theory and Practice: Volume 1, Realism and Naturalism*. Cambridge UP, 1981.

Williams, Raymond. *Drama from Ibsen to Brecht*. Penguin, 1983.

https://theodora.com/encyclopedia/d/drama.html

http://www.historyworld.net/timesearch/default.asp?conid=static_timeline&timelineid=769&page=1&keywords=Drama%20timeline

Shaw George, Bernard. "The Quintessence of Ibsenism." https://warwick.ac.uk/fac/arts/english/currentstudents/undergraduate/modules/fulllist/special/endsandbeginnings/quintessenceofib00shawrich.pdf

Shaw George, Bernard. "The Quintessence of Ibsenism." https://www.litencyc.com/php/sworks.php?rec=true&UID=7514

Chapter 4

World Drama: Contemporary Expressions Across Countries

Theatre in the Later 20th Century Europe

The Age

The 20th century witnessed drastic and imminent changes in all spheres of human connections and communication because existing ideologies were being questioned as never before. Modernism was based on the belief that a rational, scientific explanation for everything could be found in a universe that had been created by God, and the prevalence of certain absolute truths expressed through language, within a comprehensible world would express concerns of the age within a finite set of rules for an ordered life. There was the sense of order and a certainty about the meaning of life; albeit, faith and science contradicted each other, and both existence and purpose of life could be elucidated.

However, as the 20th century progressed religious certainty was questioned and the world after the First World War (1914-18) were wary of religious beliefs and practices of the Church. The society suffered from poverty and social unrest due to increased political activism throughout the world. Economic collapse, the barbarism and genocide during Hitler's rule in Europe during the Second World War (1939-45), disillusionment with existing unstable or dictatorial forms of government, spiritual aridity, racial and ethnic tensions, sexual and gender inequalities, poverty and unemployment, famine and man-made calamities accelerated frictions and hostilities among nations of the world and resulted in unfathomable apprehensions and turbulence worldwide. To add to woes of masses, technological advancement and improvisations as well as mass communication systems turned the world into a network that operated in a clandestine manner and exacerbated the worsened political scenario.

Postmodernism

As a result of the social and philosophical shifts that overtly challenged the inherent order in modernism, postmodernism held the belief that there were no clear or fixed truths, only immediate sensory experiences, that is, truth is something that could be felt, not believed. Metanarratives that explained existence failed to give a succinct purpose for existence. There was nothing outside of human life that provided a set of values by which life could be lived, or a framework of good or bad that could be ascertained. Man lived in a world of images created by himself and those images did not provide any external explanation to instill a sense of what living was all about.

The world was a place where humans were largely engaged in the business of exercising power over one another and oppressing the weak. The world had turned a violent place to co-exist and it catered to the fulfillment of selfish interests and parochial alliances of those in power. Religion was an instrument that spread dogmatic principles and the sacred was no longer eulogised. The German philosopher Friedrich Nietzsche (1844-1900) is credited with outlining the ideology that is known in the Western world as postmodernism in his novel *Thus Spake Zarathustra* (1855). He is remembered for his dictates that "there are no facts, only interpretations" and "that this old God liveth no more. He is dead indeed".

Postmodernism in Theatre

The long-established rules of drama were challenged and many new forms of theatre developed; however, the popularity of the well-made play continued for a longer period of time. The British playwrights J.B. Priestley (1894-1984), Noel Coward (1899-1973) and Terence Rattigan (1911-77) considered theatre the appropriate vehicle for conveying information. Noel Coward's *The Vortex* (1924), the comic plays *Fallen Angels* (1925), *Hay Fever* (1925) and *Blithe Spirit* (1941) and the play *Cavalcade* (1931) were quite popular. Terence Rattigan's plays discussed issues of homosexuality, which was quite uncommon. His play *Separate Tables*, performed in 1945 dealt with the theme of isolation and frustration as a consequence of imposing rigid social conventions. *Ross*, performed in 1960 analysed the life of T.E. Lawrence of Arabia and *Bequest to the Nation*, in 1970 explored the intimate and covert aspects of the life of Lord Nelson. *Cause Célèbre*, the radio play broadcast in 1975 was his final work.

With the publication of the Hungarian-born British dramatist Martin Esslin's (1918-2002) book *The Theatre of the Absurd* (1962), a new category of drama called Absurd Drama emerged and announced such an approach to theatre that theatrical depictions had never perceived of or experimented before and this novel outlook at drama shattered the conventional notions of presentation of the existing theatres. Absurdism rebelled against conventional theatre and hence it is called an anti-theatre.

Language became meaningless, stage actions either went beyond or contradicted words spoken by characters. The characters talked in a fragmentary manner to fill the emptiness between them. Existence was depicted as excruciating, bewildering, troubling, and obscurely threatening. The implied meaning of words conveyed more meaning than what was actually being said. Mime, ballet, acrobatics, conjuring and clowning appeared prominently on the stage to project the senselessness and meaninglessness of existence in a world that was largely incomprehensible and alienated.

The Irish writer Samuel Beckett (1906-89) produced *Waiting for Godot* in 1935, *Endgame* in 1957, *Krapp's Last Tape* in 1958 and *Happy Days* in 1961, wherein he examined the pointlessness of life in a world that was largely absurd. Battered characters in barren landscape struggled to make sense of their lives. Eugene Ionesco (1909-94) the Romanian dramatist came out with *The Bald Soprano* in 1950, *The Chairs* in 1952 and *Rhinoceros* in 1960 to project man's inability to communicate meaningfully. His plays were characterised by bizarre themes such as the plight of the inhabitants of a small, provincial French town, metamorphosed into rhinoceroses in his play *Rhinoceros*. Jean Genet (1910-86) wrote about pertinent social issues and inquired into the plausible solutions to ameliorate the conditions of the people in the collective imbroglio, in *The Thief's Journal* (1940), *Death Watch* (1954), *The Balcony* (1956), and *The Screens* (1961).

Other playwrights who could be bracketed within the Theatre of the Absurd were Max Frish and Friedrich Durrenmatt of Switzerland, Fernando Arrabel of Spain and Edward Albee of America. Existentialist dramas of Jean-Paul Sartre, the plays of Arthur Miller and Tennessee Williams that were realistic and symbolic in nature, and the surrealist plays of Jean Cocteau expressed the disillusionment and pessimism of the 20th century.

Drama in the Latter Half of the 20th Century

The Age

It was a time of increased political and social tensions and uncertainties not only in Britain but across the whole of Europe and the Western world. The so-called cold war between the United States and Soviet Russia and respective allies that began in 1947 extended up to 1991. The breaking up of the Communist Soviet Socialist Republic into independent states, the issuance of *glasnost* (openness) and *perestroika* (restructuring) broke down the iron curtain that the Soviet Union had erected. Conflicts in Korea, Vietnam and Afghanistan emerged and these countries were declared perpetual war-torn areas due to the interference of armed forces of the United States and the Soviet Russia.

Possession of nuclear weapons by both sides was denounced because they were used for destructive purposes. Mass public movements in the form of social protests and marches were held in both the countries to stop the unauthorised infiltrations by both sides and concentrate on internal affairs of their citizens, public grievances, and work to address social and economic inequalities within their countries. In Europe, the Suez crisis of 1956, caused unrest in the Middle East when Britain and France failed to keep control of the Suez Canal.

The New-wave Playwrights

A post-war generation of middle-class, intellectual authors and playwrights referred as The Angry Young Men came into prominence in the 1950's led by John Osborne and the novelist Kingsley Amis (1922-95). John Osborne (1929-95) invented the kitchen-sink drama that was set in everyday working-class life and dealt with the anger felt by the people whose lives were controlled by power. His *Look Back in Anger* (1956), and *The Entertainer* (1957) are some of the finest works that probe the disillusionment, frustration and anger of middle-class sections of the society that struggles to cope with the failings of the political and social systems. Other plays by him include *Luther*, *Inadmissible Evidence* and *A Patriot for Me*.

The Absurd dramatist Harold Pinter (1930-2008) brought out *The Birthday Party* in 1958, *The Caretaker* (1960), *The Dumb-Waiter* (1960) and *The Homecoming* in 1965. He conjoined both the absurdist and the kitchen-sink styles of drama to create a sense of the uncanny and all his plays bear undertones of menace that is disturbing and unnerving. He is the inventor of a device known as the 'Pinter Pause', where actors use the technique of a deliberate silence to build up tension in a scene. The lofty position held by Harold Pinter is evident in the inclusion of the adjective 'Pinteresque' in *The Oxford English Dictionary*, which denotes the discernible style of Harold Pinter that includes elements of possessing the sense of menace and delivering dialogue interspersed by many pauses.

The British playwright Arnold Wesker (1932-2016), associated with the Angry Young Men group of writers wrote *The Kitchen* in 1957, Chips with Everything (1962), and The Roots Trilogy—*Chicken Soup with Barley* (1958); *Roots (*1959) and *I'm Talking about Jerusalem* in 1960. Joe Orton (1933-67) wrote black comedies that shocked, outraged and amused audiences and the adjective 'Ortonesque' is occasionally used to refer to works of similar styles. His important full-length plays *Entertaining Mister Sloane* (1964), *Loot* (1965) and *What the Butler Saw* (1969) were appalling black comedies about sexual avarice, violence and moral corruption and degradation and the one-act play *Funeral Games* (1968). All plays of Orton were true depictions of moral and social depravity, corrupt forces of power and the thriving of the rich at the expense of the poor.

The Period of the 1960s and Beyond and Theatre

The end of the 1960s was a defining period that bore testimony to the definite turn to violence with protests in all countries of the world against the Vietnam war, communist oppression and authoritarian governments. Feminist movements had gathered force and the new freedom that women had gained was reflected in intellectual, academic, social and political circles. Theatres were not censored and controversial topics of religion, politics and sex were discussed overtly. Homosexuality was acknowledged and the depiction of nudity on the stage was legalised.

The English playwright Edward Bond (b. 1934) described himself as a writer of a rational theatre that contradicted premises of the Theatre of the Absurd. He resorted to deploy theatre to analyse the society and describe a world ruined by the dominant capitalism that necessitated immediate action to salvage the loss rather than delve into individual isolation of characters and alienation in a society to address the onslaught of existential angst. He called his dramatic method "the Aggro technique" that was employed in his play *Saved* (1965). The play was internationally acclaimed for its fight to abolish theatre censorship, which eventually took place in 1968.

Sir David Hare (b. 1947) talked about several issues of political interest of the Middle East and similar to David Edgar his plays originated from agitprop theatre. *Via Dolorosa* (1998), *Racing Demon* (1990), *Murmuring Judges* (1991), and *The Absence of War* (1993) discussed current political issues that afflicted the nation. David Edgar (b. 1948) described actual political and social upheavals that affected countries of the world. *Destiny* (1976) discussed political campaigns, the bye-elections in the West Midlands and the rise of right-wing extremism in Britain during the mid-seventies. *The Shape of the Table* (1990) and *Playing with Fire* (2005) analysed political manoeuvers in several parts of Europe and Britain.

Tom Stoppard (b. 1937), the Czech-born British key playwright of the National Theatre, best known for the plays

Rosencrantz and Guildenstern are Dead (1967), *Travesties* (1974), *Arcadia* (1993), and *The Coast of Utopia* (2002) showed initial affiliation to the Absurd Theatre, but shifted to a distinct category of the "plays of ideas" that examined philosophical concepts and made them entertaining through the clever use of word play and jokes. His popularity rested in the fact that he was one of the most internationally performed dramatists of his generation. Alan Ayckbourn's (b. 1939) *The Norman Conquest Trilogy* (1973), *Bedroom Farce* (1975), *Woman in Mind* (1985), and *Private Fears in Public Places* (2004) among others are considered significant for their comic presentations of moral choice in common parlance.

The abusive language of John Osborne's *Look Back in Anger* (1956) and Edward Albee's *Who's Afraid of Virginia Woolf?* (1962), pauses and intermittent silences of Harold Pinter's plays and the orgiastic recklessness of Julian Beck's *Paradise Now!* (1968) reflect elements of the Theatre of Cruelty. The British playwrights' David Storey's *Home* (1971); Sir Alan Ayckbourn's trilogy, *Norman Conquests* (1974), and David Hare's *Amy's View* (1998) worked on Realism from the dimensions of psychology, politics and society.

John Arden (b. 1930) produced the plays *Serjeant Musgrave's Dance* (1959) and *The Happy Haven* (1960), neither being didactic nor impressionistic in depiction. He made a break with realism in *Serjeant Musgrave's Dance. The Waters of Babylon* (1957) was a grotesque satirical play that dealt with corruption at the government level.

Theatre from Other Parts of the World: An Overview

Germany

Goethe who wrote from the 1770s to the early 1800s was one of the most eminent German writers. His poetic drama *Faust* narrated the tragedy of a man who sold his soul to the devil to attain worldly desires and regain his youth. In the 1890s, Gerhart Hauptmann (1862-1946) initiated the mode of dramatic presentation called Naturalism in the *German theatre*. His work *The Weavers* was a socially committed play. The contribution of Bertolt Brecht (1898-1956) that spanned for almost thirty years from the 1920s through the 1950s featured his plays *Mother Courage, The Caucasian Circle,* and *The Good Woman of Setzuan* among others, and thereby revolutionised German theatre with the introduction of the Epic theatre.

Heiner Müller (1929-95) ingrained Brecht's notion of "Kopien", the German equivalent for "copying", whereby the text by other writers could be "used, imitated or rewritten" and he used the materials as primary texts for his creations. His work, says Banham "marks beginning of a tradition of densely poetic dramaturgy based in the logic of association, rather than linear "dramatic narrative." For over fifty years, Müller remained one of the most celebrated playwrights and his drama was labelled "postdramatic theatre" by Hans-Thies Lehmann in 1999.

France

Moliere, Voltaire, Victor Hugo and Alexander Dumas produced important drama in France from the 17th to the 19th centuries. The French theatre of the 20th century was occupied by the plays of Jean Giraudoux (1882-1944), Jean Anouilh (1910-87), Jean-Paul Sartre (1905-80) and Samuel Beckett that were unique in presentation and new in subject-matter. Giraudoux's *Tiger at the Gates, The Madwoman of Chaillot,* and Jean Anouilh's *The Lark, Antigone,* and *Becket* were staged in several countries around the world. Anouilh was the most popular dramatist with nearly 50 dramatic works to his credit. His plays did not give importance to social relations, but they were bitter satirical portrayals of morality.

Jean-Paul Sartre's *No Exit* and *The Flies* are plays that follow the existential mode of dramatic presentation. Musicals *Les Misérables* and *Miss Saigon* by Alain Boublil and Claude-Michel Schonberg enthralled audiences in the latter half of the 20th century. Samuel Beckett's plays were originally written in French, but they were translated into several languages and staged worldwide.

Italy

Plays by Luigi Pirandello, written in the 1900s were filled with intrigue and controversial issues. They also portrayed complexities of human relationships and identities of people who may not be true to how they appear, which means he expressed the ways in which man portrayed the changing perceptions of reality. *Six Characters in Search of an Author* (1921), *Naked Masks* (1916-24) and *Right You Are, If You Think You Are* (1917) Dario Fo (1926-2016), the recipient of the Nobel Prize for Literature in 1997, contributed substantially to the theatre during the last quarter of the 20th century with more than eighty plays, and some along with his wife and actress Franca Rame. His most popular plays, *Morte accidentale di un anarchico* (*Accidental Death of an Anarchist,* 1970), and *Non si paga, non si paga!* (*We Can't Pay? We Won't Pay!,* 1974) were performed in several international forums.

Spain

Poet and dramatist Garcia Lorca (1898-1936) portrayed the Spanish country people, nationalistic spirit and the life of the gypsies in his plays. His popular plays were *Blood Wedding, Yerma* and *The House of Bernardo Alba*. José Echegaray, who won the Nobel Prize for Literature in 1922, employed the free verse form and imagery of the Romantics, but his plays dealt with controversial issues. His significant play was *The Passion Flower* (1922).

Russia

Many Russian playwrights followed the lead of the other European writers in producing plays that took for their subject, everyday lives of the middle-class and the poor for serious realistic dramas. Ivan Turgenev (1818-83), with his important play in the Russian naturalistic style, *A Month in the Country* (1850) that dealt with issues of economic divide and poverty. Nikolai Gogol (1808-52), in his play *Gogol's Government Inspector* (1836) satirised the politically corrupt Imperial Russian bureaucracy.

Anton Chekov (1860-1904) projected the harsh realities of the lower middle-class and the peasant life, marked by objectivity and unsentimental depiction. His play *The Seagull* (1895) was important because he pioneered what was called "the indirect action play". His later plays *Uncle Vanya* (1897), *The Three Sisters* (1901) and *The Cherry Orchard* (1904) brought out the concept of dramatic realism.

Konstantin Stanislavsky (1863-1968) and Vladimir Nemirovich-Danchenko (1858-1943) together founded the progressive theatre company called the Moscow Arts Theatre in 1837 to stage the realistic theatre performed by actors who were rigorously trained. His acting career began in his family's amateur theatre group called The Alekseyev Circle. Maxim Gorky (1868-1936), the greatest writer of the new realistic theatre in Russia, dealt with injustice, violent crime, adultery and corruption in his plays such as *The Philistines* (1901) and *Enemies* (1906).

Czechoslovakia

The Ĉapek brothers, in the former Czechoslovakia achieved fame in the 1920's and 1930's with expressionistic plays that indulged in social issues. The theme of the play *Rossum's Universal Robots*, futuristic in projection, explained how the world would change drastically when robots would eventually take over humanity.

Ireland

The plays of W.B. Yeats and Lady Gregory combined dance, poetry and myth. Some of the plays were *At the Hawk's Well*, *Spreading the News* and *Hyacinth Halvey*. J.M. Synge wrote in the early 1900s and his plays *The Playboy of the Western World* and *Riders to the Sea* are prominent plays. Sean O'Casey wrote *Juno and the Paycock* and *The Plough and the Stars*. The late 20th century Irish playwrights include Brian Friel and Brendan Behan. Friel's *Dancing at Lughnasa* (1990) and Martin McDonagh's *Leenane* trilogy (1990) discussed contemporary themes employing wit, irony and satire.

China

Chinese drama had always been traditionally linked to the policies of the government and the country's political situation. When the Japanese invaded China in 1937, playwrights wrote plays on nationalistic grounds and reworked the old ones for patriotic propaganda. Peking Opera, developed in China in the 19th century incorporated diverse facets of historical drama, spoken drama, song drama, dance drama and ballet. Costumes were stylised, traditional characters were represented and social classes were depicted throughout the dramatic performances. The makeup for characters included symbolic colours and designs that represented different human qualities.

Japan

Three major forms of drama, unique to Japan and produced before international audiences were Noh, Bunraku and Kabuki. Devised by the fourteenth-century actor Zeami Motokiyo, Noh combined lyrics, dance and music to events of the story that are portrayed. Almost 600 years old, this form of drama is enacted in its traditional form even in modern times. Performers were men and the subject matter of the Noh play was the life of Gods, brave warriors, and the nobility. Three parts of the Noh are jo-ha-kyu. "Jo" is the introduction, "ha" is the body and "kyu" is the conclusion. This structured form of drama usually begins with the story of a God and evolves to include a warrior play, a love story with a beautiful woman and ends with a frenzied dance by a God or demon.

Bunraku or the Japanese doll theatre presented performances by wood carved marionettes as tall as four foot with realistic, moveable eyes, eyebrows and mouth handled by men only. Three puppeteers dressed in black held a puppet each close to their bodies and moved around the stage. Dialogues were rendered by specialised chanters that appeared on to the stage to perform each scene.

An innovative form of drama performed by men only, Kabuki combined the elements of Noh and Bunraku, but differed in the use of elaborate make-up, brightly-coloured costumes, assorted music, vocal renditions and exquisite stages settings specially designed to promote its production.

African Drama

Drama, in Africa owes its rich diversity and complexity to the indigenous performance traditions that include music, dance, mime, and story-telling. The African theatre is syncretic in that it combines the traditional with the modern art forms to provide a wholesome combination that appeases the mind, soul and the body. Pre-colonial African performances included complexity of forms that employed the regional language to set of symbols.

Drums, dances, masks and masquerades such as the Pende Masks, and the Yoruba Egungun along with the Bamana or the Bambara puppets were deployed in religious and social dramas and performed at religious occasions too. Initiation ceremonies for youngsters, called the Rites of Passage; preparation for training in hunting and wars; celebrations honouring the dead and social gatherings were occasions when performances were conducted.

In 1927, G.B. Sinxo's *Debeza's Baboons* became the first play in Xhosa language to be performed. H.I.E. Dhlomo (1903-56) published the first drama in English by a black person, *The Girl Who Killed to Save: Nongquase the Liberator* in 1935. However, with the official advent of colonialism in 1885, the World Wars and the independence movements in the 1950s and the 1960s, the subsequent civil wars and apartheid, performances turned into sites of reinforcement, resistance and subversion of the existing social orders (Drewal 15). The Negritude Movement coined by Aimé Césaire purposefully included the offensive term Negro in 1932, and carried forward by Léopold Sédar Senghor, Léon Gontran-Damas, the Black literature in Paris from 1932 to 1966 turned the venue for serious depictions of Black solidarity against the disruptive forces.

The Independence Movement that includes Edward Blyden, W.E.B. Dubois, Haile Selassie, Kwame Nkrumah and Sékou Touré known as Panafricanism, the Mau-Mau Uprising, National Theatres and National Ballets, the travelling theatre companies in Nigeria such as Duro Ladipo and Hubert Ogunde along with television groups and the introduction of Nollywood used for social commitment. Dramas employed surrealistic techniques to raise social concerns and criticised politics of the time. Wole Soyinka, Ngugi wa Thiongo, Ama Ata Aidoo, Femi Osofisan, and Bernard Dadié were some of the prominent dramatists of Africa.

Black consciousness movement gave rise to the political theatre that fervently advocated the use of theatre to unite the black population and remind them of history, servitude, forced assimilation and lost culture to resist further dehumanisation. Dance and music in energetic tempos to sonorous beat movements were infused with theatre. Banham and Plastow notice that certain playwrights in Zimbabwe use "Ndenglish", a deliberate mixing of Ndebele and English, "and in [some] southern African plays...we see a basic English script which utilises many indigenous language terms as well as a street language which draws on multiple tongues."

The Nigerian playwright, poet, author, teacher and political activist and Nobel Prize Laureate for Literature in 1986, Wole Soyinka wrote around 29 plays. Some of his plays include *The Swamp Dwellers* (1958), *The Lion and the Jewel* (1959), *The Road* (1965), *Madmen and Specialists* (1970), *Opera Wonyosi* (1977), *A Play of Giants* (1984), and *King Baabu* (2001) to name a few.

Guillaume Oyono Mbia (1939), African dramatist and short-story writer, one of bilingual Cameroon's few writers to achieve success both in French and in English created comedies that played well both on stage and on radio. *Trois prétendants...un mari* (*Three Suitors...One Husband,* 1962), *Until Further Notice* (1967), *Notre fille ne se mariera pas*! (*Our Daughter Will Not Marry*!, 1969), and *His Excellency's Train* (1969) are notable plays. His plays centred on themes such as the confrontation of youth and adult, and modernity and tradition.

Drama in the United States of America

The American company managed by David Douglas was the first professional company to produce plays in the American colonies. The first American play was *The Prince of Parthia* by Thomas Godfrey in 1767, in Philadelphia, which imitated the British blank verse tragedies and had only one performance. *The Contrast* by Royall Tyler was the first comedy to achieve professional success in the United States. The first theatre in America was built in Williamsburg, Virginia in 1716. The first actors on American stages were John Drew and Luis Lane. Lane became the first female American actor manager. Edwin Booth (1833-93) was one of the greatest romantic actors in America during his period.

American Playwrights

American playwrights continued to follow the prevailing conventions of drama for some time until the 20th century when theatre became more innovative and experimental in theme and technique. Eugene O'Neill's (1888-1953) *The Emperor Jones*, *The*

Iceman Cometh, Days without End, The Hairy Ape, and *Long Day's Journey into Night*, written in the Expressionistic technique presented man's struggle with destruction and deception of the self and the chances of redemption. His full-length play in the Naturalistic tradition was *Beyond the Horizon.*

In 1949, Arthur Miller (1915-2005) wrote the classic tragedy that explored the American Dream in *Death of a Salesman*, and the other moral and political tragedies, *The Crucible* and *All My Sons. All My Sons* was a drama modelled on Ibsenism. While *The Crucible* entailed the Salem witchcraft trials of 1962, used as a parable for McCarthyism in America in the 1950s, the play *The Misfits*, a screenplay was written for his wife Marilyn Monroe. Tennessee Williams' (1911-83) *American Blues, Battle of Angels, The Glass Menagerie,* and *The Streetcar Named Desire* portrayed diverse aspects of human life.

As the 20th century progressed, playwrights concentrated on social issues that plagued the American society. James Baldwin's *Blues for Mister Charley* and *Amen Corner* were important influences on the Civil Rights Movement of the 1960s. Thornton Wilder examined life in a small town in the classic *Our Town.* Clifford Odets brought out *Waiting for Lefty* and *Country Girl.* Susan Gaspell wrote plays that influenced the feminist movement in the early 20th century. Her most important work was *Alison's House.* Alice Childress dealt with racism in her plays *Wine in the Wilderness* and *Trouble in Mind.*

Australian Drama

Robert Sidaway (1758-1809), an ex-convict set up the first theatre in Australia in 1796; however, it was closed down due to a spate of robberies in the houses of the patrons. Later, from 1834 to 1914, several theatres were built, where around 600 plays were staged. "The Film", an organisation that was famous for commercial productions was founded by J.C. Williamson and Maggie Moore. What was described as the "golden age of melodrama" witnessed the contribution from George Darrell, Alfred Dampier, Garnet Walsh and Bland Holt who popularised "Australian characters: the bushman, the new chum, the girl of the bush and the loyal 'mate'—and the status of the local actor-manager" (Morley 53).

Louis Esson was considered the father of Australian theatre of the twentieth century. Esson's plays *The Woman Tamer* (1910), *Dead Timber* (1911), and *Mother and Son* (1923) gained popularity because they subverted masculine roles. Pioneer Players (1922), co-founded by Esson was a gathering formed to produce and promote the plays by Australians. Australian Drama nights was promoted by William Moore between 1909 and 1912. Reflexive drama was encouraged and developed by the journalist Leon Brodzky through his Australian Theatre Society (1904). The earliest of Esson's plays were presented by McMahon of the Melbourne Repertory Theatre.

Katharine Susannah Prichard, in *Brumby Innes* criticised sexual exploitation of women, racial discrimination and domestic violence. The New Theatre produced *Waiting for Lefty* (1936), *The Thirteen Dead* (1936), *War on the Waterfront* (1939) and *Reedy River* (1951). From the 1930s to the radical 1960s and 1970s playwright-novelists such as Betty Roland, Dymphna Cusack and Frank Hardy contributed to drama. Henrietta Drake-Brockman's *Men Without Wives* (1944), Elaine Ackworth's *Composing Venus* (1995), and Patrick White's expressionist drama *The Ham Funeral* (1947) were popular.

The Union Theatre Repertory Company (UTRC), established on the campus of Melbourne University and the Australian Elizabethan Theatre Trust, was set up under the guidance of British expatriate Hugh Hunt, where Ray Lawler's *The Summer of the Seventeenth Doll* (1955) was enacted. National Black Theatre produced *Basically Black* (1973), that featured Jack Charles and Bob Maza, and performed Robert Merritt's *The Cake Man* (1974). Jack Davis, Australia's leading indigenous playwright, produced his trilogy with the Black Swan Company in Western Australia. Andrew Ross worked with Jimmy Chi, and Nicholas Parsons and Bryan Brown in the productions of *Dead Heart* in 1993 and 1996 respectively.

Women Playwrights and Practitioners of the 20th Century

Joan Littlewood (1914-2002) was one of the most influential British theatrical directors of the 20th century. She instituted a company in Manchester called Theatre Workshop in 1945. Her productions include *Oh! What a Lovely War* (1963) that used

Brechtian techniques such as newspaper headlines, direct address, popular songs of the period and other devises to disparage the First World War. The other prominent productions were *The Quare Fellow* (1956) and *The Hostage* (1958) by Brenda Behan, and *A Taste of Honey* (1958) by Shelagh Delany.

Known as the playwright of women's self-hood, the Afro-American Lorraine Hansberry wrote about a variety of social issues such as equality for women and family solidarity. Her play *A Raisin in the Sun* (1959) discussed the lives of minorities and women. Ntozake Shange projected the predicaments of the Black community, issues of race and Black power in her works. She is internationally acclaimed for her play *For Colored Girls Who Have Considered Suicide When the Rainbow is Enuf* (1976).

The Radical Feminist Theatre

Women's Theatre Group (1973) and Monstrous Regiments (1975) were the theatre groups that encouraged women writers to resuscitate women's hidden history, discover and encourage women writers, give women opportunities for work especially in technical areas, which had always been male preserves and put real women on the stage without projecting stereotypical representations of women.

England's Caryl Churchill (b. 1938), recognised the founder member of the Joint Stock and Monstrous Regiment Theatre companies linked feminism with a socialist view of society. Her best known plays include *Top Girls* (1982), *In a Light Shining in Buckingham Shire* (1976) and *Cloud Nine* (1979). Pam Gems (b. 1925) wrote plays like *Queen Christina* (1977), *Piaf* (1978), and *The Blue Angel* (1991), where historical figures as successful women played the dominant role and their lives propagated how women could overcome troubled backgrounds to achieve success through resilience and determination.

The Cuban-Mexican experimentalist dramatist Maria Irene Forńes (1930-2018), in *Fefu and Her Friends* (1977), and the American realist playwrights Beth Henley, in *Crimes of the Heart* (1978); Marsha Norman, in *Night Mother* (1982), and Wendy Wassertein, in *The Heidi Chronicles* (1988) analysed several feminist themes. The British dramatist Sarah Kane (1971-99) developed a unique style of blending the Expressionist techniques and the Jacobean tragedy and earned a critic's comment on her theatre to be "In-Yer-Face-theatre". Her works include *Blasted* (1995), *Skin* (1997), *Crave* (1998), and *4.48 Psychosis* (2000) that shocked the audience with brutal and powerful images of rape and torture. Expert monologists such as Eve Ensler, in the *Vagina Monologues* (1996) produced women-centred one-man shows.

Drama in the Last Decades of the 20th Century

The period chiefly concentrated on rights of marginalised sections of the society especially women, homosexuals, the ethnic population, and the racially discriminated. Experimental dramas by groups as Beck's Living Theatre and Jerzy Grotowski's Polish Laboratory Theatre merged several aspects of performance art, improvisations in technique, elements of postmodernism and media and the other categories of avant-garde theatre.

Tectonic Plates (1988) by the Canadian writer-director Robert Lepage; the one-man shows of the monologists such as Eric Bogosian, and Spalding Gray; the transgressive dance-dramas of Charles Ludlam's "Ridiculous Theatre" to which the play *The Mystery of Irma Vep* (1984) belonged along with the multimedia experimental theatre of Robert Wilson in *White Raven* (1999) conjoined several modes of presentation and received critical acclaim.

New York's La MaMa (1961) and Mabou Mines (1970-) were theatre groups that produced innovative dramas. James Baldwin's *Blues for Mr. Charley* (1964), Amiri Baraka's *Dutchman* (1964), Charles Gordone's *No Place to be Somebody* (1967) and Ed Bullins' *The Taking of Miss Janie,* produced in 1975 drew the attention of the audiences worldwide to controversies and apprehensions of the Black Americans.

Conclusion

Diverse ways to represent life on stage through art found drama to be one of the prominent modes of presentation that incorporated elements related to sight, sound, light and colour variations. Drama that was once a mere stage presentation with the plot, characters, sound and light to appeal to the audiences gradually turned complex due to the interplay of different constituents of drama to serve purposes suitable to the changing times. Drama became a mode of communication that was not restricted to a unidimensional approach to understand its multidimensional appeal.

Theatre emerged as one of the most effectual prolific art forms that transformed the conventions of theatricality. The twentieth century produced some of the most versatile dramatists that not only concentrated on themes of plays written by them but also on innovative ways in which plays could be rendered to the audience so that the desired effect could be produced.

Dramatic representations are unique in terms of themes, characterisation, settings, costumes, music and other paraphernalia. From Europe, drama travelled across countries that welcomed the stagecraft, infused it with distinct perceptions and offered a rich platter of savory recipes that left connoisseurs, amateurs and the common man in a state of absolute bliss. Drama also opened gates to several commitments that raised consciousness among marginalised sections to revolt against atrocities, which earned the support of the world. Possibilities of drama were wide-reaching and enigmatic and it was left to dramatists to decide the appropriate mode of presentation to suit their intentions.

Glossary

Agitprop : A popular form of political theatre that emerged in the 1930's that discussed several issues concerning marginalised sections of the society.
aridity : barrenness
unfathomable : profound
clandestine : concealed
exacerbate : worsen
eulogise : extol or glorify
dictates : pronouncements
metamorphose : transform
censor : amend or edit
manoeuvre : move skillfully

orgiastic : debauched or wanton
dramaturgy : practice of dramatic composition

References

Banham, Martin. *The Cambridge Guide to World Theatre*. Cambridge UP, 1995.

Banham, Martin, and Jane Plastow, editors. *Contemporary African Plays*. Routledge, 1989.

Drewal, Margaret. "The Sate of Research on Performance in Africa." *African Studies Review,* vol. 34, no. 3, pp. 1-64.

Maria, Lilla Crisafulli, and Keir Elam, editors. *Women's Romantic Theatre and Drama: History, Agency, and Performativity*. Ashgate, 2010.

Morley, Michael, editor. *The Continuum Companion to Twentieth Century Theatre*. Colin Chambers, 2002.

Styan, J.L. *Modern Drama in Theory and Practice: Volume 1, Realism and Naturalism.* Cambridge UP, 1981.

Wright, Elizabeth. *Postmodern Brecht: A Re-Presentation*. Routledge, 2016.

https://www.britannica.com/art/dramatic-literature

https://www.britannica.com/art/dramatic-literature/Drama-in-Western-cultures

https://www.britannica.com/art/Western-theatre/Theatre-of-the-20th-century-and-beyond

https://theodora.com/encyclopedia/d/drama.html

http://www.historyworld.net/timesearch/default.asp?conid=static_timeline&timelineid=769&page=1&keywords=Drama%20timeline

Shaw George, Bernard. "The Quintessence of Ibsenism." https://warwick.ac.uk/fac/arts/english/currentstudents/undergraduate/modules/fulllist/special/endsandbeginnings/quintessenceofib00shawrich.pdf

https://www.litencyc.com/php/sworks.php?rec=true&UID=7514

Chapter 5

Drama of the Nineteenth Century in Europe and Henrik Ibsen

Nineteenth Century Drama in Europe

Myths, legends, anecdotes and pantomime shows along with stock characters formed an integral part of the European drama until the 19th century. Due to the widespread political revolution in the mid-19th century, plays written during the period focused on miserable lives of the people who belonged to the lowest strata of the society. A radical transformation in dramatic representation emerged with the rise of the bourgeois drama that was instrumental to the beginning of modern drama.

With the rise of Romanticism and its preference for commonplace incidents and ordinary lives of individuals, the 19th century writers romanticised mundane lives of people and this initiated the drive to glorify the outlaw, which in a way foresaw the rise of the impending revolution in literature and other art forms.

Ideas that propagated Romanticism emerged early in Germany in the work of three major playwrights Gotthold Ephraim Lessing (1729-81), Johann Christophe Friedrich von Schiller (1759-1805) and Johann Wolfgang von Goethe (1749-1832). These writers admired Shakespeare and advocated diversity and freedom in theatrical productions. While Goethe chose mythological figures as his subjects, Schiller preferred patriots of European history, the most prominent being Joan of Arc and William Tell.

The Closet Drama

During the early nineteenth century, many plays called closet dramas were written to be read rather than performed. Writers intended to explore philosophical issues through poetic dialogue rather than think about practical problems of staging plays. Since these dramas were written in freestyle and retained as manuscript publications with characters and extensive stage directions, the plays could be imagined as if they were being performed on stage. Lord Byron's *Manfred: A Dramatic Poem* (1817) and Shelley's *The Cenci* (1819) imitated Shakespeare. Milton's *Samson Agonistes* (1671), the earliest closet drama and Shelley's *Prometheus Unbound* (1819) were based on Greek tragedies. The two parts, *Faust, Part 1* (1828-29) and *Faust, Part 2* (1832) of *Faust*, a tragic play by Johann Wolfgang von Goethe were acclaimed closet dramas. Other prominent closet dramas are Robert Browning's *Strafford* (1837) and *Pippa Passes* (1841).

During the English Civil War, Thomas Killigrew (1612-83) wrote several closet dramas. His closet dramas, the ten-act double plays unintended for the stage were *Thomaso, or the Wanderer*, a comedy based on Killigrew's experiences in European exile; *Bellamira Her Dream, or Love of Shadows*; and *Cicillia and Clorinda, or Love in Arms* were heroic romances. However, Aphra Behn later adapted *Thomaso* for her successful *The Rover* (1677).

George Eliot's *The Spanish Gypsy* (1868), Michael Field's *Stephania* (1892), and Augusta Webster's *A Woman Sold* (1867) that critiqued the social, cultural and ideological restrictions imposed on women of their time were dramas meant for private reading or performing. It is quite interesting to note that several women writers in the 16th and 17th centuries resorted to closet dramas, since they were restricted from openly staging their social and political protests. Some prominent women dramatists who wrote Closet dramas included Jane Lumley (1537-78), an English noble; Elizabeth Cary (1585-1639), an English poet, dramatist, translator, and historian, who was recognised the first woman who had written and published an original play in English, *The*

Tragedy of Mariam; Margaret Lucas Cavendish (1623-73), the English aristocrat, fiction-writer, and playwright; and Anne Finch (1661-1720), the English poet and courtier.

William Robertson Davies (1913-95), the Canadian novelist, playwright, and critic, in *A Voice from the Attic: Essays on the Art of Reading* (1990), disapproved the closet drama and described it as "Dreariest of literature, most second hand and fusty of experience!"

Theatrical Production in Europe in the 19th Century

Lighting effects were introduced and geographical locales were reproduced on stage. Scenic constructions along with lighting devices and several actors and musicians on the stage added to the faithful representation of several scenes. Large-scale panoramas associated with historical films were staged with ease. Extravagant staging presentations enhanced the credibility of performances and the rise of stardom was inevitable. The popularity of actors, the phenomenon of stardom, and star power enhanced the role of the theatrical professional—the director whose job to coordinate the performances of actors became prominent.

During the late eighteenth century and the early nineteenth century, the affluent families that settled in Paris turned the face of the city from a township to a flourishing urbane locale that was glamourous and appealing. Groups with political leanings and particular social inclinations such as Conservatives, Liberals, Democrats and Republicans emerged in France and other parts of Europe that projected their divergent visions of society and government rule and competed with each other to gain the support of the citizens. The period witnessed the rise of a new urban class worker, drawn by rapid industrialisation and the ideals of French revolution who joined hands in forming various alliances and confederations that aligned with groups of political parties.

In the mid-19th century, huge profits reaped from the proliferation of industries in France and England, and the emergent ruling class with uncontrollable power attached greater importance to wealth than intellect or power, and this change severely affected dramatic productions. Drama catered to the interests and tastes of the rich, and modern drama was reduced to a saleable product.

The Boulevard Theatre

The Boulevard Theatre rose to prominence under French dramatists Eugene Scribe (1791-1861) known for the perfection he brought into the well-made play, Alexandre Dumas (1824-95) and Victorien Sardou (1831-1908) who also played a significant role in the development of the well-made play. Well-made plays involved intricate plots and featured stock characters that led to dramatic revelations that were impulsive. Unbelievable coincidences with stock characters occupied a major part of the well-made play that showcased rewards towards the end.

This theatre focused on commercial productions for profit rather than the development of theatre as art, and hence focused on issues and themes related to middle-class lives. Dramatic presentations included the sympathetic portrayal of mundane routines of the ordinary people and later the conservative middle class. Later, melodrama, farce and well-made plays turned to project the lavish upper-class world of privileges, funded by their money and power and ignored heritage. The new elite engaged in amusements that were shunned by old aristocrats who found them more frivolous than serious.

The theatrical partnership of the dramatist W.S. Gilbert and the composer Arthur Sullivan, popularly known as Gilbert and Sullivan jointly wrote comic operas between 1871 and 1896 that won international acclaim. Some of the comic operas in two acts with music by Arthur Sullivan and a libretto by W.S. Gilbert include *H.M.S. Pinafore or, The Lass That Loved a Sailor* (1878); *The Pirates of Penzance*; *or, The Slave of Duty* (1879); *Princess Ida* (1884); *The Mikado or, The Town of Titipu* (1885). Oscar Wilde, wrote *The Importance of Being Earnest* (1895) towards the end of the century.

Introduction to Modern European Drama

Modern theatre is believed to have developed in the mid-19th century with the introduction of the plays of Henrik Ibsen, the Norwegian playwright who infused drama with his radical bent of thought. While J.T. Grein, a Dutchman introduced Ibsen to the

English audience in 1890, William Archer, the dramatic critic in England championed the cause of Ibsen for theatrical productions. Realism in plot, use of dialogue, deft characterisation, and themes on social issues that had psychological repercussions gained such relevance that they carried away sensibilities of the people and these plays, popularly termed "a drama of ideas", achieved wide acclaim.

Characters in Realist plays vacillated with ideas and struggled against forces of tradition and society. Ibsen's ideas were bold experiments to project his theories through his unique technique of ideas. His dramas shook the clutches of stardom and crushed the stronghold of the commercial minded theatre-managers because the new drama restricted stifling the power of true dramatic art. Modern drama, with the advent of Ibsen, transpired successful in eliminating artificiality in the arts, and simultaneously promoting the genuine worth of drama.

On the one hand, William Archer promulgated plays of Ibsen and on the other, George Barnard Shaw introduced the real spirit of Ibsen into English drama. Plays of Shaw were inspired by John Galsworthy who gave a version of realism in drama, which did not possess the reformist zeal of a propagandist. This infused realism was described as naturalism—the attempt to present "both fare and foul, no more no less." The naturalistic play is intended to be objective and impersonal and both Harley Granville Barker and John Galsworthy were absolutely passionate about the presentation of the naturalist drama. Barker rebelled against the despotism of Victorian convention over the individual and Galsworthy resisted the inhumane and mighty social forces that crushed the individual.

The Contribution of George Bernard Shaw

George Bernard Shaw (1856-1950), one of the foremost Anglo-Irish playwrights who wrote almost fifty plays for the stage was influenced by Ibsen and European naturalist writers. He produced his collection *Plays, Pleasant and Unpleasant* (1898) that mainly dealt with serious and debatable issues in the society. *Widowers' Houses* (1892) exposed the exploitation of working classes by rich landlords. *The Philanderer* (1898) inquired the relationship between sexes. *Mrs. Warren's Profession*

(1898) voiced the problems of the prostitutes and questioned the attitude of the society towards prostitution. The play in turn highlighted economic deprivation and the lack of opportunities available for women at the time. *The Man of Destiny* (1897) brought out ideals of liberty, honour and reputation, which was presented through an imaginary conversation between Napoleon and a mysterious woman.

Arms and the Man (1894) advocated the futility of war, reality and heroism at the cost of human lives. *Candida* (1898) questioned the notions of marriage and the relationship between husband and wife. The play *You Can Never Tell* (1897) discussed notions of independence and marriage. *Caesar and Cleopatra* (1898) told the story of the young Queen Cleopatra's love affair with the much older Roman Emperor Julius Caesar and *Pygmalion* (1913) was a comic classic about an English professor's efforts to transform a Cockney flower girl into a duchess. Its popular musical *My Fair Lady* (1956) was later adapted as a movie in 1964. Shaw won the Nobel Prize for Literature in 1925.

Two prominent concepts in Shaw's plays were "Life Force" and "Thinking Person's Society". The notion of "Life Force" held the belief that humanity possessed the innate capacity to improve and emerge stronger despite oddities in life. The conception of "Thinking Person's Society" was that out of thousand people, 700 would not think, 299 were idealists and only one person would think. Shaw attempted to transform idealists into thinkers through his dramas.

The Revival of Poetic Drama

An important facet of modern drama was the rebirth of the poetic drama along with the naturalistic and realistic plays. Plays of W.B. Yeats (1865-1939) were poetic to a certain extent, but the Irish theatre drifted towards realism. In England, poetic drama was introduced by Stephen Phillips (1864-1915) whose blank verse plays were enjoyed during the initial years of the century. John Masefield (1878-1967) and John Drinkwater (1882-1937) revived the poetic drama. Drinkwater's *Abraham Lincoln* (1918), his *magnum opus* on the American president and his other plays *Cromwell* (1921) and *Mary Stuart* (1922) projected lives of notable public stalwarts. His successful comedy is *Bird in Hand* (1927).

Masefield chose Biblical and historical characters for his experiments with lyric meter, but later projected simple rustic folk. His best poetic plays were *The Tragedy of Nan* (1909) and *The Tragedy of Pompey the Great* (1910). James Elroy Flecker's (1884-1915) verse drama *Hassan: The Story of Hassan of Baghdad and How He Came to Make the Golden Journey to Samarkand* (1922) and T.S. Eliot's *Murder in the Cathedral* (1935) appealed to the masses and reaped huge success.

Realism in Theatre

The realist movement in literature first developed in France in the mid-nineteenth century and spread to England, Russia, and the United States. Realism in the theatre projected real-life situations with faithfulness and presented minute details with accuracy in performances and texts. Playwrights dealt with real and contemporary situations and themes in the society and disregarded precepts of the well-made play. Common and everyday language in dialogues replaced ornate poetic wordings and extravagant phraseology. To appear closer to life, depictions on stage incorporated movements and gestures that were natural and stage backdrops imitated commonplace surroundings. Henrik Ibsen and August Strindberg from Scandinavia, Anton Chekov and Maxim Gorky from Russia were prominent playwrights.

Naturalism in Theatre

Naturalism was inspired by formulations and methods of natural science, especially Charles Darwin's view of nature, which directly influenced art and literature. Naturalism was more faithful in its presentation of the reality of life than Realism. Characters were seen vulnerable to heredity and environmental factors that were provoked by the discord between their distinctive instincts and external social and economic conditions. Therefore, the characters had little control of their will and their fate. A new mode of dramatic presentation that dealt with themes centring on real contemporary society, treated in action and dialogue that looked and sounded like casual and ordinary behaviour and speech developed.

Zola named his technique "slice-of-life", and the naturalistic strain of drama was propagated by August Strindberg in Sweden with *Fröken Julie* (Miss Julie, 1888). Writers included Gerhart Hauptmann in Germany, Henry-François Becque in France, and Maxim Gorky in Russia.

Similarities between Realism and Naturalism

Both these categories of dramas depicted real life events that could befall even the members of the audience and therefore the focus was on the everyday situations in lives of individuals, families and societies. Playwrights found ample and appropriate subject matter because the society struggled and fought against oppressive governing systems. With the advancement of science and technological developments that included innovations, the questioning attitude of the people approached fresh domains of enquiry into human life.

Differences between Naturalism and Realism

The naturalist drama that developed during the nineteenth century gave a lot of importance to characters in a drama that were considered a part of nature, which transferred the genetic material and only the strongest survived. Naturalism was more objective, scientific, and methodical in its approach to art than Realism.

Realistic plays centered around characters that made attempts to break free from unpredictable circumstances and they earned the sympathy of the audience. Naturalistic plays considered the conflict between individual desires and the role of the environment surrounding the characters' lives that made them incapable of controlling their will. Moreover, Naturalism was based on scientific determinism that governed physiological nature rather than individual moral or rational attributes.

However, with the passage of time the elements of both these types of plays intermingled and diverse characteristics of either plays overlapped. Important playwrights that incorporated elemental aspects of both Naturalism and Realism in their plays were Emile Zola, Jean Jullien, and Andre Antoine from France; Ivan Turgenev, Anton Chekov, Constantine Stanislavsky and Maxim Gorky from Russia; August Strindberg from Sweden; Henrik Ibsen from Norway; and George Bernard Shaw from England.

Drama in Norway in the Nineteenth Century

The Norwegian state had formed its constitution in 1840, and Danish language became its official medium of communication. Björnstjerne Björnson (1832-1910), was a powerful leader, who fought to establish Norway as an independent country in 1905. The language and literature of Norway was principally Dano-Norwegian. Among the early Norwegian authors, the most famous was Ludvig Holberg (1684-1754), often referred as "the Moliere of the North". Two writers, the Danish Romantic poet and playwright Adam Gottlob Oehlenschläger's (1779-1850) Romantic plays celebrated the Scandinavian era of Vikings from the 8th to the 11th centuries inspired Ibsen's earlier works, and French playwright Eugene Scribe's (1791-1861) dramas influenced Ibsen at later stages of his development as playwright. Björnson popularised indigenous Norwegian literature. His novel *Sunny Hill* (1857) exposed hardships of peasants.

The Contribution of Henrik Ibsen

George Bernard Shaw, in a lecture on Ibsen, claimed the Norwegian playwright Henrik Ibsen as "the leader of a vanguard of 'modern' Victorians who at the fin de siècle championed socialism, feminism and new forms of artistic expression" (Ledger 1). This meant that Ibsen had exerted an indelible influence on the Victorian cultural mode during the 1880s and 1890s. He had initiated a 'new realism' to the stage, which critically examined lives and values of the bourgeois class and blatantly rejected romantic plots that had prevailed in Britain at that time. Ibsen lived in Italy and Germany and his cosmopolitan outlook on life enabled him to challenge existing social circumstances and take a critical stance to "dissect modern life and its problems" (Ledger 4). George Bernard Shaw, Thomas Hardy and a few other writers imbibed the spirit of Ibsen and wrote plays that broke the cultural establishment of the society and that move established Ibsen as an "advanced" and "emphatically modern phenomenon" in respect of the significant implications in lives of women, in particular.

The Problem Play

Ibsen magnetised the audience who were spellbound with the problem play or the drama of ideas where the chief emphasis was on the presentation of a social or psychological problem that was intertwined with the theme of the play. With succinct characterisation and dense plot structure, problem plays were powerful dramas, wherein their emotional impact or appeal underscored the imminence of the theme or problem. Although Ibsen presented problems, he rarely provided solutions because he believed that "a dramatist's business is not to give answers but only to ask them." Ibsen emphasised the role of the audience and their reception was crucial for the development of his plots in all the dramas he produced.

Ibsen's dramatic career that extended to about fifty years could be demarcated into three phases that varied markedly in respect of themes and nature of dramatic production. However, a rigid compartmentalisation could severely affect identifying the undercurrents operating in each play that would in turn provide a parochial understanding of the artistic ingenuity of Ibsen and his theatrical mode of presentation. The three periods were:

Period of Folk Stories, Historical Plays and Epic Poetical Dramas (1850-73)

In *Catiline* (1850), the first play of the period he expressed his sympathy for *Catiline* (68-62 BC) and in *The Vikings of Helgeland* (1858), a tragedy for Julian the Apostate (361-63 AD). The historical characters that staged political and religious rebellion respectively were pivotal to the plot of the plays. *The Feast at Solhaug* (1855), a poetic drama and *The Pretenders* (1863) based on early history of Norway were considered the best of Ibsen's dramas for the intricate plot and characterisation. The two verse dramas *Brand* (1866) and *Peer Gynt* (1867) stood out as plays that profoundly influenced the drama of the period. Marked by the romantic spirit of vitality and poetry projected through the idealism of romanticism and lyricism respectively. *Love's Comedy* (1862) was a satire and *Lady Inger of Ostraat* (1855), emerged a powerful romantic drama of intrigue with psychological undertones. The period culminated with the colossal drama *Emperor and Galilean* (1873), where Ibsen employed historical facts to explore ideas and present the confrontation between determinism and free will.

Period of Realistic Dramas—Problem or Thesis Plays (1877-90)

Through *Pillars of Society* (1877) and *A Doll's House* (1879) Ibsen introduced social problems that plagued the society. In *Ghosts* (1881), *The Lady from the Sea* (1888) and *Hedda Gabler* (1890) psychological problems of characters were projected. All these plays, set in realistic backgrounds expressed concern for contemporary life situations. Ibsen proposed his themes or problems to the audience through the employment of realistic characters, effective dialogues and straightforward plots. Plays such as *Rosmersholm* (1886) and *The Lady from the Sea* (1888) used symbolism to some extent to represent struggles of characters. In all plays of this period, characters were represented as struggling or fighting for reclaiming individuality and self-expression, while confronting enforced and established social conventions; their opposition being extended to the society.

Period of Symbolic and Abstract Dramas (1892-99)

The Master Builder (1892) showcased an ageing architect who had renounced love to devote himself completely to art. In a similar strain, the play *John Gabriel Borkman* (1896) exposed a financier who had sacrificed his love for the sake of amassing a fortune. Both plays extensively used symbolism that served Ibsen's purpose of exploring inner recesses of the individual mind that grappled with its thoughts, but in the process dramatic action was subordinated. In *When We Dead Awaken* (1899), designated a surrealist play, Ibsen defended the right to defend individual aspirations, pursuits and happiness against all impeding conditions and restrictions imposed in a modern society. However, towards the close of the play the protagonist realised that art cannot replace love and symbolically, the dead cannot be resuscitated.

Conclusion

The advent of the modern period corroborated the phenomenal role of the Norwegian playwright Henrik Ibsen that ushered a novel and unique approach to confront contemporary issues. By adopting a method of presentation that was effective enough to shake the production industry of its complacency, the dramas of Ibsen captured the attention of stalwarts like Shaw and Thomas Hardy, who not only endorsed the spirit of Ibsen's plays but also employed some of his dramatic notions in their own art. The Problem plays of Henrik Ibsen penetrated into common issues of gender inequality, social and psychological problems that affected common lives, but were marred by stardom and cheap sensationalism. The potential to create awareness about real problems of the society made the Problem play the most sought after mode of dramatic presentation. Moreover, the birth of verse drama effected a novel outlook of dramatic art and characterisation.

Glossary

bourgeois	: belonging to the middle class
instrumental	: serving as a means of pursuing a particular notion
mundane	: dull
impending	: about to happen
propagate	: spread and promote
panorama	: view of the whole area
Closet drama	: Episode 15, the "Circe" episode of James Joyce's *Ulysses* (1922) was considered a closet drama, because it was written in dramatic form, but turned out rather difficult to perform.
Naturalism	: In 1867, the French novelist Émile Zola announced the rejection of all artifice in theatrical performances too and insisted that plays be faithful records of behaviour that would predominantly involve a scientific analyses of life. Zola's Thérèse Raquin (1873), the dramatisation of his own novel that was written in 1867 represents the first consciously naturalistic drama.
Realism	: Realism as a movement began in France in the latter part of the 19th century and first appeared as a response to the novel social and artistic conditions of the time. By 1860, the movement had framed certain dictums that considered truth to be verifiable by science, that the scientific method based on close observation was capable to solving problems in the society and the purpose of art was to better conditions of mankind.
Maxim Gorky	: Pseudonym of Aleksey Maksimovich Peshkov (1868-1936). Russian short-story writer

and novelist, who became popular with his naturalistic and sympathetic stories of tramps and social outcasts and later wrote novels, and plays, including his famous The Lower Depths. From an impoverished family, nearly always hungry and dressed in drags, he was quite familiar with the seamy side of Russian life. He was often beaten up by his employers too. The bitterness of these early experiences later led him to select the word gorky ("bitter") as his pseudonym.

intricate : very complicated
frivolous : not serious or purposeful
transpired : emerged
facet : an aspect or feature of something
amass : accumulate or gather
underscore : emphasise
immediacy : urgency or excitement
complacency : uncritical satisfaction
alluring : attractive or fascinating

References

Fort, B. Alice, and Herbert S. Kates. *Minute History of the Drama*. Grosset and Dunlap, 1935.

Ledger, Sally. *Henrik Ibsen*. 2nd ed., Atlantic, 2010.

Maria, Lilla Crisafulli, and Keir Elam, editors. *Women's Romantic Theatre and Drama: History, Agency, and Performativity*. Ashgate, 2010.

Styan, J.L. *Modern Drama in Theory and Practice: Volume 1, Realism and Naturalism*. Cambridge UP, 1981.

https://www.britannica.com/art/dramatic-literature

https://www.britannica.com/art/dramatic-literature/Drama-in-Western-cultures

https://www.britannica.com/art/Western-theatre/Theatre-of-the-20th-century-and-beyond

https://theodora.com/encyclopedia/d/drama.html

http://www.historyworld.net/timesearch/default.asp?conid=static_timeline&timelineid=769&page=1&keywords=Drama%20timeline

Chapter 6

Modern Drama of Europe and Henrik Ibsen: Contribution and Influence

Dramatists Henrik Ibsen, Emile Zola, George Bernard Shaw, Antonin Artaud and Konstantin Stanislavsky announced the rise of modern drama with the emphasis on techniques of realism and naturalism. Diverse attributes of Ibsenism, Wagnerism, Realism, Symbolism, and Naturalism occupied the center-stage of drama, and provided scope for innovations in dramatic technique. The developments like Expressionism and the Epic theatre formulated by Erwin Piscator and Bertolt Brecht among others influenced the drama of the twentieth century.

The foremost intention of the modern theatre was freedom from adherence to regulations that existed in dramas of earlier times, namely the realisation of unities of time, place and action and the depiction of tragedy through noble characters. The French dramatist Victor Hugo (1802-85), in his romantic play *Hernani*, premiered in 1830 flouted conventions of drama and employed a radical form and style that later became the impetus for Zola's Naturalism, Ibsen's critical Realism and Strindberg's Expressionism.

Gassner observed that "beneath the surface of action, dialogue, characterisation, style lay intellectual visionary conviction of radical thoughts of Hegel, Nietzsche, Darwin and

Marx" that became cornerstones in efforts to explore boundaries of art and expose various facets of the society. Gassner reiterated that modern theatre propagated the idea of freedom that later turned to the production of plays related to adversities of common man in diverse situations.

Playwrights from different parts of the world such as Ibsen, Strindberg, Chekov, Shaw, Gorky, Sean O'Casey, and Arthur Miller to name some of the prominent dramatists had the courage to move beyond rules and theories to create dramas that penetrated into imaginations and found greater freedom of expression. Ibsen, Hauptmann, Gorky, Chekov and Shaw explored several styles of writing and technical innovations and brought out inherent contradictions in the society, political and social discontent, social unrest and inner turmoil of the times. Crombrich's comment that "...drama originates in our reactions to the world, not in the world itself" captures this mood appropriately.

Modern drama was primarily a mélange of genres that blended dramatic techniques. Realism, Naturalism, Symbolism, poetic drama and Existentialism employed divergent strategies with regard to acting, music, lighting, design, costume and architecture that succinctly outlined objectives of each type of drama.

The Early Plays in Norway

The first Danish-language theatre opened in 1722 in Copenhagen. The Norwegian playwright Ludvig Holberg (1684-1754) contributed extensively to drama. His comic epic *Peder Paars* (1719), a parody of Virgil's *Aeneid*, was the earliest classic of the Danish language. His contribution to drama, especially the comedies was so profuse that he came to be known as "Molière of the North." His most important works included *Den politiske kandestøber* (*The Political Tinker*, 1722), *Den vægelsindede* (*The Scatterbrain*, 1723), *Jean de France* (1723), *Jeppe på bjerget* (*Jeppe of the Hill*, 1723), *Ulysses von Ithacia* (1725), *Den stundesløse* (*The Fussy Man*, 1731), and *Erasmus Montanus* (1731). His satirical novel about an imaginary voyage is *Nicolai Klimii Iter Subterraneum* (*The Journey of Niels Klim to the World Underground*, 1741). Henrik Ibsen admired the works of Holberg for their witty satire, sympathy for women, and the call for social reform.

Holberg's contribution to drama was phenomenal; however, dramatic compositions after his death were principally depictions of Norwegian ballads and folk tales of ancient times that continued for a long time in Norway. Significant dramas were tragedies that were never written in prose but in verse because it was preferred by the noblemen or upper classes of the society. Theatre had never witnessed any change in the mode or presentation of tragedy until Henrik Ibsen revolutionised the mid-19th century European theatre with his realist plays.

The Drama of Henrik Ibsen: A Brief Sketch

Theatre underwent ramification under Ibsen, whose profuse contribution to drama for about fifty years and his unquestionable influence on the dramatists of several parts of the world remained unparalleled. Martin Lamm remarked, "Ibsen's work is the Rome of Modern Drama; all roads lead to it and away from it" (75). However, the progress of the dramatist as the forerunner of a decisive stride away from the subject-matter and techniques of dramatic production of his predecessors was gradual.

In 1851, Ibsen was assigned the post of dramatic author at the Bergen theatre where he had to spend six years in poverty and artistic depression because he could not express his ideas at that time. The change in theatre did not materialise until many years in future because of the influence of tradition and dramatic principles, and Ibsen continued to write about folk tales and legendary ventures of ancient Norway as well as on nationalism for some more time. *Catiline*, a rhymed verse tragedy set in Rome was written in 1849. *Lady Inger of Ostraat*, in 1854 was the first play that Ibsen wrote in prose. However, he could not dispense with the hackneyed theatrical devises used in mid-19th century tragedy. *The Feast at Solhaug* (1855), a comedy written partly in rhymed verse and partly in prose was set in 14th-century Norway.

Ibsen was appointed artistic director at the Norwegian theatre in Christiana in 1857, and in the same year, he completed *The*

Vikings of Helgeland that was based on his reading of N.M. Petersen's translations of the Icelandic chronicles. In 1862, he published *Loves Comedy* and in 1863, *The Pretenders*. Sometime later, he moved out to Italy to relieve himself from stagnancy and boredom. The first play that Ibsen wrote in Italy was *Brand,* in 1866 as an epic quartet, which was followed by *Peer Gynt* in 1867 and *Emperor and Galilean* in 1873.

Realist Plays

The year 1869 marked a watershed in Ibsen's dramatic career with *The League of Youth* that showcased elements of realism for the first time. The play was his maiden attempt at writing a play entirely in modern colloquial dialogue. He mentioned to Hegel, his publisher that the new dramatic endeavour "... will be in prose and written entirely with the stage in mind" (Ledger 18). The source of the realist prose dramas were the Norwegian newspapers that were not meant to satiate "an idle curiosity for news...but...drawn more closely and intensively into life in Norway and thus feel strengthened..." (18). The new modern drama was a deliberate turn from the so-called romantic ventures and the nationalistic quagmire of Norwegian ballads and folk tales to a new form of drama that experimented with contemporary socially relevant themes. Brustein accorded Henrik Ibsen of introducing the "theatre of revolt" (4) in prose and initiating the theatre as a forum for debating on contemporary social, political, and intellectual issues in the latter half of the nineteenth century in England and Europe.

A Doll's House was one of Ibsen's epoch-making realist-problem plays, the others being *The Pillars of Society* (1877) and *An Enemy of the People* (1882). Contemporary social problems were represented through incidents in the life of an individual character in each play. Ibsen frequently focused on socially representative types and typical characters who personified a general social problem. *A Doll's House* effected drastic political, cultural and social transformations, wherein Marxists, socialists, Fabians, and feminists, in unison hailed Ibsen as the spokesman for their various grounds of ideologies and protests. The model for Nora Helmer was a young Norwegian woman Laura Kieler, who admired Ibsen's plays and wrote a proto-feminist novel called *Brand's Daughters* in response to Ibsen's play *Brand* (1866).

Eleanor Marx, the daughter of Karl Marx was the first to translate Ibsen's plays into English. The other feminists and novelists such as Olive Schreiner, Edith Lees Ellis and Emma Frances Brooke attended the theater releases of Ibsen's plays. Ibsen did for European drama what the French dramatist Gustave Flaubert (1821-80) had done in 1856, with the introduction of literary realism for the novel. However, Ibsen's frank depiction of violation of moral codes of patriarchal society, discussions of free love, the concept of open relationships, illegitimate relationships, and extra-marital affairs in his plays were disparaged.

An Enemy of the People questioned differences between the freedom of speech of every individual and needs of the majority. The play articulated the dilemma of how to harmonise individual freedom and concerns with the interest of the wider community. Eleanor Marx first translated *An Enemy of the People* in English, then translated it as *An Enemy of the Society* though she disliked the play.

Stanislavsky played the role of Dr. Stockman, the protagonist of the play at the Moscow Arts Theatre in 1905. In his autobiography *My Life and Art,* Stanislavsky recalled the performance of the play, which took place on the day of an anti-revolutionary massacre in Kasansky and the entire audience rose from their seats and the performance had to be stopped. Dr. Stockman's final utterance in the play, "The fact is you see that the strongest man in the world is he who stands most alone" (222), meant that the struggle between individual rights and social acceptance was perpetual. Such struggles acquired political dimensions that hampered social relations. However, his daughter Petra stood with him with her advanced political thinking that was evident by her firm stand against political corruption as well as compromise to deter any untoward incidents.

The Psychological Plays

Little Eyolf (1894) was one of Ibsen's late plays that had immense psychological depth. Ibsen's middle and late plays tended to end with a discussion of a relationship that had serious implications with regard to the theme of the play. The conversation between Rita and Alfred Allmers towards the end of the play is an example of one of the most moving and memorable scenes in Ibsen's theatre. The resolution of Nora Helmer at the close of the play made her a realist character that represented the anguish of women of the period. Hedda Gabler, in the play *Hedda Gabler* was a less representative realist character than a psychological case study, which was similar to the portrayal of Rebecca West in *Rosmersholm* in 1886.

In *John Gabriel Borkman* (1896) and *When We Dead Awaken* (1899), Ibsen explored the wounded masculine psychology by penetrating its darkest recesses. Ibsen made a dramatic shift from plays of social criticism of his middle period towards an intense focus on individual subjectivity during the later phase of his career. In *John Gabriel Borkman* and *When We Dead Awaken*, Ibsen concentrated on the inner conflict of the mind rather than the outer realm of human experience by using symbolic modes of dramatic representation.

The act of climbing mountains by the protagonists towards the end of both novels symbolically represented the journey from liberty and sexual fulfilment, and the desire for power and success to death. The act was the culmination of the destructive wounded masculine ego that ruined even the feminine energy. The futility of the journey undertaken was symbolic of man's unreasonable quest for the unattainable at the cost of genuine happiness and freedom.

In *The Lady from the Sea*, the sea symbolically represented freedom and sexual liberty and Ibsen used the mermaid myth to structure his account of Ellida's imprisonment in her marriage to Dr. Wangle. In *Little Eyolf* (1894), the unwelcome rats can be readily identified with Eyolf, the unwanted child, the loathsome thing, which the rat-wife offered to get rid of. The rat-wife was a complex character that arose from the unconscious and altered a dull bourgeois domestic life into a living nightmare. Both plays portrayed women who were unwilling to adopt motherhood and that created an upheaval in the society, especially after the plays *A Doll's House* and *An Enemy of the People* that had featured bold and radical women that took decisions that were contrary to the expectations of the society.

Plays of Ibsen in Chronological Order

- *Catiline* (1850)
- *The Burial Mound* (1850)
- *St. John's Night* (1853)
- *Lady Inger of Ostraat* (1855)
- *The Feast of Solhaug* (1856)
- *Olaf Liljekrans* (1857)
- *The Vikings at Helgeland* (1858)
- *Love's Comedy* (1862)
- *The Pretenders* (1863)
- *Brand* (1866)
- *Peer Gynt* (1867)
- *The League of Youth* (1869)
- *Emperor and Galilean* (1873)
- *The Pillars of Society* (1877)
- *A Doll's House* (1879)
- *Ghosts* (1881)
- *An Enemy of the People* (1882)
- *The Wild Duck* (1884)
- *Rosmersholm* (1886)
- *The Lady from the Sea* (1888)
- *Hedda Gabler* (1890)
- *The Master Builder* (1892)
- *Little Eyolf* (1894)
- *John Gabriel Borkman* (1896)
- *When We Dead Awaken* (1899)

The Drama "Ghosts"

Introduction

The Pillars of Society (1877), *A Doll's House* written in 1879 and the play *Ghosts* (1881) extended Ibsen's new realistic techniques in prose with the focus on middle class life. The play

Ghosts (1881) regarded as Ibsen's naturalistic play broke all the conventional social and literary codes and inflamed the bourgeois society that could not accept the depiction of moral and social depravity on the stage. The play was banned in several countries across the European continent because it directly addressed the inheritance of syphilis and questioned the concept of a traditional bourgeois family. With *Ghosts*, Ibsen had introduced a new realism to the stage with its critique of lives and values of the bourgeois class.

The Title "Ghosts"

Gengangere (Ghosts), that literarily means "those who come back" was first published in 1881 in Oslo. It was written in the official language Dano-Norwegian, *Riksmaal*. The first English translation of the play was printed in *Today*, a socialist journal by Mrs. Franceslord in 1885. It was translated by William Archer in 1888. Modern translations of the play can be found in several editions of Oxford University Press, and Penguin Books among others.

Structure of the Drama

The play, in three acts has an intricately organised structure, which observes the classical unities of time and place. The entire action of the play occurs within less than twenty-four hours and takes place in one room in Mrs. Alving's house. Each act begins with a conversation that introduces the main motifs and sets up a crisis, which is to be resolved. Each act ends in a moment of dramatic suspense.

Character List

- Mrs. Alving, the widow of Captain Alving, who was formerly Chamberlain to the King
- Oswald Alving, her son, an artist
- Pastor Manders, the pastor of the parish
- Jacob Engstrand, a limp carpenter
- Regina Engstrand, Engstrand's daughter, Mrs. Alving's servant

The Background to the Drama *Ghosts*

The play revolves around about the gradual revelations of the past events and their consequences on lives of characters. Mrs. Helena Alving spends her entire life serving her dissolute husband, Captain Alving, who is dead for almost ten years now. She plans to construct an orphanage to commemorate her husband's death with his fortune in order to protect the honour of the family and dissuade her son from inheriting anything that belonged to his father. Oswald, Mrs. Alving's son is an artist in Paris and has begun to make a name for himself. He seldom returns home, but agrees to come for the dedication of the orphanage. The action of the play starts on the day before the orphanage is to be dedicated to her husband.

A Brief Summary of the Drama

The conversation between the carpenter Engstrand and his daughter Regina, the young housemaid at Mrs. Alving's close on his intentions of building the seaman's home for her benefit. Manders and Helena had been lovers, but they parted ways because her family married her off to the captain, who was quite affluent. Pastor Manders advises Mrs. Alving about her duties to her late husband and son as well as her son's responsibilities within Norwegian conventions. At this point, Mrs. Alving discloses the concealed aspects of her life to the clergyman.

She was dissatisfied with her married life because of her husband's wanton ways. In order to keep his behaviour from triggering a public scandal, she forced her husband to allow her complete control of the household. She organised his activities so that local society believed he was an honest and worthy resident. She even drank with him in their home to keep him from getting drunk in public. She was so frightened of consequences of their life on their son Oswald that she sent him away for his education at an early age to Paris.

Regina is the daughter of Captain Alving and Johanna, the housemaid; a scandalous affair that dates back several years and remains secretive. Johanna hurriedly marries the limp carpenter Jacob Engstrand, who accepts the proposal because she comes with three hundred dollars, given by Mrs. Alving to keep the affair undisclosed. Mrs. Alving later provides for the illegitimate daughter of her husband Regina and brings her up as a housemaid.

Oswald, captivated by Regina's beauty tries to seduce Regina, who happens to be his half-sister, a fact he is unaware of. Mrs. Alving is upset because effects of past events seem to be surfacing in her life causing her distress. Her firm belief in traditional beliefs come in her way of enjoying life, but they never affect her husband, who remains unfaithful to her till death.

Pastor Manders and Mrs. Alving are anxious about Oswald's interest in Regina; however, they are interrupted by Engstrand, who in intent on securing money from Manders for the seafarer's home he intends to build in the hope of starting a fresh life for Regina. Oswald reveals to his mother that he has contracted syphilis, a disease that affects the brain. Obviously, the doctor's claim that it is inherited from his father confuses him; moreover, in spite of being a celibate it is improbable too. Mrs. Alving is shocked, but she does not disclose his father's waywardness to her son.

Seeing the intimacy between Oswald and Regina growing intense, Mrs. Alving decides to reveal to both of them the truth about Regina's birth and hence the improbability of their relationship. The unforeseen burning down of the orphanage disrupts her thoughts. Manders and Regina discuss the cause of the fire and the effects of the incident are reflected in the final scene of the play. The fire enables Engstrand to obtain money from Manders. Mrs. Alving discloses the truth of Regina's birth and Oswald requests his mother to take away his life and save him from pain and suffering. The play ends with Mrs. Alving contemplating putting her son to death.

Conclusion

The onus for initiating modern drama is attributed to Henrik Ibsen, who emerged as one of the most influential dramatists in the world. His realistic dramas not only addressed the dramatic stagnancy of the nineteenth century in Norway, but also revolutionised drama and its facets in Britain in those times and the other parts of Europe. The themes in his plays have social, political and individual implications that are evidences of his continuous engagements with concerns that affect the common man. His plays inspired feminists of that period who considered him the spokesperson in their fight for equality and economic freedom. This is not to say that his influence has declined in contemporary times, but his initial steps of a radical change in several dimensions of the society have far-reaching consequences in the present.

Glossary

evince	: prove
adversity	: hardship
turmoil	: havoc
Wagnerism	: The music, theoretical writings, political ideas, and aesthetics of the German composer-conductor and essayist Richard Wagner (1813-83) are collectively referred Wagnerism. The Symbolist movement in art and literature was influenced by Wagner during the second half of the nineteenth century. The French poet and art critic Charles Baudelaire was one of Wagner's early admirers.
mélange	: combination
ramification	: consequence
quagmire	: muddle or morass
Ludvig Holberg, Baron Holberg (1684-1754)	: Most of the plays have been translated into English in Jeppe of the Hill and Other Comedies (1990); a translation of Den vægelsindede appears in Three Danish Comedies (1999); and Den stundesløse is translated in Four Plays by Holberg (1946).
Niels Klim (1741)	: Originally written in Latin and later published in Dutch (1742), the novel has been referred "a Danish Gulliver's Travels".

disparage	: criticise
perpetual	: continual
deter	: dissuade
untoward	: unpleasant

References

Ledger, Sally. *Henrik Ibsen*. 2nd ed., Atlantic, 2010.

Martin Lamm. *Modern Drama*, translated by Karin Elliot. Philosophical Literary, 1853.

Robert Brustein. *The Theatre of Revolt: An Approach to the Modern Drama*. Little, Brown and Co., 1962.

Shaw, George Bernard. "The Quintessence of Ibsenism." https://warwick.ac.uk/fac/arts/english/currentstudents/undergraduate/modules/fulllist/special/endsandbeginnings/quintessenceofib00shawrich.pdf

Styan, J.L. *Modern Drama in Theory and Practice: Volume 1, Realism and Naturalism*. Cambridge UP, 1981.

Zuck, Virpi, editor. *Dictionary of Scandinavian Literature*. Greenwood P, 1990.

https://theodora.com/encyclopedia/d/drama.html

https://www.litencyc.com/php/sworks.php?rec=true&UID=7514,

Ghosts https://www.gutenberg.org/files/8121/8121-h/8121-h.htm

Chapter 7

Ghosts

Act-I

The scene opens in Mrs. Alving's country house in western Norway. The atmosphere is gloomy and it is raining outside. Regina, the young and beautiful housemaid sees her father Jacob Engstrand outside the house. He visits her clandestinely to disclose his intentions to build a home for sailors and seeks her help. Regina is wary of her father's claims and refuses to oblige. She sends him away quickly when she sees Pastor Manders approaching the house. The nature of their discussion interrogates Engstrand's actual relationship with Regina.

Pastor Manders complains about the weather and simultaneously discusses Oswald's home-coming from Paris with Regina. He reminds Regina about her duty towards her father, which she politely refrains to talk about and leaves the discussion to call for Mrs. Alving and by this time, he is politely let in by Mrs. Alving.

Mrs. Alving greets the Pastor, who notices certain books on the table that could probably be some recent novels on matters of sex or certain contemporary anti-religious philosophical works. He delivers a firm lecture deriding such books, but Mrs. Alving refrains from defending her act. She mentions that the society should respect opinions of others and frankness about individual thoughts is important. Moreover, she is not bound to account to everybody for what she reads, thinks and believes. Pastor

Manders respects not only conventional moral standards but also opinions of the upper-middle classes. Manders is unaware of the irony of his defence of the social order, which suggests that such an order is part of God's providence.

Pastor Manders then discusses the establishment of the new Captain Alving Foundation, an orphanage to be set up with the fortune left by the late captain. When Manders shows her the documents related to the orphanage, she does not claim responsibility for its management. She initially thinks that the building must be insured but accepts Manders argument that the act of insuring the building would mean insufficient faith in the Providence of God at least by some people. When Mrs. Alving warns about Engstrand's deceitful nature because he started a fire at the carpenters' shop, the pastor supports Engstrand who had approached him earlier as a part of mending his ways.

When Oswald comes in smoking a pipe, the pastor immediately senses a close resemblance between him and his late father. Manders is critical of life abroad, which in his opinion is immoral and Oswald mocks at the pastor's parochial moral beliefs. Oswald disagrees with the pastor, who compares him to the Biblical Prodigal Son who returns home after leading a depraved life. Oswald is nervous, looks unhealthy and appears aggressive. He causes grief to his mother by narrating an event in his early childhood when his father forces him to smoke a pipe until he becomes sick. He finds it difficult to reconcile this memory with his mother's account of his respectable father.

He expresses his disgust that in spite of being sick when young, he is forcefully sent to Paris to get educated, and has lived alone for a long time; moreover, the reason for sending him away still remains unexplained. He recounts life in Paris, particularly the common-law marriages or live-in relationships without marriage ties of some of his artist friends, which in his opinion are quite decent and honourable despite their irregularities. He adds that respectable Norwegians act immorally when they are abroad and the pastor takes their word and moral uprightness for granted. Apologising for his outspokenness, he leaves.

Pastor Manders gives Mrs. Alving a sermon on marital duties and perils of sending her son abroad at an early age to be educated. He criticises Mrs. Alving for returning to him, her lover of many years for refuge from her husband Captain Alving even after being married to him for almost a year. He prides himself on having saved her virtue and reputation by sending her back to her husband. She listens to his speech in silence and discloses the truth that the captain was unfaithful to her and never mended his ways till death, a fact she hid from everyone, including the pastor and her son.

She adds that Captain Alving even carried his dissipations home, which she endured for a long time for the sake of family honour. Mr. Alving is the real father of Regina, from Johanna, a servant in the Alving household. Mrs. Alving gives the servant three hundred dollars to hush up the affair. Johanna hurriedly marries Jacob Engstrand, a limp carpenter and the impression created is that an English seaman had deserted her and offered money as restitution for the misfortune. The drunkard carpenter agrees to the marriage for money. Mrs. Alving is critical of middle-class marriage with respect to the commodification of women that is unfair.

Mrs. Alving reiterates that the orphanage is built with captain Alving's fortune so that Oswald will inherit nothing from his father. She suggests that the memorial to Captain Alving is founded under the pretext of family honour and respect for her husband because she does not want to disclose the truth about her husband's degenerate ways for fear of shame and reproach from the society.

Mrs. Manders understands that Oswald is attracted to Regina and his advances remind her of a similar scene between her husband and the servant many years ago. When Mrs. Alving gasps in horror as they bear witness to Oswald's approach to Reigna, Manders comes to believe that Regina is Captain Alving's daughter. Both the pastor and Mrs. Alving see "ghosts", since Oswald and Regina seem to re-enact the incidents of the past. Mrs. Alving understands that the remnants of the memories that she had hoped to bury would stay and they would continue to haunt her.

Critical Analysis

The gloomy weather outside forebodes dreariness. The opening act introduces the main characters of the play as well as their dispositions. Though Mr. Alving lives a comfortable life, she is dejected. The opening scene shows her rather disturbed because her son has returned home from Paris, quite ill. Mrs. Alving is stoic because all these years she has guarded the secret of her husband's immoral life from her son and the society and suffered disgrace all alone. The immoral relationship of Captain Alving and Regina's mother causes distress to Mrs. Alving, who views this as hypocrisy of marriage that is upheld by conservatism. She is unable to come to terms with her husband's ways and decides to prevent their son from acquiring his father's ways.

Mrs. Alving's distress is her helplessness because she is neither able to marry Manders, who she loved nor live happily married. She is unable to restrict her husband's depravity, but emerges a strong woman who boldly faces criticism from the pastor, and refutes the pastor's claims that she is disinterested in the matters of the family. Ibsen will later expand this theme to include the traditional outmoded thoughts and values that rule Pastor Manders and enhance the tragic effect to Mrs. Alving's life. Mrs. Alving sees similarities in Regina's plight, Regina's mother's and her own when Oswald tries to seduce Regina. She admits that revealing the truth about the family to Regina and Oswald would avert anything untoward.

Jacob Engstrand is a rogue who is not respectable and he is able to frame a good opinion about himself by deceiving the pastor. Mrs. Alving is more quick to realise deceptive ways of Engstrand than the pastor who is clearly deceived by Engstrand's arguments. The pastor is clear about his intentions in trying to reform the people of his parish, but he is weak enough to recognise deceit and people who put on appearances. He considers behaving or thinking in a different manner, improper. Mrs. Alving is shrewder than the pastor, who is gullible.

Act-II

The second act opens after lunch when Mrs. Alving sends Regina off so that she can talk to Pastor Manders. She insists that Regina cannot be allowed to stay with her anymore and she gives him details about the marriage of Regina's mother to Engstrand. She mentions: "I'm afraid Regina stayed at home for too long", which implies that she is worried about Oswald's affair with Regina, which not be encouraged given the nature of their relationship. She calls herself a coward for hiding the truth of Regina's birth and wishes she were brave enough to allow Oswald and Regina to marry, but this would mean acting against ethics and her conscience. She questions the moral order of the world, and the society's respect for law despite several unfortunate situations and inconsistencies in marital relationships. She elaborates that everybody is ruled by "ghosts...by dead ideas and dead beliefs". She explains that the world should not be ruled by ideas and beliefs from the past, which stand between human beings and truth.

Pastor Manders is shocked to hear about Mrs. Alving's disadvantaged life and for a moment recalls his own struggle to contain his emotions when she approaches him to escape from her depraved husband, and he persuades her to return. Mrs. Alving remains unemotional and interrupts the painful discussion and mentions about the similarities between her son's approach to Regina and her husband's to Johanna. To the pastor's question on the carpenter's readiness to marry a fallen woman for a few hundred dollars, Mrs. Alving readily counters that she lived with a fallen man, an unscrupulous person who would not correct his ways. The pastor, however does not find any similarity between the two situations and this could be seen as his failing.

The pastor is aghast when Mrs. Alving refuses to abide by his moral teaching and admits that he had to fight against love. He convinces himself that he always considers her another man's wife. She realises that the pastor had suppressed his emotions entirely and renounced his happiness for her sake. Pastor Manders regards their sacrifice unwanted and the marriage to Mr. Alving, a disaster. Mrs. Alving finds that marriage could be the only solution for Regina's secure future, despite her radical ideas and the fact that she realises herself as sold into marriage. Their conversation is interrupted when Engstrand approaches the pastor to request him to take part in the opening of the orphanage.

The pastor rebukes Engstrand for not disclosing the truth about his marriage to Johanna. The scheming old man dupes the pastor by telling him how the considers his marriage an opportunity to save and raise up a poor fallen woman. He tortures Johanna though, and the poor woman dies young leaving behind Regina. Engstrand describes his virtues and requests the pastor's approval for the proposed seafarer's home. He asks the pastor to conduct a prayer service for him at the orphanage.

Engstrand, realising that the pastor is disturbed because Engstrand accepted the money offered at marriage and sacrificed honour, quickly admits of having used the money for the child. Manders is impressed and asks Engstrand to forgive him for having misjudged him and readily agrees to consider helping the projected seamen's home. While the pastor is naive, Mrs. Alving recognises that Engstrand is manipulative and crafty. She also understands that it is too easy to deceive the pastor.

Worried about Oswald's habit of having drinks often, Mrs. Alving requests him to reveal his mind. Oswald, who is restive, petulant and depressed is uncertain how much he means to her since she sent him away from home for so long. He used to have severe headaches and ailments as a child, but his mother, unmindful of his physical ailments had sent him away from home to Paris and he had to endured the pain all alone. She was not there to comfort him or nurture him to health. He discloses that he suffers from a deterioration of his mental processes. The headache has intensified and the possibility of respite or improvement in his condition is rather thin.

The doctor he consults in Paris says the illness is inherited from his father, and the doctor makes the allusion to the Bible: "The sins of the fathers are visited on the children." While announcing the Ten Commandments to Moses, God says: "For I the Lord, thy God am a jealous God visiting the inequity of the fathers upon the children". Oswald, believing in his mother's account of his father's integrity, cannot accept the doctor's claims. Oswald idealised his father and reacted violently to the doctor's suggestion. He says: "I nearly hit him in the face". Oswald blames himself for trying to lead a full and happy life in Paris. He could probably have contracted the illness from his artist friends, albeit being extremely cautious and apparently leading a celibate life.

Mrs. Alving, Regina and Oswald have champagne together when Oswald mentions of Regina's attractiveness. He wants to go away with her because he can neither put up with the gloom and rain of Norway nor see his mother see him deteriorate. He mentions: "I can't remember ever having seen the sun." The sun is the symbol of joy of living Oswald find in Paris but not in Norway. Regina is "full of the joy" of living, a characteristic he finds among the people of Paris. He says that while people at home complain about misery and the drudgery of work, in Paris work and life are things to be enjoyed. Mrs. Alving cannot accept that "salvation" may lie in joy and thinks of salvation in terms of religion. Ironically, Oswald uses "salvation" to mean someone who will take his life when the time comes.

When Mrs. Alving is about to tell them the truth about their relationship, Pastor Manders returns after conducting the evening's prayer and tells them that he has decided that Regina help Engstand with the Seaman's Home; however, Oswald discloses his intention of marrying Regina, probably to use her services than to love her. Mrs. Alving is interrupted the moment she is about to disclose the truth of their relationship when the orphanage starts to burn down and she has to hasten out. The Pastor sees this incident as divine judgement on the impiety of the household, although he regrets that the building is not insured.

Critical Analysis

Mrs. Alving realises that her inclination towards outdated notions of morality, ideas and beliefs have wrecked her life and left her confounded. The repeated reference to the word "ghosts" indicates that she in under the grip of convention and social codes. While endeavours to save her family from disgrace and its possible recurrence through her son has made her take tough decisions, she finds that in the end, her efforts are in vain. The Captain Alving Foundation is to safeguard her husband's immorality, maintain his public image and keep her son away from his father's disgraceful inheritance.

Her son is down with a gradual deterioration of his mental faculty, which is inherited from his father and the irony is that while she has been able to save her son from the fortune of his father, she is not able to rescue him from the deadly disease. In the effort to save her son, she has put him in danger. He seems to blame her for sending him away from home though he used to be a sick child. The time at home with his parents could have been a better choice than the company of friends away from home.

Oswald finds that "light and sunshine" in his paintings give "a feeling of holiday", the opposite of life in Norway. He will find his view of the "joy and delight to be in this world" destroyed by the "ghosts". The reference to the sun in the drama not only suggests the joy of living in Paris but also stands as the symbol of truth that Mrs. Alving is still keeping away from him. While at the beginning of the act, Oswald mentions that he cannot live "without a glimpse of the sun", towards the end of the play, the sun rises too late for him.

Mrs. Alving understands what Oswald means by "joy of life", which is quite similar to her husband's claim because she gives more importance to her duty as wife and mother. The joys in her husband's life are beyond moral and social codes, and her presence hampers his high spirits. She is indirectly responsible for the tragedy of her life. Unlike her husband, she is a coward who cannot lead the life of her choice because of her respect and concern for conventional modes of thought and behaviour.

Act-III

Mrs. Alving and Regina watch the entire building burn down to ashes. Mrs. Alving mentions: "There's nothing to save." This implies that nothing in the building, and the replica of deception, which the orphanage stands for, remains. Engstrand blames the pastor for accidently starting the fire, and then offers to take the blame entirely upon himself. He mentions: "Someone I know has taken the blame for another man once before". Engstrand could be referring to his responsibility for Johanna's pregnancy. By making such a comment, mention some critics Engstrand could be making a blasphemous comparison of himself to Christ.

Engstrand claimed that Manders lit the candles, extinguished one with his fingers and threw the wick away. The pastor, who is utterly confused owns responsibility for the same. Engstrand's excitement is revealed as he mentions: "We've got him now, my girl!" This indicates that it was indeed he who has started the fire, or that he plans to profit from it. Mrs. Alving is not interested in the construction of the orphanage and she is confused with what has to be done with the money set apart to meet the expenses at the orphanage. Engstrand is successful in his efforts to squeeze money from the pastor in return for the blame he takes for the cause of the fire. He decides to name his Seaman's Home as Chamberlain Alving's Home. He promises everyone that this place would be worthy of the Chamberlain's memory, which is probably a dig at the Alvings'.

Oswald, who is overcome with the heat of the fire shows signs of mental degradation. Regina is disturbed to learn that Oswald is gravely sick. When Oswald requests her to stay back to help him, she does not reply. Mrs. Alving exposes her husband and eventually the secret of Regina's birth is revealed. Regina is ashamed of her mother's true character, which is explicitly revealed when she says: "So my mother was like that" and decides to leave the place to make her own way. She decides not to stay back at Mrs. Alving's because of the nature of her relationship with Oswald and his ailment. Similar to Engstrand, she plans to use the pastor to get some of money from the Alvings. She is angry by her lowly upbringing and decides to become rich by adopting any means. She claims that she can always go to the Chamberlain Alving's Home and make a living, which shocks Mrs. Alving.

Oswald neither sympathises with his father nor loves his mother. He feels he has to think more about his physical and mental ailments. He desperately asks his mother, "And what sort of a life have you given me?" He not only thinks of his inherited disease but his unhappy early separation from his home. Mrs. Alving is unhappy that she "didn't bring any sunshine into his life". She tries to comfort him with the hope and promise that soon he will see the "sun", which means that he will get well soon. Oswald tells his mother of the dread he constantly feels about his death, which may not be quick but slow. He will eventually sink into a permanent state of mental degradation from which he may never recover until death would release him.

The dawn breaks forth in bright sunlight and the rain stops. Oswald suddenly goes berserk and without hesitancy he asks his mother: "Mother, give me the sun." Rather than face an unpleasant death, he wishes for a dose of morphia so that he can be released of suffering and he wants his mother to administer the dose of the drug. Mrs. Alving frantically looks for the pills, and as the curtain falls, she stands staring at him in horror, and says: "Yes! No, no" that suggests that she is undecided whether to put him to death.

Critical Analysis

Engstrand's assurance that his sailor's home will be worthy of the late Mr. Alving's memory, who is one of the most depraved persons in the society, is considered one of the finest examples of dramatic irony. Ibsen uses Engstrand, who is the epitome of treachery to satirise the pretense in the society. The ease with which Engstrand deceives the pastor is probably the most unbelievable part of the play. The theme of the "ghosts" surfaces when Regina decides to take care of herself, though she may not end as fortunate as her mother. The emphasis on the outspread theme of the "ghosts" comes when Oswald shows pity for the memory of his father.

Mrs. Alving's efforts to instill love in Oswald for his father is in vain and she realises and the more she attempts to seek liberation the more she is controlled by the "ghosts". When she asks him if he loves her, he simply answers that he knows her at least but hardly knows his father. Several critics have denounced the ending of the play because it involves mercy killing. The critic Ledger mentions that whenever Ibsen was asked the question whether Mrs. Alving will give him the pills or not, he grew extremely impatient and sometimes discourteous (23). The question is irrelevant because once Oswald is dead the tragedy of Mrs. Alving is complete. All that she lived and worked for, her son, would evaporate. She would be left with nothing, not even the memory of his love. Even before his mind was destroyed he was still too sick to think of anybody but himself.

In *The Oxford Ibsen*, James McFarlane quotes William Archer, one of Ibsen's first English admirers and translators, who reports a conversation with Ibsen about the question of Mrs. Alving's decision in the end:

> Ibsen said: "I don't know. Everyone must work that out for himself. I should never dream of deciding such a difficult question. Now, what do you think?". "I (Archer) said that if she did not come to the rescue it was no doubt that the result of a *gengangere* a ghost, still walking in her—always assuming I added that the disease was ascertained to be absolutely incurable. He said he thought the solution perhaps lay there: that the mother would always put off coming to the rescue on the plea that while there is life, there is hope." (475)

Mrs. Alving's tragedy is that of a woman left completely alone to deal with the "ghosts", the dead ideas and beliefs and that will appear to smother her. The venereal disease, the corporeal ghost symbolises dead impressions, notions and insensible conventions. Pastor Manders too lives for these conventions, but his life is spiritually dry, which is entirely devoid of any love in the true sense of the word. However, Mrs. Alving lives only for the love of her son.

Mrs. Alving strives to follow her dead ideas and beliefs despite the recognition to a certain extent that upholding conventions to maintain her late husband's reputation and concealing the truth from her son and his half-sister is pointless. Towards the penultimate stages of the play, when the edifice of falsehood, symbolised by the orphanage is engulfed by fire, Mrs. Alving's understanding is completely realised.

Conclusion

The introductory scene presents the major characters, who are involved in the plot of the play that revolves around the Alving family. Mrs. Alving, the wife of the late Captain Alving is unhappy because of the shame her husband has brought the family, and which she has concealed to save the family honour. She discloses the truth about her husband's wantonness to Pastor Manders, who she loves, but cannot marry. Regina, the young housemaid is the daughter of her husband by their servant Johanna, who readily accepts the three hundred dollars given by Mrs. Alving to conceal the relationship and marries Engstrand to save herself of disgrace.

Engstrand, who values money more than honour accepts Johanna as his wife. Mrs. Alving intends to build an orphanage in memory of her husband with the fortune he has amassed. Her decision is proof that she rejects her husband's earnings and in turn ensures that her son does not inherit anything from his father. Meanwhile, Engstrand expresses his wish to build a lodging for sailors, but Regina is suspicious about her father's plans for her future.

Mrs. Alving disapproves of the relationship between Regina and her son. She intends to send her away to avoid further issues. Her unhappiness and view of life is apparent when she explains that each person in this world lives in pretence and the fear of public opinion. Her life is wasted because she has put up with her disgraceful husband all these years. Under the pretext of family honour, she is to construct an orphanage with her husband's wealth and under his name, while the truth is that she neither wants to own nor give her son anything that belongs to Captain Alving.

Jacob Engstand intends to use Regina's charm to seduce sailors and the home that he has decided to build would serve the purpose. Oswald discloses to his mother that he suffers from deterioration of the mind, but he is not sure how he has caught the ailment. Mrs. Alving is shocked, but she decides not to disclose to Oswald the truth about his father's similar condition, which means that his illness is inherited from his father. Mrs. Alving decides to disclose the relationship of Oswald and Regina, but a sudden fire at the orphanage stops her and she rushes out.

Mrs. Alving sees her efforts to construct the orphanage to maintain the dignity of her family go up to flames. Engstrand dupes the Pastor and tells him that the fire at the orphanage was accidentally started by the Pastor, but owns responsibility for the same and regards his deed as a generous act. Engstrand is responsible for the destruction of the orphanage, and his treachery is considered a derogatory act because his intention is to obtain money for the home for sailors from the pastor by cheating on him. The pastor is too naive and agrees to help Engstrand.

When Mrs. Alving reveals to Regina that Mr. Alving is her father from an illicit relationship with the maid Johanna, Regina decides to leave the house, or obtain money from the Pastor or stay at the house of sailors even if it is immoral. Engstrand and Regina are corrupt because they find means to become affluent through any means. Oswald is shocked when Regina deserts him and now he wants to put an end to his degenerate condition. He asks his mother to alleviate him from pain by putting him to death by administering morphia; however, Mrs. Alving stands aghast, shocked and undecided.

Glossary

evince : prove
adversity : hardship
turmoil : havoc
ramification : consequence
parochial : narrow
quagmire : muddle or morass
disparage : criticise
perpetual : continual
deter : dissuade
untoward : unpleasant
inconsistency : unpredictability
fallen woman : disgraceful or disreputable woman
rebuke : scold
manipulative : scheming
crafty : cunning
restive : agitated
petulant : sulky or moody
congenital : inherited or hereditary
syphilis : A hereditary disease, this bacterial infection that spreads by unprotected sex

deteriorate : weaken
albeit : although
celibate : refraining from marriage and sexual affairs
afflicted : badly affected with
dig : ridicule
rotting : decaying

Glossary from the Text

Act-I

Asleep? At this hour: indicates that Oswald could seriously ill.

rendezvous: 'meeting' in French. Regina intends to show-off her education.

Back to town: indicates a place called Bergen, where it rains hard.

Fi donc!: shame (French). Regina believes that Oswald will take he to Paris.

Pied de mouton: (French) clumsy ox!

Savoir vivre: (French) good breeding.

that can pay just as well: Engstrand has no moral ethics about Regina's becoming a prostitute. He thinks it's fair because her mother earned money in a similar manner.

What a child owes its father: Engstrand could be referring to a child's duty towards its parents.

Filled out?: Regina's reference to her sexual attractiveness embarrasses the pastor.

a single man: Regina doubts Engstrand to be her father.

These books?: Probably referring the kind of books she could have been reading, which the pastor considers indecorous.

Lowering our Poor Rate: the good upper-middle classes, who opinion Manders values, hope to pay lower taxes because of the orphanage. Ibsen in indirectly satirising the social conventions of the Norwegian clergy of his time.

one would almost think you were afraid: Mrs. Alving is afraid that Engstrand would reveal that he is not Regina's father.

soul and body unharmed: Mrs. Alving does not realise how sick her son is; however, she notices that Oswald looks sick. The illness is inherited and not from his stay away from home.

something Oswald must have dreamed: Mrs. Alving tries to repudiate her son any memories of his father.

to think that the authorities permit such things: Manders believes in controlling individual freedom. This is the point where he contradicts with Oswald.

the wonderful, free life: Oswald loves the life abroad and to prove his stand, he criticises the Norwegians abroad who pretend to be respectable, but they are unscrupulous and immoral.

It's not a wife's place to judge her husband: Manders agrees to the subordinate position of women in society.

You've evaded everything in your life that was difficult: Pastor Manders refers to the luxurious life of Mrs. Alving, unaware of her difficulties and duties in life. Mrs. Manders has not disclosed the truth about her husband, which is the only fact that she has not confided to anyone.

whose life has no effect on his reputation: the life of Mrs. Alving projected in contrast to how his life was actually spent.

A piece ·of unseemly high spirits: Manders cannot agree with Mrs. Alving's experiences.

I didn't want Oswald…father: Though Mrs. Alving tries to keep Oswald away from his father, she cannot prevent him from inheriting the fatal disease from his father.

The Orphanage was to refute all the rumours: the memorial to Capt. Alving is based on a lie.

my purchase price: Mrs. Alving comments that middle-class marriage treats the woman as an object to be bought.

everlasting rain: Oswald is upset by the gloomy weather outside and the melancholic atmosphere at home.

Bien: (French) good.

Let me go!: an echo of Regina's mother's words. Oswald's real motive is to marry Regina and ask her to end his life when the time comes. This remains unknown and unfulfilled.

Ghosts!: the pair is re-enacting the past. Mrs. Alving realises that what she hoped to bury is alive.

Act-II

Ghosts!: the pair is re-enacting the past. Mrs. Alving realises that what she had hoped to bury is alive.

[the wet mist]: reference to the moral gloom that pervades the house

She must leave this house: Mrs Alving decides for Regina without considering her wishes.

Yacht: Engstrand believes the story about a foreigner with a yacht who was the actual father of Johanna's child. He had boasted about good sum given by the foreigner to Johanna in Act One.

I should have never hushed up the truth: Mrs Alving reconsiders not having spoken the truth regarding Capt. Alving all these years. She now feels she needs to escape the confines of the image of the respectable home she has tried to build.

Coward that I am: In Act One Mrs. Alving admitted to being a coward because she held on to ideas that she had feared to express. Now, in spite of her shock at the affair between her son and Regina and illness of her son, she cannot disclose the truth.

he's not going to ruin that poor girl's life: Mrs Alving notices similarities among her experiences, Regina's and her mother's many years before.

and who was it that arranged the world like that: the disorder of the world shows God, who appears malevolent.

haunted by ghosts: Mrs. Alving repeats this expression when she notices that it is not only the characters and situations of the past that seem to creep up, but also the ideas and beliefs from the past that obstruct human beings and truth.

afraid of the light: implies the truth that is disclosed only towards the end of the play.

it would be best if we could get her settled-suitably married: in spite of Mrs. Alving's modern outlook and the realisation that she had been sold into marriage, she can think of marriage only as a solution for Regina's welfare.

a sort of orphanage too: Engstrand manipulates the truth and calls his brothel an orphanage. The irony is that Mrs. Alving's orphanage and Engstrand's brothel are built on the grounds of deception.

without a glimpse of the sun: the sun rises too late for Oswald.

vermoulu: (French) worm-eaten.

It's all been my own fault!: Mrs. Alving cannot allow Oswald to believe in his father's debauchery, but she does not disclose the truth.

the one thing I have in the world: Mrs. Alving has sacrifices her life to Oswald, but he understands this only when he is at home.

the lamp: represents a slight ray of hope; feeble light.

a punishment for sin: the belief among the Protestants that man in born in Original Sin and must suffer in order to find salvation. For Oswald, work implies the joy of artistic creation.

everything that matters to me will be turned into something ugly here: The weather and the society depress Oswald. He is thoroughly disturbed and home does not provide comfort.

I see now for the first time: For the first time, Mrs. Alving realises the futility of the deceptive life she has led all these years. Now she can disclose the truth about her experiences.

a judgement on this wicked house: The clergyman gives a religious interpretation.

And not insured!: The pastor realises that the orphanage should have been insured.

Act-III

worthy of his memory: The seaman's home, which is actually a brothel is more suited as a memorial to Capt. Alving because he remained degenerate throughout his life.

[all the doors are open]: Suggests the destruction of Mrs. Alving's constructed edifice of a fake image and the subsequent exposure to the world of reality.

Ghosts!: the outdated notions than Mrs. Alving has held so long.

you'll see the sun: Mrs. Alving is optimistic that her son would be better off.

cherry-coloured velvet curtains: refers to the sensory impressions of a brain that is incapable of rational thought. While this phrase conveys Oswald's artistic sensibility, his mother can only scream in horror.

And what sort of a life have you given me?: Oswald is unhappy because his disease is inherited and he has been away from home without the love or care of his parents. Mrs. Alving's purpose in sending her son away from home has turned futile.

[the glaciers and the peaks]: The reference to the rising sun amidst the mountains is the first glimpse of the real world beyond the hypocritical home constructed by Mrs. Alving. The sun that appears after long hours of rain towards the end of the play signifies Oswald's release from pain forever. Ibsen has used the mountain in other plays to refer to the unattainable ideals that man strives for.

"Mother, give me the sun": The sun that once represented joy of living, towards the end of the play represents the opposite, death, which would assure his sanity.

References

Ledger, Sally. *Henrik Ibsen*. 2nd ed., Atlantic, 2010.

McFarlane, James Walter. *The Oxford Ibsen: Pillars of Society, A Doll's House, Ghosts*, vol. 5. Oxford UP, 1961.

Meyer, Michael. *Henrik Ibsen: Ghosts*. Methuen, 1973.

Styan, J.L. *Modern Drama in Theory and Practice: Volume 1, Realism and Naturalism*. Cambridge UP, 1981.

"Ghosts". https://www.gutenberg.org/files/8121/8121-h/8121-h.htm

https://www.britannica.com/biography/Henrik-Ibsen

https://www.britannica.com/art/dramatic-literature

Chapter 8

A Critical Study of the Play *Ghosts* and Henrik Ibsen as a Dramatist

The Two Interlinked Storylines of the Play *Ghosts*

Ghosts is primarily the story of Mrs. Alving, who desperately attempts to impose her will on the household and fails to come to terms with circumstances in her life. The story begins with Captain Alving, Mrs. Alving and Pastor Manders in their youth that continues with experiences of Oswald and Regina, the housemaid. The second story centers on the life of Engstrand, Regina's father who plots to get money from Pastor Manders for his seamen's home. The two plots are entwined in the play, and each act develops both the plots concomitantly.

While the main story is a tragedy, the instances of Engstrand's deception contributes to the story crucially with regard to relationships and true love. Both the stories are concerned with the importance of pretense, appearances and falsity at the expense of truth in society. Both the stories mention about the rights and duties of parents and children. The home Engstrand wishes to build is a satirical contrast to the orphanage Mrs. Alving has built. While Mrs. Alving's intention is purposeful and moral in nature, Engstrand's plans are carnal and appeal to baser instincts of man. Ibsen's view that the scoundrel Engstrand thrives, but Mrs. Alving deteriorates is a rather bitter portrayal of an insensible society.

Significance of the Title "Ghosts"

Ghosts means "those who come back" that refers to people, ideas or beliefs from the past that affect the present. Mrs. Alving uses the word "ghosts" for the first time when she hears Oswald trying to seduce to Regina. At that moment she recalls similar scenes between her husband and Regina's mother. Psychological reactions of the young pair of lovers are visitations by ghosts of their parents. The play suggests that parents' attitudes influence children. In this sense, Oswald's tendency to drink heavily and Regina's decision to move to the seamen's home could be attributed to the inclinations of their father and mother respectively.

In the second act of the play, Mrs. Alving repeats the word "ghosts" when she speaks to Pastor Manders about incestuous relationships that continue to haunt and frighten her. Her reference is to attitudes children inherent from parents and redundant conventional ideas and beliefs upheld by the society. Mrs. Alving has been taught that men are naturally sinful and women must suppress their emotions and work dutifully because life is a battle of tears for women. Though she has fought emotionally to reject some old ideas, she still believes in preserving the reputation of her family. Pastor Manders is also haunted by "ghosts" of acceptable social conventions and shouldering one's burdens.

Mrs. Alving uses the word "ghosts" for the last time in the third act. She tells Oswald that he should love his father, but Oswald refuses to comply with an old "superstition". The orphanage, her memorial to "ghosts" of her past has been destroyed, but she realises that she is still not entirely emotionally free from the weight of the past. She tries unsuccessfully towards the end of the play to make Oswald say that he loves her, which shows that she still clings to such beliefs.

The title of the play is significant of ways in which individual freedom is impeded by heredity, convention, religion and emotions yielded by past lives. Such "ghosts" cannot be destroyed. Even after Mrs. Alving's disclosure, Oswald is destroyed by his parents, "ghosts", that is events of the past.

Character-Sketch

Mrs. Helena Alving

Ghosts revolves around unfortunate incidents in the life of Mrs. Alving, the central character of the play. Mrs. Alving at the beginning of the play appears to read books that disagree with conventional morals, but she never discusses what she reads with others. She spends her entire life defending her husband's reputation and she believes that life and work are more of duty than enjoyment, which is in direct contrast to her husband's views.

She disapproves of her husband's infidelity and takes a harsh stand that unfortunately separates her from her husband and her son. She fails to realise her son's need for love and prioritises moral principles over affection and she sends him away from home at an early age. Though she is successful in preventing her son from inheriting his father's fortunes, she is unable to free him from inheriting his father's illness.

Her lack of education and experience makes her condemn herself for her moral strictness, later in life. In spite of her disastrous marriage, she thinks of arranging a marriage for Regina as a way of securing her future. She is shrewd to identify fraudulent moves of Engstrand, but she is helpless in that she cannot prevent him from stop scheming against her family. Towards the end of the play, she reveals that her intentions would live through her son, who she expects to act like a loving child, not realising that he has little affection for her. She instils the hope of a new life in her son, and in the end remains undecided whether to put him to death. The play is essentially her tragedy.

Pastor Manders

The pastor is of the same age as Mrs. Alving and they loved each other. Her marriage to Captain Alving makes him suppress his emotions and he believes in the moral principles maintained by the middle-class bourgeois, which is disdained by Oswald. He is scorned by Oswald for giving in to appearances than the truth. He is gullible and easily manipulated by Engstrand. The pastor seems to trust more in God's Providence than be practical.

Oswald Alving

A young man in his late twenties, Oswald has spent very little time at home and hardly knows anything about his parents. He is captivated by life in Paris and deliberately sets out to shock Manders by expressing his preference for live-in relationships than marriage. He plays with Regina's affections, failing to realise their connection, until his mother discloses his father. Oswald is self-centered, but he cannot be blamed because he is sure that nothing can cure him.

To his mother, Oswald represents freedom, joy and truth that she seeks. Through him, she wants to create a life that she has not been able to lead. To Regina, Oswald is her chance to better her status in the society, which is thwarted by the truth their relationship. To Manders, Oswald is initially a symbol of the stability of the bourgeois family, but later he appears to be full of vices. At the end of the play, Oswald represents the silent and unfortunate sufferer for no fault of his, but his father's.

Jacob Engstrand

He is a wily and old limp carpenter, who is interested only in finding enough money to become the owner of a brothel. To achieve his end, he plays on the naivety of Pastor Manders and presents himself as a poor sinner in order to make Manders think he should be safe and uses the fire at the orphanage to blackmail Manders. He lacks moral principles and chooses his words and gestures to meet his ends. In the end, he succeeds in his endeavour to construct the home for seamen, with the financial support of the pastor, who fails to realise Engstrand's real intentions.

Regina Engstrand

A young and attractive nineteen-year-old housemaid at the house of Mrs. Alving, she desperately wants to better herself and escape her low position in the society. Her only asset throughout the play is her youthful attractiveness that both Oswald and Engstrand want to make use of to achieve their personal goals. She flirts openly with Oswald to secure herself but when she realises that he is too ill to recover and he is her half-brother, she deserts him forever. She repeatedly talks about her unhappy childhood that was shattered by Engstrand who mistreated her mother. She is more condemned than anybody in the play because her future would end in the brothel, the proposed Seamen's Home.

Captain Alving

He has been dead for ten years when the play opens, and the construction of the orphanage in his memory is to conceal his despicable nature. From Mrs. Alving, his immorality is revealed and the relationship between Regina and Oswald becomes evident. He is seen as the "ghost" that haunts the entire family and influences their behaviour. While Oswald has unpleasant memories of his father, Mrs. Alving's life experiences lead her to self-discovery. The unscrupulous life of the captain and Mrs. Alving's response to life, later become the cause of the tragedy in her life.

Themes in *Ghosts*

Free-will and Determinism

Ghosts could be interpreted to discuss the twin issues of free will and determinism, which was considerably debated during the 19th century. Ibsen strives to remain aloof from problems of individuals and destiny, and neither recommends a particular line of conduct nor advocates the position of any characters in his plays. He poignantly portrays the specific moment of crisis in lives of individuals faced with their own past experiences within the family and in the society.

Ibsen, aware of Charles Darwin's (1809-82), *Origin of Species* (1859) presents evidences of the contribution of genetic inheritance in the life of every individual in some of his plays. Ibsen is conscious of the extent to which society shapes individual thoughts and limits the range of choices. He understands that man's conduct is chained by heredity and environment and it is a daunting task to be able to exercise freedom. In *Ghosts*, Mrs. Alving wants to be free from constraints of the society, and has intellectually rejected many of its dictates; however, she is emotionally unable to break traditional life and hopes to find liberation through her son.

Heredity

Oswald's hereditary disease may be interpreted as the equivalent of the Christian concept of Original Sin that the sins of the fathers are visited upon their children. The sin of Adam and Eve brought death into the world, means that man cannot escape from mistakes of the past either committed by his family or the whole human race. Heredity influences the Alving family and the notion of moral guilt from previous generations binds with the future. Oswald suffers from a physical disease and his childhood isolation influences his thoughts and character. Regina rejects the idea that Engstrand may be her father for she detests his moral and physical decadence and does not want to inherit them. Oswald does not want to be reminded of his father, but he inherits his physical ailment.

Religious Beliefs and Societal Conventions

The play satirises the provincial Norwegian society of Ibsen's time, which is evident in the portrayal of Pastor Manders who is completely bound by social conventions. The "ghosts" are often the outmoded ideas that Manders upholds such as the sanctity of the marriage vow, the subordination of women to their husbands, the refusal to accept new ideas and the narrow conventionality of town life.

Ibsen was disgusted with the moral weakness of the clergy. He satirises the clergy's respect for appearance and conventions and support of the middle-class social order but its blindness to the real nature of men. Pastor Manders does not insure the buildings because he wants to appear trustful of divine Providence!

Marriage

Ghosts is a criticism of the conventional middle-class marriage that is primarily based on monetary consideration. Mrs. Alving says that her family urges her to marry the captain because he is wealthy. Marriage is a matter of financial security, not love. She yields to a marriage for money and remains untruthful to her emotions. Once married she finds that she is expected to accept whatever her husband does. Oswald contrasts the supposedly respectable married men who behave wantonly while abroad with the unmarried couples in Paris in living-in relationship, whose union is based on love.

The Status of Women in Society

Ibsen is sensitive to lives of women that are fettered by conventions of the society. Women's progress in society is the struggle for personal emancipation that becomes an overwhelming task because of the pressure to remain within accepted social norms and limited access to education. Regina, for instance cannot attain independence unless she attaches herself either to Pastor Manders or Oswald, or decide to become a prostitute.

The Issue of Putting One to Death on Request

The final scene of the play raises the issue of putting another person to death on request. Oswald chooses not to live a rotten life and procures enough morphia to kill himself. Although he has accepted the doctor's diagnosis that the next attack would be fatal, he does not administer the poison himself prior to the attack. He wants to force someone else to take up this responsibility. If he is weak, his mother is also weak and the play ends without resolving this question.

The individual's need to assume responsibility for one's own self and the impossibility of ever freeing oneself from fate is one of the principal arguments of Ibsen. He raises the question of the moral and legal acceptability to end life in the face of incurable illness and the effects of the decision on the individual and the family.

The Symbols in the Play *Ghosts*

Dominant symbols in the play have immense psychological relevance. It has been raining from the beginning of the play. The gloomy atmosphere pervades the entire play that is built on secrecy, guilt, treachery and moral depravity. The rain represents immorality and conservatism. The sun, which is the symbol of truth, life and energy, ironically shines only after Oswald is decapacitated and when Mrs. Alving reveals the past. Towards the end of the play, Oswald requests his mother to give him the sun, which is the life-force and creative energy; however, in effect, he is asking for death.

The orphanage stands for reverence to social convention under pretension, and fear of humiliation, but its destruction symbolises Mrs. Alving's decision to destroy her husband's false reputation, which she has tried to maintain throughout her life. She the courage to break down walls of hypocrisy and realises that family honour cannot be purchased. The construction of the Seamen's Home is emblematic of the victory of baser instincts of man over ideals.

The Dramatic Art of Henrik Ibsen

The Influence of Henrik Ibsen on Modern Drama

The school of naturalism to which Ibsen's *Ghosts* belongs, is strongly associated with novels of Emile Zola. It was mainly at Zola's prompting that the play was initially staged in France in 1890. *Ghosts* is a self-consciously new naturalistic form of theatre but retains the classical unities of time and place. It is probably Ibsen's most economically-constructed play. Ibsen is unconcerned with historic figures from a mythical past, but portrays lives of the ordinary citizens of the 19th-century Norway. It is the first tragedy to have been written about the unheroic, unexceptional middle-class people who speak the plain, idiomatic prose.

Ibsen's central observation in *Ghosts* is that the most dreadful human suffering is lived out everyday in the most ordinary circumstances. This essentially makes the play a modern tragedy. Ibsen was acutely conscious about the way in which "ghosts" broke out the dominant moral and aesthetic codes of his day. He was horribly disappointed that the liberal newspapers and cultural commentators in Norway had not supported him over the controversy aroused by *Ghosts*.

Mrs. Alving is a portrait of what Nora Helmer, the heroine of *A Doll's House* might have become had she stayed with her husband and children instead of slamming the door on her domestic life, mentions Ibsen. Writing to Countess Sophia Aldersparre on 24 June 1882, Ibsen remarked: "I had to write *Ghosts*. I couldn't stop at *A Doll's House*; after Nora I had to create Mrs. Alving" (Ledger 32). Mrs. Alving's decisiveness and moral courage are indicated by her earlier attempt to leave her husband whatever be the social consequences.

It is only because Pastor Manders insists, she returns to the marital home that she relents; a decision, which she later regrets. She has spent her life nursing an immoral and diseased husband, sending her son away from home for protecting him from the morally debased influence of his father. In the period of her husband's physical decline, she has handled the family estate single-handedly, taking on traditionally masculine responsibilities and sheltering her family from ignominy.

Heredity theory adversely influenced Ibsen's drama because of the view that biological and social evolution theories did not always comes to term with racial and social improvement, but they led to racial degeneration. The role of heredity theory that influenced the 19th century is prominent in *Ghosts*. Oswald's condition is the result of inheritance and his friends who do not bother to get married are far better than him.

Oswald's failure is more due to biological inheritance than social oppression. Regina, the illegitimate daughter of Captain Alving appears to have inherited her mother's weakness for sexual advances. The influence of heredity theory on the play is intricately bound up with its standing as a naturalist drama. The realism of the play emphasises the physical basis of human life, and ways in which social relations are entrenched in biology.

Techniques Employed by Ibsen in His Plays for Character Analysis

Ibsen deploys three different tactics to examine the characters in his plays. The first technique is through the process of a gradual revelation of past events. Such a technique would keep the audience informed about the nature of each character progressively. This method also traces the development of the character throughout the play either due to the revelation of past events and its effect in the present or by a reassessment of known facts. The best example is Mrs. Alving's realisation towards the close of the second act that it is her sense of duty and respect for tradition that are responsible for her unsuccessful marriage and the moral dissoluteness of her husband.

The second technique employed by Ibsen to describe character is through action as in *Hedda Gabler*, where Hedda's dangerous play with her pistols reveal the destructive tendencies in her extremely neurotic character. In *An Enemy of the People*, Dr. Stockmann's dance with his wife at the close of the first act brings out his optimistic nature.

The third technique is the effective use of opinions of others to describe a character. In *Rosmersholm*, Brendel describes the editor Mortens Gaard as one who is capable of living his life without ideals. In *An Enemy of the People*, the editor Hovstad describes his printer Aslaksen as "chicken-hearted" and "a coward".

Thematic Association in Plays of Ibsen

Close analyses of Ibsen's major plays would unravel a thread of association in the themes he discusses in his plays that evince the wide range of issues he chooses to comment on.

Brand (1886) and *Peer Gynt* (1867) are concerned with opposing but complementary themes. The protagonists in both plays are concerned with self-realisation but they fail until the very end to come to terms with their distinctive personalities. While Brand finally sees his tragic fault in the last scene, Peer Gynt, towards the end of the play perceives that he has yet to develop to set an identity for himself.

In *Pillars of the Society* (1877), Ibsen attacks the falsity prevalent in society and takes up contemporary parochial notions on marriage and womanhood. In *A Doll's House* (1879), he shocks the theatre with Nora shutting the door, leaving her husband and children for searching for her identity. In *Ghosts* (1881), Ibsen entails the lies that permeate the society that surface as "ghosts" or dead ideas and beliefs of the past that smother individual right to enjoy life. Rather than the theme, the subject matter related to the venereal disease causes great commotion in his times. *An Enemy of the People* (1882) discusses the similar theme of outmoded ideas and beliefs that thrive on majority opinion and strongly advocate wrong ideas.

In *The Wild Duck* (1884), Gregers Werle, in his quest to bring truth to the Ekdal Home, ends up ruining what he is seeking to elevate. Through the character of Dr. Relling, Ibsen presents the idea that illusions are important for people to maintain their happiness and every man encounters an illusory phase in his life. *Rosmersholm* (1886) discards social messages and provides a psychological insight into the character Rebecca West that ends with the realisation of the self. However, excessive individualism takes away life and the drama ends in a catastrophe. The theme of realisation forms the basis of *Hedda Gabler* (1890), where Hedda to a greater extent than Rebecca West suffers from excessive individualism. *The Master Builder* (1892) and *John Gabriel Borkman* (1896) deal with individualism and the social responsibility of an artist.

Conclusion

Henrik Ibsen's contribution to drama is phenomenal since he uses his Problem plays to project several issues prevalent in his times. His plays pose questions on several grave concerns that are supposedly invisible, and the insensitivity of the society to address issues is not ruled out. To foreground the inherent contradictions of the practices of the times, Ibsen uses his characters that expose the drawbacks of tradition and convention. Most of his plays replicate real problems that exist in the society and hence the audience is able to appreciate and emulate the efforts of Ibsen to reveal the inconsistencies that plague the social order.

The effective use of dialogues, well-etched characters, and symbols intensify the magnitude of contemporary problems presented and invite critical appraisal. Ibsen stands out as an exemplary dramatist who is not only sensitive to issues of the times but also conscious of the role of the dramatist; however, his ingenuity lies in the fact that he stands as an observer who notices, and points out to drawbacks of the society and seeks answers from the audience. Ibsen's holistic approach to drama accounts for his role as a modern dramatist.

Glossary

satire	: ridicule, mockery
carnal	: bodily, erotic
baser	: dishonourable

visitation	:	visit
evince	:	demonstrate
inclination	:	predisposition, tendency
providence	:	divine intervention
unscrupulous	:	unprincipled
poignant	:	emotional and distressing
replicate	:	reproduce

References

Ledger, Sally. *Henrik Ibsen.* 2nd ed., Atlantic, 2010.

Meyer, Michael. *Henrik Ibsen: Ghosts.* Methuen, 1973.

Styan, J.L. *Modern Drama in Theory and Practice: Volume 1, Realism and Naturalism.* Cambridge UP, 1981.

https://www.britannica.com/biography/Henrik-https://www.britannica.com/art/dramatic-literature

Chapter 9

Modern Drama: The Emergence of Epic Theatre

Introduction

Modern drama that emerged in the nineteenth century and continued to evolve consequently, employed several dramatic techniques that were principally the manoeuvres created by playwrights to suit their purposes and achieve the desired end. Modern drama was an amalgam of several artistic movements such as Realism, Naturalism, Symbolism, Expressionism, Surrealism and Existentialism that contrived unique ways to depict a generation of disillusionment and disintegration. In this regard, Sir Arthur Pinero mentioned: "The art—the great and fascinating and most difficult art—of the modern dramatist is nothing else than to achieve the compression of life which the stage undoubtedly demands, without falsification."

Modern drama engaged with controversial subject matters and used innovative forms of expressions that urged the audience to challenge the existing social order and project a distinctive view of life. The emergence of cities, preference for industry to agriculture for survival, and scientific and technological advancements worked in tandem with the formation of social classes, and gave rise to diverse and discordant themes in drama, and hence they were either banned or even censored.

The well-made play and melodrama, which were prominent theatre forms during the 19th century were scoffed at by modern playwrights. While Henrik Ibsen and George Bernard Shaw adopted conventions of these plays, and made effective use of these dramas to highlight social and psychological issues, August Strindberg preferred the drama of logic. Anton Chekov used understatements and nuances as experimental forms in his drama, and avoided the deployment of stock characters in his plays.

Theatrical Forms

Naturalism originated in France in the 1860s and drew impetus from Darwin's theories, notions of survival of the fittest, natural selection and dependence on the environment. Therefore, science and social behaviour, influenced by biological factors effected the naturalist theatre that opposed the Romantic view of subjectivity, emotion and individual experience. André Antoine's Théâter Libre in Paris, J.T. Grein's Independent Theatre in London, Otto Brahm's Freie Bühne of Berlin and Konstatin Stanislavsky's Mosco Art Theatre offered the platform to experiment with this mode of dramatic presentation. The emphasis was given to realistic stage settings the actors' psychology and emotions. By enacting plays of Ibsen, a new generation of female actors such as Eleanora Duse, Elizabeth Robins and Eva Le Gallienne displayed their artistic talents and earned reputation.

Aestheticism, a French movement, which was primarily opposed to the dominance of science and the dissent of works of art without any moral purpose by the middle-class of the time, advocated that the end of art is pleasure and it had no moral aim "outside its own being" (Abrams 4). The slogan "Art for Art's Sake" proposed that the beauty of works of art was accentuated over their use for social or political propaganda.

Walter Pater introduced the dictates of French aestheticism into Victorian England and writers such as Charles Swinburne, Oscar Wilde, Arthur Symons and Lionel Johnson emphasised the autonomy of art. Symbolism was associated with the contribution of Maurice Maeterlinck (1862-1949) of Belgium, Madam Rachilde (1860-1953) of France and William Butler Yeats (1865-1939) of Ireland. The movement relegated direct, common speech and insisted on the employment of mysticism, subjectivity and suggestion in drama.

Avant-garde Movements

The predominant facet of modernism is the observable avant-garde, which is French for "advance-guard." The term was originally used to denote the vanguard of an army, that is the segment of an army, which marched forward ahead of the rest. The term was applied to art in France in the early 19th century and subsequently reached Italy, Germany and the other countries in Europe.

Abrams mentions that a small group of artists and authors intended to break away from convention deliberately. He adds: "By violating the accepted and properties of not only art but of social discourse, they set out to create ever-new artistic forms and styles and to introduce hitherto neglected, and sometimes forbidden, subject-matter" (*A Glossary* 227). The term avant-garde attained a dual signification. It was associated with both the historical movements that commenced in the latter half of the 19th century and ended in the 1930's as well as the continued attempts of profound and revolutionary innovation and change in art, literature and fashion in the later twentieth century.

Avant-garde art probably gained ground in the 1850's with the realism of the French painter Gustave Courbet (1819-77), who was strongly influenced by early socialist ideas. Thereby several forms modern art appeared that revolutionised artistic expressions. While Cubism focused mainly on innovations of form, Futurism, De Stijl or Surrealism had firm social agendas. Futurism, Vorticism, Dadaism, and Anarchism effected crucial innovations in aesthetic form and content, and concomitantly engaged the viewers by the deliberate employment of appalling tactics and techniques. Avant-garde, a conscious and deliberate break with prevalent standards, not only challenged convention but also framed innovative strategies to present drama. However, several avant-garde practices and depictions raised controversies and they were resisted.

Futurism, the Italian movement in the arts commenced with efforts of F.T. Marinetti (1876-1944) in 1909, who intended to integrate arts, technology and industry and denounce past culture that was considered oppressive in every form. Marinetti used puppets, machines and inanimate objects instead of human characters on stage. That way, the dynamism and energy of the modern world could be encapsulated. "'Designed analogies', the pictograms where shape analogically mimics meaning; *dipinti paroliberi*, the literary collages combining graphic elements with free-word poetry; and *sintesi*, the minimalist play" were among some innovative genres presented by the Futurists (britannica.com).

Considered the British counterpart to Futurism, Vorticism was launched by the artist, writer and activist Wyndham Lewis in 1914 in London to produce art to capture the dynamism of the modern world. Lewis, however, was inimical to the Futurists. Lewis introduced many of these ideas in the short-lived but highly influential magazine, *Blast*. It is believed that the movement culminated with the First World War, albeit Lewis made attempts to revive the art with the formation of Group X in 1920. The new movement, which was directed to the revival of tradition art-making rejected the avant-garde.

Dadaism emerged in 1916 out of repugnance with the inhumaneness and destructiveness of the First World War. It is believed that when a paper knife inserted into a French-German dictionary pointed to the French word *dada* ("hobby-horse"), the term was considered apposite by the group of young artists to present their anti-aesthetic creations and protest activities. The group expressed its disgust for bourgeois values and the consequences of World War I.

Dadaists embraced socialism to destroy the formation of societies based on class distinction. They propagated "negative art and literature" (Abrams 392) that presented themes that shocked and perplexed the audience that was exposed to the false values and rationality of thought of the modern bourgeois society. Nonsense poems, musical pieces and masked performances of Dadaism, influenced by the Romanian dramatist Tristan Tzara (1896-1963) flourished in Zurich during the period of the First World War. Dadaism included the contribution of Marcel Duchamp, Man Ray and Max Ernst.

The prime apologist of Surrealism, the French painter and writer André Breton (1896-1966) employed Freud's psychoanalytical and dream theories in the dramatic presentations and Antonin Artaud (1894-1948) of France invented the Theatre of Cruelty in Italy that was enthused by ancient rituals as well as the film comedies of the Marx Brothers. The word 'surrealist', which suggests 'beyond reality' was coined by the French avant-garde poet Guillaume Apollinaire in the play *The Breasts of Tiresias* written in 1903. The play was performed in 1917 with the subtitle *Drame surréaliste* and a preface, whereby he conceived the word "surrealism" to elucidate his new style of drama.

The Surrealist movement transformed the literary, artistic and philosophical discussions by delving into inner recesses of the human mind that functioned in tandem with the rational and irrational expressions. Breton proposed that surrealism was a means of reunifying the conscious and the unconscious realms of experience so intimately and totally that the world of dream and fantasy, and the everyday rational world would be linked in "an absolute reality, a surreality." While the word 'surreal' ordinarily means 'strange' or 'dreamlike', the word 'surrealist' is associated with philosophy and the surrealist movement.

The Contribution of Erwin Piscator to Epic Theatre

The German dramatist Erwin Piscator (1893-1966) was admired for the extraordinary Expressionistic techniques he conceived for the stage. He was the originator of the Epic theatre, which was later improved and developed by Bertolt Brecht (1898-1956). Piscator became an actor and a director at the Hof Theatre in Munich. The "proletarian theatre" was founded by Erwin Piscator and Hermann Schuller in March 1999 in Berlin. In the book *The Political Theatre* (1929), Piscator outlined the basic tenets of this theatre.

The "Program of the Proletarian Theatre" asserted that the plays were proclamations that endeavoured to intervene in contemporary events to act politically. Art was subordinated to the revolutionary goal of propagating the idea of class struggle. The proletarian theatre emphasised the gradual doing away with the bourgeois professional actor and the emergence of the proletarian actor, who must not become so absorbed in his role that he would forget to make everything an expression of the proletarian idea.

Piscator was one of the liveliest and the most persistent advocates of the "direct action" of literature and especially when the proletarian theatre had finally failed because of the revocation of his license in 1921. "Direct action" demanded a "revolutionary professional theatre", that aimed to politically enlighten the masses. In contrast, the proletarian lay theatre penetrated the working class as a whole with propaganda. But "direct action" could not be achieved with an enlightened passive audience, and hence the active participation of the audience became inevitable. Further the boundary between audience and stage had to be removed to a great extent. Piscator believed that he could bring this about through the stage action and by staging the masses, they could be activated and enlightened.

Technological innovations such as the use of projections and boards, lights, and the use of film were used by Piscator so that the whole drama could be lifted out of its original plane onto the higher plane of the "didactic drama". Technical innovations, efforts to bring to the stage the life of reality and to include the masses in the action were actually not as novel as they seemed in Germany, and the audience came out of complacency and reacted to stage presentations.

The idea of creating and experiencing a "total theatre", where an absolute theatrical effect was to be produced saw Piscator experimenting with optical, acoustical and mechanical devises. However, his extensive use of deafening loudspeakers, blinking lights, blaring sirens, and revolving sets failed to convey the message appropriately to the audience. During the Nazi period, he fled to outskirts of Germany and travelled to Russia. His directed the only film *Vostaniye rybakov* (*The Revolt of the Fishermen*) in 1934 and returned to Germany in 1951 as the director of the theatre Volksbühne in West Berlin. He produced Rolf Hochhuth's *Deputy*, which was based on the role of Pope Pius XII during the Third Reich, and *The Investigation* by Peter Weiss that dealt with horrors of the Auschwitz concentration camp.

Brecht pointed out: "The most radical attempt to endow the theatre with an instructive character was undertaken by Piscator" (6). He praised Piscator for using the stage innovatively and bringing in several contemporary discussions of political implications. Piscator's theatrical presentations were predominantly political in nature and depicted class inequalities in the society, which expressed his considerations for the German working class. However, Brecht noticed that though experiments of Piscator changed the creative process entirely, it resulted in "complete chaos in the theatre" due to the use of complex technicalities for the stage, relegation of aesthetic aspects and the involvement of several academics of diverse disciplines (6).

Bertolt Brecht and Epic Theatre

Piscator taught Brecht the importance of using film and other art forms in the theatre, which led to collaborations with composers including Kurt Julian Weill (1900-50) of Germany. Brecht developed the Epic theatre that employed techniques, which interrupted the flow of plot and acting and emphasised contemplation rather than observation of spectacles.

Brecht appeared on the dramatic forefront with a unique concept in drama that distanced sympathy from the performance. In respect of the move to introduce a new kind of drama, Brecht mentioned: "The whole debacle started when I wanted to have my plays staged properly and effectively and so-oh misery!—in order to define a neo-Aristotelean dramaturgy I developed—oh calamity!—a theory of the epic theatre" (*Brecht* 1). Emotional identification with characters and purgation of emotions were disregarded and the viewers were made to critique the show in the attempt to jolt them from their complacency.

In the article "On the Experimental Theatre", Brecht maintained that the conventional theatre was morally and intellectually degrading because "the more the public was emotionally affected, the less capable it was of learning" (9). The principal function of the theatre in that sense destroyed the ability of the audience to perceive and comment on the performance.

The Epic theatre concentrated to arouse the spectator from the complacent mood and destroyed what could be the designated the usual way of observing a thing that hindered the identification between the stage and the audience and united them in mutual enjoyment. Brecht opposed the naturalistic theatre that attempted to portray truth on stage. He intended a certain kind of distancing of a certain degree by the spectators from what was happening on the stage. That way, the spectators entered into an unusual dramatic experience, grasped things and remained uncontrolled by the events. Brecht termed that experience as 'Verfremdungseffekt'—usually referred in English as the "Alienation effect", which later became the cornerstone of epic theatre.

The active participation of the audience was preferred and the reaction of the audience was quintessential for alienation technique. The theatre introduced the element of detachment that commenced with a procedure that involved the revival of the banal and mundane thing which appeared strange and evoked a sense of wonder and curiosity among spectators. The close episodic structure of his plays led the spectators to see, to ponder and to comment on events staged. The complete effect of the theatre was achieved by the juxtaposition of contrasting episodes. Dramatic illusions were projected by the use of glaring and stark lighting, empty stages, placards that announced changes of scenes, bands that played music on stage, long pauses and gestures.

The Differences Between the Epic and the Dramatic Theatres

Thomson and Needle, in *Brecht* noted that Brecht used the name "Aristotelian Theatre" as well as "Dramatic Theatre" to explain the conditions under which the Epic Theatre was established (187). He used the word "dramatic" to elaborate "a way of *telling* a story" in theatrical terms and for a reason he could not agree with, he used the word "Culinary" to express his contempt for dramatic theatre (187). In his book *A Short Organum for the Theatre*, Brecht mentioned that a genuine story emerged only if the experience of real life was used without the importance given to the succession of events or the need to make complete sense of the play. That way, the story unfolded in an incongruous way and the specific scenes sustained their unique meanings. The scenes aroused a host of ideas and the total effect, the story unfolded without cheap romanticisation of incidents and resulted in an ending in which everything essential for the drama was solved. Brecht insisted on a story that was not fallacious or fabricated (279-80).

Epic theatre was in principle opposed to dramatic theatre. This disagreement was essentially based on Brecht's argument that dramatic theatre maintained the present circumstances and remained ineffective to depose the power structures as well as dismantle the class system inherent in the society. In contrast, Epic theatre persistently interrogated the status quo, enabled and enhanced critical thinking, and resorted to future action for a radical transformation of the society.

Some of the differences between the dramatic and the epic theatres enumerated by Brecht are:

Dramatic Theatre	Epic Theatre
plot	narrative
implicates the spectator in a stage situation	turns the spectator into an observer
wears down his capacity for action	arouses his capacity for action
provides him with sensations	forces him to take decisions
experience	picture of the world
the spectator is involved in something	he is made to face something
suggestion	argument
instinctive feelings are preserved	brought to the point of recognition
the spectator is in the thick of it, shares the experience	the spectator stands outside, studies
the human being is taken for granted	the human being is the object of the enquiry
he is unalterable	he is alterable and able to alter
eyes on the finish	eyes on the course
one scene makes another	each scene for itself
growth	montage
linear development	in curves
evolutionary determinism	jumps
man as a fixed point	man as a process
thought determines being	social being determines thought
feeling	reason

(*Brecht* 37)

These differences could be explicated. The plot or the story line in a dramatic theatre maintained the interest of the readers or even viewers that were motivated by the desire to find out what would follow. In contrast, the Epic theatre engaged with the narrative and concentrated either on how the incidents would unfold or the way the story would be narrated. For Brecht, the spectator was primarily the observer who remained aloof from the situation and watched the happenings in a detached manner. Dramatic theatre concentrates on *catharsis*, the purging of emotions and feelings that left the person clear after the pouring out of emotions and instilled the sense of complacency. In the Epic theatre, the audience is forced to confront the situation, adopt a perspective and frame an individual opinion.

The dramatic theatre played with emotions of the audience that changed according to the situation and prevented the spectator from taking a stand. The Epic theatre considered the opinion of the audience to be crucial because it enabled critical thinking and evaluation of the situation. Dramatic theatre involved the audience completely in the plot and they empathised with the experiences of the protagonist. However, the Epic theatre provided an enigma that depended on the working of the mind of the audience that perceived, contemplated, and comprehended situations that were staged. Each participant in the audience would come up with individual perceptions of the play.

While the dramatic theatre suggested possible reasons for the occurrence of certain events, Epic theatre presented the arguments succinctly. Epic theatre depicted the action and the dialogue. Dramatic theatre achieved the emotional realisation of the experience of the dramatic theatre. Epic theatre delved into and interrogated the reasons for the emotions that led to the discovery of the origin of the problem or injustice that was rampant in the society. In a dramatic theatre, the common experiences of the audience were shared, whereas in the epic theatre the differences in the perceptions of the audience were revealed. While the audience in the dramatic theatre involved in the plot that unfolded, in the Epic theatre, a certain kind of estrangement of the audience was accomplished.

Circumstances of individuals, in dramatic theatre were taken for granted, but the Epic theatre concentrated on how to effect a change in the object of inquiry, the character. The dramatic theatre focussed on the conclusion of the story, whereas the Epic theatre converged on the details of the story and the path traversed by the story. The dramatic theatre used discrete acts and scenes to maintain continuity and facilitated validation of the events on stage, but the Epic theatre stated that a spectator who walked into a theatre at any time should be able to comprehend the scene. The Epic theatre used the technique of hosting a series of scenes where one scene followed another; yet, they remained independent of each other. To achieve this end, technology was extensively used.

In the dramatic theatre, the story unfolded itself through a linear narrative that proceeded from one scene to the other, and the action led to its consequences and so on. In the Epic theatre, the story unfolded in a manner where the focus was not on the end, but on the achievement through the narration, and thereby on questions it raised. Dramatic theatre supported the belief that events were completely determined by previously existing causes. It presupposed the absence of free will and randomness of events that affected life. Epic theatre put forth events without explaining the background or past events.

The Epic theatre reiterated that man possessed the ability to change and extend the change to the society he inhabited. Thoughts determined feelings and man was capable of approving or disapproving a situation and made efforts to change them. Dramatic theatre generated feelings, however Epic theatre initiated reasoning whereby an event or a situation was questioned. In the Epic theatre, the individual might not take anything for granted; nevertheless, the possibility of radical change was apparent.

Conclusion

The theatre of the nineteenth century initiated fresh insights into the development of artistic presentation in literature. The contribution of Naturalism, Symbolism, Aestheticism, avant-garde movements and the Epic Theatre were so profound and phenomenal that they transformed nuances of dramatic presentation forever and augmented the scope of dramatic forms in the subsequent periods all over the world.

The Epic Theatre under Piscator was principally political and the use of technology and film transformed drama; however, the advent of Brecht inducted the use of the stage quite differently in that it concentrated on effects that would propel the audience to respond rather unemotionally to scenes that unfolded as unique parts of the narrative. That way, the audience would maintain an objective stance and reason out depictions on stage rather than partake of the plot emotionally.

The Epic Theatre intended to distance the audience from the dramatic performance so that the possibility of either questioning or adhering to the presentation was achieved. The desired effect was not a passive acceptance of events as they unfolded but a transformation of the way the audience received the message conveyed.

Glossary

manoeuvre	: move carefully to achieve an end
amalgam	: combination
discordant	: conflicting
nuances	: shades
accentuate	: emphasise
relegate	: downgrade
mysticism	: mystical quality
suggestion	: implication
concomitantly	: simultaneously
Marx Brothers	: The popular American comedy team of five brothers that gave over thirty performances on stage, radio and the screen. Chico Marx, Harper, Groucho, Gump and Zeppo enthralled the audience with songs, dances and musical fortes. The three of their greatest comedies included *Monkey Business* (1931), *Horse Feathers* (1932), and Duck Soup (1933).
apologist	: advocator
concocted	: devised
optical	: visual
acoustical	: aural
mechanical	: power-driven

Kurt Julian Weill (1900-50)
: German-born American composer who created a revolutionary kind of opera of sharp social satire in collaboration with Bertolt Brecht. Mahagonny (1927) sharply satirises life in an imaginary America that is also Germany. Weill then wrote the music and Brecht provided the libretto for *Die Dreigroschenoper* (*The Threepenny Opera*, 1928), which was a recasting of John Gay's *Beggar's Opera* (1728) with the 18th century thieves, highwaymen, jailers, and their women turned into typical characters in the Berlin underworld of the 1920s.

complacency : smugness
appalling : dreadful
inanimate : lifeless
enthused : stimulated
juxtaposition : contrast
depose : overthrow
dismantle : demolish
enigma : mystery
apparent : obvious
Dadaism : Refers to any form of art that is innovative and either introduces or explores new forms or subject matter. It first appeared in connection with art in France in the first half of the nineteenth century, and is usually attributed to the influential French thinker Henri de Saint-Simon (1760-1825), one of the precursors of Christian socialism. He believed in the social power of the arts and saw artists and considered them important just as scientists and industrialists and leaders in building a new society.

In 1825, he wrote : "We artists will serve you as an avant-garde, the power of the arts is most immediate: when we want to spread new ideas we inscribe them on marble or canvas. What a magnificent destiny for the arts is that of exercising a positive power over society, a true priestly function and of marching in the van [i.e. vanguard] of all the intellectual faculties!".

Surrealism : Surrealism developed primarily out of the earlier Dada movement in art and literature between the World Wars Europe. The French poet and critic André Breton initiated the movement with the publication of *The Surrealist Manifesto* in 1924. Whitney Chadwick made an insightful analysis of the contribution of the women artists and surrealists in her pioneering book *Women Artists and the Surrealist Movement* (1985). Critics are divided in their opinions regarding the end of the movement with the death of Breton in 1966, while some others contend that it still remains a powerful force in drama.

Futurism : Futurism was launched by the Italian poet Filippo Tommaso Marinetti in 1909. On 20 February he published his "Manifesto of Futurism" on the front page of the Paris newspaper *Le Figaro*. In the Manifesto, Marinetti asserted that "we will free Italy from her innumerable museums which cover her like countless cemeteries". His intention was to involve modern technology and the arts and announce the creation of a modern world that was least oppressive. Innovation in arts and culture, desire for change and adoption of technology were principal to the Futurists.

Vorticism : The British movement that corresponded to Futurism was introduced by Wyndham Lewis in 1914. The movement declined during the First World War, although efforts were made by Lewis to revive the movement in 1920. The revived group called Group X, concentrated on traditional production of art instead of avant-garde.

References

Abrams, M.H., and Geoffrey Galt Harpham. *A Glossary of Literary Terms*. 11th ed. Cengage Learning, 2015

Brecht, Bertolt. *Brecht on Theatre*, translated by John Willett. Methuen, 1964.

Demetz, Peter, editor. *Brecht: A Collection of Critical Essays*. Prentice-Hall Inc., 1962.

Gascoigne, Bamber. *Twentieth-Century Drama*. Hutchinson and Co., 1974.

Needdle, Jan, and Peter Thomson. *Brecht*. Basil Blackwell, 1981.

Styan, J.L. *Modern Drama in Theory and Practice: Volume 1, Realism and Naturalism*. Cambridge UP, 1981.

——. *Modern Drama in Theory and Practice: Volume 2, Symbolism, Surrealism, and the Absurd*. Cambridge UP, 1981.

Thomson, Peter, and Glendyr Sacks, editors. *The Cambridge Companion to Brecht*. Cambridge UP, 1994.

Watson, J. George. *Drama: An Introduction*. Macmillan, 1983.

Willet, John, editor and translator. *Brecht on Theater: The Development of an Aesthetic*. Hill and Wang, 1964.

Williams, Raymond. *Drama from Ibsen to Brecht*. Penguin, 1973.

Brecht, Bertolt. "On the Experimental Theatre." *The Tulane Drama Review*, edited by Bertolt Brecht and Carl Mueller, vol. 6, no. 1, Sep. 1961, pp. 2-17. The MIT Press.

https://www.jstor.org/stable/1125000?seq=1

http://tenstakonsthall.se/uploads/139Brecht_A_Short_Organum_for_the_Theatre.pdf

https://archive.org/details/in.ernet.dli.2015.225314/mode/2up

https://www.britannica.com/art/dramatic-literature

https://www.britannica.com/biography/Bertolt-Brecht

https://www.britannica.com/biography/Erwin-Piscator

https://www.rem.routledge.com/articles/vorticism

https://www.rem.routledge.com/articles/overview/futurism

https://www.britannica.com/art/Dada

https://www.britannica.com/topic/anarchism/Anarchism-in-the-arts

Chapter 10

The Contribution of Bertolt Brecht to Drama

Brecht: The Dramatist

Brecht devised the stage to reform conventional theatre and associated to bring about social and ideological changes into his theatre for political causes. Initially, he studied medicine and served in an army hospital in 1918. He produced his first play *Baal* in 1923. His achieved fame with the play *Drums in the Night* in 1922. *A Manual of Piety*, 1927 was his collection of poems and songs and in 1924 he launched his first professional production, *Edward II*. He expressed his antagonism for the bourgeois class and associated with the Dadaist group that endeavoured to destroy the false standards of bourgeois art through mockery, and subversive satire. He came under the influence of Karl Korsch the Marxist scholar who taught him the principles of Marxism.

In 1928, along with the music composer Kurt Weill, Brecht wrote the satirical ballad opera *The Threepenny Opera,* and in 1930, he came out with the opera *Rise and Fall the City of Mahagonny.* "Lehrstücke", the "exemplary plays", which were plainly didactic works for performance to the accompaniment of music by Weill, Hindemith, and Hanns Eisler were written and performed. The didactic plays helped Brecht discover his own style of theatre in entirety. Initiated by Piscator he not only developed his theory of "epic theatre" but also turned a Marxist in those times.

The play *He Who Said Yes* (1930) was a didactic play that lamented the "sorrowful ways of the world" (Gascoigne 128) by depicting only a particular harsh reality of life; *Leben der Revolutionärin Pelagea Wlassowa aus Twer* (*The Mother: Life of the Revolutionary Pelagea Vlassova from Tver*, 1932) based on the adaptation of Maxim Gorky's novel *Mother* was a critique of capitalism that revealed the disadvantaged sections of the society that were adversely affected by its onslaught.

During the years Brecht went into exile to Scandinavia (1933-41) and later to the United States (1941-47), and produced his collection of poems *Svendborger Gedichte* (1939); the incomplete novel *Die Geschäfte des Herrn Julius Caesar* (*The Business Affairs of Mr. Julius Caesar*) in 1957 that detailed a scholar researching a biography of Caesar dating several years after the Emperor's slaying; *Mutter Courage und ihre Kinder* (*Mother Courage and Her Children*, 1941), an exemplary anti-war chronicle play of the Thirty Years' War; the drama *Leben des Galilei* (*The Life of Galileo*, 1943), which outlined the principal contentions between science and religion, and led the scientist Galileo to face a trial towards the end; and *Der gute Mensch von Sezuan* (*The Good Woman of Setzuan*, 1943), a fable play against the backdrop of pre-war China.

Brecht left the United States in 1947 and produced *Antigone-Modell* (1948), which was adapted from Hölderlin's translation of *Sophocles*. First produced in English, in 1948, *Der kaukasische Kreidekreis* (*The Caucasian Chalk Circle*, 1949), depicted the theme "Whatever there is shall go to those who are good for it". The drama depicted the struggle for possession of a child between its aristocratic mother, who deserted it, and the servant girl who nurtured it. *Herr Puntila und sein Knecht Matti* (*Herr Puntila and His Man Matti,* 1948), was a Volksstück (popular play) about a Finnish farmer who oscillated between rude soberness and drunken good humour; *Der Aufhaltsame Aufstieg des Arturo Ui (The Resistible Rise of Arturo Ui*, 1957) was a parable play of Hitler's rise to power located in pre-war Chicago.

Brecht published his salient theoretical work the Kleines Organon für das Theater ("A Little Organum for the Theatre") in 1949. The same year he staged *Mother Courage and Her Children* with his wife Helene Weigel at the Deutsches Theater, which later helped him establish his own theatre company the Berliner Ensemble and he finally settled down in Berlin.

The Fundamental Aspects of Brecht's Dramatic Theory Proposed in "A Little Organum for the Theatre" (1949)

A playwright who advocated Marxism, Brecht denounced the Aristotelian principle that the audience should be able to perceive what was happening at that moment. He construed that if the audience emotionally partook of the emotions of the heroes of the past, like Hamlet, Othello, King Lear or Oedipus, then they would be refuting the Marxist notion that human nature was not constant but dependent on changing historical conditions. Hence Brecht reasoned out that the theater should not make the audience emotionally associate with characters on stage, but rather they should be rendered capable of following the method adopted by the epic poet's art.

The effort was to make the audience realise that the depictions on the stage were actually accounts of the bygone events that should be viewed in a critically detached manner. The "epic" theater that was narrative and nondramatic in nature was therefore based on detachment, principally the *Verfremdungseffekt* (Alienation effect). This effect was achieved through several devices that prompted the spectator to comprehend that a demonstration of human behaviour, basically scientific in spirit, which was being presented before him was not an illusion of reality. That meant that the theatre was only an acting that was staged and not the world itself.

The Dramatic Art of Bertolt Brecht

Brecht attacked the conventional theatre of the Greeks and Schiller as well as the theatre of Wagner and the well-made play that were quite prominent during his time. Epic acting, along with captions and writings that were projected up on the stage to the accompaniment of songs, music, choreography and scenic design worked against the fable. Improvisations induced by Brecht's epic drama commented on certain events of the play that caused alienation and transformed the ordinary, natural and expected incidents to appear surprisingly new and strange commented certain critics of the nineteenth century.

The German for strange is *fremd* and Brecht's notion of *verfremdungseffekt* is referred to in English as the Alienation effect. The intention of this 'making strange' was to force the audience to respond intellectually to the action of the play with the intention to question the action rather than respond to it emotionally and accept it. To achieve that end, Brecht thought it would be sufficient to break the illusion of the theatre wherein spectators would get so engrossed in the play that they would temporarily forget where they were. Alienation techniques affected the total structure of the play for they weakened tight construction of the plot, challenged the inevitability of events that followed as distinct units, employed interruptions, which divided the play into almost autonomous parts and hence contributed to the decline of the appeal of dramatic illusion.

The most plausible explanation for the invention of the Alienation effect, in the opinion of Brecht was to remind the audience that they were sitting in a theatre. Brecht left the stage apparatus visible, presented a synopsis of each scene on a placard or had narrators talking directly to the audience. His technique, mentioned Gascoigne failed to eliminate the emotional involvement of the audience with a character and that aspect was considered one of the major paradoxes about Brecht's theatre (124). Instead of inspiring the audience as he intended to, he actually ended up exciting an international audience of intellectuals.

The apparent 'failure' (124) was the consequence of a misjudgement in Brecht's theory added Gascoigne. Brecht was wrong to equate empathy, the inseparable part of theatre with illusion, which was a comparatively upstart factor and a peculiar reserve of Naturalism, which Brecht's technique opposed. Gascoigne noticed: "There is alienation in Greek tragedy, in medieval Mystery plays and in the Noh plays and in Jacobean dramas. None of these earlier theatres relied on illusion yet they all caused emotional involvement" (124).

The epic method of acting was a unique strategy of Brecht's overall scheme of alienation or estrangement. Brecht, the creator of epic theatre considered the actor to be a figure who demonstrated on the stage and concomitantly preserved his own individuality. Brecht described the fundamental quality of the epic with the German word *zeigen*, which meant "to point to, to refer to, as a teacher would point to an interesting drawing on his blackboard" (*Brecht* 4).

The epic quality of Brecht's theatre was a decisive turn against an audience that was desirous for illusion because it dwelled on the past. Brecht endeavoured to make it succinct to the spectators that they were in fact not witnessing real events on stage, but listening to "an account...of things that have appeared in the past at a certain time and a certain place" (4). The epic theatre therefore intended to obliterate illusions and exposed the audience to the reality of the depictions on stage.

Brecht opposed the dramatic theatre that sought to tranquilise the audience with emotional empathy and theatrical illusion that they sat quiescent throughout the performance. Brecht preferred to ignore the fact that in a traditional theatre the spectator only intermittently yielded to theatrical illusion. Brecht believed that the theatre must be radically cleansed of the relative and the sporadic interventions as well as the elements of empathy and illusion because they were so toxic that a man would lose his ability to think critically. The epic theatre in which the union of stage techniques and Marxism was achieved, helped retain detachment, sobriety, coolness and a critical bent of mind.

Alienation effects showed relations and events in a new light for they demonstrated that the world was changeable, and alerted the audience for practical political action. The reason for action along Communist lines was left unexplained by Brecht. In his "Little Organam for the Theater" (1949), he employed the terms "enjoyment" and "pleasure" and shunned any theatrical efforts that included the didactic that fell short of contributing to the pleasure of his senses. Shortly before his death in 1956, Brecht seemed to be ready to dispense with the term "epic" altogether as a meaningless endeavour and instead announced his theatre to be "dialectical theatre". The intention behind the formulation of this transformed form of presentation, nevertheless remained unclear.

Categorisation of Brecht's Dramas

Brecht's plays fall into three sequential groups mentions Gascoigne: "There are the earliest, written in the wild and whirling spirit of the twenties full of excitement but lacking control, mixing satire and indulgence almost inextricably" (121). The dramas *Baal* (1922), *Drums in the Night* (1922), *A Man's a Man* (1926), *The Threepenny Opera* (1929), and *Rise and Fall the City of Mahagonny* (1929) belong to this category. Brecht's plays, until 1929 took little interest in the society, which he was satirising, but the mounting threat of Nazism made him embrace Communism.

During the second phase, primarily in the thirties he began his series of didactic plays designed for performance in schools. Each of these drams invariably brought out some crucial aspects of life or themes related to Communism, but almost invariably they revealed the moral paradox of life. *He Who Said Yes* (1930), *The Measures Taken* (1930), *The Seven Deadly Sins* (1933), which was a ballet with songs; and *The Horatians and the Curiatians* (1934) belong to this group. To the last group of dramas is *Puntilla and his man Matty* (1940), *Mother Courage and Her Children* (1941), *The Good Woman of Setzuan* (1943), *The Life of Galileo* (1947) and *The Caucasian Circle* (1948). These dramas were based on serious issues of contemporary relevance that sought the opinion of the audience. The third period saw Brecht at the pinnacle of his dramatic career. Issues related to war, suffering of women, his political commitment, his opinion on scientific development, and the conflict between idealism and practicality of life were depicted.

A Concise Analyses of Some Plays of Brecht

Baal portrayed the sinking life of the drunken poet Baal, who was also licentious. Drawing on the energetic love of protagonists that professed their homosexual affiliations, the play explored the degradation of the anti-hero who was against the social trappings of a bourgeois society. Baal's debauchery ended in his desolate and disgraceful death in a forest hut. *Drums in the Night* celebrated a soldier's homecoming, marriage and revolution with an undercurrent of cynicism. A soldier who returned from war found his fiancée pregnant. He abandoned her in disgust to fight in the Communist apprising in Munich; however, disenchanted there he returned to marry his fiancée.

The Threepenny Opera, which was based on John Gay's play *The Beggar's Opera* exposed vices of the capitalist bourgeois and successfully employed caustic lyrics to the present ironic situations in which lives of various characters were situated. *Rise and Fall the City of Mahagonny*, an opera was a critique of the chaotic and immoral Weimar Republic in Berlin in the 1920s. The plot revealed the ugly side of an unstable government with unethical political agendas, imminent economic crises and widespread social ills such as prostitution and bribery.

The Horatians and the Curiatians substantiated that the soldier who won against an opposing force could have broken the code of honour and moved away at a strategic moment. In *The Exception and the Rule*, the case of a merchant who shot the Coolie who offered him a drink in the desert because he mistook the water bottle for a stone and the offer for an attack is analysed. To prove his plea of self-defence the merchant found himself in a paradoxical position of having to prove to the judge that the Coolie had every reason to hate him. In *The Measures Taken*, a young Communist was put to death by his comrade, his vice being the practice of the normal virtues such as expression of sympathy and honesty for sufferers and his protest against isolated cases of injustice that endangered the wider Communist cause.

The Seven Deadly Sins showed how a young girl's attempts to avoid vice turned out a careful avoidance of virtue upon scrutiny. Anna the young woman and her relations had to build their little house, so she gave up her pride, which had earlier prevented her from stripping in a night club. Her fight with anger at the sight of injustice meted out to her is carried down by the dramatist to expose the seven deadly sins that misdirected her life and exposed false standards of the society.

The four major plays of Brecht—*He Who Said Yes, The Caucasian Chalk Circle, The Good Woman of Setzuan*, and

Mother Courage and Her Children gave more prominence to the dialogue than technical aspects of the alienation effect such as leaving the stage machinery visible to the audience. The dramatic style developed in didactic plays broadened the nature of characters depicted in plays and infused new life into them.

Characters in *He Who Said Yes* expressed their anguish at the deplorable condition of the world of which they were a part of. The fact that those who did good would benefit was the theme of *The Caucasian Chalk Circle*. Shen Te, the heroine of *The Good Woman of Setzuan* suffered for her goodness. She disguised as the tough Shui Ta, her supposedly shrewd male cousin to fight against Shen Te's detractors. The Gods who had earlier helped her with a fortune with the smile of goodwill left her to solve her dilemma.

Mother Courage loved her children, yet she profited from the war which killed all three of them. As a column of troops passed by, she heaved off her tragedy to join them and moved back to the way of life which had caused her ruin; that was the only life she has known. The tragic irony which resulted from the death of her children in her life became complete in the last scene of the play.

The mother Pelagea Vlassova, in *The Mother* journeyed through misfortunes from the death of her son to her illness, while fighting illiteracy that is expressed through good humour and wily activism. The play suggested that to become a good mother was to struggle not only for the family but for all working mothers without complaining about the deplorable situations they faced. The play *Life of Galileo* traces the career of the great Italian natural philosopher Galileo Galilei who was tried by the Roman Catholic Church for propagating his scientific discoveries. The play put forth the themes of the conflict between dogmatism and scientific evidence, and the value of constancy of purpose and devotion to work in the face of oppression.

The short scenes in all his plays contained the essence of the plays. Marked by precision and movement, the plays denounced sentimentality that is evinced by their tough simplicity. Such movements formed the dramatic backbone of Brecht's plays just as the portrayal of characters was pivotal to his depiction of the style of acting.

The Good Woman of Setzuan

Introduction

Brecht began writing the drama during his days in exile in Denmark in 1938 and completed the work in 1939 after moving on to the United States to escape the Nazi persecution and the World War. Besides, he also completed the dramas *Mother Courage and Her Children* and *The Caucasian Chalk Circle*. The plays opposed fascism and capitalism that reflected man's quest for power. The evidences of man's quest for power and dominance were the Second World War and bombings at Hiroshima and Nagasaki. The cruelty of mankind propagated by these incidents led Brecht to critically and sceptically comment on widespread violence and the unfathomable destruction of a humane society. The drama *The Good Woman of Setzuan* expresses the shock and grief that Brecht experienced in those times and debriefs the innate goodness of man.

Other dramas such as *The Threepenny Opera* and *Mother Courage and Her Children* also raised moral, ethical and social concerns and the feeling of insecurity as a result of disgust and anguish at the confounding realities of a world that was lurching under the constant threat of rising fascism and dictatorship. Brecht had earlier intended to title the play *The Good Woman of Setzuan* as *Die Ware Liebe*, a phrase which translated in English to "the product love," "the product that is love," or "love as a commodity." Though the protagonist of the play strived hard to be good to everybody, Brecht asserted the protagonist had to pay a heavy price even in the face of love.

A Brief Summary of the Drama and the List of Characters

The Good Woman of Setzuan, a 'parable in ten scenes", was produced in 1943 and published in 1953 as *Der gute Mensch von Sezuan*. The drama has been translated into English with alternative titles such as *The Good Person of Szechwan* and *The Good Soul of Szechuan*.

Set in China against the backdrop of the First and the Second World Wars, the drama portrays the abject poverty-stricken people of the province of Setzuan. Shen Te, the protagonist is a poor but kind prostitute who is forced into the profession. Her willingness to shelter the three Gods who visit her city with the task to find people on the Earth "living lives worthy of human beings" and check whether goodness prevails in the world, earns her money, which she uses to purchase a tobacco shop to earn her livelihood.

Her relatives and other customers take advantage of her kindness and exploit her. Realising that her business could end a failure, she adopts an alter ego. Disguising as a man and acting out the role of Shen Te's cousin Shui Ta, she tactfully and shrewdly extracts the money swindled from her and teaches the detractors a lesson. Her appearance and the simultaneous disappearance of Shen Te force the people to think that Shui Ta could have murdered his cousin. Towards the climax of the play, Shen Te reveals the truth of her disguise and her intentions.

Character List

- Wang: A poor water-seller in Setzuan, who interacts with Gods in dreams.
- First God, Second God and Third God: They arrive at the city of Setzuan in the Prologue.
- Shen Te/Shui Ta: Shen Te is a former prostitute who has bought a tobacco shop with the money Gods gave her after she let them spend the night in her home when no one else would welcome them. Since Shen Te is being taken advantage of her good nature, she invents a male alter ego, Shui Ta, her supposed visiting cousin, who is shrewd and cunning in business and clever at deceiving Shen Te's deceivers.
- Mrs. Shin: The former owner of Shen Te's tobacco shop.
- Unemployed Man: He enters Shen Te's tobacco shop asking for a free cigarette, which he gets.
- Carpenter: He had installed shelves in the tobacco shop before Shen Te purchased it.
- Mrs. Mi Tzu: Shen Te's landlady.
- Yang Sun: An unemployed pilot and Shen Te's lover.

- Old Whore: She is annoyed with Shen Te for deserting prostitution and running a successful tobacco shop.
- Policeman: He arrests the boy who steals food from the bakery.
- Old Man: He is a carpet-seller.
- Old Woman: She enters the tobacco shop to buy a cigar for her husband.
- Mr. Shu Fu: A barber who wants to marry Shen Te.
- Mrs. Yang: Yang Sun's mother.

Conclusion

Bertolt Brecht was one of the important advocates of the Epic theater that shook the drama of contemporary times because it discarded the emotional attachment of the audience with the depiction of situations on the stage. That way, the audience interacted rationally to the drama and framed individual opinions based on a critical outlook.

Brecht's dramas could be demarcated into three periods that ranged from Marxist viewpoints, discussions on political issues to individual sufferings on account of being victims of their circumstances. Nevertheless, didactic plays of Brecht cast the individuals within specific situations and called for reasonable explanations to their conditions.

Rather than being swayed by tragic incidents in lives of characters, the audience assessed situations they saw and they were encouraged to frame individual opinions either in support or otherwise of the narrative or characters as they unfolded throughout the drama. Brecht devised several tactics to engage the audience in the make-believe world of the theater without getting passively involved in the happenings on stage. The Alienation effect that he propagated contributed to the efficacy of responses of the audience.

Glossary

subversive : destabilising

critique : evaluate

onslaught : attack

construed : to understand
choreography : composition
illusion : delusion
debrief : question
plausible : probable
didactic : moralising

References

Brecht, Bertolt. *Brecht on Theatre*, translated by John Willett. Methuen, 1964.

Brecht, Bertolt. "On the Experimental Theatre." *The Tulane Drama Review*, edited by Bertolt Brecht and Carl Mueller, vol. 6, no. 1, Sep. 1961, pp. 2-17. The MIT Press.

Gascoigne, Bamber. *Twentieth-Century Drama*. Hutchinson and Co., 1974.

Giles, Steve, and Rodney Livingstone, eds. *Bertolt Brecht: Centenary Essays*. Rodopi, 1998.

Jameson, Fredric. *Brecht and Method*. Verso, 1998.

Needdle, Jan, and Peter Thomson. *Brecht*. Basil Blackwell, 1981.

Styan, J.L. *Modern Drama in Theory and Practice: Volume 2, Symbolism, Surrealism, and the Absurd*. Cambridge UP, 1981.

Thomson, Peter, and Glendyr Sacks, editors. *The Cambridge Companion to Brecht*. Cambridge UP, 1994.

Willet, John, editor and translator. *Brecht on Theater: The Development of an Aesthetic*. Hill and Wang, 1964.

https://www.jstor.org/stable/1125000?seq=1

http://tenstakonsthall.se/uploads/139Brecht_A_Short_Organum_for_the_Theatre.pdf

https://archive.org/details/in.ernet.dli.2015.225314/mode/2up

https://www.britannica.com/art/dramatic-literature

https://www.britannica.com/biography/Bertolt-Brecht

Chapter 11

The Good Woman of Setzuan

Prologue and Scene 1

Prologue

It is evening time and Wang, the poor water-seller stands at the gates of Setzuan to address the audience and introduce himself. He says that water is scarce and he has to walk miles to procure water; however, when water is available he is not able to make profit or provide for himself. This means that he has been living in poverty for quite some time without any help of any sort. This condition has prevailed in his province for many years and the people of the locality believe that only divine intervention could save them. Wang has lately heard a rumour from a merchant that Gods are due to visit the province soon and hence he has been waiting for them at the gates to be the first person to receive them.

Wang instantly recognises the three shabbily dressed "illustrious ones" to be the Gods he has been waiting for. He prostrates before them and promises to be at their service. He tells them that only he knows about their arrival to the city. The first God requests Wang to find a house nearby to shelter them for the night. When Wang proceeds to Mr. Fo's house, the nearest one, the servants refuse because he is not at home. Later the widow Su tells Wang that she lives in an untidy and tiny room. Mr. Tscheng refuses to help them and says: "Spare us your Gods! We have other troubles!".

The Gods are denied a place to stay by almost everybody and they move away from Wang to discuss the situation on their own. The second God says that they have been turned away from three villages so far—Schun, Kwan and Setzuan, but the first God reassures others that the "good person" they have been searching for would be just be anywhere near. Wang tells the Gods that the three provinces have to put up with "accidental circumstances" and that is the reason for not being able to find a night's place to stay.

The third God unfurls a scroll that highlights their purpose of visit. They have come down to ascertain whether the world can remain as it exists at present. The Gods are determined to leave the world as it is only if sufficient number of people are seen to be living "worthy" lives. Though the third God thinks that Wang is a good person, the second God refutes when he notices that the measuring cup in which Wang gives them water contains a false bottom. The first God insists that they would definitely find a person who "can *be* good and *stay* good".

Wang admits to the Gods that he cannot find a place for their stay. The moment Wang notices a villager he asks him if he would seize the "rare opportunity" to provide shelter to the Gods who are in search of a shelter for the night. The man suspects Wang, who he thinks is trying to deceive him into hosting "a gang of crooks". Wang is desperate and he tells the Gods that there is just one person now in the village who could help them-Shen Te the prostitute, who would never turn down a guest at night. Shen Te refutes Wang's request to take in the Gods for the night because she is expecting a gentleman with money, which is needed to pay her rent the next morning otherwise she would be thrown out of the house. When Wang begs her help, she agrees, but decides to hide until the gentleman caller would leave and then receive the Gods.

Wang is relieved and he breathlessly tells the Gods to wait for some time until their stay is tidied up. While the Gods take rest, Wang assures them that they would be staying with "the finest human being in Setzuan". When the Gods ask Wang about life in Setzuan, he tells them that both the good and the bad people face hardship. Just then, Shen Te's visitor whistles out to her, but she does not appear at the window and he leaves.

Shen Te calls out to Wang who doesn't seem to hear her and when she walks down the street in search of him, Wang thinks she too has deserted them and feeing utterly ashamed, laments that he has "failed in the service of the Gods" and runs away to his stay, a sewer pipe near the river to hide from the Gods. Shen Te meanwhile returns to find the Gods sitting in the doorway. She introduces herself and invites them to share her "simple" room. The Gods, realising that Wang has abandoned them, leaving behind his carrying pole, carry it along with them so that Wang could get it from Shen Te later.

The lights dim and a streak of light that appears later, announces a new morning. The Gods, pleased with Shen Te's hospitality thank her for accommodating them, and call her a "good human being". Shen Te reveals to them that she had declined to help them earlier at Wang's request, so she was not a good person. The first God reassures her that to deny first and then to complete a good deed is not an offence. Her act of kindness testifies that some good people can be found in the world.

When the Gods get ready to set out, Shen Te tells them that she is not sure about being a good person as the Gods have found her to be, for she has to sell herself to make a living and she does not respect her parents; moreover, she often tells lies and steals from her neighbours. The first God, alarmed insists that her thoughts are the "misgivings of an unusually good woman". When the Gods prepare to leave, Shen Te says she doesn't know how she would be able to continue to be good when things are quite expensive and the cost of living rising up each day. The second God asserts that they do not "meddle with economics". The third God however proposes that Shen Te could be better off if she has more money. The Gods discuss for a minute and then the first God approaches Shen Te and shoves money into her hands declaring that they have paid her for the room. Shen Te gladly accepts the money and the Gods depart.

Scene 1

Shen Te stands beside her tobacco shop in the morning and informs the audience that Gods have given her over a thousand silver dollars for their one-night stay. She has invested some amount as rent for a tobacco shop and the attached rooms and hopes "to do a lot of good" in her new venture. Mrs. Shin the previous owner of the shop had visited her the previous night for some rice to feed her children. She has arrived again in the morning to crib about Shen Te's taking over her and her "innocent children's home". She is unhappy that Shen Te considers the shop a "dump" when she is struggling to survive with her children as they are forced to stay in a shack because of Shen Te. Shen Te gives Mrs. Shin some more rice, which Mrs. Shin willingly accepts.

An elderly couple along with their nephew arrives and they congratulate Shen Te on becoming well-off. The couple request her to allow them a night's stay with her because they are homeless. When Mrs. Shin enquires about the elderly couple, Shen Te tells her that the couple had sheltered her when she had first arrived at Setzuan. In an aside, Shen Te discloses the truth that the couple had in fact thrown her out on the street, when she couldn't pay them. Shen Te offers them the little room behind the shop for their stay.

Soon an old, ragged, unemployed man enters the shop and asks if she has any damaged cigarettes, which he can get for free. The old woman who had arrived earlier with her old husband mocks at the man for asking for cigarettes instead of bread. Shen Te gives the man a pack of cigarettes and thanks him for being the first customer and hopes that he would bring her luck with the days' business. The man leaves the place lighting his cigarette, without thanking Shen Te. The elderly couple advise Shen Te to "learn to say no" to customers if she has to become successful because being "too good" would not help her prosper.

The carpenter Lin To announces himself and rebukes Shen Te for stocking the shelves without paying for the ledges. Though Shen Te insists that the payment she had made for the shop included the furnishing, the carpenter refuses to listen to her claims and demands a hundred silver dollars. Shen Te requests the carpenter not to be restive because she has just started her business, but the carpenter begins to rip off the shelves from the wall. The old wife tells Shen Te to allow her husband to settle the dispute. Though the carpenter finds it hard to believe that the old man is Shen Te's relative, he puts the shelves down and prepares a bill stating the amount that is due to him. Shen Te gets concerned about the Gods' opinions about her failure to pay the carpenter because he ought to be paid for the work he has done and he too has a family to feed.

A man and a five-month pregnant woman enter the shop and express their anger with the old husband and his wife for "hiding out" from them. The old woman mentions that the man is her brother Wung and the temperamental woman, his wife, and Shen Te welcomes them in kindly. Mrs. Mi Tzu the landlady enters the shop with an agreement and asks Shen Te for references. When Shen Te is about to declare that she does not have anybody, the old husband introduces himself as Ma Fu, a tobacco dealer. When Mrs. Mi Tzu mentions that two references are required, Shen Te, with downcast eyes reveals her cousin Shui Ta who lives far away in Shung who should give an undertaking. When the family members in the shop agree that Shui Ta is an honourable person, the landlady agrees to get the document duly signed from him as soon she meets him.

A very old man, the grandfather of the large family enters the shop with a young boy and the niece of the elderly couple. The wife asks Shen Te for the key of the shop to disallow other "unwanted guests". The family revels by opening bottles of wine and smoking cigarettes taken from the shelf without Shen Te's permission. The nephew is apprehensive about the arrival of "the strict Mr. Shui Ta", but his family's reassurance that Shui Ta is in fact a fake, brings him relief. Shen Te stands staring helplessly at the family with the carpenter's bills and the landlady's lease at hand, too fatigued and stunned to say anything.

When the sister-in-law suggests a song to elevate Shen Te's dejection, the grandfather wails and sings "Song of the Smoke" that suggests that smartness is insufficient to become rich and his condition is similar to "smoke" that "float[s] free into every colder coldness", forlorn and desolate. The husband expresses grief that in spite of trying out being both good and crooked, he has not been successful. The niece mourns that the future looks bleak for the younger generation. Though several opportunities are made available for them, each entrance is "nix", which suggests "nothing" and leads nowhere.

The family gathering suddenly turns violent and in fury, some of the members throw up Shen Te's display items. Though she pleads with the family not to destroy the gift from the Gods, they do not bother. The sister-in-law laments that the shop will soon become over-crowded when the other members of the family would join them. Shen Te stares is disbelief when a knock on the door announces the arrival of an uncle, an aunty and some children. When the wife requests them to be let in, Shen Te agrees reluctantly but remarks that even when a "lifeboat" is sent down, men "greedily hold on to it as they drown". This means that men would never leave their hold on money or a sudden fortune even if it is not their own. Given a chance to exploit others, men would be more ready to plunder than think about the consequences.

Scene 1a

The scene shifts to Wang, who has been hiding from the Gods for four days below a bridge and crouching by the river. He soon falls asleep and his dream is revealed to the audience. The three Gods appear before him and Wang apologises for his inability to find a single room for their night stay. The first God explains about Shen Te and the Gods sing a song to reprimand him for his "hasty judgement" of others, and Wang immediately asks for forgiveness. The first God commands Wang to return to Setzuan and give them information on Shen Te's tidings. The first God insists that Wang gives importance to Shen Te's act of goodness because "no one can be good for long if goodness is not in demand." The Gods assert that their intention is to search for more good people in the world like the good woman of Setzuan so that complaints regarding good people not being able to live on earth would end and the Gods disappear.

Analyses

The Prologue exposes how the people are ensnared by capitalistic forces that drive them to vindicate their stand against their response to the situation. Wang, the poor water-seller is forced to depend on the suffering of the people for sustenance, which indicates that to survive is to depend on betraying the common man. This circumstance is quite intimidating because the essence of humanitarian concerns is at risk and the ugly face of capitalism has infringed upon human sensibilities. Wang's difficulty to find a shelter for Gods shows how the people are so absorbed in their own struggles that they fail to recognise how narrow and selfish they have turned out.

The Gods' arrival announces their task to find out if an iota of humanity exists in the world or whether the world should be made over. The main purpose of their visit is to ensure whether a small amount of goodness and kindness remains on earth so that they can depart with the assurance that whatever happens, the human race would sustain on altruistic grounds. The prostitute Shen Te's initial refusal to accommodate the Gods reflects her dire necessity to survive odds at the cost of her chastity and the way capitalism has eroded principles and values that are to be cherished.

The Gods are aware of the plight of the citizens that has driven them to become greedy, distrustful and isolated. Wang is aghast that he cannot help the Gods and hides from them. His departure would not affect the Gods' mission and they are thankful to Shen Te for giving them a place to stay for the night. Recognising that poverty is the primary cause of Shen Te's desperateness, they give her a good amount of money so that she can continue to be good, albeit they appear least concerned about her moral depravity, which is the result of her desperate necessity to survive under bitter and critical conditions. Moreover, they do not want their choice of the good person to be proved otherwise.

In the first scene, Shen Te's altruism is portrayed. Her status in the society does not prevent her from helping even those who have been cruel to her and she even uses the money given by Gods to help the other villagers in need. Shen Te provides for several persons such as Mrs. Shin, and the poor couple and their extended family. Her acts of kindness turn out burdensome when many people take advantage of her wealth and good nature. She is advised by the old couple to remain cautious and prudent while helping others.

The carpenter's claims and the landlady's contract demonstrate that financial debts and commitments should be dealt with firmness. The arrival of the character Shui Ta would henceforth prove decisive throughout the drama. The fact that close relatives unify and prevent the other desperate relatives from joining them and the "Song of the Smoke" sung by some of the family members express their dissolute conditions and expose the stark realities of capitalist forces that have wrecked ordinary lives. On the one hand is material comfort and on the other, goodness. While wealth denotes power, greed and visibility, goodness is attributed with sympathy and kindness; however, both are pitted against the other. Under the given situation, Shen Te's limits of being good to her fellow countrymen are put to test by Brecht.

Shen Te is dumbfounded when the "lifeboat" of her wealth has made her neighbours cling on "greedily" to her fortune even at the cost of their impending doom. Shen Te becomes aware of how judgemental people become when wealth, power and greed take control of their lives as evidenced by the attitude of the family and the others when Shen Te earns a fortune. Scene 1a reveals that the Gods demand Wang to keep them updated about Shen Te's acts of goodness because her behaviour from this point onwards in her life would be significant for them. Nevertheless, they maintain that their mission of finding other good persons like the good woman of Setzuan is yet to be completed.

Conclusion

Driven by poverty, the people of Setzuan are not only discourteous to strangers but also disbelieve and disapprove of their own villager. Women like Shen Te are forced into prostitution and men like Wang cheat the villagers of money by fraudulent methods. The Gods' visit to Setzuan is one way of making the audience realise the need for living with values and principles even in times of adversity. Brecht portrays how several people take advantage of Shen Te's goodness and demand shelter and money from her. Shen Te becomes critical of those who cling on greedily to generosity even when they know that they are being unfair to the generous person.

Shen Te realises that her goodness is being pushed to the limits and this necessitates the arrival of Shui Ta, her cousin to manage the business and take control of the situation. The Gods are certain that Shen Te is good, but they decide to keep a close watch on her movements with the help of Wang. While acts of goodness are on one side of the scale, wealth is on the other. It's to be seen whether Shen Te can act prudently to safeguard her wealth and use the fortune to her benefit, and simultaneously remain good to everybody.

Glossary

restive	:	impatient
sewer	:	drain
ledges	:	rack
revel	:	merry-making
apprehensive	:	worried
nix	:	nothing
lease	:	agreement
iota	:	a little amount of
pitted	:	opposed
albeit	:	although
vindicate	:	defend
infringe	:	interfere with
altruism	:	selflessness
prudent	:	sensible

Glossary from the Text

Prologue

illustrious ones: reference to the Gods

accidental circumstances: Wang gives excuse for the inhospitable people due to certain desperate situations in the provinces of Schun, Kwan and Setzuan.

stomachs rumble even on the emperor's birthday: Shen Te says that everybody feels the pangs of hunger.

We mustn't meddle with economics: The second God says that they are not supposed to enquire about matters related with money. Their mission is to find out a good human being in the world.

Scene 1

But for the young I hear, the door is open/ It opens, so they tell me, upon nix: The young niece expresses the opinion that in spite of promises for the young, of greater opportunities for them, the doors open up to nothing.

The rats climb on to the sinking ship: The sister-in-law mentions that are already too many people in the house and if the number of people increases, they would all be uncomfortable.

The little lifeboat/ Is quickly sent down/ Too many people greedily/ Reach for it as they drown: Shen Te mentions that her wealth is a lifeboat that is a gift of the Gods, but many greedy people are interested in her fortune even though it could be the reason for their downfall.

Scene 1a

No one can be good for long when goodness is not in demand: The Gods say that it is important to be good; however, if fewer number of people possess this quality then people would stop being good and the good ones would not be able to survive on earth.

References

Demetz, Peter. *Brecht: A Collection of Critical Essays*. Prentice-Hall Inc., 1962.

Gascoigne, Bamber. *Twentieth-Century Drama.* Hutchinson and Co., 1974.

Needdle, Jan, and Peter Thomson. *Brecht.* Basil Blackwell, 1981.

Styan, J.L. *Modern Drama in Theory and Practice: Volume 2, Symbolism, Surrealism, and the Absurd.* Cambridge UP, 1981.

https://www.britannica.com/art/dramatic-literature

The Good Woman of Szechwan https://pdfs.semanticscholar.org/82d6/8ed23db277c702a1f467266d5a1f21b65cd3.pdf

Chapter 12

The Good Woman of Setzuan

Scenes 2 and 3

Scene 2

It is early morning, and the inmates of Shen Te's tobacco shop are awakened by a knock at the door. When the wife opens the door, Shui Ta, Shen Te's cousin enters the shop with the carpenter. On enquiry, Shui Ta mentions that he is Shen Te's cousin. The niece and the nephew are baffled because they are sure that Shen Te does not have a cousin and the story of Shui Ta is a fake one. The brother and the nephew jeer at Shui Ta to prove his identity, but Shui Ta stands firm and orders everybody to wake up and get dressed so that he can open the shop. Though the husband points out that the shop belongs to Shen Te, Shui Ta refuses to listen and carries on with the work in the shop.

When the sister-in-law demands to see Shen Te, Shui Ta conveys the message that his cousin wants him to open the shop for her this day and he is entrusted to convey the message to the family residing in the shop that "This is a tobacco shop, not a gold mine." This means that the shop is the only means of income for a poor woman and the family staying in the shop should not hinder the progress of the shop and it's unfair to live on somebody else's income. The family is shocked and outraged. While some of the members of the family go out in search of Shen Te, the young boy goes out to steal breakfast for the family from a nearby bakery.

As Shui Ta begins tidying up the shop, the carpenter hands over the bill of a 100 silver dollars to Shui Ta, who laughs at the bill and offers to pay him 20 dollars only. The carpenter justifies his stand by saying that the shelves are made of walnut, and he has four children and his wife to care for, but Shui Ta does not agree to pay such a huge amount. He insists the carpenter should take the racks away, and the carpenter agrees to remove them and seeks help from the husband and the wife.

When the couple help remove the ledges, the carpenter rebukes them by saying that the boards are "spoiled", and they would only "fit this dump", referring to the shop because they could be of "no use anywhere else". Instantly, he realises that his claims are baseless, and accepts 20 silver dollars from Shui Ta then leaves the shop saying that the money would at least help him fetch drinks if not provide for his family. The husband and the wife are jubilant to have got rid of the "scamp".

After doing away with the carpenter, Shui Ta asks the family in the shop who he calls "thieves and parasites" to vacate the premises immediately. The husband and the wife are furious, and they refuse to move out. Shui Ta opens the door to receive the policeman waiting outside. Now, the husband and the wife are terrified of being caught and sentenced to prison if the boy returns with the stolen food tucked up under his shirt.

Shui Ta invites the policeman into the shop and considers this a courteous gesture because as the owner of the small shop, he has to be on good terms with the resident policemen. The husband and the wife realise that Shui Ta has set a trap for the young boy. As soon as the boy rushes into the shop with the stolen pastries, he is caught red-handed by the policeman who questions Shui Ta about the happenings in the shop. Shui Ta expresses regret that his store is involved in the petty theft. The policeman orders the boy, the husband and the wife to accompany him down to the police station.

Now that the shop is evacuated, Shui Ta manages to organise the shop. Mrs. Mi Tzu is alarmed at the sight of the policeman and the thieves being hauled away from her property. The landlady is disgusted with Shen Te and criticises her because of the dubious means by which she has come to occupy the shop on contract basis. Mrs. Mi Tzu demands an advance half-yearly payment of two hundred dollars, which is quite pricey. Shui Ta explains to her that his frequent customers are only the sack makers at the cement factory who smoke a lot when they get exhausted, but they do not earn much. Mrs. Mi Tzu is disinterested in the conversation and refuses to lower the rent.

The policeman interrupts the discussion and returns to the shop to officially felicitate Shui Ta's help to catch the thieves. Though the policeman expresses his gratitude to Shui Ta and considers him an honourable and upright person, Mrs. Mi Tzu does not come to terms with Shui Ta and leaves the shop sulkily. Shui Ta discloses to the policeman that Shen Te did not earn a "respectable" living until recently and she would not be able to afford the rent. The policeman declares that if Shen Te will not be able to arrange for a credit to pay the landlady, then the only way out would be to find her a husband.

An old woman enters the shop to buy cigarettes for her husband on their fortieth wedding anniversary. He enquires with the old woman if an advertisement in the paper inviting suitable alliances would suit Shen Te's needs. He does not wait for an answer and quickly drafts: "What…decent…man with small capital…widower…not excluded…wishes…marriage…into flourishing tobacco store?.... Am pretty…pleasant appearance…." Shui Ta is appalled and takes note of the fact that everybody needs luck to survive in desperate conditions and thanks the policeman for finding a way out of the difficult situation.

Scene 3

It is evening and a young man Yang Sun, dressed is tattered clothes watches a plane fly overhead in the park where he spends time. He moves towards a tall tree and takes out a rope, however he stops when he sees two women approaching him. One is an old woman and the other is the young niece from the family that had stayed in Shen Te's shop. As the young woman tries to lure Yang Sun, he realises that they are prostitutes. The old woman tells the niece that she shouldn't expect anything from him because he is unemployed and looks desperate.

The women do not bother him anymore and Yang Sun throws a noose over the branch of the willow tree, but the sudden arrival of the two women announcing that it would rain any time interrupts him. Just then, Shen Te enters the park and the old woman immediately recognises the "gorgon" who threw the niece's family out to the streets, but the niece corrects her saying that it was Shui Ta, Shen Te's cousin who was cruel to them.

Yang Sun gets disturbed when the women arrive and urges them to set off quickly. The two women curse him and leave him alone. Shen Te notices Yang Sun's attempt to commit suicide and dissuades him from taking his life. Yang Sun tells Shen Te to leave him alone, but he quickly calms down when it begins to rain and he asks Shen Te to take shelter with him beneath the tree. When Shen Te asks him the reason for attempting to take his life, he discloses that he is a jobless pilot—"a mail pilot with no mail". Since the government has enough "flyers" and his service is not required.

Shen Te sympathises with Yang Sun, and comforts him but Yang Sun is quite sure that she cannot understand his situation. Shen Te recalls an incident in her life as a little girl when she had a crane with a broken wing as her playmate that would not bother about its own condition, but she could see how restless the bird would turn during autumn and spring when it saw the other birds fly across the sky. Shen Te begins to cry and Yang Sun comforts her as he wipes her face with a handkerchief.

When Yang Sun asks him why she saved him, Shen Te tells him that the weather was the reason for the thought of death. Shen Te makes a relevant statement that "with all the misery" in the world, "a very little [more] is enough" to make men throw their lives away. There is no end to the miseries in the world but when the situation becomes unbearable, and the level of endurance has reached its limits, the individual gets frustrated and resorts to self-destruction.

Yang Sun enquires about Shen Te's life, and she replies that there is nothing interesting in her life except the shop she owns. Yang Sun asks if she walks the streets, and Shen Te discloses that she used to before beginning her tobacco business. Yang Sun realises that the change in her life is due the "gift of the Gods" which Shen Te does not deny, but Yang Sun finds it hard to believe her. Shen Te confesses that she has decided to break the vow of celibacy she had made when she opened the shop and get married. Yang Sun and Shen Te share some intimate moments before Yang Sun breaks away from her. They share certain facts about their lives. Yang Sun says that he has friends but they are tired of hearing his complaints about being out of work. Shen Te mentions about a cousin in town, who would never return.

When Yang Sun implores her to speak more about her life, she tells him the incident when she received a penny from a poor man when she was a little girl. She mentions that it is amazing that only those who have very little are more generous than the wealthy. A drop of rain falls down on her and Wang enters singing "The Song of the Water Seller in the Rain". He wails that nobody buys water from him because it rains and wishes for seven rainless years so that everybody would beg for water from him.

Shen Te runs to Wang to tell him about his pole at her shop and Wang thanks her for keeping it. She insists on buying water from Wang for Yang Sun because he has been working hard for long. Though Wang suggests that he could just pour water through Yang Sun's mouth, Shun Te refuses to listen because she wants to help him out of his difficult times and tells him about the "bold" flyer who is unemployed. By the time she fetches water for Yang Sun, he is fast asleep.

Scene 3a

The scene shifts to Wang's home, the sewer pipe. The Gods visit Wang in his dreams once again to enquire about Shen Te. Wang tells them that he saw her with Yang Sun, who she loves. Moreover, she has been helping others in every way she can being kind and considerate to those who cannot afford to buy tobacco. The family of eight are again housed in her place and she even purchased a cup of water from him when it was raining. She is now called "the Angel of the Slums".

Probably the only person who dislikes her is the carpenter who refuses to acknowledge that Shen Te has paid her dues to him. When Wang tells the Gods that Shen Te's cousin, Shui Ta paid the carpenter less than what he demanded for the job of fixing the shelves, the Gods get angry. The second God declares: "One pays what one owes!" and demands that Shui Ta must never "cross her threshold" again, since he exerts a negative influence. The first God, however admits that he doesn't know what is "customary" in the "unintelligible" realm of business.

The Gods seem to notice that of late, they have been sent away by the rich to the poor who don't have enough space in their homes to shelter more number of people. Nobody is heroic anymore claims the first God and they get ready to depart, when Wang calls out to the "illustrious one" and points out not to ask too much from people at one time.

Analyses

Brecht reveals the dark side of capitalism that has gripped the society and each person struggles in a different manner to survive. While the rich are insensitive and selfish, the poor turn out to destroy their character in order to survive. However, Shen Te appears confident and turns out to be the source of strength to her neighbours. She has managed to survive and pulled through goodness, desperation and adversity to take hold of her life. In scene 2, Shen Te dons the role of Shui Ta her cousin to execute what Shen Te could not do. Through her alter ego Shui Ta, she is able to take charge of the shop authoritatively, dictate the family, make demands and have her voice heard. She becomes practical while dealing with her business and gets things done according to her requirements.

As Shen Te, she maintains her goodness and as Shui Ta does everything to secure her wealth and run the shop with a profit motive. Shui Ta is so commanding that everybody obeys him without questioning him, quite unlike Shen Te who used to be ruled by others. While Shen Te is too good, impractical and sensitive, Shui Ta is sensible, practical and rational. Shui Ta is able to argue and force his opinions on others, but Shen Te is emotional and weak.

Shui Ta is so bold that he makes shrewd decisions and is cunning enough to unnerve and dislodge the family in the house.

He wins over the carpenter who had taken advantage of Shen Te's goodness. Through the guise of Shi Ta, she emerges victorious in making things come her way and deciding for herself without consulting or heeding anybody. The people around Shen Te become greedier and Shui Ta becomes more prudent. Though Shui Ta does not prefer marriage to be a solution to Shen Te's financial problems, because he believes that Shen Te should resolve her issues as a woman and not in the guise of a man. Shen Te realises that a lot of thinking goes in to maintain a balance between making wealth and saving oneself from drowning.

Scene 3 exposes the miserable lives of poor men and women who grope in darkness not knowing how to survive. Without distinctions of age and character, men and women are forced to take extreme steps from suicide to prostitution to end their sufferings. Shen Te sympathises with Yang Sun and they exchange several moments of their life in a bid to get to know each other better. Shen Te emerges the sole source of comfort to Wang as well as Yang Sun because she sees them as equal sufferers in the game of life. While Yang Sun struggles to cope with poverty and the inability to fly, and decides to end his life when all the doors of survival close before him, the other struggles to sell water, a basic necessity of life.

Shen Te loves Yang Sun and decides to marry him, and she purchases water from Wang so that he will not go home empty-handed. Brecht uses the technique of analogy when Shen Te describes to Yang Sun how she can understand what it feels not to be able to fly anymore. She tells him about a crane with a broken wing that used to be "very good-natured about our jokes," but becomes restless when it sees other cranes that fly across the sky during spring and autumn. After telling Yang Sun that he only wanted to kill himself because of rains, Shen Te sings to the audience, breaking the imaginary fourth wall that lies between characters in a play and the audience watching them.

In scene 3a, Shen Te's acts of kindness are accepted by Gods who visit Wang in his dreams to know about her good deeds. Though they infer that the carpenter is the only person who is dissatisfied with Shen Te, they do not agree with Shui

Ta's decision on the carpenter. The inherent paradox of life is brought out by Brecht when the rich, who can afford to help the poor are disinterested, and the impoverished ones who are full of sympathy wish they could help others but cannot.

Conclusion

Every deprived person in Setzuan is desperately fighting to take hold of life during these trying conditions. Shen Te, realising that her boat of survival could sink in the rising waters of greed and people who take undue advantage of her kindness appears as her alter ego Shui Ta, the cousin who lives far away. He distances each and every person who has caused distress to Shen Te and keeps her boat of life afloat.

The disguise works well to ward off the guests who take shelter in Shen Te's shop, the carpenter is paid what is rightly due to him and the young boy who is used to thieving is caught by the policeman and along with the man and his wife is taken to custody. The rich landlady who fails to see Shen Te's suffering insists on the getting the fixed amount of rent because of Shen Te's previously disreputable life. However, the prevalent conditions in Setzuan also force men and women to take drastic steps in life. While the young boy becomes a pilferer at a young age to feed the family, the old woman and the niece become prostitutes to feed themselves, and the jobless pilot Yang Sun attempts suicide.

Men and women, irrespective of age are either out of work or they turn into anti-social elements. Yang Sun is rescued by Shen Te and they decide to live together. Shen Te helps Wang by buying water from him realising the difficulty he is facing during rains. Wang is happy that Shen Te has not changed a bit even after securing good fortune and informs the Gods how she has been doing acts of kindness for the people around her.

Glossary

pricey	:	high or expensive
pilferer	:	thief
haul	:	drag
alter ego	:	double

Glossary from the Text

Scene 2

A blanket ten thousand feet long/ Which would simply cover all the suburbs: Refers to the inability of one person alone to meet diverse needs of many people.

The shelves are walnut: The shelves are made of the wood of the walnut tree.

She's ruined: Shui Ta mentions that because of Shen Te's good nature, people take advantage and she will be ruined.

scamp: rogue

gabbles: speak nonsense; blabber

I'm not a monster but I got to be careful: Mrs. Mi Tzu says that she does not intend to frighten anybody with her words, but she has to be careful to whom she would rent the tobacco shop.

usury: overcharging

She'll work her fingers to the bone to pay the rent on time: Shui Ta suggests that Shen Te would work hard to pay the rent on time. Mrs. Mi Tzu could consider reducing the amount to be paid as rent for such a sincere, humble and hard-working person as Shen Te.

I feel like a man who dealt with the rats, only to find himself with rivers to cross: Shui Ta tells the policeman that he could oust the people who stayed in the shop and the wily carpenter by being hard and cunning. However, now the lines are drawn against him and he has to swim across several rivers to emerge successful.

With horror I see how much luck one needs to keep above water: Shui Ta remarks in astonishment that in order to survive, one needs luck by the side. He is fortunate to have a friend like the policeman to suggest ideas to Shen Te's problem of paying a high rent to Mrs. Mi Tzu.

Scene 3

tearoom: tea shop or café

they don't tire of fishing for victims: Yang Sun calls the prostitutes "vultures" who do not get tired of trapping men.

flier: pilot

What are lawns and hedges thinking?/ What are fields and forests saying?/ "At the cloud's breast we are drinking!/ And we've no idea who's paying!": The song implies that nature receives anything in plenty unlike man who detests anything that is surplus.

Scene 3a

What does business have to do with an honest and dignified life?: The first God says that he does not know anything about business, and cites the examples of the Seven Good Kings and the Kung of Just.

References

Demetz, Peter. *Brecht: A Collection of Critical Essays*. Prentice-Hall Inc., 1962.

Gascoigne, Bamber. *Twentieth-Century Drama*. Hutchinson and Co., 1974.

Morley, Michael, editor. *The Continuum Companion to Twentieth Century Theater*. Colin Chambers, 2002.

Needdle, Jan, and Peter Thomson. *Brecht*. Basil Blackwell, 1981.

Styan, J.L. *Modern Drama in Theory and Practice: Volume 2, Symbolism, Surrealism, and the Absurd*. Cambridge UP, 1981.

https://www.britannica.com/art/dramatic-literature

The Good Woman of Szechwan https://pdfs.semanticscholar.org/82d6/8ed23db277c702a1f467266d5a1f21b65cd3.pdf

Chapter 13

The Good Woman of Setzuan

Scenes Four and Five

Scene 4

The scene opens in the morning on a square, which has two other shops near Shen Te's—a carpet shop and a barber's. The grandfather, the sister-in-law, the unemployed man and Mrs. Shin wait outside Shen Te's shop eagerly for her return. The sister-in-law says that Shen Te has been out all night and Mrs. Shin laments that Shen Te has been moving around with a man. Just then, Wang is thrown out of his shop by Shu Fu the barber for pestering his customers into buying his "smelly" water and in a rage, he burns Wang's hand with a hot curling iron. Wang wails in acute pain and the unemployed man tries to rescue the poor water-seller. Mrs. Shin and the sister-in-law are aghast and mention that had Shen Te witnessed the brawl, she would have attended to Wang with a bandage.

Shen Te, arrives looking ecstatic, and addresses the audience. She says that her life will change for the better because she is in love. She approaches the shop and distributes rice to everybody gathered outside her shop and darts to the carpet shop. Shu Fu admires her beauty and declares that he is in love with her to the people who have gathered. The old man and the old woman, the owners of the carpet shop offer Shen Te a discount on a shawl she selects because they know that her good deeds "eat [her earnings] all up." They enquire whether her new lover would help her pay the rent, and Shen Te replies that Yang Sun is penniless. The old woman offers her 200 silver dollars required to pay the rent for six months and in exchange asks Shen Te to pledge the stock of tobacco. Shen Te considers the offer and wishes the Gods listen to their offer.

Shen Te shows the money offered by the old woman to the people gathered outside the shop. Mrs. Shen points out Wang's injury and Shen Te regrets not having attended on him earlier. She suggests taking Wang to the doctor, but the unemployed man insists on visiting the lawyer instead so that the "filthy rich" barber could be sued, but since nobody claims witness to the incident, nothing can be done. Shen Te accuses everybody present for being selfish and ignoring Wang's suffering. When Shen Te offers to endorse the crime, Mrs. Shin warns her against bearing false witness. The sister-in-law says that Shen Te cannot change the world. Shen Te is disgusted and orders everybody to leave her alone. She expresses her grief to the audience that nothing moves her countrymen to do a good deed.

Mrs. Yang, a frail, old woman who is Yang Sun's mother comes to the square in a hurry with the information that Yang Sun has just received an offer to work as a pilot, but the director of the airfield demands 500 silver dollars. She says that Yang Sun has been nicknamed "Dead Flier of Setzuan" and she hopes this opportunity would help him recover the job and get rid of the label. Shen Te gives Mrs. Yang the 200 silver dollars given to her by the old couple stating that she can repay them with the tobacco stock. She also discloses that she knows "someone who can help" them with the remaining 300 silver dollars. They see a plane flying overhead and Shen Te, in elation mentions that soon Yang Sun will be able to carry "friends in faraway lands/ The friendly mail!".

Scene 4a

Shen Te comes on to the stage singing "The Song of the Defenselessness of the Gods and Good Men" with Shui Ta's mask in her hands. The song states that one's usefulness can be proved only with the help of "strong helpers", which means that Shui Ta's strong support would be beneficial for her. Both the good people and the Gods are "powerless" during these difficult times. She desires that the Gods initiate an expedition with "battleships, bombers and tanks" to destroy all the bad in the world and shower peace and prosperity on all.

She puts on Shui Ta's mask and finishes the song in his voice. The impressive Shui Ta declares that to help "one poor man" "twelve others" should be trampled up on and "Luckless brothers/ By trampling down a dozen others." Shui Ta considers it rather unfortunate that to help a few underprivileged people, some others have to suffer. He enquires why Gods don't "stand by the good men with their bombers" or work to set matters right.

Scene 5

The scene is set in Shen Te's tobacco shop. Shui Ta is at the counter of the shop and Mrs. Shin is seen tidying it up. She advises Shui Ta to watch over Shen Te because she has been moving out with a man of late; moreover, the wealthy barber has an eye on Shen Te and wants to marry her. When Shui Ta does not respond, Mrs. Shin leaves. Yang Sun's voice is heard down the street and Shui Ta immediately runs into the shop to groom himself and set the disguise and laughs emphatically at his appearance.

Yang Sun enquires about Shen Te whose absence is evident. Yang Sun inspects the stock of tobacco and asks if he can "squeeze" 300 silver dollars out of it. Shui Ta asks Yang Sun not to get restive and wait until Shen Te makes arrangements. Yang Sun is insensitive when he believes Shen Te to be the kind of woman who would "keep a man waiting". When Shui Ta enquires to Yang Sun about requirements to get reinstated into the job of the pilot, Yang Sun discloses that he intends to bribe the airfield commander into firing a pilot whose family depends on his sole income and securing the job for himself.

Shui Ta asks Yang Sun if he has plans to marry Shen Te after she gives up her possessions and neighbourhood and moves to Peking where he would work. Shui Ta calculates that Shen Te might be better off in Setzuan after paying 200 silver dollars and running her tobacco business with Yang Sun beside her. When Yang Sun scoffs at the idea of handling a tobacco business, Shui

Ta mentions that he is willing to sell out the stock as cash since Shen Te would more interested to listen to her heart and have the "right to love" than think about safeguarding her life alone.

Mrs. Mi Tzu arrives asking after the rent and Shui Ta tells her about the change in Shen Te's plans. Shen Te is moving to Peking with her lover and she will be putting up the entire stock for sale. Shui Ta asks for 500 silver dollars in exchange for the stock. Mrs. Mi Tzu agrees for 300 silver dollars, but Shui Ta affirms that the amount is insufficient. When Yang Sun agrees to Mrs. Mi Tzu's offer, Shui Ta pulls him aside and discloses that the tobacco stock is pledged to the old couple who had lent Shen Te the initial 200 silver dollars. Yang Sun enquires if there is any written document as proof, and when Shui Ta mentions that there isn't any, Yang Sun informs Mrs. Mi Tzu that 300 silver dollars would suffice. Mrs. Mi Tzu promises to return a day after with the amount.

Yang Sun tries to find out where they could raise 300 silver dollars in the meantime, but Shui Ta says that there isn't anybody who can help them. He asks Yang Sun if he has enough money to provide for Shen Te for the first few weeks in Peking. Yang Sun says that he would either "dig it up" or "steal it". Shui Ta mentions that Yang Sun will have to meet expenses related to their travel. Yang Sun discloses to Shui Ta that he would be leaving Shen Te behind, for he has no intentions of carrying a "millstone" around his neck. When Shui Ta asks him how Shen Te will live, Yang Sun entrusts Shui Ta to find a way to support her.

Shui Ta asks Yang Sun if he would leave 200 silver dollars at the shop until Yang Sun produces proof of two tickets to Peking because his cousin could change her mind and she may not be interested in selling the shop. Yang Sun insists that Shen Te will do anything for him. Shui Ta suddenly declares that his cousin has common sense, but Yang Sun argues that being a woman, Shen Te lacks common sense because she is easily fooled by the promise of love and sexual pleasure. Yang Sun takes a cigar from the shelf and asks Shui Ta to inform Shen Te that he would like to marry her. He asks Shui Ta to arrange for 300 silver dollars and leaves the shop.

Mrs. Shin, having overheard the entire conversation from the room at the back of the shop mentions that she cannot believe that Yang Sun could behave in such a nasty manner and retreats. Shui Ta, enraged at Yang Sun's claims runs around the shop declaring, "I've lost my shop! And he doesn't love me!" repeatedly and suddenly stops and calls out to Mrs. Shin.

Shui Ta recalls that he grew up penniless and now he is strong enough to endure any pain. Shui Ta says that Shen Te possesses the mental strength to turn her face away from the cunning Yang Sun who she loves to preserve her dignity and marry the barber who loves her sincerely; albeit love is the most vicious threat that could weaken this strength. Mrs. Shin asks Shui Ta to discuss marriage plans with Shu Fu and make arrangements for the wedding between Shen Te and the barber, and scurries off to fetch him.

When Mrs. Shin returns with Shu Fu, Shui Ta tells him that Shen Te is in danger because she has lost her shop by being excessively good and she is in dire need of money to get the shop back. Shu Fu insists that he is more attracted to her good nature than anything else. Her charitable and selfless nature is so alluring that he is ready to help her open a shelter for the homeless at the cabins he has nearby. Shui Ta is impressed and mentions that it would be an honour for Shen Te to accept the offer made.

Wong and the policeman enter looking for Shen Te and Shu Fu pretends to be busy in the shop. Shui Ta informs them that Shen Te is not at the shop and instantly runs to the back of the shop to fetch Shen Te's shawl for Wang. When the policeman asks Shui Ta if Shen Te had witnessed the skirmish between Wang and the barber, Shui Ta declines, but Wang refuses to change his stand. Shui Ta responds that Shen Te had enough problems and it would be unfair to force her to lie. Wang throws the sling in disgust and the policeman warns him not to tarnish the character of his neighbours.

Shui Ta apologises to Shu Fu for the furore. Shu Fu points to the shawl Shen Te purchased for her lover and asks Shui Ta if Shen Te would be ready to move out with him. Shui Ta mentions that Shen Te may need time to resolve the confusion regarding her choice of a life partner. Shui Ta suggests that he takes Shen Te for a warm supper to propose to her and discuss their future plans. Shu Fu agrees to Shui Ta's proposal and suggests that she deserves to be taken to a "high class" restaurant. Shui Ta then leaves him in search of Shen Te. Meanwhile, Shu Fu rehearses his proposed dinner plans with Shen Te. He would behave decently with her, not feel her, but engage in discussion about their future over adorable chrysanthemums that would beautify their supper table. He hopes to win her love by giving importance to her wishes and caring for her.

Mrs. Shin appears on stage from the back of the shop and the two engage in a short conversation. When Shu Fu enquires about Yang Sun's character, Mrs. Shin asserts that he is a "worthless rascal", and just then Yang Sun enters. While Mrs. Shin threatens him by saying that she would call Shui Ta, Shu Fu tells him that the siblings are in an important discussion and they should be left alone. When Yang Sun tries to barge his way to the back, Shu Fu obstructs him. Shu Fu declares that he and Shen Te are to be engaged, which Yang Sun finds hard to believe, and as they scuffle Shen Te emerges from the room at the back of the shop.

Yang Sun asks Shen Te to reveal the truth about the present situation. Shen Te says that she agrees to go by her cousin's plans of helping the poor with Shu Fu's help. Yang Sun is aghast and pleads with her to recall hours they had spent together and cherish their intimate moments. Shen Te gets so involved in memories that she announces to accompany Yang Sun to Peking. Yang Sun is relieved and takes possession of the keys of the shop. He dictates Mrs. Shin to clean the shop and leave the keys under the mat after the day's work.

Yang Sun accompanies Shen Te out of the shop. Though Shu Fu tries to influence Shen Te by suggesting that her cousin disagrees with her, she says that her cousin is mistaken. To the audience Shen Te says that it would be better for her to love without "count[ing] the cost," without taking into account how wise her move could be and whether he really loves her. Yang Sun replies, "That's the spirit".

Scene 5a

Shen Te, dressed in her wedding gown stands in front of the curtain on the stage. She informs the audience that an unfortunate incident has happened. She happened to meet the old carpet dealer's wife who expressed concern over her husband's health because of "worry and excitement" over the money they had lent her. The old woman requests her to repay the money and Shen Te promises to return the amount after her wedding. Shen Te is dissatisfied that she has allowed Yang Sun to whizz her away "like a small hurricane" and forgot her assurance to the old carpet dealers. Shen Te makes known that Yang Sun plans to work in a cement factory rather than "owe his flying to a crime". She is on her way to her wedding and cannot vacillate "between fear and joy" at this time.

Analyses

Shen Te's love affair becomes the talk of the neighbourhood, and her inability to help the needy always is considered her selfishness. While nobody wants to help the other, the entire responsibility is put on Shen Te. Shen Te is happy that she can devote her time and money to help the deserving, even though the others feel she sparingly does so. Probably for the first time, she gets financial help from the old couple that sells carpets and she sincerely hopes the Gods would recognise their goodness too. Shen Te continues to do good for others, but this makes her neighbours self-centred and expect more from her.

The song in the next scene is sung by Shen Te initially and then Shui Ta takes over. Shen Te realises that she needs Shui Ta's backing for her sustenance. Shui Ta's approach to life and business would help her in dealing with several issues that she would not have been able to face otherwise. Shui Ta is unhappy that in order to serve the deserving people, she is forced to put others into trouble.

While Shui Ta is practical and shrewd, Shen Te is emotional and these contradictory attributes are housed in Shen Te, who is ultimately swayed away by Yang Sun's words. Shui Ta exposes the cruelty of Yang Sun who is only interested in Shen Te's wealth to pursue his dreams. Yang Sun unwittingly discloses his real intentions to Shui Ta because he is supposed to be a man like him. The desire to fly becomes a symbol of dreams nurtured by capitalism at the expense of others. Yang Sun looks up on Shen Te as a means to reach his desired end even at the cost of love.

Shui Ta is caught between protecting Shen Te's finances from Yang Sun's deception and being loyal to Yang Sun. Shui Ta cannot withstand Shen Te's emotional outburst and gives in to emotion instead of practicality. Yang Sun has been using Shen Te to fulfil his requirements and he is quite hopeful that Shui Ta would support him. He gravely insults Shen Te and even Mrs. Shin disapproves of his meanness. Shen Te considers marrying the barber who she does not love more acceptable than giving in to the cunning Yang Sun to uphold her dignity, but she needs to become hard at heart to execute her plans. Marrying a person who does not take advantage of her goodness is better than one who does. At times, it is important to sacrifice love for the sake of survival.

Shui Ta hands over Shen Te's shawl to Wang to use it as a sling but does not want Shen Te to lie for Wang. Shui Ta is aware that it is impossible to remain good throughout. Shen Te has to play a careful game to maintain her finance and survive a loveless marriage. Shen Te gives in to Yang Sun despite the odds and declares that Shui Ta goes "wrong" while taking certain decisions for her. Shen Te listens to her heart and dismisses Shui Ta who thinks for her.

Shen Te has to help her disloyal lover, serve the greedy neighbours and carry on with her deception to safeguard her interests and well-being. Shen Te realises that it is impossible to be simultaneously good to oneself and the world. Her masquerade is the reason she is able to carry on, otherwise she would have turned an absolute failure without being able to look into the reality of situations and characters including her lover.

Conclusion

Shen Te is not only exposed to the dark side of Yang Sun but also the sincerity of the barber's love. She painfully realises the empty words of Yang Sun that are built on false love. In a bid to safeguard herself, she accepts financial help from the old carpet sellers. She cannot trust Yang Sun anymore because he depends on her money to get the job of the pilot. Yang Sun intends to bribe the commander to secure his job at the cost of another person's livelihood.

Yang Sun turns out utterly despicable and Shen Te has to think twice before deciding to move out with him. There are several unfortunate people in the world who survive on goodness showed by others, but there are some others who always suffer for the well-being of a few, and this could be the law of the world. While Shen Te gauges her chances of living life according to her dictates, she cannot listen to her rationale self.

She Te discloses that Yang Sun has agreed to work in the cement factory rather than chase his dreams of flying high by adopting fraudulent means. Though her conscience pricks her for not being loyal to Shui Ta and the old couple that lends her money, she is sure that she would find ways of bringing Yang Sun to the right path. Shen Te reveals that Yang Sun has agreed to work in the cement factory and has given up the job of a mail pilot because it would cause distress to others.

Glossary

aghast : shocked
brawl : fight
indignant : outraged
skirmish : conflict
scuffle : fight

Glossary from the Text

Scene 4

Unbelievable behaviour: Mrs. Shin cannot understand how Shen Te could ignore those who depend on her and settle down in life without thinking about them. She is considered selfish.

What a scandal: the sister-in-law mentions that Shen Te has not returned home at night and staying outdoors for long hours is not considered moral. Her affair with a man is scandalous and her attitude is incorrect. In fact, those waiting for She Te's return need the customary service from her; they do not love her but depend on her to satisfy their needs. Who is more selfish is the question that is raised by Brecht.

light-headed: Shen Te considers herself unsteady and frivolous after falling in love with Yang Sun.

And if there is no revolt, it were better that the/ City should perish in fire before night falls!: Shen Te is shocked that there is nobody to stand up for Wang and sue the barber. She believes in fighting tyranny and injustice. These lines echo Brecht's belief in Communism and the need to destroy fascist forces, which requires revolt against existing social, economic and political conditions.

perjury: false swearing

Nothing moves their hearts: Shen Te is disappointed because the poor do not defend themselves or unite against tyranny. Their heads turn up when they need food, otherwise their heads are perpetually held down.

Scene 4a

Why then don't the gods speak up in their heaven/ And say that they owe the good world to good men?: Shui Ta knows that the world has both the good and the bad people. He cannot understand why the Gods don't work to set the world on the right path by punishing the bad. He cannot understand why the Gods do not defend the good and speak for them in heaven.

Scene 5

A real live store: Yang Sun inspects the shop and he is impressed and plans to squeeze money out of the shop to meet requirements for his job.

At first she'll only be a millstone round my neck: Yang Sun wants Shen Te to give him money so that he can become a pilot, but she does not intend to take her with him immediately because he may not be able to cover up the initial expenses. He regards her a burden that cannot be carried along for the moment.

Scene 5a

Shall I be strong to bring the good in him: Shen Te hopes mend Yang Sun's ways and turn him into a good person.

References

Demetz, Peter. *Brecht: A Collection of Critical Essays*. Prentice-Hall Inc., 1962.

Gascoigne, Bamber. *Twentieth-Century Drama*. Hutchinson and Co., 1974.

Needdle, Jan, and Peter Thomson. *Brecht*. Basil Blackwell, 1981.

Styan, J.L. *Modern Drama in Theory and Practice: Volume 2: Symbolism, Surrealism, and the Absurd*. Cambridge UP, 1981.

https://www.britannica.com/art/dramatic-literature

The Good Woman of Szechwan https://pdfs.semanticscholar.org/82d6/8ed23db277c702a1f467266d5a1f21b65cd3.pdf

Chapter 14

The Good Woman of Setzuan

Scenes Six and Seven

Scene 6

Shen Te and Yang Sun celebrate their wedding in the side room of a cheap restaurant in town in the midst of a few guests. The priest stands alone in a corner. Yang Sun, in a dinner jacket tells his mother that Shen Te has disagreed to sell the shop because someone has requested to return the amount that is lent. Mrs. Yang is annoyed and asks her son to postpone the wedding, but Yang Sun reassures her that he has requested Shui Ta to settle the matter and arrange for the amount at the wedding ceremony and Mrs. Yang expectantly awaits Shui Ta's arrival.

Shen Te tells the audience that she believes she has made the right decision and Yang Sun has given up the desire to fly again for her sake. She asks Yang to drink a toast "to their future" with her. Mrs. Yang is upset that Shui Ta has not arrived with the promised amount. Shen Te is bewildered that Mrs. Yang expects Shui Ta at the wedding and at Yang Sun's suggestion, she is ready to wait for another 15 minutes for his arrival.

Mrs. Yang excitedly informs the guests that her son is a mechanic and a pilot and soon she along with the young couple would move to Peking. Yang Sun is stunned that Yang Sun hasn't disclosed to his mother that he intends to give up the job of a pilot. Yang Sun needs the money anyway to secure the job. Shen Te is upset, but Yang Sun insists that he needs to move out of

Setzuan. Shen Te reminds him that she has promised the old woman that she would return the money. Yang Sun is critical of Shen Te's attitude and says that Shui Ta could be on his way with the money he had discussed with him.

Shen Te announces that her cousin cannot attend the wedding because he can't be where she is. She exposes Yang Sun's purchase of one ticket to Peking and his decision to leave her back. Yang Sun takes out two tickets from his pocket and says that he sold his mother's furniture to get the second one and he does not want to let his mother know that she would be left behind. When Shen Te questions about the old carpet sellers' condition, and whether the money is returned to them, Yang Sun expresses concern about his own.

When a waiter requests for the amount to be paid for the wedding party, Mrs. Yang assures him that the someone is on the way with the money. The priest leaves to officiate another wedding and make arrangements for a funeral the next morning. Mrs. Yang reassures the guests that the priest would return. Yang Sun requests the guests to leave because the priest has left the place and Shui Ta has not yet reached the restaurant. While the guests leave, Shen Te asks if she should leave too, but Yang Sun pulls her across the room and tears up her dress.

Yang Sun sings "The Song of St. Nevernever Day", in which the talks of things that would never materialise such as the day a poor woman's son would sit on a throne made of gold, goodness would be rewarded and badness would cost one's head, men would turn so good that they would live without batting an eye and make the earth a better place to live, and on this day the idle man would find work and become a pilot so that the woman can rest. All these would happen only on Nevernever Day at the "first cock crow". Towards the closing stages of the song, Mrs. Yang understands that Shui Ta will not turn up with the money.

Scene 6a

The scene shifts to Wang's home, the sewer pipe, and the Gods visit Wang in his dreams. Wang tells the Gods that Shen Te has invited trouble for herself because she has followed the commandment "love thy neighbour" too sincerely. Wang tells the Gods that Shen Te is too good and Gods have to interfere and help her out. The first God states that they are no longer going to intervene in the affairs of human beings because the third God's eye that is black now is the result of involving in a fight earlier.

Wang is perturbed and he says that Shen Te may lose her shop if the Gods do not come to her rescue. The first God asserts that Gods help those who help themselves and the second God proposes they help her. The third God concedes that they have been unsuccessful in finding any other good person on earth. The first God suggests that "the heavier the burden the greater will be her strength!" This means that the more intense her problems would become the better she would come out. The first God assures that issues would be resolved and they fade away.

Scene 7

There is a cart with some equipment and the backyard and Shen Te and Mrs. Shin are seen taking down clothes from the line. Mrs. Shin asks Shen Te to "fight tooth and nail" to retain her shop. Shen Te is determined to sell the stock of tobacco to Mrs. Mi Tzu and repay the old couple. Mrs. Shin is worried that without a husband, a job and a shelter Shen Te would become a destitute. Mrs. Shin pulls out Shui Ta's pants off the line and says that he has many sets of pants and he must have left these after his previous visit. Shen Te collects them in a hurry from Mrs. Shin and retreats.

Shu Fu arrives and tells Shen Te that he is aware of her sacrifice for the old couple and she is truly "the Angel of the Slums". He appreciates her efforts in helping the poor in every possible way and providing for them every morning without fail. He says that he cannot allow Shen Te lose her shop and cause the disappearance of "the good woman of Setzuan." He takes his cheque book and gives Shen Te a blank cheque so that she could fill out "for any sum" and "full of veneration" leaves them.

Mrs. Shin asks Shen Te to fill in thousand silver dollars in the cheque and draw the amount quickly. Shen Te is unable to make up her mind because she cannot forget Yang Sun. Shen Te feels dizzy and stumbles under the weight of the clothes. Mrs.

Shin expresses doubts of pregnancy, and if so Shu Fu will not permit her to have the money. Shen Te caresses her stomach in the excitement of bringing a blessed boy into the world who, she envisions would surmount mountains and become a flyer one day. She imagines holding the hands of a small boy, showing him around the town and acquainting him with his neighbours.

Wang enters holding a boy, and introduces him as the youngest son to Shen Te tells her that the carpenter having lost his business and home has his other three children begging on the streets. Shen Te takes pity on the boy and says that he can stay in Shu Fu's cabins. She too may have to reside there because she is in the family way. Shen Te enquires about Wang's hand, which is battered but just fine and asks him to fetch Mr. Lin To the carpenter. Shen Te asks Wang to sell a cartful of tobacco and use the money to treat himself. Wang is happy that Shen Te is still good and hurries off to do as Shen Te has suggested.

The husband, wife and nephew enter, each dragging a huge sack and they request Shen Te if they could store them in her new home because she is giving away the tobacco shop. Shen Te agrees and promises to claim that they are hers. The husband tells Shen Te that sacks are loaded with tobacco and she could start a tobacco factory. Shen Te stocks the sacks in the backroom and agrees to think about the suggestions at Shu Fu's cabin.

The carpenter's son in the meantime eats scraps of food from a nearby pile of dump. Shen Te is so shocked at the sight of the child eating the waste that she runs to pull him away. She gives an extended speech and declares that she would turn a tigress if she ever has to defend her son from such a disgrace. She picks up Shui Ta's pants and says that her cousin must come back for the last time to straighten matters.

Mrs. Shin, the sister-in-law and the grandmother enter the stage. They lament that the tobacco shop is to close down and they have to languish in Shu Fu's cabins. The sister-in-law says that the cabins are "damp rat holes with rotten floors!" The barber has offered the cabins because his supplies of soap got mouldy in the rooms. The unemployed man requests Shen Te to call on Shui Ta to prevent the closing down of the shop and save them from penury.

When Wang enters with the carpenter's three children, Shui Ta arrives and enquires about the crowd gathered. Wang informs him about the situation and their shift to Shu Fu's cabins. Shui Ta tells him that the cabins have another purpose and nobody would be allowed to stay there unless they are ready to work for Shen Te in making tobacco. The carpenter and the unemployed man express their willingness to work and go in to fetch the three bales of tobacco.

Mrs. Mi Tzu comes with 300 silver dollars for Shui Ta, who changes his mind into sign the lease rather than sell the shop. When Mrs. Mi Tzu asks for an advance payment of the rent, Shui Ta pulls out Shu Fu's cheque and writes down 10,000 silver dollars. He promises Mrs. Mi Tzu that she will have six months' rent credited by night. Mrs. Mi Tzu is amazed that Shen Te has discarded Yang Sun for Shu Fu and generalises that young girls are "fickle and superficial" and leaves.

The carpenter and the unemployed man drag the three sacks of tobacco on the stage and begin to work. Though the carpenter is unhappy, Shen Te reminds him that he has a family to feed. The sister-in-law recognises her family's sacks, but Shui Ta's clever move to call the police to confiscate the illegal goods makes her silent.

Shui Ta shows the carpenter and his children, the sister-in-law, the grandfather and the unemployed man Shu Fu's cabin, but asks Wang and Mrs. Shin to stay behind. The old man and the old woman enter and notice that Shui Ta has arrived. They mention that Shen Te was supposed to hand over something to them. Wang's assurance that Shui Ta would leave quickly and things would get better soon is supported by Mrs. Shin and the old couple is satisfied.

Scene 7a

The Gods appear worn-out from extensive travel to Wang in his dreams. Wang tells the gods that he has been seeing a bad dream about Shen Te, where she is by the riverside at a place where "those who commit suicide are found". She wobbles hopelessly as she carries something along the muddy bank. When Wang calls out to her, she explains that she must get the Gods' "package of rules" to the other side of the river without getting wet otherwise the writing would be wiped off. Wang pleads with the Gods to relax rules a little because the times are unfavourable. The Gods reply that their interference would intensify problems and rules must stay.

Analyses

Yang Sun insults Shen Te for being good by being in debt rather than helping him out and allowing him control of her financial commitments. He does not realise that Shen Te and Shui Ta is the same person. Though Shen Te looks elated about getting married, she is quite nervous about the decisions she takes as Shui Ta and her obligations as Shen Te. Yang Sun's deceit is revealed when he tries to convince her that she is neither an efficient businesswoman nor a good decision-maker. His intention is to manipulate things and maintain contact with Shui Ta who is shrewder and smarter than Shen Te with little idea of the truth of Shui Ta's identity.

Yang Sun is self-centred and does not think of anybody except himself. He does not realise that he owes his life to Shen Te and exploits her good nature. He insults Shen Te to the extent that he earns the wrath of Yellow Street and the entire neighbourhood that considers her the "Angel of the Slums". While Shen Te is careful about maintaining her business and caring for the deserving, Yang Sun's aim is flying high at the expense of others without considering the plight of the helpless including his mother.

As expected by Shen Te, the wedding does not materialise and Yang Sun blames Shen Te for his downfall and thwarting his right over her money. Yang Sun turns berserk and violent and his song of self-pity is not only mean but also directed to his weak emotional state. He sings that the poor would never rise to become rich, the good would never be rewarded, the corrupt would never change and his dreams of becoming a pilot would never be realised.

Wong knows that Shen Te is entrapped among her love for Yang and his treachery, the money she owes the old couple, the pitiable condition of Shu Fu and the practical decisions of Shui Ta. He tells the Gods to lend her a helping hand, but they believe that her adversity would make her stronger and better. The fact is that the Gods are thoroughly famished with the world and they hope they need not interfere with the problems of men.

There are hints that her dual identity could be exposed when Mrs. Shin finds Shui Ta's clothes at the backyard. Shu Fu emerges truly concerned about Shen Te who he respects and admires for her selfless service. When he understands that her shop would be sold, he hands her a blank cheque to help her with as much money as she wants. Brecht symbolically uses flying to denote that the child's dreams may not be fulfilled if Shen Te is not steadfast and resolute at this moment.

The carpenter who tries to swindle Shen Te is on the streets. Had Shui Ta given him the amount the carpenter had asked for, he probably would not have landed on the streets. Brecht draws on the fact that it's only by feeding on others that the world survives and it is hard to find honest workers. Wang realises that the only person who has been sincere and concerned about others welfare in times of misfortune and hardship is Shen Te. Though Shen Te does not want Shui Ta's help, she understands that at this point in life, only his presence would save her from disaster.

Shui Ta's ruthlessness and her own necessity to safeguard the future of her unborn child makes her plan to rent the shop than sell it and make her dependents work for her. She makes use of the illegal stock of tobacco to restart the business with Shu Fu's money. It appears as if he intends to kill his sister's love for business. Shui Ta does not mince words or allow anybody to sit idle. He extracts work from all those who lived on Shen Te for free. However, only Mrs. Shin sees Shen Te through Shui Ta, but she keeps the secret to herself.

Wang expects the Gods to protect Shen Te who seems to be reeling under the mantle of goodness thrust on her by the Gods. He requests the Gods to amend the rules in her favour, but they do not relent because they realise that they can do little to change or better human beings. The Gods prefer to remain as aloof as possible from humans and figure out how mankind would find solutions to problems

Conclusion

Yang Sun is anxious about his future as a pilot and demands money from Shen Te. His intention is to use her money for his benefit and keep her away from him for a while and entrust her with Shui Ta. However, his demand of 500 silver dollars is beyond Shen Te's capacity and their wedding is stalled because Shui Ta does not bring the balance of 300 silver dollars as promised at the wedding. Yang's unscrupulousness is exposed and he stands out as the most ignoble person in the entire neighbourhood.

Shen Te becomes pregnant with Yang Sun and the news is kept discreet. Shen Te sees distress everywhere including her own life. She decides to bring Shui Ta back and reclaim the lost business with his shrewd moves. Shui Ta spares no time in collecting all the resources and putting them all to suit his purposes. Though Wang pleads with the Gods to show mercy on Shen Te who is suffering for being good, the Gods decide to leave Shen Te to emerge stronger and better. They find that the world has fewer good people and their interference would not resolve matters. They decide to stand apart and watch the happenings objectively without bending or changing any rules of life in anybody's favour.

Glossary

envisions	:	visualise
surmount	:	overcome
fickle	:	indecisive
wobble	:	tremble
resolute	:	determined
steadfast	:	firm

Glossary from the Text

Scene 6

She's got a thick head: inflexible or stubborn; overly willful or obstinate.

Shoptalk: conversation about occupation or business at social occasions.

Here's a plane darling, but it's only got one wing: Yang Sun is upset that he has to return 200 dollars to Shen Te and doubts whether Shui Ta would arrive with 300 dollars to enable him to become a pilot and fly with Shen Te to Peking.

It's going to be a scandal: Mrs. Shin suspects something wrong about the marriage because Shen Te is waiting to get married but Yang Sun is waiting for Shui Ta, which suggests that he does not love her but requires money from her family. For Yang Sun, money is love.

She wants to see her falcon in the clouds: Yang Sun realises that Shui Ta will not bring him 300 dollars, and his bride cannot do anything about it because she cares more for the poor people of Setzuan than him. Without the money, her ambition to see him fly cannot happen. Falcon refers to Yang Sun.

Scene 6a

Nonsense, weak and wretched man! Lice and doubts, it seems have almost eaten you up: The Gods say that Wang talks nonsense because he has become weak and his doubts about the welfare of Shen Te have a great bearing on his thoughts.

Suffering ennobles!: The second God mentions that human beings become nobler only when they learn to suffer and overcome difficulties.

Scene 7

It all comes from poverty: Shen Te supports Yang Sun and does not hate him though he is a depraved person because she realises that poverty has made him a scoundrel. She has several reasons to hate him but when she sees the real reason behind his behaviour she can only pardon him and love him.

Extended naturally, a hand gives and receives with equal ease: A hand gives and receives when the help is natural; however, the same hand has to strain a lot to grab greedily. It's tempting to give and pleasant to be kind. A good word pronounced is similar to a sigh of gratification.

Mr. Shu Fu steps into the flier's shoes: Mrs. Mi Tzu cannot believe that Shen Te has changed her mind about Yang Sun so quickly. To accept the offer from Shu Fu to stay in his cabins and carry on with her business is to prefer Shu Fu. Young girls are too quick to change lovers and they are inconsistent and playful.

Scene 7a

O, shame! I'm sure you'll understand my worries: In his dreams, Wang is worried that the Gods who had given her money in return for her kindness in allowing them to stay at night are now torturing her with work that is too burdensome. She is given the task of carrying the "package of rules" to the other side of the river without getting the book wet lest the water may wipe away the text.

References

Demetz, Peter. *Brecht: A Collection of Critical Essays*. Prentice-Hall Inc., 1962.

Gascoigne, Bamber. *Twentieth-Century Drama*. Hutchinson and Co., 1974.

Needdle, Jan, and Peter Thomson. *Brecht*. Basil Blackwell, 1981.

Styan, J.L. *Modern Drama in Theory and Practice: Volume 2: Symbolism, Surrealism, and the Absurd*. Cambridge UP, 1981.

https://www.britannica.com/art/dramatic-literature

The Good Woman of Szechwan https://pdfs.semanticscholar.org/82d6/8ed23db277c702a1f467266d5a1f21b65cd3.pdf

Chapter 15

The Good Woman of Setzuan

Scenes Eight and Nine

Scene 8

Shui Ta has emerged as a flourishing young businessman with a tobacco factory established in Shu Fu's cabins and many women and children work together. The carpenter, his three children, the sister-in-law, and the grandfather are among the workers. Mrs. Yang and Yang Sun appear on stage. Mrs. Yang informs the audience that ever since Yang has started work in the tobacco factory, he has transformed into a "model citizen". Shui Ta has allowed Yang Sun to repay the 200 silver dollars he owes to Shen Te by employing him in the factory, a move directed against the charge of "breach of promise of marriage". The hard work has paid off and Yang Sun is now an honest foreman in the factory. Yang Sun leads a group of workers and they sing "The Song of the Eighth Elephant."

The song is a parable about a man named Mr. Dsching, who had seven wild elephants and one tame number Eight, who was in charge of guarding and inspecting the work of the other elephants. Number Eight worked hard even though the other elephants grew tired. The chorus sings, "Seven are no match for one, if one has the gun". As the workers sing together, Shui Ta ambles among them smoking a cigar. Mrs. Yang tells the audience that Shui Ta is a man of great wisdom and strength because he did not make "fantastic promises" like his cousin but "forced him into honest work".

Scene 9

It is raining outside and Shen Te's shop looks elegant with club chairs and fine carpets. Shui Ta has grown fat and he is seen sitting on a chair talking to the old man and the old woman, while Mrs. Shin is looking on. Shui Ta mutters angrily to the old couple that he cannot disclose where Shen Te is. The old woman tells Shui Ta that she wants to thank Shen Te in writing that 200 silver dollars she owes them has been received. Shui Ta tells them that he does not have her address and sends them away. Mrs. Shin informs Shui Ta that the couple lost their shop while waiting for the money because they could not pay their taxes. When Shui Ta replies that they should have come up to him for help, Mrs. Shin informs him that people detest approaching him.

When Shui Ta says that he feels dizzy, Mrs. Shin replies that he could be in the seventh month of pregnancy. Shui Ta is afraid that people would notice the bulge, but Mrs. Shin assures him that everyone would mistake the swelling to be the outcome of being rich. Shui Ta says that he does not intend to meet the child and asks Mrs. Shin for any rumours being spread about him. Mrs. Shin says that so long as Shu Fu doesn't learn the truth, they have nothing to worry about and offers Shui Ta a cup of tea.

Just then, Yang Sun enters dressed in a suit and Mrs. Shin puts on a pair of gloves and leaves the place. Yang Sun mentions that Mrs. Shin is cheating on him. He takes a paper from his briefcase and tells Shui Ta that his absence is making things difficult in the factory. The police are bent on shutting down the factory because it has twice the number of permitted workers. Yang Sun offers to bribe Mrs. Mi Tzu into letting their company use her buildings to house the large number of workers in exchange for his sexual favours. Shui Ta firmly denounces this idea.

Wang knocks at the door and enters stating that he has been searching for Shen Te who was last seen six months back and there are rumours that something has happened to her. He says that he sees rice at the doorstep of the shop just as it used to be when Shen Te provided for the needy. Wang says that people believe she is in Setzuan, probably hiding a pregnancy. Yang Sun is shocked. When Shui Ta calls Wang a liar, he says that "a good woman isn't so easily forgotten" and leaves the place hastily.

Yang Sun, left alone wonders where Shui Ta would have sent the pregnant Shen Te away so that he wouldn't get to know about a son being born to him. He suddenly hears a sob from the back room, which surprises him because he knows that Shui Ta never weeps. Yang Sun admits to have seen bowls of rice at the doorstep. As Shui Ta steps out from the back and opens the front door, listening for something, Yang Sun enquires what is going on.

Shui Ta probes whether Yang Sun has forgotten his dreams of flying and he replies that he has neither lost interest in flying nor in Shen Te. Yang Sun expresses doubts whether Shen Te is kept locked up somewhere by Shui Ta, and if so it would create mayhem. Shui Ta offers to promote Yang Sun in exchange for dropping the enquiry, but Yang Sun admits that he would like to see Shen Te and moves out.

As Shui Ta wraps up Shen Te's clothes in her old shawl, he hears voices. Mrs. Mi Tzu and Shu Fu enter enquiring why they have been sent for. Shui Ta says that the factory is in trouble and it needs more space to accommodate the large number of workers otherwise it could be shut down by the police. Shu Fu disagrees the way Shui Ta has been managing the resources provided to Shen Te because Shui Ta seems to be consuming all the favours Shu Fu has showered on Shen Te.

Shui Ta disagrees with his cousin having dinner with him citing financial difficulties as the reason. He has made use of the cabins given to Shen Te and turned them into a factory, and has lent 10,000 silver dollars to Mrs. Mi Tzu by filling the blank cheque he had given Shen Te. However, Shen Te is not to be seen around. Shui Ta assures him that Shen Te's arrival is just round the corner.

When Mrs. Mi Tzu arrives and demands for Yang Sun, Shui Ta, in the effort to save the establishment, promises Mrs. Mi Tzu that Yang Sun will call on her the next day if she agrees to tell the police that Shui Ta is taking over her buildings. Shu Fu supports the move because they could have Yang Sun posted elsewhere by the time Shen Te returns. When all matters are set to be resolved, a group of people announce the arrival of the police.

Yang Sun, Wang and the policeman enter the shop with Yang Sun's complaint that Shui Ta has kept Shen Te locked up in the room at the back of the shop because he has heard sobs come from the room. Word spreads and the entire neighbourhood gathers in front of Shen Te's shop. Though the policeman finds the room empty, Yang Sun comes out with Shen Te's bundle of clothes stashed away by Shui Ta. Wang and the crowd suspect foul play and declare that Shui Ta could have murdered Shen Te and hidden the corpse. When the policeman commands Shui Ta to disclose where he has hidden Shen Te, Shui Ta denies and he is taken away to the station. Shui Ta mentions that there are efficient judges who will fight the case for him.

Scene 9a

The Gods appear worn-out and exhausted to Wang in his dreams. He tells them about Shen Te's sudden disappearance and blames Shui Ta, who he says has been arrested in this connection. Wang tells the Gods that he dreamt of Shen Te telling him that she had been made a prisoner by Shui Ta. Wang implores the Gods to help in finding her. The Gods mention that Shen Te is the only good person that have encountered during their travels across the world so far and now that she has vanished, the first God says that "all is lost". The first God finds fault with the world that is filled with "misery, vulgarity and waste". The third God bemoans that it's always the one performing good deed that suffers in the end. The Gods feel miserable and the first God says that their hopes lie in finding Shen Te, the only good person they have been able to come across during their extensive travels. Their only hope in moving out from the earth is in finding out this one good person, Shen Te.

Analyses

Shui Ta is a prominent businessman who makes everybody work tirelessly for meagre wages. There is no charity and the factory is a soulless enterprise with Shui Ta's iron fist keeping the entire neighbourhood under his control. Though the 'Song of the Eighth Elephant" expresses solidarity, it also indicates how capitalism pitches workers, friends, and countrymen against one another.

The people seem to miss Shen Te's warmth and presence as much as they hate Shui Ta for his cold and indifferent attitude. Shen Te does not want the child to know about Shui Ta and his bad deeds. Mrs. Shin is the only person who knows about Shen Te's disguise and she seems to be taking advantage of this. Brecht implicitly states that both the good and the bad deeds are two sides of a coin that however exist alongside each other. Shen Te's goodness is evident because she is unable to refrain from feeding the poor even in the guise of Shui Ta.

Shui Ta is barely able to cope with financial, legal, and emotional upheavals and he seems to be giving in to his greedy and unscrupulous neighbours and workers. As Shui Ta is making desperate "dirty" moves to survive, the problems around him are mounting up from all sides and it seems his life is suddenly getting out of his control. To disclose Shen Te would be to put her reputation at stake. His intentions to maintain his identity are in conflict with demands of the people who perceive his hand either in hiding Shen Te or murdering her.

The Gods are despondent because the only good person on earth Shen Te is now missing and their aim is to find her at all cost. The Gods have given up the hope of finding other good persons and they have resolved to leave the earth and get themselves entangled with the degenerate ways of the world. The moment they get hold of Shen Te, they would depart to heaven.

Conclusion

There is widespread belief that Shui Ta is hard-hearted and a task-master. The neighbourhood misses the caring and affectionate Shen Te. Now, each person whether a child, an old person or a woman has to work to earn a livelihood. The times have changed and people realise nothing comes free. Yang Sun has changed a lot and he works to repay what he owes Shen Te. Shui Ta is more successful than ever, but he is torn between love and duty, service and disservice, and punishment and pardon.

He realises that he cannot carry on for long because of the weight of burden that he seems to be carrying as Shen Te is. The Gods understand that the problems of the world cannot resolved unless each individual decides to change for the better rather than remain selfish and uncaring. Shen Te's disappearance causes unrest among the Gods because they may have to rebuild the world.

Glossary

ambles	:	strolls
pitches	:	places
stashed	:	hidden
unscrupulous	:	opportunistic
at stake	:	at risk
perceive	:	sense

Glossary from the Text

Scene 8

A noble man is like a bell. If you ring it, it rings, and if you don't, it don't, as the saying goes: Mrs. Yang compares a noble person to a bell that rings only when someone hits at it; otherwise, it is quiet. Here, Shui Ta is the noble person who takes an immediate action only when somebody requires his help.

Scene 9

I should give you an adequate position, could I count on your giving up all future investigations concerning your one-time future wife?: Shui Ta tells Yang Sun that he would be promoted if he does not probe into what has happened to Shen Te.

And if, instead of me, the firm threw you out?: This means that Yang Sun aspires to be in Shui Ta's position if he has to keep quiet about Shen Te's whereabouts and if he is thrown out, then he will bring the police.

Scene 9a

The world can't be lived in, you've got to admit!: The third God fears that their commandments have become so deadly that their moral values have to be discarded. The people in the world are so busy trying to save themselves from wrong-doings. Good thoughts land people to the depths of worry and good deeds bring misery, so it's too difficult to survive in this world.

No, it's people who are worthless: When the third God say that the world is a cruel place for man to survive, the second God mentions that the people are worthless, which is the reason for the difficulty in survival. The third God says that the world is too frigid and the people are too weak.

References

Demetz, Peter. *Brecht: A Collection of Critical Essays*. Prentice-Hall Inc., 1962.

Gascoigne, Bamber. *Twentieth-Century Drama*. Hutchinson and Co., 1974.

Morley, Michael, editor. *The Continuum Companion to Twentieth Century Theater*. Colin Chambers, 2002.

Needdle, Jan, and Peter Thomson. *Brecht*. Basil Blackwell, 1981.

Styan, J.L. *Modern Drama in Theory and Practice: Volume 2: Symbolism, Surrealism, and the Absurd*. Cambridge UP, 1981.

https://www.britannica.com/art/dramatic-literature

The Good Woman of Szechwan https://pdfs.semanticscholar.org/82d6/8ed23db277c702a1f467266d5a1f21b65cd3.pdf

Chapter 16

The Good Woman of Setzuan

Scene 10

The scene shifts to the courtroom and everybody is anxious because Shui Ta has decided to expand his tobacco business by opening twelve new shops. His status and power at present, many believe are clear indications that he would not be punished and the rumour that he has bribed the judge persists. Mrs. Shin is reported to have carried a fat goose to the judge's kitchen as a bribe. The old woman says that Shen Te's absence is obvious and Wang, utterly desperate mentions that only the Gods can find out what would have happened to her.

The policeman announces the arrival of the panel of judges. Unknown to the people, the three Gods, dressed in judges' coats move to the seats and in undertones mention about their badly forged certificates and their shabby attire. Wong is relieved when he sees the Gods disguised as judges and they exchange smiles. The policeman brings in Shui Ta, now called "The Tobacco King" who nearly faints when he recognises the "judges".

The first God asks Shui Ta to defend that he is not guilty and to testify for him, the policeman vouchsafes that Shui Ta was a man of principles who would never harm his cousin. He was a "respectable and law-abiding citizen". Shu Fu too and Mrs. Mi Tzu bear witness to the fact that Shui Ta could never be guilty of such a crime because he is the Vice-President of the Chamber of Commerce, and an honest member of the community who regularly contributes for charity purposes.

For a fair hearing of the case, the Gods have to listen to both approvers and disapprovers of Shui Ta. When the first God asks if there is anyone with "*less favourable evidence*" against Shui Ta to come forward, Wang, Lin To, the old man and the old woman, the unemployed man, the sister-in-law and the niece oblige. The policeman discreetly tells the first God that whatever they would tell would be unsubstantial. The witnesses call Shui Ta a cheat, a thief, a liar and a murderer. The first God thanks them for their testimonies and the lets Shui Ta speak is defense of himself.

Shui Ta stands for himself by recalling several "dirty" jobs he has undertaken in order to help Shen Te and this could probably be the reason that they despise him. However, those who testify against him say that he has been deceitful and his support of the corrupt Yang Sun is further proof of Shui Ta's fraudulent ways. When Shui Ta tries object their claims, Yang Sun rises up to defend Shui Ta.

He recalls hearing Shen Te's sobs from the back room of her shop and he is sure that she is alive. Shu Fu affirms that Yang Sun would recognise Shen Te's voice because he has made her cry several times. Yang Sun answers that he has never stepped in her way because Shui Ta wanted her to be with Shu Fu and that's the reason why Shui Ta has sold her to Shu Fu.

Shui Ta claims that the money he procured in the exchange was used for the benefit of the poor and for Shen Te so that she could continue being good. Wang accuses Shui Ta of destroying "a little fountain of goodness" that the shop, the gift of the Gods symbolised. Shui Ta defends his stand by stating that he did his best save the fountain from running dry because doing only good deeds often ruin the good person, "good deeds mean ruin". Wang insists to know Shen Te's whereabouts and the crowd in unison demands the same. Shui Ta gets frustrated and in anger yells that had Shen Te stayed back, everybody would have shredded her to bits.

When the crowd becomes relentless, Shui Ta declares that he wants to confess only in the presence of the judges. The policeman orders everybody out and Shui Ta professes to the Gods, who are the judges that he is Shen Te in disguise. He removes his mask and clothes to reveal Shen Te behind the camouflage and the Gods are astonished. Shen Te discloses that the Gods' plea "to be good and yet to live" has torn her in two parts because she could not be good to herself and the others at the same time.

It is difficult to survive in this world because it is an arduous endeavour to live between misery and despair that the world is filled with. Shen Te asserts: "Whoever helps the lost is lost himself", which means that it is easy to lose oneself while trying. Add the semi-colon after asserts to help those who are struggling themselves and the journey often makes a person rude.

Shen Te is amazed to disclose that "it was when she was unjust that she ate good meat". She says, "Something must be wrong with the world" and enquires why "malice is rewarded" and good deeds are punished. She regrets that she has to behave rather ruthlessly but her intentions are good. She has to provide for her neighbours, keep her lover, and provide for her child and hence she is too weak, too "poor and small" to follow the Gods' instructions. The first God requests Shen Te not to sound miserable and make her life dreary, for the Gods are delighted to have located her.

Shen Te asks the Gods how they could be happy to have her back when she is the "bad man" who has committed grave injustice against her neighbours. In reply, the Gods point out that she is also the good woman who has sacrificed a lot for everybody around her. The first God announces that Shen Te is just confused and then proclaims that the world should not be changed. Suddenly, the stage lights up in a pink hue and music plays in the background. The first God says:

> This little world has much engaged us.
> Its joy and sorrow have refreshed and pained us.
> Up there, however, beyond the stars,
> We shall gladly think of you, Shen Te, the good woman
> Who bears witness to our spirits down below,

Who, in cold darkness, carries a little lamp!
Goodbye! Do it well!

When the first God makes a sign, the ceiling opens and a pink cloud comes down. The Gods ascend onto the cloud to reach heaven and they ask Shen Te not to lose courage. All the people gathered outside except Wang are awestruck with the happenings. Only Wang understands what happens. He beckons the people to respect the Gods, who have arrived to help them. Everybody including Wang is exuberant to see Shen Te safe in the courtroom with the Gods.

As the Gods ascend, Shen Te requests the Gods to instruct her the ways to help the old couple that lost the shop, the water-seller whose hand is mashed, the barber to whom she is betrothed but does not love and the cruel Yang Sun who she loves and the child she will bear soon. The Gods advise her to continue to be good. When Shen Te says that she will need the help of her bad cousin, the first God says that she can call him only once a month. Though Shen Te cries out and pleads with them to stay back, they leave her singing "The Trio of the Vanishing Gods on the Cloud" a brief song in which they assert:

Our anxious search is over now
Let us to heaven ascend
The good, good woman of Setzuan
Praising, praising to the end!

Epilogue

The Epilogue, addressed to the audience succinctly points out to the "bitter ending" of the play without any resolution. The actor who addresses the audience speaks on behalf of the entire team of artists that they are disappointed as the audience is because "the curtain closed, the plot unended" as no solution as yet has been provided by the Gods to make the world a better place to live in. The epilogue seeks the opinion of the audience to determine what factors could bring about a drastic change to the prevailing conditions—change is human nature, the interference of "bigger, better Gods or none" that is the path of atheism, the option of materialism or what else.

The question whether it would be possible for humans to be both good and rich remains. The dramatist says: "Ponder my friends,/ How man with man may live in amity/ And good men-women also—reach good ends./ There must, there must, be *some* end that would fit." He urges the audience to help look for plausible ways to make the world a suitable place where everybody gets the opportunity to live with dignity.

Analysis

All the poor people of the neighbourhood that are Shen Te's well-wishers want Shui Ta to be punished, but they are sacred of his influence and status in the society. The trial scene raises apprehensions that the rich and corrupt would be left unpunished for their crimes while the poor and virtuous would face the consequences. The Gods reappear as judges to listen to complaints lodged against Shui Ta and they are desperate to seek Shen Te and make sure this one good person on earth has not disappeared.

While the poor justify that Shui Ta is absolutely dishonourable and dishonest, his wealthy associates and the policeman testify his good nature. Shui Ta has earned disrepute among the working-class, but his opinions are highly appreciated among the businessmen and the rich. Though Shui Ta tries his best to point out reasons for his crudity, the poor people of Setzuan disagree with him at every instance. Brecht uses the imagery of the fountain to denote that amassing a fortune would not serve the desired end always as evinced in the case of Shui Ta and Shen Te.

Appearing undisguised, and standing alone before the Gods, Shen Te laments that the world is neither full of happiness nor scrupulous for a person like Shen Te to be good at all times and at all places as the Gods decree. The act of doing good could become the cause of good persons' fall into the nadir of hopelessness. Dark forces of capitalism would engulf people who would turn their own enemies, provided men learn to alternate between being good and otherwise. Just as Wang profiteered people in their bad times, Shui Ta has probably exerted power and influence when he thinks only of his motives and requirements.

When Shen Te pleads with the Gods that she is not an entirely good person, and requests the Gods to help her with her choices in the future, the Gods ascertain that it would be good that Shen Te decides how her problems could be solved because there can never be a truly good person. The Gods decipher that Shen Te's circumstances, her sense of solidarity, attitudes and her individuality are things that she can resolve for there can never be any other exemplary person as "the good woman of Setzuan" on earth.

The Epilogue is a concise monologue that captures the helplessness of the dramatist to arrive at a conclusive explanation to ways in which humanity can survive and thrive without compromising on any values and principles. Brecht entrusts the audience to suggest how greed, wealth, identity, gender and religion can play dominant roles to initiate human beings to live amiably. Brecht suggests that the welfare of the world lies in the hands of human beings who have to live up to save humanity. It's not the duty of the Gods or the parable to suggest solutions but the sincere efforts of human beings themselves to find solutions to these issues and make the world a safe place to live with pride and honour.

Conclusion

The entire neighbourhood is anxious to know what happened to Shen Te who has not been in their midst for a long time. They have all assembled at the court to discuss the wrongs meted out to them by Shui Ta and hope a favourable decision is taken by the judges, who are none other than the Gods in disguise. However, Shui Ta is defended by the law and the rich and he too stands up for himself by providing appropriate arguments against the charges levelled against him. However, all the discussions finally end with the noticeable absence of Shen Te, the saviour of the neighbourhood and Shui Ta's suspected role in either concealing her or doing harm to her.

At the request of Shui Ta, Shen Te reveals her dual identity only to the Gods and she explains the reasons why she had to visit the neighbourhood thrice as Shui Ta. Remaining good at all times, doing good to all and to oneself, taking care of business while helping the poor are contradictory notions that cannot be successfully carried out without being harsh or practical. She has done just that, but in doing so has not been able to be good as the Gods demanded from her. The Gods understand her plight, but they do not blame her. The first God says that she is just confused, not defeated or without the sense of purpose and their presence is not required; nevertheless, the world need not be changed. They reveal themselves to the people who enter the courtroom and marvel at Shen Te's presence.

The play however ends on a rather dismal note and the Epilogue speaks of the inability of the fable or actors to find a solution to end miseries of the world. The quest for a permanent solution to miseries of the world rests with the people who have to think rationally and logically and come up with the most viable strategies.

Glossary

forged	:	fake, phoney
attire	:	outfit, apparel, dress
testify	:	give evidence
vouchsafe	:	approve
discreet	:	subtle
testimony	:	proof, evidence
procure	:	obtain
profess	:	confess
arduous	:	strenuous, difficult
hue	:	shade, colour
exuberant	:	excited
betrothed	:	engaged to be married
nadir	:	depths
solidarity	:	harmony
amiably	:	cordially
parable	:	fable

Glossary from the Text

Scene 10

What good is a fountain if you can't get at the water?: Shen Te's shop symbolises the fountain that quenches the thirst of the needy. If the shop does not provide shelter to the poor, then it is useless. Shen Te's shop was refuge to the needy, but under Shui Ta's control it becomes a place where they are exploited.

A load of good intentions weighed me down to the ground: Shen Te is distressed because she could not bear the weight of being good to herself and the world at the same time.

Should the world be changed? How? By whom? No! Everything is in order!: The first God mentions that no change is required in the world because human beings are capable of taking care of themselves. Shen Te appears confused, but not defeated for she possesses the ability to run her life and business simultaneously. They give her the confidence to move on.

Who, in cold darkness, carries a little lamp!: The first God mentions that the tribulations of the world have engaged them for quite some time and he is sure that the world does not require their presence anymore She is the lady with the lamp who brightens the lives of the poor and the distressed.

Epilogue

We wished, alas! Our work might be commended/ We're disappointed too.: One of the audience mentions apologetically that the entire team has not bene able to resolve the issue of devising ways to make the place fit for everybody to live amiably because the Gods have not helped them. The audience is urged to seek ways to improve upon the existing conditions of the world so that every human being gets the opportunity to live to the fullest.

References

Demetz, Peter. *Brecht: A Collection of Critical Essays*. Prentice-Hall Inc., 1962.

Gascoigne, Bamber. *Twentieth-Century Drama*. Hutchinson and Co., 1974.

Morley, Michael, editor. *The Continuum Companion to Twentieth Century Theater*. Colin Chambers, 2002.

Needdle, Jan, and Peter Thomson. *Brecht*. Basil Blackwell, 1981.

Styan, J.L. *Modern Drama in Theory and Practice: Volume 2: Symbolism, Surrealism, and the Absurd*. Cambridge UP, 1981.

https://www.britannica.com/art/dramatic-literature

The Good Woman of Szechwan https://pdfs.semanticscholar.org/82d6/8ed23db277c702a1f467266d5a1f21b65cd3.pdf

Chapter 17

A Critical Study of *The Good Woman of Setzuan* and Bertolt Brecht as a Dramatist

Themes in *The Good Woman of Setzuan*

Goodness

The central question of the drama is whether a person can be wholly good under any circumstance. Shen Te struggles to remain good to others and herself, but she inevitably fails. The conditions of the society force her to adopt strategies that make her compromise many times and at other times reveal that pains and efforts she takes to be good are actually worthier than being good. Moreover, Shen Te has apprehensions about being a good person because she involves in activities that she thinks are not appropriate to be designated as a good person.

The Gods intend to leave the world as it is, if they are able to convince themselves of finding one soul that fits into their concept of a good person in the course of trying times and mounting pressures. Shen Te's acts of goodness begin with giving shelter to the Gods for a night when they are refused by every household in Setzuan and the neighbouring villages. She acknowledges that she has her own misgivings about being good for she sells her body for a living, lies often and covets her neighbours' things. She is critical about herself and assesses whether she could be labelled good.

Disguised as Shui Ta, he explains how he has to encounter difficult situations to provide for others without causing harm to himself. He realises that those who seek help from Shen Te are unmindful of the troubles they cause her, which adds to her woes. Shen Te wrestles with the two selves that take refuge in her and maintains balance between what she does for herself and others. Shui Ta is a practical and cautious hard taskmaster who plays his game with accuracy. He can look into the heart of the matter, which Shen Te cannot because she is caring, emotional and sensitive; albeit the opposing qualities rest within the same person.

The Gods understand Shen Te's predicament and give her the permission to be good and assure her that Shui Ta could visit her once a month so that she could plan her manoeuvers and take help from Shui Ta to execute them properly. Nobody can be completely good; therefore, goodness shouldn't go unrewarded. Brecht neither suggests a permanent solution to Shen Te's dilemma nor provides a happy ending to the play, but believes in collective effort of mankind to better themselves amidst changing conditions. Ultimately, it's the quest for goodness that plays a vital role for the prevalence of humanity.

Capitalism and Corruption

Setzuan is in the grip of capitalism that is evident in the way the people cheat on others, take advantage of others, take interest in individual profit, behave immorally, pilfer, and accept and offer bribe. It is ironic that the good suffer and the bad thrive. Given the circumstances, Wang, Lin To, Mrs. Mi Tzu, Yang Sun, Shu Fu and all the members of the family either try to deceive others or do not own responsibility for their actions, hence they cannot be called good persons.

Shen Te is forced into prostitution to make ends meet and pay her rent, but the Gods shower their favours on her. She becomes the owner of the tobacco shop, but soon finds herself in the midst of the hungry and the greedy that seek her favours alone. Her struggles and pain are overlooked and in order to safeguard herself, she dons the role of the shrewd and practical cousin Shui Ta. She learns the lesson that to be good and remain generous in a corrupt society is to drown oneself and to remain afloat is to exploit, become ruthless and demanding, which as Shui Ta she succeeds.

While the poor struggle, the rich hoard the resources. Shen Te must choose to protect her interests or be engulfed by poverty and despair, which she does not intend to become. This is the reason why she invents Shui Ta, her alter-ego. His entrance marks Shen Te's way in to capitalism. He amasses wealth, gains control over the poor, exploits women and children in his tobacco factory and imposes his dictates to make their lives miserable. He turns a ruthless boss and a swindler who cannot tolerate indolence. Shui Ta is the tool that Brecht employs to show how society rewards the owners and landlords but ignores workers who toil under extreme conditions.

Brecht is the commentator who suggests that even the good and the hard-working feel the pressures of capitalism and to survive inhospitable conditions is challenging for it may involve getting lost in the quagmire of helping another in the effort of saving oneself. Though Brecht's characters fail to provide answers to the questions posed by capitalism, Brecht advocates upholding moral values and principles to combat capitalism, greed and corruption. This could perhaps be the only way "to help good men arrive at happy ends".

Dual Identity

Shen Te realises that she has to take a tough stand to save her interests. As Shen Te, it would be difficult because she is an upstart tobacco-shop owner who climbs up the social ladder only because of divine intervention. Her kind and good-nature accommodates the less privileged ones, but she is taken advantage of and ridiculed by the rich and the poor. To protect herself and to cater to needs of others and fight injustice, she creates her alter-ego, Shui Ta.

Shui Ta wades through the rough waters of capitalism, greed, corruption and injustice to turn shrewd, self-imposing, tactful, unapologetic, pragmatic and crude and becomes a successful businessman who puts Shen Te's enemies in their places. Brecht creates the dual identity to accomplish what Shen Te finds difficult to do as a woman and the dual self is considered a masquerade that has an identity which is markedly different from the original one. The masquerade helps Shen Te escape the drudgery of existence and at the same time take control of the circumstances that weigh her down.

The disguise could also be seen as a way in which the need for a masculine self becomes inevitable as Mrs. Mi Tzu enquires for male references from Shen Te to authorise the lease. Shen Te's imposing cousin Shui Ta shrugs off all those who cause trouble to Shen Te including Mrs. Mi Tzu. Shui Ta is able to decipher machinations of Yang Sun, negotiate and manage a business firm, consolidate property and wealth, have profitable conversations with difficult men, and adopt the traditional male role that gives him a dominant position in society, which could never have been realised as Shen Te. Shui Ta becomes the vent through which Shen Te releases her inner frustrations and fights pressures of being good despite all odds by adopting a dual self that would allow her to manage the daunting task.

Divine Intervention

The issue of being good forms the background of the play because the Gods want to test whether any good persons could be found on earth; if not, the world has to be rebuilt. However, there is just one person Shen Te who is good, and the Gods feel that their incessant search for other good persons would definitely prove fruitful; nevertheless, they fail to find someone better than or equal to Shen Te. It could be inferred that the Gods do not want their choice of the good person to go wrong, otherwise they may have to bend rules of their book because they will have proof that their rules have failed humanity.

The Gods constantly appear in Wang's dreams to know more about Shen Te and her doings. Their wanderings ultimately drain them off and they confess that nobody can be so good as Shen Te and her reservations about being good as Shui Ta are inconsequential. The agree with Shen Te that nobody "can be good and yet [...] live [for themselves]" at once. The Gods prefer to "go back to [their] void" than spend time on earth solving man's issues because they realise the futility of such a move.

The human world is so full of misery and drudgery created by men themselves that it would be better if men come together to ameliorate their conditions than crave divine assistance.

Character Analysis

Shen Te

The protagonist, a prostitute who is chosen by the Gods to be a good person because she gives them shelter for the night when they are refused by everybody else and she is given a good amount to improve her life. She later becomes the owner of a tobacco shop, but she is swindled by many because of her generosity and compassion. The task assigned to her to remain good at any cost lands her in trouble and she is considered meek.

Shen Te is determined not to give in to the unscrupulous characters and moves ahead with the mission entrusted to her through her alter ego Shui Ta. Shen Te possesses the grit to restructure her business and becomes confident to handle the pressures of being good and rational at the same time with the help of Shui Ta. Shen Te is emotionally weak because she gives in to Yang Sun's advances and becomes pregnant, but keeps the matter clandestine.

She does not pretend to be good and requests the Gods to help her maintain her good reputation while still accomplishing deals and negotiations that are profitable for her to steer ahead of capitalistic aspirations. She gets so tired of her disguise that she ultimately goes after the Gods seeking their interference to rescue her, only to find the Gods ascending heaven without offering any solution. Through the character of Shen Te, Brecht exposes struggles encountered by women to survive the onslaught of capitalism, oppose the constraints of femininity, and adopt unusual strategies to rise above societal constrictions.

Shui Ta

The dominant and commanding alter-ego of Shen Te and steers her boat of life to victory over her detractors and the capitalistic society that take undue advantage of her. Shui Ta is an emergency entrant when Shen Te finds that being sympathetic and thoughtful about others would sink her life because the others are unmindful of her own battle. Shui Ta is supposed to be Shen Te's cousin who lives far away, and visits her thrice through the course of the drama. The last time he spends almost six months in Setzuan and becomes a successful and ruthless businessman, and an important link to capitalist endeavours.

Shui Ta finds practical solutions to Shen Te's problems beginning from those who are bent on duping her to unearthing Shen Te's lover Yang Sun's real intentions. He successfully squeezes information from Yang Sun about his future plans and avoids further pitfalls in Shen Te's financial affairs by extorting work from Yang Sun and each and every poor person of Setzuan in the tobacco factory. He not only becomes a successful business tycoon but also turns an oppressor of the people of Setzuan who hate him.

Shui Ta becomes aware of his power and the concomitant jeopardy to his position when is he is suspected of murdering his cousin Shen Te. He understands it proper to disclose his identity only to the Gods because the disguise has made him not only "bad" but also play "dirty" to safeguard Shen Te's interests. The Gods do not rebuke Shen Te but consider her as good as before, but insist that Shui Ta should visit her only once a month. Shui Ta brings order and stability in the life of Shen Te, and it could be inferred that in future too his presence would have a positive impact on the decisions she takes in life.

Wang

The poor water-seller of Setzuan who welcomes the Gods and struggles to find a home for their night stay. He is not considered a good person by the Gods because he dupes his fellow countrymen by serving them water in cups with a false bottom. He earns his livelihood only when there is drought and he curses his neighbours if they do not buy water from him when it rains. His survival is at the expense of others' suffering and never asks the Gods for help. Unfortunately, he meets with a nasty mishap with the barber Shu Fu when he enters the shop to sell water and has his hand burnt smashed by a hot iron.

This incident depicts the ugly side of capitalistic forces that overpower small businessmen who struggle to survive. He respects Shen Te because she has always been kind to him, but despises Shui Ta. He acts as the informer about Shen Te's good deeds when the God's visit him in his dreams at night. From Wang's opinions of Shen Te, the Gods plan their future action. He is the first to declare that Shui Ta could have committed a grave crime, and admits that only the Gods can save Shen Te's life.

Yang Sun

He is the most despicable character in the drama who is self-centred and untrustworthy because he loves Shen Te for the wrong reason. He first appears crestfallen because he is unable to secure the job of a pilot that requires money. On the verge of taking his life by hanging, he is saved by the timely interference of Shen Te, who not only gives him courage to live but also starts loving him. Yang Sun, however is selfish and cruel, and intends to acquire money from Shen Te to bribe his way to become a "flyer".

The unsuspecting Yang Sun is caught by Shui Ta to whom he discloses the intention of his relationship with Shen Te and his future plans. Though Shen Te realises that he is a rogue, she becomes pregnant with his child. While Shen Te forces him to quit the idea of becoming pilot, Shui Ta makes him work in his tobacco factory and deducts the money he owes Shen Te from his wages. His hard work makes him an honest and upright foreman in the factory. He gets upset when he hears the news of Shen Te's pregnancy. He suspects that Shui Ta would have caused Shen Te harm and calls the policeman to get Shui Ta arrested.

Shu Fu

A wealthy barber who falls in love with Shen Te because she is good, kind and considerate though he knows that she is in love with Yang Sun. He is heartbroken when Shen Te rejects his offers for Yang Sun, but he remains faithful to Shen when he sees her in distress after it becomes that she would lose her tobacco shop. He offers his cabins as shelter for the destitute and gives her a blank cheque to withdraw the amount she requires. He causes serious harm to Wang's arm when the poor water-seller tries to sell water in his shop. Here he is selfish and ruthless.

Shu Fu expects Shui Ta to understand his feelings for his cousin, but Shui Ta makes use of his cabins and money to get rich and employ the poor. Shu Fu is unable to fulfill his dreams to marrying Shen Te though Shui Ta supports him. Though Shen Te discovers that Yang Sun is a fraud, and Shu Fu truly loves her, she is unable to love him, but makes use of his money to thrive. This is how women often sacrifice principles to survive dark forces of capitalism.

Music in *The Good Woman of Setzuan*

Brecht produced *The Good Woman of Setzuan* and authorised two versions of the play set to the musical accompaniment of the Swiss composer Huldreich Georg Früh on its maiden release in 1943 and Paul Dessau later in 1947. The songs included in the play inform the attitudes and moods of the characters or comment on the action. In scene 1, the grandfather's song "The Song of the Smoke" explains that being clever does not bring success or assure survival during the present conditions and his efforts are in vain. Just as the grey smoke floats into the colder recesses of corners, his boat of life seems to be moving into the rough waters.

The husband says that in spite of trying out both just and crooked means of survival, his efforts have borne no fruit. The young niece complains that despite the information that several opportunities have been opened for the young, all the doors lead nowhere. The refrain "So what's the use?/ See the smoke float free/ Into ever colder coldness!/ It's the same with me" denotes that people of all the age groups have little chances of gainful employment and hence they struggle to survive the harsh conditions.

This scene closes with a song by Shen Te: "The little lifeboat/ Is swiftly sent down/ Too many people greedily/ Reach for it as they drown". The lines explain how the tobacco shop, her lifeboat sent by the Gods is occupied by the greedy, who will not be able to survive because it would be too difficult to provide for everyone. Her despair and plight, however are ignored by the rude family that occupies her shop. In scene 1a, the Gods despise Wang for being a coward and having little faith in Shen Te. They call him "a weak man" because he takes hasty decisions and always expects the worst.

In scene 3, Wang sings "The Song of the Water Seller in the Rain" presents an ironical situation where Wang desperately searches for someone who would buy water from him when it's raining. The futility of his hard work when water is not in demand is highlighted by the song. Wang's poverty is revealed when he dreams of seven rainless years and people begging for water from him.

The song also contrasts nature, which appreciates what it receives in plenty, and humankind, which does not require anything that is available in surplus. Shen Te mentions that Yang Sun's decision to end his life is because of the rains and she sings to the audience that the miseries in the world make life unbearable and ends in its destruction. Yang Sun remains indifferent to her words but when she sings a few lines to show why she would not be a prostitute anymore, he responds.

Shen Te, in scene 4 laments that the poor would never raise their voice to help the others when required because they lift their head only to beg. When she sees the smashed hand of Wang, she says that the poor are scared to rebel against injustice and crime. The need of the hour is to revolt against injustice, but the poor would never unite and dare to raise their concerns and this is pitiful. She sings: "When injustice is done there should be revolt in the city." The lines echo Brecht's call for revolution to change the existing circumstances so that man would be able to survive without the fear of capitalism.

The theme of "The Song of Defenselessness of the Gods and Good Men", in scene 4a is about the stronghold of capitalism. The first part of the song is sung by Shen Te with Shui Ta's mask in her hand. She speaks that even the Gods and the good men are so helpless that they cannot support or protect anybody from the evils of capitalism. She says: "Alas, the commandments of the Gods/ Are no use against want", which implies that the rules of the Gods do not help anybody in times of necessity. When the song is sung in the guise of Shui Ta, it turns into an ironic revelation that in order to help save one life, a dozen others have to be sacrificed. He wonders why Gods do not stand by the good men and fight to end suffering.

When the carpenter's youngest son, in scene 7 is seen eating waste from the garbage to satisfy the pangs of hunger, Shen Te rushes to him in horror and grabs him. Her long speech decrying the inhumaneness and the helplessness of the society, her resolution for preventing her son from facing such a plight and expressing anger against the cruel forces of capitalism is rendered with the background music of "The Song of Defenselessness of the Gods and Good Men."

In scene 6, Yang Sun's song "The Song of Saint Nevernever Day" is about the endless wait for times to change. Just as the poor cannot even think of becoming rich, his aspiration of flying will not be realised because he does not have money to buy the job. However, the fact that the intends to bribe the commanding officer to secure the job by taking away somebody else's is a cruel facet of life. The endless wait to secure life at all costs is evident in the song sung at the chapel at the wedding of Shen Te and Yang Sun, eventually the marriage is not solemnised because Shui Ta does not reach with the money.

"The Song of the Eighth Elephant", in scene 8 urges the workers to work diligently. As a foreman, Yang Sun directs the workers to sing to make them work faster. The song is about the eighth lame elephant that works even after the other seven elephants that are hard-working and wild are worn out because he has tusks and they give him the upper edge over the others. Though he is lame, he is servile and continues to work because of his powerful tusks, which means power is important.

The last song is in scene 10, when the Gods sing "The Trio of the Vanishing Gods" that marks their return to the heavens. They confess that they do not wish to stay on earth anymore, lest their "good woman" may cease to be good. They say: "If we watch our find too long/ It will disappear." They prefer to remain ignorant of any change in her so that they may not have to change their Book of Rules. They shower praises on "The good, good woman of Setzuan" and disappear.

The songs in the drama manifest despair or unfulfilled desires that play a crucial role in the lives of the characters. At times, songs reveal the pathos of characters that are caught in such situations that they fall short of verbal expression only. Music augments emotional upheavals that characters are forced to put up with. The use of music is one of the characteristic features of epic theatre that also involves lighting and stage settings to enhance the epic quality of the presentation.

The Role of the Gods

The Gods are set on a mission to find out a good person on earth so that they can convince themselves that goodness still prevails on earth and they need not change rules in their book. They find Shen Te to be a good person, and give her enough money to make her life. They continue their search for other good persons and entrust Wang to report them in his dreams about Shen Te's good deeds after she becomes wealthy. While the first God is bent on continuing their search for other good persons, the second God does not want to take responsibility of solving man's issues, and the third God is seen as the most empathetic of the three and suggests they help mortals on earth.

The Gods' discussions in Wang's dreams reveal that their travels in search of good persons are futile and makes them weary. Ultimately, they come to the conclusion that Shen Te is the only good person on earth, but they do not stay back to listen to her woes. They believe that Shen Te is capable enough to resolve her problems, but insist that Shui Ta should visit her only once a month.

Brecht introduces the Gods to show that men's actions are always gauged, but the Gods cannot help men who have created problems that end in misery and suffering for the others on earth. Their swift ascent to heaven to return to their "void" rather than stay back to help men out of complications exposes their disgust at mankind. Their only consolation and hope is Shen Te, who emerges good despite her misgivings, which are not considered grave by the Gods.

The Function of the Epilogue

The epilogue, rendered by one of the actors on stage is an apology to the audience because "the play is still in need of mending", which means that the play needs to be worked on for not addressing the problem at hand and leaving the plot "unended". However, the "bitter ending" of the play is attributed to the need for the audience's response to the situation and solutions to the questions posed by the drama. The actor is uncertain about what could bring both happiness and plenitude to the mortals—Providence of God, atheism, or a materialistic attitude.

Human beings must think of ways to live in harmony with others. The prosperity of the society rests in the well-being of both men and women. "There must, there must, be *some* end" to achieve both contentment and abundance and ensure that human beings live amicably and maintain the dignity of every individual irrespective of gender or class distinctions.

The epilogue is considered the representative of Brecht's epic theatre that makes people ponder over contemporary questions of social, political and economic relevance. A society under capitalism would tend to serve the interests of the privileged few and the skewed distribution of resources would inexorably lead to chaos. To maintain the dignity of mankind and ensure equity of resources, man has to devise strategies. The welfare of the world lies in the ability of man to take wise decisions, advocate peace, and work for the larger interests of the society at large.

Symbols

Water

Water is a natural life-force that forms the bedrock of civilisations but its availability and usage in capitalist society turns crucial for Wang the water-seller, who presents the dilemma of his profession. He commodifies this natural resource and ekes his living in the society when water is scarce, but when it rains he is barely able to support himself. His dilemma is that he can survive only at the expense of his neighbours' suffering in the given conditions. Water metaphorically represents one aspect of capitalism that forces one to survive only at the disadvantage of the other.

Flying and Planes

Yang Sun's desire to fly is a dream that he pursues to the extent of betraying his lover, his mother and bribing the commanding officer. Though he knows that he cannot be reinstated, he decides to end his life without thinking about his aged mother. Shen Te gives him the hope of a better future, and hands over 200 silver dollars, but Yang Sun demands 300 silver dollars more. This means that his demands exceed the means; however, he is obstinate and stoops too low to cheat Shen Te, and later unknowingly reveals to Shui Ta.

His marriage to Shen Te is stalled because Shui Ta does not bring the 300 silver dollars promised. Shen Te persuades him to take up a job at the tobacco factory, where he is forced to settle the dues to Shen Te. The extent to which man degrades and dreams get crushed in a capitalistic setting is revealed. The dream of flying could be considered an act of escapism from problems, which is first revealed in his attempt to take his life and the planes are symbolic of unfulfilled desires.

The Good Woman of Setzuan as an Epic Drama

The epic theater is a radical form of theater that compulsively breaks with the Aristotelian theater in terms of narrative, depiction and purpose. The importance given to logical connection between scenes, unities of drama and characters is revolutionised to incorporate social, political and economic conditions of the society and provides a realistic portrayal of characters to conditions set in a far-away locale expressed in the form of a fable. Moreover, the inclusion of devices like aside, songs, music, unnatural lighting, episodic structure and address to the audience are some of the distinguishing features of the drama.

The Good Woman of Setzuan, which is a parable in ten scenes is set in Communist China between the two World Wars. The story revolves around the responses of characters of the drama whose behaviours are analysed against a capitalistic background, and the visit of Gods in search of a good person in the world is invented by Brecht to explicate the purpose of his drama. The changing behaviours of the characters in the given context are considered crucial because the drama intends to make the audience react to situation where their opinions are involved to effect a change in the way of thinking.

Shen Te the protagonist is deemed a good person by the Gods who gives them shelter when all the others turn away from helping them. She is given a reward to survive, but she is obliged to help her neighbours. She is unable to be good and remain rich at the same time, and invents a cousin Shui Ta, her alter-ego to stand for her through the tough times. Shui Ta's scheming manoeuvers help Shen Te to take over the reins of life and business.

While Shen Te is able to provide for herself, Shui Ta is able to make the others work for their living in the tobacco factory. Shui Ta becomes an inevitable part of Shen Te's life. The drama ends in the courtroom, where Shui Ta discloses her true identity to the Gods who appear as judges. They encourage her to be good and allow Shui Ta to visit her once a month. It is revealed that people like Shui Ta are necessary in a materialistic world and they leave Shen Te to resolve the impasse.

The drama is a critique of capitalism that projects the need for a Communist agenda. A universal human predicament is presented and the audience is challenged to think and propose possible solutions to the problems that are educed from them. In this way, the audience participates in the process of changing the world for the better. The audience is not emotionally strangled but intellectually stimulated to analyse and predict the future of the world. The audience would critically observe the happenings on the stage and eventually become a part of the actual processes around them.

Brecht's Dramatic Theory

Brecht's dramatic theory is the outcome of his strenuous practice with the stage, actors and directors. As the critic Demetz contends: "About 1930, he conceived and developed the concept of epic theatre. In the notes to his drama *Mahagonny* he emphasizes that 'the modern theatre is epic theatre'" (106). The concept of the epic theater originated from his extensive travels, especially in Munich and Berlin, in 1924 when the word "epic" was already in usage with experiments being initiated by Wedekind, Döblin, Paul Zech and Alfons Paquet, and stage directions designed by Erwin Piscator (106).

Luigi Pirandello announced the method of acting, which was both critical and analytical. The discussions around the inclusion of pathos and the technical innovativeness of the Japanese Noh play helped Brecht to combine Marxist ideas and employ them in his plays. Brecht firmly believes that "Art is not a mirror held up to reality, but a hammer with which to shape it." He rejects the dramatic theater of Aristotle and challenges the characteristics, qualities, and purpose of dramatic theater.

Brecht's concept of "Verfremdungeffekt" from "verfremdung", which means alienation is a translation of the Russian word *ostrannenie,* mentioned as early as 1917 by Victor Shklovsky, one of the principal exponents of Russian Formalism in his essay "Art as Artifice". Brecht's use of the word "verfremdung" appears around 1936 only and hence the concept of alienation was not conceived by him. To Shklovsky, the word alienation denotes the transformation of an ordinary or automatic experience into a sensation that is poetically sensed and envisioned.

When Russia was steeped in socialist realism, Brecht was in Moscow and he realised that the word "alienation" was most suited to his dramatic technique (Demetz 108). His observation of the Chinese actor Mei Lan Fang, who created scene in a critical and aloof manner without makeup, costume or lighting enthralled him to such an extent that he accorded the greatness of the actor in his essay "The Alienation Effect in the Acting Art of the Chinese" (1936) and later in 1940 in "A Little Description of a New Technique of Acting", he added that "the Chinese art of acting is masterly in its gesture by openly observing his own movements, the Chinese actor arrives at the effect" (108).

While Shklovsky attaches a purely aesthetic quality to the word Alienation that is also closely related to imagination, Brecht gives it an interpretation closely related to the human society. Brecht prefers to portray than imagine through art, and art is considered a critical reproduction of reality. The alienation effect is used by Brecht to etch a permanent mark in the mind of spectators so that scenes depicted on stage are independent in themselves and do not lead one to the other.

The epic theatre casts the character as an object of investigation, who is susceptible to change and develops through the entire process. Through the use of gestures, the actor builds scenes to demonstrate patterns of behaviour that are related to conditions depicted. This way, empathy on the part of the audience could be avoided and reducing the drama to a mere subjective response is averted.

The most important part of Brecht's theater is that he considers theater an inevitable part of a scientific endeavour, a mode of "emancipation out of nature into production; it is the task of the one as well as of other to make the planet on which we live livable" (Demetz 110). Art and science are similar because they endeavour to sustain and entertain life, which are the two cardinal aspects of human existence. Art possesses the capability to portray reality effectively and science explores all the aspects of nature for human benefit. Brecht never speaks of drama, but only theatre. He enjoys confronting critically whatever he wants to have. The meaning and essence of the drama is defined by Brecht on the basis of the theatrical production, which means performance.

The Uniqueness of Brecht's Artistic Style

One of the most unique aspects of Brecht is that he is an exceptional poet with a range of expressions and diverse moods. Esslin calls Brecht "a poet, first and foremost" and Hannah Arendt mentions that Brecht is a poet par excellence. His dramas are an amalgamation of musical combinations and visual effects mingled with scornful humour and depictions of lively characters that enhance the quality of his productions. His dramas are known for their clarity and close-knit sequences. He is also known for developing a theory for the stage by working on his faults.

Brecht the artist depicts socialist realism and employs unique and diverse artistic devices to enhance the quality of his dramas. His intention is to use drama as a tool for propaganda and instruction that beseech both readers and the audience to comprehend, analyse, conclude and predict the outcome of his presentations. A tireless worker, an ardent dramatist and a perfectionist, he writes endlessly and meticulously to place his characters within social circumstances described accurately (Demetz 56).

He takes interest in comments related to all the aspects of a dramatic presentation but discards historical anachronisms and erroneous local realities identified. Infused with the facet of abstraction to serve the purpose of instruction, his plays give more importance to depicting ideas than blatant generalising.

An Advocate of Socialist Realism

Brecht is not only one of the most sensitive writers of the 20th century but also the advocator of socialist realism. Socialist realism implies a true representation of life and manners through art that is divested in social approaches and thereby posits intellectual response to situations. The fact that society acutely determines the fortunes of man is embedded within the pleasure derived from art.

The awareness of dialectical rules of the progress of the society helps the society determine the fate of man. Characters and events are established historically; however, the dynamic nature of this determination is decisive for art. Newer modes of representation and expression are explored and diverse viewpoints are ascertained, especially the opinions of the working class that are also aimed at the betterment of the society at large.

Works of art thus created open wider dimensions of thinking and elucidate thoughts that invigorate the minds to think about a society that is free from exploitation and the abilities of the artist would wade through uncharted waters of creativity. Social realism could be a tool that works for social reforms that have never before been harnessed. Artistic innovation and new expressive methods serve as inevitable facets of artistic expression.

Conclusion

Brecht deserves acclaim as a dramatist that uses his dramatic prowess to defy classical notions of drama and evolves an unusual stance that has left an indelible mark in the annals of dramatic history. Notwithstanding innumerable theatrical experimentations with form and content, let alone dramatic devices and choice of stage properties, the effect of the epic theater in minds of the audience cannot be overlooked.

Brecht is so involved in his theater that he sees through the mind of the audience and enthralls them more to ponder over depictions on stage rather than beseech their observation. The power of a dramatist lies in the ability to transform an experience into an everlasting question of invaluable relevance and Brecht does just that.

The stage, for Brecht is the space where the characters break the fourth wall between them and the audience, and thereby the audience is given the freedom to express their opinions without emotional entanglements of any sort. The active participation of the audience in turn would invite conflicting judgements or suggestions that would affect the entire population to rise and act in the interests of the common man. Brecht uses machinations of drama to search for possible answers to his inquiries of contemporary bearings.

Glossary

inevitable	:	unavoidable
misgivings	:	doubts
albeit	:	although
indolence	:	sloth; laziness
combat	:	to battle
quagmire	:	predicament; dilemma
masquerade	:	impersonate
weigh down	:	burden; overloaded
daunting	:	formidable
inconsequential	:	insignificant
drudgery	:	labour
clandestine	:	concealed; covert
detractor	:	enemy
servile	:	submissive
extort	:	obtain by force or threat
pitfall	:	danger
mishap	:	casualty
amicably	:	cordially
representative	:	mouthpiece
skewed	:	lopsided
elicit	:	extract; educe

blatant	:	obvious
anachronism	:	chronologically out of place
prowess	:	expertise
indelible	:	enduring; lasting
annals	:	records
beseech	:	implore
machination	:	manoeuver

References

Demetz, Peter. *Brecht: A Collection of Critical Essays*. Prentice-Hall Inc., 1962.

Esslin, Martin. *Brecht: The Man and His Work*. Doubleday and Company, 1960.

Gascoigne, Bamber. *Twentieth-Century Drama*. Hutchinson and Co., 1974.

Morley, Michael, editor. *The Continuum Companion to Twentieth Century Theater*. Colin Chambers, 2002.

Needdle, Jan, and Peter Thomson. *Brecht*. Basil Blackwell, 1981.

Styan, J.L. *Modern Drama in Theory and Practice: Volume 2: Symbolism, Surrealism, and the Absurd*. Cambridge UP, 1981.

Willet, John. *The Theatre of Bertolt Brecht*. New Directions, 1959.

https://www.britannica.com/art/dramatic-literature

The Good Woman of Szechwan https://pdfs.semanticscholar.org/82d6/8ed23db277c702a1f467266d5a1f21b65cd3.pdf

Chapter 18

The Theatre of the Absurd

Introduction

Repercussions of the two World Wars in Europe were the destruction of conventional values and principles in life, the sense of alienation and desolation, suspicion and lack of meaningful communication. Moreover, the decline in religious sentiments and the concomitant growth of science along with the emergence of a totalitarian power structure changed the world forever. Man, in the post-war world had to face a fragmented self and the future seemed uncanny. The world appeared largely irrational and meaningless, and existence in such a world was agonising. This sense of the meaninglessness of human life was expressed in works of literature under the term "absurd".

The Literature of the Absurd in Western Europe

The literature of the absurd incorporates several works in drama and prose fiction that proposes to highlight the human condition as absurd or out of harmony and an incongruous strategy is adopted in works to present this universal condition. The movement gained prominence after the French philosophers Jean Paul Sartre (1905-80) and Albert Camus (1913-60), depicted the alienated condition of the human beings that survived in a tormented world after the World Wars and devoid of truth, value or inherent meaning. Human life is a series of purposeless and insignificant endeavours that emerges from nothingness, moves from nothingness and ends in a similar manner, and human existence is characteristically anguished and absurd.

Camus, in *The Myth of Sisyphus* (1942) elucidates the condition:

> A world that can be explained by reasoning, however faulty, is a familiar world. But in a universe that is suddenly deprived of illusions and of light, man feels a stranger. His is an irremediable exile, because he is deprived of memories of a lost homeland as much as he lacks the hope of a promised land to come. This divorce between man and his life, the actor and his setting, truly constitutes the feeling of Absurdity. (42)

Camus reiterates the story of the absurd hero Sisyphus who is perpetually sentenced to roll a rock to the top of a mountain and watch its descent. Completely aware of his miserable condition, he struggles to emerge victorious, but ultimately realises that his success lies in his acceptance of his wretched plight. He could free himself from the stronghold of his plight only if he learns to come to terms with the senselessness and nothingness of his efforts.

Camus considers the absurdity of human life as the outcome of the dichotomy between human thoughts and the world that it is part of. The emotional vacuity of man works in tandem with the indifferent attitude of the people and creates an absurd world that is caught between indecisiveness and irrationality. In *Thus Spake Zarathustra* (1883-85), the German philosopher Friedrich Nietzsche (1844-1900) declares "God is Dead", which captures the despondency in a world torn down by the World Wars thereby destroying reasoning and disconnecting human life.

A related explanation to the universal human condition is given by the French author Eugene Ionesco in his essay on Kafka. Ionesco defines the term absurd as something which is "...devoid of purpose.... Cut off from his religious, metaphysical, and transcendental roots, man is lost; all his actions became senseless, absurd, useless." Ionesco adds that "People drowning in meaninglessness can only be grotesque, their sufferings can only appear tragic by derision" (qtd. in Esslin v).

The Theatre of the Absurd

Camus regards art the avenue for man to give vent to his frustration in the face of absurdity of life. The artist who experiences isolation conveys his thoughts in his works that represent his freedom to explore subjective passions. The critic Martin Esslin (1918-2002) coined the term "The Theatre of the Absurd" for several dramatic works written from 1950 to 1960 that hold the view that the human situation is primarily out of harmony.

The "absurd" plays of the Irish dramatist Samuel Beckett (1906-89), the French playwrights Eugene Ionesco (1909-94), Arthur Adamov (1908-70), and Jean Genet (1910-86), and the British Harold Pinter (1930-2008) among others share the opinion that man inhabits a world, which is incomprehensible and purposeless and leaves him confounded, anxious, perturbed and threatened.

Other prominent playwrights associated with this theatre are the British playwrights Tom Stoppard (b. 1937) and N.F. Simpson (1919-2011), the American dramatists Arthur Lee Kopit (b. 1937) and Edward Albee (1928-2016), the Swiss Friedrich Dürrenmatt (1921-90), the Spanish Fernando Arrabal (b. 1932), the French dramatists Boris Vian and Jean Tardieu (1903-95), the German Peter Weiss (1916-82) and the Czech Václav Havel (1936-2011).

The beginnings of the Theatre of the Absurd are ingrained in the avant-garde experiments in art during the 1920s and the 1930s. The traumatic experiences of nuclear extermination and genocide propelled by the Second World War shook the world of the remnants of religious faith, values and conventions, and foregrounded the precariousness of human life and its essential futility and unpredictability. The Theatre of the Absurd endeavours to raise that consciousness and exposes the vulnerability of the human race that gropes in a mechanical world controlled by forces that are megalomaniac, insensitive and diabolic.

The absurd plays employ an innovative form that directly shocks the viewer, shaking him out of his complacency and concerns with the mundane routine activities. Traditional methods of storytelling, art forms and depictions lose their significance and they are replaced by representations that overtly challenge convention. The anti-theatre is surreal and illogical and projects a universal condition that does not necessitate conflict, dialogues, plot or characters so to say.

Language is reduced to meaningless exchanges because words fail to put across the depth of human emotions. Words are insufficient to project an utterly incomprehensible world that is devoid of meaningful communication. Clichés, rantings, slogans and technical jargons that parody, distort and break down thought patterns replace conventional dialogues in an effort to make people aware of the limits of the language to authentically project the morbid world and penetrate into the predicament of the human situation.

Rational thought, conventional speeches, and well-constructed dialogues are considered ineffective to bring out the understatements and the implied meanings that the theatre indulges in. To transcend the conventional tropes of thought and language is to bring to the fore the essence of the theatre that uses connotations and suggestions to mean and imply through poetic imagery.

The drama relishes the unexpected and the illogical. Rational thought is replaced by nonsense that opens fresh doors of implications through comedy. Dramatic conflicts are avoided because they are trappings of a world governed by establishments and when every situation is rendered meaningless, conflicts are insignificant and hence unnecessary. Frantic performances of characters on stage accentuates the fact that nothing would change their existence. Absurd dramas deliver an atmosphere, and involve the audience in a situational experience.

Stage elements of movement and light that incorporate mime, ballet, clowning, slapstick comedy, conjuring and acrobatics to create abstract scenic effects. Visual experience is more important than the role of language, which is secondary. Absurd drama conjures up an allegorical vision of the world that has never been experimented before.

The Precursors of the Absurd Drama

- **Nonsense literature:** The French Renaissance writer Francois Rabelais (1494-1553), the English writer Lewis Carroll (1832-98) and the English writer and poet Edward Lear (1812-88) wrote nonsense fiction. John Keats, Victor Hugo, Lord Byron, and Thomas Hood among others wrote nonsense poetry. The German poet Christian Morgernstern (1817-1914) perfected the art of nonsense poetry. Eugene Ionesco was influenced by the dialogues of the Marx Brothers' films written by the American humourist and screenwriter S.J. Perelman (1904-79).
- **Allegory, Dream and Myth:** English dramatists John Webster and Cyril Tourner, the Spanish dramatist Pedro Calderon de la Barca (1600-81), the German playwright Jakob Biedermann (1578-1639) wrote allegorical dramas. The decline of allegory witnessed the emergence of fantasy in drama exemplified by Jonathan Swift and Hugh Walpole.

  The Absurd Theatre also drew upon transcripts of dreams, character transformations, nightmares and fascinations seen in works of August Strindberg, Dostoevsky, James Joyce and the Jewish Franz Kafka (1883-1924). These writers explored the subconscious mind to derive a universal implication of their own subjective preoccupations. Kafka, in his dramas introduced nightmares and obsessions in the otherwise mundane life of man.

  The French symbolist writer Alfred Jarry (1873-1907) created Ubu Roi the eponymous character, a mythical form framed around the terrifying and grotesque archetypal image of the cruel nature of man. Ubu Roi proclaims himself king of Poland and unleashes terror on the subjects. Through this character, Jarry objectively presents the wavering psychological states of the mind of a man.
- **The European Avant-garde in the 20th Century:** The Surrealist movement emphasised the role of the subconscious after Freud and introduced myth and dream in dramatic presentations. The Dadaist movement

gave importance to nonsensical dialogues to shock the bourgeois audience and make a deliberate turn from artistic conventions.

The French dramatist Antonin Artaud (1896-1948) filled the stage with magic and mysticism to probe inner recesses of the human mind. He called for producing collective archetypes for creating a new mythological tradition. He used gestures, light, sound-effects, and rapid movements to externalise the internal world of man. Under Artaud, theatre transcended the confines of language for expressing ideas. In Germany, Brecht used humour, clowning, and music to present thoughts and realities of life rather objectively, and hence his plays resembled Absurd dramas.

The Political Situation in Eastern Europe

Russia promulgated Soviet socialism because the defeat of Nazis was imminent. The Russian army was so powerful that Stalin was able to establish the principles of the Soviet administration with an iron fist throughout Central Europe. Rumania, Poland, and Czechoslovakia that were under the control of feudal monarchies, the quasi-authoritarian rule, and the parliamentary version of governance respectively came under militant Soviet rule. Drastic transformations in the political and economic spheres of influence altered the bureaucracy of countries that had severe ramifications. People were confounded with the new regime and they felt that their existence was incomparably meaningless.

While the Western world posed questions related to the existence of man and the prevalence of injustice and suffering in the world, the Soviet government in the Eastern part of the world declared that the Marxist ideology possessed the capacity to eradicate suffering and injustice. However, the notion and practice of this system of thought was far more depressing than the philosophical systems it seemed to outdo.

The Marxist ideology dominated every domain of public and private interest and people were forced to abide by directives enshrined in its manifesto savour its contribution to the society at large, albeit the people became aware of the absurdity of the claims made. Millions were forced to act against their will or nature, and this created unrest throughout East Europe.

The Rise of the Theatre of the Absurd in Eastern Europe

In the initial decades of Communist rule in East European countries, feature films depicting happy, hardworking workers in steel factories or tractor drivers eulogising tractors and becoming a part of the Communist Party were common. All the art forms were employed to serve national and political interests, that is the spread of communist ideology.

Experiments in the arts and the theatre were considered bourgeois excesses and they were absolutely denounced by Joseph Stalin (1878-1953), the secretary-general of the Communist Party of the Soviet Union (1922-53) and premier of the Soviet state (1941-53). Several harsh political, cultural and social decrees of the Stalinist regime resulted in the exploitation of art for ideological and propagandist ventures.

With the demise of Stalin in 1953, artists could write about their experiences without fear of being either persecuted or exiled. In 1956, the defeat of the Hungarian revolution and the series of political upheavels in Poland ended in the introduction of several liberational practices within the Soviet Bloc. Czechoslovakia announced democratic policies in the period between 1962 and 1963 and the revival of art forms was one of the major outcomes. The Absurd plays were either translated or published, and staged only in Poland and Czechoslovakia during this period.

During the 1960s, the West European absurd drama was denounced by most of the countries in East Europe because the dramas were regarded nihilistic and anti-realistic by most of the governments in East Europe. Several East European theatrical producers were hesitant to jeopardize their careers by staging plays that were condemned by their respective administrative systems.

During this period, the English theatre critic and writer Kenneth Tynan (1927-80) criticized the absurd dramas of Ionesco and "warned his readers of the danger that Ionesco might become the messiah of the enemies of realism in the theatre" (Esslin

125) and this anti-realist indictment was seriously taken in by the bureaucracy to condemn the Absurd dramas.

The fear that the Western absurd plays might be unacceptable to the general public who were accustomed to the realist dramas and the consensus that the plays may be avant-garde and arcane for the audience dissuaded their production. Stalin's death and the liberalisation policies of the governments instilled confidence in the people that the anguish was only a matter of time. In the long run, man's concerted efforts would set matters right. Seen from this perspective, the Western absurd plays were perceived to be pessimistic, negative, hopeless and detrimental.

Both the East and the West European countries underwent the anguish of existence that stemmed from their fear of death and the desire for salvation from a real situation. While the absurd situation in the West was the expression of distress and annoyance over the rather insipid life they led, the East confronted the harsh Marxist precepts. It could be ascertained that reformists and liberal Marxists in Czechoslovakia were under the impression that the experience of absurdity of the human condition in the West was due to the decline of capitalism and this was irrelevant in the East since the socialist parties had found a solution in the liberal policies announced by the government after Stalin's death.

The East European Absurd plays endeavoured to stage the disconcert with the Marxist regime and hence they were considered constructive, in contrast to the Western absurd plays that were pessimistic and destructive. Later, however several critics realised that the absurd drama of the West attempted to play constructive roles.

In 1956, Samuel Beckett's *Waiting for Godot* was produced in Poland followed by Slovakia in 1969. The play was well-received by the Polish and the Slovak general public that saw signs of hope in a seemingly hopeless world. Similar to the rousing response to the play by inmates of the prison inmates at California, the East European public were responsive to the questions posed by the drama that brought them closer to the pressing concerns of everyday life because they lived under such conditions.

It is observed that while the absurd drama in the West had spent itself by the 1960s, the eastern counterpart continued to stage such dramas even in the 1970s. While the absurd dramas in the West projected the universal predicament of man in an irredeemable situation that was intangible and mysterious, the dramas in the East presented the individual who was ensnared within the mechanistic social system.

The absurd dramas of the East were concrete and realistic to a certain extent in contrast to the West, where a theoretical background to the situation was deciphered. The absurd dramas of the East projected the essential tragedy of the human situation that was the consequence of a faulty and corrupt social system and the dramas were successful in communicating the absurd situation more candidly than the West because they faced the miserable condition almost everyday.

Not late, Russia invaded Czechoslovakia in 1968 and the liberationist policies were immediately stalled. The country was thrown into a state of stagnation under the new policies of the regime that disapproved the liberal reforms spearheaded by artists and intellectuals who were either made homeless overnight or forced to leave the country. While several writers and artists who were banned continued to write in Czechoslovakia, and their works were subsequently produced and staged in the West. The absurd playwrights in Poland who were undisturbed continued to work relentlessly and published and produced their works in Poland.

The absurd dramatists of the West namely Samuel Beckett, Harold Pinter, and Eugene Ionesco expressed their solidarity with writers of the East, especially Václav Havel. Beckett's short play, *Catastrophe* (1982), was dedicated to Havel when he was made a political prisoner in Czechoslovakia. Some of the noted East European dramatists are Slowomir Mrozek (b. 1930), Tadeusz Rozewicz (b. 1921) and Vaclav Havel (1936-2011).

The Absurd Theatre in the United States of America

The American stage was largely influenced by cultural changes due to the immigrant settlements and the intelligentsia, and hence along with the technological advancements, the influence of the theatre was replaced by the cinema and television. Many dramatists resorted to invent new modes of presentation to attract the audience and they ingrained ideas from the Italian dramatist Luigi Pirandello (1867-1936) and the German playwright Bertolt Brecht (1898-1956). Several dramatists devised strategies to expose man's anguish and engaged the audience to comment on the happenings on the stage.

Abstractions replaced realistic and naturalistic plots and the belief in the American dream that spread cultural and social disharmony after the First World War became so intense that the desire to live a life of plenitude became a myth. Several dramatists employed this concept by engaging in a "metatheatre" that was coined by the Jewish-American playwright and critic Lionel Abel (1910-2001) and described as reflecting comedy and tragedy concomitantly, and the audience can laugh at and empathize with the protagonist (Abel 23).

While Europeans suffered existential anguish due to excruciating war experiences and debilitating policies of the government, the Americans felt insecure restless as a consequence of being unsuccessful in fulfilling the American dream. The Americans dispensed with the Freudian understanding of human nature and found the European notion of man's life amidst misfortune inexplicable. Hence, ideas of the search for reality or the sense of being did not surface in American absurd dramas.

The Absurd theatre in America could be considered postmodern in the sense that it celebrated the notion of unfulfilled desires and questions national and political ideals. Culture, which consisted of symbols and rituals were evident in the cultural codes that sustained meaning in a performances on stage. Each play contained implications that engaged with different facets of the American culture.

American literature, grounded on the precepts of Puritanism and morality and the philosophical postulations of the Age of Reason, was repudiated by the French. The American dream pervaded the American life and hence only a handful of dramatists attuned to the absurd tradition because they had not experienced loss of meaning or purpose in life as the European countries had.

The American plays were didactic and intended to reform the society. Some of the prominent dramatists include Robert Hivnor (b. 1916), Carson McCullers (1917-67), Neil Simon (b. 1927), Maria Irene Fornes (b. 1930), Jack Richardson (1935-2011), John Gaure (b. 1936), and Arthur Kopit (b. 1937).

The British novelist Christopher Bigsby (b. 1941) mentioned that the American theatre was not adept to expose the absurd situation because "Its actor training was committed to psychological veracity, its theatrical tradition at odds with the absurd denial of social conflict and more fundamentally absurdism" (125). Ernest Hemingway, in *The Old Man and the Sea* (1952) noted that man had to struggle against odds to become successful, and each person fought a unique battle, however nothing remained forever in the end. Ideas of material prosperity and technological development as crucial markers of individual identity in the American society formed the basis of Eugene O'Neill's expressionist play *The Hairy Ape* (1922).

This situation was appropriately explained by Edward Albee who contended that art philosophically explored where the man tried to make sense of his senseless position in the world bereft of moral, religious, political and social structures that crushed under existential crises.

The optimism of the American dream appeared a delusion that surfaced as the aftermath of the reckless assassinations of President John F. Kennedy and Martin Luther King Jr., and the Vietnam war. The inevitable social and political changes impinged on the American faith in society and political stability. The disillusionment at the non-realization of the American dream proved crucial for the evolution and advancement of the absurd theatre.

Devoid of any comic elements in the plot and the absence of grotesque or surreal settings, the tragic situation of man was highlighted in the backdrop of the American myth, which relied on cultural codes. Without poetic images, the narrative was conversational and extended dialogues that projected familial discord, marital issues and social disparity. The audience was exposed to the frustration of the characters on stage and they empathised with them. The pessimistic approach to degraded values in life, the futility of the pursuit of the American dream and the frustration due to unemployment and hopelessness were captured by the dramatists.

While the American absurd theatre brought out the frustration at the decline of moral and cultural values due to the failure to realise the American dream, the European theatre concentrated on the inability to communicate in a world that was war-torn and susceptible to further annihilation.

The American theatre was more didactic, but the European one was grounded on a philosophical approach that relied on existentialism. The settings of the American stage were realistic with social elements that played a dominant role. Plays often lacked the artistic refinement and complexity of the European stage, and it not only condemned man's deplorable condition but also strived to undermine the decadent society.

Conclusion

The Theatre of the Absurd is considered the appropriate mouthpiece of an era that witnessed the devastating wars and mentally, spiritually, morally and physically decapitated innumerable lives. The irredeemable human condition is expressed by this theatre that invented stage techniques and situations and presented dramas that were irrational or absurd themselves.

These dramas exposed the hollowness of the society that failed to recuperate from the emotional and mental tortures they were subjected to. While Western Europe succumbed to the crises that emerged out of the desperateness of war and the inevitable consequences of religious disbelief and social alienation, Eastern Europe reeled under the harsh Soviet dictates that seemed to provide the panacea to the ensuing deplorable condition in the world.

However, though many East European countries tried to break free from the Soviet stronghold, they were only further steeped in inconsiderate circumstances under the post-Stalinist governments. The absurd theatre in America exposed the human condition that could not make up to realise the American dream of material success and prosperity. While the European theatre was more philosophically inclined in projecting a world that underwent existential anguish that left an emotional lacuna, the American counterpart was more edifying in that it exposed the unsuccessful individual within undesirable social circumstances.

Glossary

repercussions	:	consequences
totalitarian	:	authoritarian
incongruous	:	absurd
vacuity	:	void
in tandem with	:	along with
derision	:	ridicule; mockery
genocide	:	massacre
impinged on	:	affected
indictment	:	accusation
messiah	:	saviour
precariousness	:	instability
megalomaniac	:	tyrannical
accentuate	:	underscore
conjuring	:	tricks
slapstick comedy	:	jest
allegorical	:	metaphoric
edifying	:	instructing

References

Abrams, M.H. and Geoffrey Galt Harpham. *A Glossary of Literary Terms.* 11th ed. Cengage, 2015.

Abel, Lionel. *Metatheatre: A New View of Dramatic Form.* Hill and Wang, 1963.

——. *Tragedy and Metatheatre: Essays on Dramatic Form.* Holmes Meier Publishers, 2003.

Bigsby, Christopher. *Modern American Drama*. Cambridge UP, 2000.

Brockett, G. Oscar, and Franklin J. Hildy. *History of the Theatre.* 10th ed., Pearson Education Limited, 2013.

Camus, Albert. *Le Mythe de Sisyphe*. Gallimard, 1942.

Crawford, Jerry L., Catherine Hurst, and Michael Lugering. *Acting in Person and in Style*. 5th edition. Waveland Press, 2010.

Esslin, Martin. Introduction. "The Absurdity of the Absurd." *The Theatre of the Absurd*. The Overlook P, 1973.

Gascoigne, Bamber. *Twentieth-Century Drama*. Hutchinson and Co., 1974.

Meserve, Walter. *An Outline History of American Drama*. Adams and Co., 1965.

Styan, J.L. *Modern Drama in Theory and Practice: Volume 2, Symbolism, Surrealism and the Absurd*. Cambridge UP, 2013.

Theatre of the Absurd. https://www.britannica.com/art/Theatre-of-the-Absurd

https://www.oxfordreference.com/view/10.1093/oi/authority.20110803095345289

https://www.bl.uk/20th-century-literature/articles/nonsense-talk-theatre-of-the-absurd

https://books.google.co.in/books/about/The_Theatre_of_the_Absurd.html?id=J7iQNBOp7Q4C&redir_esc=y

Chapter 19

The Dramatists of the Theatre of the Absurd: An Overview

Introduction

The perception of metaphysical anguish at a disillusioned period of human history that has rendered the world incomprehensible and senseless is the pertinent concern in the dramas of Beckett, Ionesco, Adamov, Genet, Pinter and the other dramatists of the absurd. Esslin points out that the Theatre of the Absurd shares similar concerns with the Existentialist theatre as well as the "poetic avant-garde", a French theatre of the period (Introduction xxiii-xv). Nevertheless, the distinctive differences among them is apparent.

A comparable feeling of the senselessness of life and the subsequent purposelessness of life and loss of values is seen in works of dramatists such as Giradoux, Anouilh, Salacrou, Sartre and Camus; however, the fundamental difference of these writers and the Theatre of the Absurd is the fact that their stage presentations reveal the use of succinct and logically construed ratiocination in contrast to the absurd dramatists that expose the similar situation by overtly forsaking elements of logic and discursive thought. Sartre and Camus use the conventional stage to express novel thoughts, but the Theatre of the Absurd endeavours to effect a unity between the universal condition and the form in which it is expressed (xxiv).

The ingenuity of the Theatre of the Absurd is that it presents the absurdity in works that are constructed within illogical and irrational frameworks using dramatic devices and images and refrain from arguing about the absurdity of the human condition. The resolution to fuse the subject matter and the form in which it is expressed is the integral point of difference between the Theatre of the Absurd and the Existentialist theatre. The Theatre of the Absurd, centred in Paris is a part of the "anti-literary movement" of the time that shares its precepts with abstract painting that rejects "literary elements in pictures", and highlights the efforts to create new forms of expression in all the art forms (Esslin Introduction xxvi).

Esslin remarks that that the "poetic avant-garde" gives importance to fantasy and dream reality, and disdains the essential unity of the plot and consistency of the characters as the Theatre of the Absurd. The presentations of the "poetic avant-garde" possess a greater lyrical quality and consist of lesser violent and grotesque elements; moreover, the plays are infused with images that carry rich verbal associations. In contrast, the Theatre of the Absurd devalues language and objectifies the images on the stage itself (Introduction xxv). Some prominent dramatists include the Belgian playwright Michel de Ghelderode (1898-1962), the French dramatists Jacques Audiberti (1899-1965), Georges Neveux (1900-82), Henri Pichette (1924-2000), and Jean Vauthier (1910-92), and the Lebanese playwright Georges Schehadé (1905-89).

The Playwrights of Western Europe and their Principal Works

Samuel Barclay Beckett (1906-89): An Irish-French poet, dramatist and critic, who was awarded the Nobel Prize for Literature in 1969, Beckett began his career as a critic and then turned to write poems and novels. He won international acclaim with his magnum opus drama *En attendant Godot* (*Waiting for Godot,* 1952) that highlighted the irredeemable human plight in the face of loss of values and principles in the world devastated after the two World Wars. Though human species had been waiting for some kind of respite or deliverance from that hopeless condition, nevertheless life moved on without any help and man continued to suffer existential "angst", which was specifically the expression of profound anxiety or dread, typically about the human condition or the state of affairs of the world.

His plays *Fin de partie* (*Endgame,* 1957), *Krapp's Last Tape* (1958), *Happy Days* (1961), the radio play *All That Fall* (1957) to name a few recorded the plight of human beings in a world that was unintelligible and their actions were primarily "out of harmony". He was also known for his trilogy of narrative prose works, erroneously labelled as novels that included *Molloy, Malone Dies,* and *The Unnamable* (1947-50) and the collection *Stories and Texts for Nothing* (1967), in which he raised the problem of the identity of the human self from within itself.

Eugene Ionesco (1931-94): Ionesco, a Romanian-born French dramatist expressed his dissent for reason and the established order. His plays examined human suffering under Nazi persecution, addressed the drab routine of human existence and the inability to make meaningful communication due to alienation. He portrayed the loss of religious faith, irrationality of thought and excessive importance to scientific advancements that had portrayed the meaninglessness of man's life.

His significant dramas included *The Bald Soprano* or *The Bald Prima Donna* (*La Cantatrice*, written 1948), *Jack, or The Submission* (*Jacques ou la soumission*, 1950), *The Lesson* (*La Leçon*, 1950), *Salutations* (*Les Salutations*, 1950), *The Chairs* (*Les Chaises*, 1951), translated as *The Future is in Eggs* (*L'Avenir est dans les oeufs*, 1951), *Victims of Duty* (*Victimes du devoir*, 1952), *The New Tenant* (*Le Nouveau locataire* 1953), *Amédée, or How to Get Rid of It* (1954). *The Killer without Reason or The Killer without Cause,* 1958 is the first of Ionesco's *Berenger Plays,* the others being *Rhinocéros* (1959) and *Exit the King* (1962).

Ionesco's dramas were characterised by a style that overtly rejected realistic theater and action and instead explored the use of comedy, exaggeration, caricature, farce and parody that gave structure to his ideas and picturised the tragedy of human existence. His dramas are called absurdist sketches or *anti-pièce* in French (anti-play) highlight the alienated existence of man and expose the futility of communication in the modern world.

Arthur Adamov (1908-70): A Russian-born French dramatist, Adamov's writings were characterised by the distressing expression of alienation. His believed that God was dead and it would be futile to search for meaning in life. He was highly influenced by the Swedish dramatist August Strindberg and Franz Kafka, and began writing plays from 1947. He was the editor of the periodical *Discontinuité,* and wrote poetry. In 1938, he suffered a nervous breakdown, and in his autobiography *L'Aveu* (*The Confession*, 1938-43), he disclosed the neurosis he suffered from and revealed his tormented psyche that pushed him to extremes of alienation. He was adept at creating visual images on the stage and hence his plays were a visual treat. His novella *Recognition* (1946) was infused with a sense of the futility of human existence.

His plays lacked a convincing plot, and presented a few unrealistic characters that together conveyed a heightened sense of loneliness as a result of loss of communication. Loaded with clichés, the so-called dialogues in his dramas were concise exchanges. His first play *La Parodie* (*The Parody,* 1950) portrays a handless clock that hangs creepily over characters who are preoccupied with the passage of time. The characters helplessly search for meaning in life, which is unattainable, albeit it exists. The plays *L'Invasion* (*The Invasion,* 1950). *A Major and Minor Maneuver* (1953), and *Everyone Against Everyone* (1953) depict the helpless human situation more realistically.

The play *Le Professeur Taranne* (*The Professor Taranne*, 1953) employs a dream-sequence that portrays a university professor unable to live up to his public role. *Le Ping-pong* (*Ping Pong*, 1955) employs a pinball machine as the central image to which the characters surrender themselves. The drama is a work of social criticism that shows man's faithfulness to false beliefs and the futility of his endeavours. In this best known play, the powerful central image is that of a pinball machine to which the characters surrender themselves in a never-ending, aimless game of chance, perfectly illustrating man's adherence to false objectives and the futility of such endeavours.

The play *Paolo Paoli* is an epic drama based on the outbreak of the First World War that portrays contemporary social and political issues. The grotesque drama *The Politics of the Outcast* (1962) is a critique of racism, while *Holy Europe* (1966) is a satire on imperialism. The burlesque piece *The Moderate* (1968) is humouristic in tone, whereas *Off Limits,* written in the same year is menacingly humouristic and exposes the tragic atmosphere of the American way of life.

Jean Genet (1910-86): A French novelist and a prominent dramatist of the Theatre of the Absurd, Genet brought out his autobiographical *Journal du voleur* (*The Thief's Journal,* 1949), which is an authentic revelation of his life as a vagabond, robber, and male prostitute in Barcelona, Antwerp and several cities between 1930 and 1939. The journal also reveals him as a connoisseur and an existentialist. He began to write in 1942 and brought out the novel *Notre-Dame des Fleurs* (*Our Lady of the Flowers*) in 1943 that succinctly portrayed the pre-war Montmartre underworld of thugs, pimps, and perverts.

His fame as an absurd dramatist rests in *Les Bonnes* (*The Maids,* 1947), where he delves into the complex problems of identity that were also the subjects of enquiry of Samuel Beckett and Eugène Ionesco. His dramas *Le Balcon* (*The Balcony*, 1956), *Les Nègres* (*The Blacks*, 1958), and *Les Paravents* (*The Screens*, 1961) are expressionistic in nature that shock the intended audience of its inherent hypocrisy and connivance. Named "Theatre of Hatred", these dramas are commentaries on social and political events that however do not inform his political inclinations.

Harold Pinter (**1930-2008**): An English playwright, who won the Nobel Prize for Literature in 2005, he studied acting for a short time at the Royal Academy of Dramatic Art in 1948 before he turned a professional actor under the name David Baron when he toured England and Ireland with various acting companies until 1959. He produced the one-act dramas *The Room* in 1957, followed by *The Dumb Waiter* in 1959, in which he introduced the element of comic menace and later, *The Birthday Party* (1958), his full-length play and *The Caretaker* (1960) launched him as a dramatist of the Theatre of the Absurd. *The Homecoming* (1965) helped establish him as the inventor of an exclusive dramatic idiom.

His plays *Landscape* (1969), *Silence* (1969), *Night* (1969), and *Old Times* (1971) did not depict physical activity on the stage, but portrayed the responses of the human mind to particular situations. Pinter's *No Man's Land* (1975), *Betrayal* (1978), *Moonlight* (1993), and *Celebration* (2000) won him accolades.

Pinter's dramas invariably featured a pair of characters whose interaction was interrupted by the arrival of a stranger that uncovered fears, jealousies, hatreds, sexual preoccupations and loneliness through strange and peculiar yet casual conversations. His distinctive colloquial "Pinteresque" speech was marked by disjointed and weird ambivalent conversation, interspersed by intermittent resonant silences. The recurrent pauses and hesitancies coupled with silences revealed not only the characters' own sense of alienation but also their difficulties in connecting with the people around them, wherein several layers of meaning remained embedded.

He wrote screenplays for *The Last Tycoon* (1976), *The French Lieutenant's Woman* (1981), *Betrayal* (1983), *The Handmaid's Tale* (1990), and *Sleuth* (2007). His verse collection *War* (2003) reflected his political stance as well as his interests in several humanitarian causes. Pinter was named a chevalier of the French Legion of Honour in 2007.

Other Dramatists of Western Europe

Apart from Beckett, Ionesco, Genet, Adamov and Pinter, the towering dramatists of the Theatre of the Absurd there were other dramatists who were influenced by them and contributed to the development of this theatre. Martin Esslin, in his *The Theatre of the Absurd*, draws together a host of dramatists who repudiated traditional drama and contributed significantly with their inimitable styles and psychological probing in the Absurd tradition.

André Pierre Gabriel Amédée Tardieu (1903-95): Tardieu is a French poet and dramatist whose short collection of plays *Theatre de Chambre* (1955) and the second volume of plays *Poems a Jouer* (1960) that were lyrical and fantastic appealed to the audience. He placed greater emphasis on the presentation of poetry on the stage through a harmonious blend of poetic language and "stage language". *Une Voix Sans Personne* (*A Voice without Anyone*) is a short play in which no characters appear.

In order to facilitate his dramatic research, Tardieu deliberately limited most of his plays to a single act and compared his short plays to musical études, which explored one technique at a time. The shortness of his plays tended to make the critics brush them off as cabaret sketches. Some critics misconstrued his art to lack seriousness or that he was unable to write longer plays.

Esslin praised veracity of Tardieu's dramatic experimentation, and referred him as "a playwright's playwright, a dedicated pioneer bent on enlarging the vocabulary of his art,". Though Esslin emphasised the importance of Tardieu's explorations as "materials for research" on which others may build, he refrained to consider them as works of art because they were "avowedly experimental" (Esslin 206-07).

The critic George Wellwarth mentioned, "Tardieu has given new life to the one-act form 'by realizing that it is inadequate for the treatment of any one theme' and by limiting himself to 'the given situation or concrete object about which he has decided to write'" (85). Wellwarth added that the one-act play should be a "self-contained entity which treats an object instead of a subject, as, for example, a situation rather than a plot (85). Tardieu also envisioned his plays as having a motif" (86).

Wellwarth insisted that that the interest of Tardieu's plays rested in the fact that that he pushed the situation beyond its logical conclusion, changing the familiar into something strange and unexpected (94). Tardieu was not interested in box-office hits and this accounted for the limited outreach of plays to a relatively small audience. This could probably be the reason why his theatre was not popular and attained little critical acclaim.

Fernando Arrabal (b. 1932): A Spanish-born French absurdist playwright, novelist, and filmmaker, Arrabal brought out his first volume of his plays in 1958, and the 1959 produced *Pique-nique en campagne* (*Picnic on the Battlefield*), an anti-war satire. However, his fame rests in *Le Cimetière des voitures (Automobile Graveyard*, 1966), a parody of the Christ story. Characters in his plays are criminals and whores. He introduced Théâtre Panique ("Panic Theatre") along with Alejandro Jodorowsky and Roland Topor in Paris in 1962. Named after the god Pan, and influenced by Antonin Artaud's Theatre of Cruelty, the group focused on chaotic and surreal performance art.

The plays *L'Architecte et l'empereur d'Assyrie* (*The Architect and the Emperor of Assyria*, 1967) and *Et ils passèrent des menottes aux fleurs* (And They Put Handcuffs on the Flowers, 1969), belonged to the Panic Theatre. In 1959, Arrabal published his novel *Baal Babylone* (*Baal Babylon*) that dealt with his nightmarish childhood in fascist Spain, and in 1970 that was later adapted into a screenplay *Viva la Muerte* (*Long Live Death*).

Wolfgang Hildesheimer (1916-91): German dramatist and essayist, Hildesheimer *wrote Spiele in dinen es dunkel wird* (*Plays in which Darken Falls*), *The Pastorale oder Die Zeit Fur Kakao* (*Pastoral or Time for Cocoa*), *Landschaft Irit Figuren* (*Landscape with Figures*), which are modern parables of life without any hope.

Norman Frederick Simpson (1919-2011): An English playwright who experimented with his stunning verbal effects manipulation of phrases and the use of illogical events to explore the absurd human condition. His significant works include *A Resounding Tinkle* (1957); *One Way Pendulum* (performed 1959), his successful work; *The Hole* (performed 1964); *The Cresta Run* (performed 1966); and *Was He Anyone?* (1973), which he turned into the novel *Harry Bleachbaker* (1976).

Tom Stoppard (original name Tomas Straussler, in full Sir Tom Stoppard) (b. 1937): A Czech-born British playwright and screenwriter whose work is marked by verbal dexterity, creative performances and structural deftness. *Rosencrantz and Guildenstern Are Dead* (1964-65) was internationally acclaimed because the drama centred around two minor characters of Shakespeare's *Hamlet*. His plays include *The Real Inspector Hound* (1968), *Jumpers* (1972), *Travesties* (1974), *Every Good Boy Deserves Favour* (1978), *Night and Day* (1978), *Undiscovered Country* (1980), and *On the Razzle* (1981). He was knighted in 1997.

- The other playwrights of the Theater of the Absurd were Dino Buzzati (1906-72), E. Zio D'Errico (1892-1972), Manuel de Pedrolo (1918-90), Gunter Grass (1927), Robert Pinget (1919-97), Boris Vian (1920-59), Max Frisch (1911-91).

The Playwrights of Eastern Europe

Slowomir Mrozek (b. 1930): Mrozek is an avant-garde dramatist. His significant works are *Policia* (*The Police*) and *The Strip Tease* (1961).

Tadeusz Rozewicz (b. 1921): Rozewicz's plays are characterised by their dream-like quality and portrayal of nightmarish events. *Kartoteka* (*The Card Index*), *The Grupa Laokoona* (*The Laocoon Group*), *Smieszny Staruzek* (*The Ridiculous Old Man*) and *Akt Rzerwany* (*The Interrupted Act*) are his prominent plays.

Václav Havel (1936-2011): The play *Zahradni Slavnost* (*The Garden Party*) is a humorous political satire which has the undertones of a Kafkesque presentation. *Vyrozumeny* (*The Memorandum*) probes the tortuous world of bureaucracy.

American Playwrights of the Theater of the Absurd

Robert Hivnor (b. 1916): His plays could be compared to Ionesco's in respect of the use of imagination and fantasy. His principal work is *Too Many Thumbs* (1947).

Neil Simon (b. 1927): Famous as an Absurd dramatist, Simon's plays deal with gender issues, infidelity, divorce, and self-interest. His major plays are *The Prisoner of Second Avenue* (1971), and *The Sunshine Boys*. The use of wit, wry humour and the mixing up of tragic and comic elements add zest to his plays.

Maria Irene Fornes (b. 1930): An avant-garde dramatist of the 1960, Fornes was influenced by Beckett. Her works are marked by Surreal elements, unconventional plot and dialogise and bizarre staging properties. Her plays include *Tango Palace, The Successful Life of 3, Promenade, Dr. Kheal, The Red Burning Light or Mission X Q3*, a surrealistic black comedy and *Aurora*, a historical fantasy.

- Other playwrights are Bruce Jay Friedman (b. 1930), Michael McClure (b. 1932), Megan Terry (b. 1932), Jack Gelber (1932-2003), Jack Richardson (1935-2011), Kenneth Brown (b. 1936), John Gaure (b. 1936), Arthur Kopit (b. 1937), Lanford Wilson (1937-2011), Israel Horovitz (b. 1939), Sam Shepard (b. 1943), David Mamet (1948) and Jean-Claude Van Itallie (b. 1936).

Conclusion

Beginning in Paris, which was considered the centre of intellectual activity during the post-war years, a radical movement in the arts and literature served as the impetus to experiment with art forms and provided opportunities to work and live nonconformist lives and agitated the world of art with newer forms of expressions. Paris was also home to receptive and reflective audiences that absorbed new ideas and demonstrated renewed interest and concern for ingenious experiments.

The Theatre of the Absurd that gained momentum and spread across the world to announce a radical approach to theatrical presentations, primarily focused on projecting a largely unintelligible world in the wake of the depressing situation after the World Wars. Essentially questioning the rationality of staging dramas in the traditional pattern when the world was in utter chaos, the absurd dramas used minimal stage properties and dramatic devices. Thereby, they inquired into the efficacy of logical thought, sensibility and reasoning in dramaturgy. The dramatists of the Theatre of the Absurd belonged to different parts of the world and they projected the irrational world in their own unique ways; nevertheless, they were part of a theatrical initiative and not a school of thought.

Glossary

étude : a short musical composition, typically for one instrument, designed to improve the technique employed or demonstrate the skill of the player.

chevalier : knight; a member of certain orders of knighthood or of modern French orders such as the Legion of Honour.

Legion of Honour : premier order of the French republic, created by Napoleon Bonaparte, then first consul, on May 19, 1802, as a general military and civil order of merit conferred without regard to birth or religion provided that anyone admitted swears to uphold liberty and equality.

References

Abrams, M.H. and Geoffrey Galt Harpham. *A Glossary of Literary Terms*. 11th ed. Cengage, 2015.

Abel, Lionel. *Metatheatre: A New View of Dramatic Form*. Hill and Wang, 1963.

——. *Tragedy and Metatheatre: Essays on Dramatic Form*. Holmes Meier Publishers, 2003.

Bigsby, Christopher. *Modern American Drama*. Cambridge UP, 2000.

Brockett, G. Oscar, and Franklin J. Hildy. *History of the Theatre*. 10th edition. Pearson Education Limited, 2013.

Camus, Albert. *Le Mythe de Sisyphe*. Gallimard, 1942.

Crawford, Jerry L., Catherine Hurst, and Michael Lugering. *Acting in Person and in Style*. 5th edition. Waveland Press, 2010.

Esslin, Martin. Introduction. "The Absurdity of the Absurd." *The Theatre of the Absurd*. The Overlook P, 1973.

Gascoigne, Bamber. *Twentieth-Century Drama*. Hutchinson and Co., 1974.

Meserve, Walter. *An Outline History of American Drama*. Adams and Co., 1965.

Styan, J.L. *Modern Drama in Theory and Practice: Volume 2, Symbolism, Surrealism and the Absurd*. Cambridge UP, 2013.

Theatre of the Absurd. https://www.britannica.com/art/Theatre-of-the-Absurd

https://www.oxfordreference.com/view/10.1093/oi/authority.20110803095345289

https://www.bl.uk/20th-century-literature/articles/nonsense-talk-theatre-of-the-absurd

https://books.google.co.in/books/about/The_Theatre_of_the_Absurd.html?id=J7iQNBOp7Q4C&redir_esc=y

Chapter 20

Samuel Beckett, the Dramatist

Introduction

Complexities of the modern age, augmented by scientific advancements, in conjunction with the literary, artistic and philosophical writings were succinctly portrayed not only in works of art but also in treatises. The period during the First World War witnessed technological advancements, initiated by the use of sophisticated weaponry. Moreover, the psychological theories of Sigmund Freud (1856-1939), the French philosopher Henri Bergson's (1859-1941) writings on time as well as the Swiss linguist Ferdinand de Saussure's (1857-1913) treatise on linguistics gained popularity. Through innovative ways, writings of the French novelist Marcel Proust (1871-1922) and the Irish novelist James Joyce (1882-1941) ushered a series of experimental techniques that transformed literature forever.

While the Irish theatre in Dublin was imbued with the Gaelic spirit, the European theatre was infused by theatrical innovativeness and intellectual unconventionalism. The Irish nationalist dramas were staged at The Abbey Theatre, the centre for Irish-nationalist drama that staged the works of Lady Gregory (1852-1932), Sean O'Casey (1880-1964), Lennox Robinson (1886-1958), and Denis Johnston (1901-84) to name a few. The works of the Italian dramatist Luigi Pirandello (1897-1936) were staged at The Gate Theatre. The Queens Theatre presented melodramas and the Theatre Royal and the Olympia Theatre primarily played popular entertainment shows known as vaudeville shows.

Nevertheless, novel ideas in art and literature that were widely designated as Modernism where extensive creativity took place between the twenties and the thirties nurtured artistic interests of several artists in and around Paris during the early twentieth century. The spirit of the age inculcated radical changes in every sphere of human influence throughout Europe.

Early Influences on Samuel Beckett

Samuel Barclay Beckett (1906-89) took his graduate and master's degrees from Trinity College, Dublin in Modern European Languages. He studied Italian and French languages and developed interest for theatre only during the ultimate years in the university. He was influenced by realistic comedies of the Irish dramatist O'Casey. However, his interest for experiments in form rather than content of the literature and art of the modern period, which were pronouncedly anti-realist influenced his dramatic creativity. The silent movies of the English comic actor Charlie Chaplin (1889-1977), the Laurel and Hardy episodes, and the laughter provoked by O'Casey's drama fascinated him.

At Trinity College, he read the French philosopher René Descartes (1596-1650), the Italian poet and philosopher Dante Alighieri, modern French poets Arthur Rimbaud (1854-91), Charles Baudelaire (1821-67), and Guillaume Apollinaire (1818-1918). A bachelor's degree with honours earned him a two-year fellowship to the prominent Ecole Normale Supérieure, the distinguished and esteemed graduate school in Paris, France.

The home of *avant-garde* in art and literature, and considered the intellectual and cultural capital of Europe during that time, Paris was swarmed by writers, artists and intellectuals in search of artistic stimulation and freedom of expression. Beckett acquainted several writers, artists and critics, and became a close associate of James Joyce. He read European philosophy and wrote fiction, poetry and criticism. During that time, his essays on Joyce and Proust were published.

Principal Works of Beckett

Beckett's return to Dublin 1930, and his subsequent posting as a teacher was however unstimulating and insufficient for nurturing his interests or talents. In 1930, he published his volume of poems *Whoroscope* based on the French philosopher René Descartes. The novel *Dream of Fair to Middling Women,* written in the mid-1930s was published only in 1992. He left for Ireland after resigning his job and later travelled across London, Paris and Germany.

Though he was psychologically disturbed and financially unsound, he continued to write. He brought out the collection of ten short stories *More Pricks Than Kicks* in 1934, which narrated the adventures of Belacqua Shuah, the protagonist, in and around Dublin. In 1935, he published the collection of poems *Echo's Bones,* and his first successful *avant-garde* novel *Murphy,* in English was brought out in 1938. By that time, Beckett had decided to settle down in Paris and write significantly.

The political situation in Europe meanwhile worsened because of Hitler's rise to power in Germany, Mussolini's in Italy, the Spanish Civil War and the impending World War; albeit the repercussions of the First World War and the Great Depression had not yet abated. While most writers held discussions and wrote and published articles on the gravity of the political situation in the world especially Europe, Beckett remained uncommitted and apolitical. He was of the opinion that "artists had no business concerning themselves with anything but art, and politics—an anathema for him—was then least of his concerns" (Bair 133). He was more interested in exposing the sufferings and inner experiences of the people who remained aloof from the society or culture and those who were neither a part of nor taken in by the mainstream culture.

However, when Germany captured Paris in 1940, he joined a clandestine resistance group, and when activities of the alliance were discovered by the Gestapo, he escaped to a mountain village called Roussillon, one of the unoccupied regions of France and took to farming for two and a half years. His next novel *Watt,* in English was written during this time but it was published only in 1953. The novel described the experiences of the protagonist amidst uncertainties and turbulence.

He returned to Paris after Germany's surrender in 1945 and wrote extensively for almost four years, the period being the most productive one. He wrote the four novellas *The End, First Love, The Calmative* and *The Expelled* (1945); the first post-war novel *Mercier and Camier* (1946 onwards), the first in French; the novel trilogy, *Molloy* (1951), *Malone Dies* (1951) and *The Unnamable* (1953); the two, three-act plays *Eleutheria* (1947) and *Waiting for Godot* (1952); several poems *Stories and Texts for Nothing*, a collection of stories that included the three short stories "The Expelled," "The Calmative," and "The End" (1946); the thirteen short prose pieces titled "Texts for Nothing" (1950-52); the short mime plays *Act without Words—Parts I and II* (1957/1960) and the other full-length plays *Endgame* (1957), and *Krapp's Last Tape* (1958).

Beckett's radio plays that were smaller did not gain popularity because they were neither staged nor published in time. *All That Fall,* his first published play in English was broadcast by the BBC in 1957; *Embers* in 1959*; Words and Music* in 1962; and *Cascando*, written in French and produced by RTF in Paris in 1964 was later translated into English by Beckett. He wrote most of these plays in French and then translated them into English. Beckett's English version of *Radio 1* was published in *Ends and Odds* in 1977. Its companion piece in the English collection *Radio 2* was broadcast by the BBC as *Rough for Radio* in 1976.

A recipient of the Nobel Prize for Literature in 1969, select archival and epistolary materials written by Beckett were published in *Dear Mr. Beckett: Letters from the Publisher, the Samuel Beckett File* (2016), in which Beckett's discussions about acting with his long-time director Alan Schneider, opinions by Susan Sontag, interviews with Eugene Ionesco and a few other dramatists of the Absurd Theatre and some controversies regarding the Grove Press are elucidated.

Beckett's Concerns in Drama

Beckett's writings not only allude to several literary sources but also philosophy and theology. His writings bear the influence of Dante, Descarte, Arnold Geulinex (1624-69), the Belgian philosopher of the 17th century, and the follower of Descarte, and James Joyce. Beckett's works portray man who is pushed into extreme circumstances that are part of realities of existence.

Beckett considers social, political and economic successes appendages of survival that are intimately related to the anguish of the human condition because there could be no answer to whether human beings do attain ultimate happiness once their objectives are fulfilled.

Beckett ponders over fundamental questions on the nature of the self, man's identity, the nature of existence of man in a world that he did not ask for, and the notion of individual subjectivity. For instance, in *Waiting for Godot*, the two individuals do not understand why they exist. Being in a world, which is meaningless and worthless is precisely absurd and hence the presence of a solitary tree on an empty stage could point to the fact that they await someone—probably the only reason why they are here. They were unsure whether Godot, who they seem to be waiting for, ever exists or has even given them such an appointment.

Beckett's preoccupation with the mystery and despair of the human condition is closely associated with his call to liberate the audience from viewing the trivialities of man's pursuit, which he considers ludicrous and senseless. His dramas incite hilarity at human frailties and futile ambitions and such portrayals reveal his intention to effect a cathartic release in an atmosphere that is rather dismal. He uses the stage to the accompaniment of sound, music and speech to portray adeptly, essentialities of his techniques to delve into his characters that expose the situation of every man.

The Principal Works of Samuel Beckett

Novels

- *Murphy*–1938
- *Watt*–1953
- *Molloy*–1951
- *Malone Dies*–1951
- *The Unnamable*–1953
- *Wow It Is*–1961

Drama

- *Waiting for Godot*–1952
- *Endgame*–1957

While Vladimir ponders whether he has met Pozzo and Lucky earlier, Estragon fails to recall having met them. A boy enters with the message that Mr. Godot "won't come this evening but surely tomorrow." He introduces himself as a person who herds Mr. Godot's goats and that his master is kind to him, but beats his brother, who is a shepherd. Vladimir asks the Boy to tell Mr. Godot that he has seen them.

As soon as the boy leaves, it gets dark and the moon rises. Estragon removes his boots and places them at the corner of the stage. Vladimir tries to lead him away, but Estragon contemplates suicide, and later sits on the mound revealing that it would be better if they parted ways. Vladimir agrees, but neither of them moves.

Act 2

It is the next day, and the scene is the same place at the same time as the previous day. The tree has sprouted a few leaves. Vladimir, frustrated walks about the stage and pauses to sing a song. Estragon has been beaten and he enters the stage dishevelled and barefoot. They embrace each other and pass time in speech because they cannot remain quiet. They discuss how to develop dialogue by contradicting and questioning each other.

Though Vladimir discusses incidents of the previous day, Estragon cannot recall anything until he is prompted. To prove his statements, he pulls up Estragon's trousers and shows him the wound from Lucky's kick and points out Estragon's boots, but Estragon denies that they belong to him. As Estragon falls asleep, Vladimir sings him a lullaby and wraps his coat around him. Though Estragon is wakes up disturbed after a nightmare, Vladimir refuses to listen to him.

A comic scene of exchange of hats between them continues with Vladimir in Lucky's hat and Estragon on his own. Vladimir tries to entertain Estragon by acting as Lucky and asks him to imitate Pozzo. Vladimir begins to dance and Estragon goes out, but returns announcing the arrival of Pozzo and Lucky. He darts to the other side of the stage, but returns as her feels they are approaching from that side too. Both of them maintain watch at either side of the stage, but nobody arrives. They engage in physical exercise, first hopping then standing on one leg, imitating the tree.

Pozzo and Lucky enter, with Lucky tied to a smaller rope and held by Pozzo, who is blind now. Lucky stops when he sees Vladimir and Estragon and Pozzo bumps into Lucky and they both fall over and lie helpless. The efforts Estragon try to help Pozzo and Lucky rise up leads to Estragon tripping over Vladimir, who had earlier fallen on the ground. Pozzo, struck by Vladimir crawls away. Estragon calls out to Pozzo and finding that he answers when called Abel and Cain, presumes, "He's all humanity".

Vladimir and Estragon get up without difficulty after this, but Pozzo falls over as soon as he is released and the two support him between them. While Vladimir and Estragon question about his blindness, Pozzo enquires about the day and time. He asks Estragon whether Lucky is hurt, suggesting that he should first tug at the rope that holds Lucky and then kick him if he does not respond. Estragon confirms that Lucky still breathes and kicks him hard till his foot huts. He goes to the mound to remove his boot, but falls asleep.

Vladimir recounts the previous day's events to Pozzo, who however fails to recall their meeting and asks Lucky to prepare for their departure. When Vladimir asks Lucky to sing a song for them before they depart, Pozzo replies that he is dumb. Vladimir is unable to believe what Pozzo has just revealed to him, but Pozzo, in a brief harangue against time, contrasts the brief hope of life and the long night of eternity. Pozzo and Lucky leave the stage, but a sound confirms that they have fallen down.

Vladimir wakes up Estragon, who continues to have problems with his boots. Vladimir comments that most people consider the nature of reality and they pass through life as though in a state of sleep, never being able to come to terms with the truth of things. The boy enters and announces that this is his first visit. He assures them that Mr. Godot would definitely visit them the next day. He mentions that Mr. Godot has no occupation and he does nothing. The boy is unable to recognise them and runs out to avoid Vladimir who leaps at him.

The sun sets and the moon rises. Estragon places his boots at the centre of the stage. Though both men decide to leave, Vladimir points out that they have to return the next day because Godot has promised to come. They have no rope and look at the tree in despair. Estragon unties the cord supporting his trousers, which fall down. They test the strength of the rope that breaks and the two men fall down. They resolve to bring a strong rope the next day and point out that if Godot does not arrive to save them, they can hang themselves. He tells Estragon to pull on his trousers and suggest they leave but they do not move.

Conclusion

Samuel Beckett is one of the most influential dramatists of the Theatre of the Absurd. His contribution to drama is phenomenal and he has been able to exert pronounced influence on other writers and artists with his unique style of theatrical presentations. In response to an age that grapples with science and religion, beliefs and values, opposes religious faith, and experiences the loss of faith in humanity, Beckett captures the inherent anguish in stage performances that are absurd, illogical and apparently irrational themselves. The effort of the artist is to exploit a medium of entertainment to reach out to the masses and announce a radical move to project the unpredictability of the human condition in a way that conjoins comedy and tragedy that intends to shock the audience and wake them up to respond to the enactment on stage.

Theatrical innovativeness is in tandem with the need to question traditional assumptions of reality, truth, time and space and use the theatre to probe the indefiniteness of all those precepts thought to be definite and unchanging. Beckett's theatre is the response of an intellectual to the growing apprehensions of a future that would direct and elicit responses from the general public regarding their perceptions of the transforming world under the given circumstances.

Rather than stand as a mere observer, Beckett intends to raise consciousness among everybody to realise the immensity of the situation of man in the wake of the World Wars. His ingenuity lies in his ability to unite theatricality with the actuality of human experiences thereby making the stage a world with the entire humanity as the characters.

Glossary

conjunction	:	combination
esteemed	:	venerated
anathema	:	loathing
clandestine	:	secret
mound	:	a round mass that projects above a surface.
apprehension	:	anxiety
Gestapo	:	The German state secret police that was organised in 1933 during the Nazi regime, which was notorious for its brutal methods and operations.

References

Bair, Deirdre. *Samuel Beckett: A Biography*. Jonathan Cape, 1978.

Bloom, Harold, editor. *Samuel Beckett: Modern Critical Views*. Chelsea, 1985.

Brockett, G. Oscar and Franklin J. Hildy. *History of the Theatre*. 10th edition. Pearson Education Limited, 2013.

Crawford, Jerry L., Catherine Hurst, and Michael Lugering. *Acting in Person and in Style*. 5th Edition. Waveland P, 2010.

Fletcher, John. *Samuel Beckett's Art*. Chatto and Windus, 1967.

Kenner, Hugh. *A Reader's Guide to Samuel Beckett*. Farrar, Straus and Giroux, 1973.

McMullan, Anna. *Theatre on Trial: Samuel Beckett's Later Drama*. Routledge, 1993.

Robinson, Jeremy. *Samuel Beckett Goes into the Silence*. Kidderminster. Crescent Moon, 1992.

Styan, J.L. *Modern Drama in Theory and Practice: Volume 2, Symbolism, Surrealism and the Absurd*. Cambridge UP, 2013.

Waiting for Godot. https://edisciplinas.usp.br/pluginfile.php/2335139/mod_resource/content/1/WAITING%20FOR%20GODOT.pdf

https://books.google.co.in/books/about/Waiting_for_Godot_Samuel_Beckett_New_Edi.html?id=nsHSXV3LWF8C&redir_esc=y

Chapter 21

Waiting for Godot: Act One

Act One

It is evening time at a country road near a tree. Estragon is seen sitting on a mound, struggling to take off his boots because he is in pain and Vladimir enters examining his hat. Estragon says, "Nothing to be done." When Vladimir enquires where Estragon had spent the previous night, he says, "In a ditch". Estragon also mentions that he had been beaten. Vladimir understands that Estragon is dependent on him and tells him that without his company, Estragon would be "nothing more than a little heap of bones".

The conversation shifts to not being able to jump from the Eiffel Tower in Paris "in the nineties" when they were more presentable. Now they appear too dishevelled to be admitted to the tower. Vladimir has prostate trouble, which is the reason for his awkward gait and frequent exits to pass water. Vladimir takes off his hat three times, peers suspiciously into it and puts them on again. Now, Vladimir mentions: "Nothing to be done." This sentence recurs throughout the drama at various instances and it is ominous because it is associated with the word "appalled," or as Vladimir calls it, "AP-PALLED." Estragon, meanwhile, takes his boot off and peers inside it, unable to find out why it had pained him.

While Estragon is concerned about the immediate, practical problems, Vladimir laments the general nature of their sufferings by recalling their better days. Estragon's foot hurts, but Vladimir is concerned about a different kind of suffering. Vladimir's thoughts shift to the Biblical concept of "Hope deferred maketh the something sick...", but he is unable to complete the proverb. The proverb fits Vladimir and Estragon's condition perfectly since they are sick at heart and their hopes of meeting Godot are forever deferred and hence their desires are never fulfilled.

Their suffering and lack of hope turn Vladimir's thoughts to the suffering of the two thieves on the cross and their lack of hope. Vladimir recalls the Old Testament about hope and the then he turns to the New Testament and the chances of hope revealed in the story of Christ and the two thieves on the cross. Just as there were two thieves now there are two men without any hope, and as one of the thieves was saved, there could be hope for either of the two men if they repent, but there is nothing to repent of, except being born.

Vladimir gives a painful laugh when Estragon mentions about repentance; however, he stifles his laughter and reminds Estragon that "one daren't even laugh any more"; one may "merely smile." Their inability to laugh indicates the graveness of their condition, the anguish, and their feeling of insecurity, which render their physical ailments insignificant. Their suffering and the appalling human predicament make Vladimir comment that there is "Nothing to be done."

Vladimir enquires whether Estragon has heard about the Gospels by Estragon says that he remembers maps of the Holy Land that were coloured and looked pretty. Estragon complains about his swollen foot and mentions about two thieves crucified along with Christ, where one was saved and the other, damned. Their conversation ends with Estragon's observation that people are "bloody, ignorant apes" because he fails to understand what they should repent about, who the Saviour is, what are they saved from, why do Gospel narratives of the scene of the Cross have different versions and what is the content of the Bible.

Vladimir also insists that Estragon would not go far if they parted. Estragon repeatedly tells Vladimir that he wants to leave the place but Vladimir reminds him that they cannot leave because they are here to meet Godot by the tree; however, they doubt whether they have arrived at the right spot on the appointed day. They are uncertain whether they had met her the previous day and undecided about the day of the week. Frustrated, they remain silent.

The silence is eerie, but it breaks when Estragon suddenly wakes up in panic over a nightmare. When Estragon tries to narrate his dream, Vladimir says that he is disinterested in listening to his friend's "private nightmares". Estragon decides to pass the time by telling a joke, but he does not complete the narration because Vladimir gets annoyed. Realising the futility of their conversation, Estragon decides to part ways, but Vladimir assures him that he would not be able to go far. They quarrel but Estragon persuades Vladimir not to leave him and they reconcile. Estragon asks Vladimir to embrace him, and recoils from the hug because Vladimir stinks of garlic. This technique is characteristic of Beckett's method of destroying man's affectations by employing the absurd and the vulgar aspects to control the action of the play.

Undecided on what is to be done next while waiting, Estragon suggests hanging themselves from the tree, since they would at least get sexually excited. However, the problem is that if Vladimir, the heavier of the two, would be the first to attempt, and if the branch does not break, then Estragon can follow him. Instead, if Estragon, the lighter of the two tries out and then Vladimir and the branch gives way, then Vladimir would be left all alone. Beckett points out that man's rational thinking could end in complexities and difficulties. Hence, they decide to "wait and see what [Godot] says."

Estragon enquires whether they are tied down to Godot. Vladimir replies that they are not, at the moment. Though Vladimir rejects the idea that they are tied down to Godot, they are tied down to the act of waiting, and nonetheless to Godot. They wonder what Godot might offer them and just what they have asked from Godot. Godot's reply was vague. They ponder whether Godot could be thinking over their matter, discussing with friends, correspondents, the banks and others. Their discussion indicates that they know little about Godot.

Getting tired of waiting, Estragon gets hungry, and Vladimir gives him a turnip, mistaking it for a carrot, and finally finds him a carrot. When Estragon mentions that the carrot that looks funny and gets worse as it is eaten, Vladimir suggests that it's just the opposite for him. Estragon repeats, "Nothing to be done." Their purposeless discussion is interrupted by a loud and painful shriek. Both are startled, and Estragon drops the carrot. They rush out together but Estragon returns to pick up the carrot, stuffs it in his pocket and runs away, then again returns to collect his boot and joins Vladimir. They huddle close, "away from the menace" and wait and watch what's approaching them.

A cry heard offstage announces the arrival of Pozzo and Lucky. Lucky carries a heavy bag, a folding stool, a picnic basket and greatcoat. He is held by a long rope by Pozzo, who also has a whip in his hand. Though Lucky crosses the stage, Pozzo, who notices the two men stops abruptly, and Lucky falls down as the rope tightens. Estragon thinks Pozzo is Godot and inquires his identity. Pozzo claims that they are awaiting Godot on his land and pulls at the rope making Lucky enter backwards. Lucky takes great effort in helping Pozzo put on his coat, places the stool down and hands over the picnic basket to Pozzo. Pozzo helps himself with some chicken and wine and makes Lucky take back the basket and stand away from him.

While Pozzo eats, Vladimir and Estragon circle about Lucky, who slumps often until the bag and the basket he has been holding for quite some time touch the ground. They notice a sore on his neck, where the rope has caused him irritation. When Vladimir and Estragon question Lucky, Pozzo asks them to leave him alone, eventually he makes demands on Lucky. Pozzo lights his pipe after eating and Estragon craves for the chicken bones and since Lucky does not oppose verbally, Pozzo allows Estragon take them.

Vladimir comments that Pozzo's treatment of Lucky is "a scandal". Pozzo, however is disinterested in the remark and rises to leave but decides to smoke a pipe and extend the conversation. To refrain from changing his mind, he makes Lucky move the stool, then sits on the stool and fills his pipe. Though Vladimir intends to leave, Pozzo insists to know about Godot who is not present. Estragon, meanwhile is curious to know why Lucky carries the luggage and does not put it down. Pozzo sprays his throat and after forgetting the question asked to him, manages to reply that Lucky hopes to impress him by offering his services so that Pozzo would not sell him at the fair. Pozzo remarks that "the best thing" to do with "such creatures" like Lucky is to kill them and Lucky weeps when his master says so.

Estragon, out of pity for the poor Lucky takes out Pozzo's handkerchief to wipe Lucky's tears, and in return Lucky kicks him at his leg so forcefully that it begins to bleed. Pozzo mentions that the pain has now been transferred to Estragon and he shifts the conversation to his association with Lucky. He mentions that he has known Lucky for nearly sixty years and he has been able to learn "beautiful things" from him. He compliments his youthful appearance that is in contrast to Lucky's. He asks Lucky to take off his hat and expose his long white hair and takes his hat off to reveal his own bald head. Vladimir reprimands Pozzo for being willing to dismiss from service "such an old and faithful servant". When Pozzo replies that he cannot put up with Lucky's awful behaviour, Vladimir instantaneously finds fault with Lucky for being cruel to "Such a good master!" Pozzo then discloses that that there is no truth in whatever he has said no far.

Pozzo and Estragon watch Vladimir go out to pass water and returns quite agitated, which is revealed when he kicks over a stool, but soon he regains his composure. Though Pozzo persuades Estragon to request Vladimir to sit down, he takes his watch and announces that it is time for him to depart. He offers to inform the men about twilight in "these parts" before leaving. While Vladimir fiddles with his hat and Estragon with his boot, Lucky falls asleep. Pozzo cracks his whip loudly and sits down to make his speech about the sky.

Pozzo concludes his speech and considers it eloquent. He asks Vladimir and Estragon to shower praise for his effort and offers to help them in every way in return. When Estragon asks for money, Pozzo ignores the request. Pozzo decides that Lucky would entertain them choosing among dancing, singing, reciting or thinking and Estragon chooses dancing and thinking. Lucky dances twice for a short time. His dance is replete with brisk movements, and it includes several nuanced movements and gestures that reflect pain, agony, strain and confusion. For this reason, the dance is diversely interpreted as "The scapegoat Agony", "The Hard Stool", and "The Net" by the onlookers. When Estragon imitates him, he falls over. Lucky is unable to carry his baggage and Pozzo struggles to think. The three men except Lucky take off their hats so that they can concentrate and Estragon simultaneously enquires why Lucky stands with the baggage. Vladimir assures him that Pozzo has answered the question and Lucky has put the luggage down to entertain them with his dance.

When Vladimir mentions that Lucky has not yet entertained them with his thoughts, Pozzo says that Lucky must put on his hat. Vladimir puts Lucky's hat on his head and Pozzo asks them to move back. He suddenly jerks Lucky's rope and asks him to think. When Lucky begins to dance instead, Pozzo pulls at the rope again and Lucky begins his rather lengthy speech. Pozzo interrupts him and makes him face the auditorium before continuing. He begins by referring to an uncaring God whose existence is doubtful. Then he shifts his observation to man who wastes his time in pining. After this, he talks about the earth that seems to be engulfed "in the great cold the great dark". Lucky's speech mocks at logical and scholarly discussions. The speech repudiates any sense of rationality in the world and this is done by subverting the logical pattern of language itself.

Hugh Kenner comments that by deriding belief in God, faith in learning and the development, the drama foregrounds the complete breakdown of Western intellectual history of several centuries (qtd. in Samuel 67). Lucky thinks aloud, in a lengthy outburst that completely frustrates the three men. In response to the speech that begins with a few sensible utterances it gradually degenerates into absolute gibberish. Though Vladimir and Estragon initially take interest, they make attempts to stop the nonsense but Pozzo remains unaffected. Utterly famished, the three men urge Lucky to stop, but he doesn't until they pounce on him to silence him and Vladimir removes his hat, and Lucky falls down.

While Vladimir peers inside Lucky's hat, Pozzo snatches it from him and tramples it under his feet. Vladimir and Estragon help Lucky to his feet, but he falls over as soon as they leave their hold on him. They raise him up and steadies him between them. Pozzo brings the bag and the basket to Lucky who drops them down first and later manages to hold on to them. Lucky stands firm after Vladimir and Estragon leave their hold on him. Pozzo cracks his whip and as he makes his way out, he notices that he has lost his watch. Vladimir and Estragon listen to his stomach in an attempt to locate the watch, but it is not found. Lucky stumbles offstage because Pozzo suddenly stops to retrieve the stool that has been left behind. Vladimir hands Pozzo the stool, which he throws at Lucky, and the two men depart.

Vladimir mentions that the arrival of Pozzo and Lucky and their antics had helped pass time, which now seems stagnant and anguishing. He recalls meeting them some time in the past, but Estragon does not. While Vladimir is doubtful about the precision of his memory, Estragon complains about his feet. A voice is heard offstage and a boy enters with a message from Mr. Godot. On Vladimir's insistence, the boy admits that has been waiting for some time, but was hesitant because he was afraid of Pozzo and his whip. Estragon, however does not believe the boy's statements and shakes him. He goes to the mound and begins to remove his boots.

Vladimir seems to recognise the boy, who says that he has never seen either men before. His conveys the message that Mr. Godot will come tomorrow and he herds Mr. Godot's goats. He discloses that his master is kind to him, but beats his brother, the shepherd. The boy is instructed to tell Mr. Godot that he has seen them and the boy runs off.

The stage is dimly lit, it is night and the moon rises. Estragon places his boots at the edge of the stage. When Vladimir asserts that he cannot move about barefoot, Estragon replies that Christ did. Vladimir mentions that things are going to be better for them because Godot will definitely turn up the next day and tries to lead Estragon away. Estragon contemplates hanging from the tree. He recalls an earlier suicide attempt, when he threw himself into the river Rhône, and Vladimir rescued him.

Though Vladimir wishes to leave, Estragon goes to the mound and considers it would be better to separate. He says: "We weren't made for the same road." However, he does not receive any answer to this. Vladimir sits beside Estragon and agrees to the suggestion of parting ways. Estragon however says it is too late to do so and proposes that they leave. Vladimir agrees but neither moves and the curtain falls.

Analysis

The master-slave relationship between Pozzo and Lucky is apparent and this could connote the imperial notion of slavery, which is just a vague supposition. The relationship between Pozzo and Lucky is subject to Pozzo's desire to control and command and Lucky's to be servile and dominated upon. In fact, Pozzo mentions that their roles could be reversed. It could be assessed that the circus-like performance with Pozzo as the ringmaster cracking his whip contributes to the comic action and seemingly nonsensical dialogues rendered by Vladimir and Estragon supplement the comedy. However, the circus could be regarded a metaphor of life because whatever is staged by the circus troop is an imitation of life with its ephemeral excitement, daring and accomplishment.

Vladimir is compassionate to Lucky and admonishes Pozzo for mistreating his servant; however, he quickly changes his mind after Pozzo mentions that he cannot bear with Lucky anymore and when Lucky behaves rudely, Vladimir reproaches him for mistreating his master for several years. It could be deciphered that Vladimir and Estragon represent humanity. The comparison of Estragon to Adam implies that he may represent all of mankind and the association of Estragon and Adam could relate to the idea of Godot as God. The arrival of Pozzo and Lucky is intended to entertain the two men, who seem to have lost sense of time, but their departure makes them gloomier. While Pozzo and Lucky are able to move, the two men cannot. They are forced to wait for Godot who sends the message that he would arrive the following day.

Estragon compares himself to Christ when he decides to go barefoot. When Vladimir tells him not to compare himself to

Christ, Estragon responds, "all my life I've compared myself to him." Estragon notices that God walked barefoot but he had the comfort of the warm climate. God's suffering ended quickly because he was crucified soon. Man's condition, in contrast is a process that extends and the long wait never seems to end. Estragon recalls an earlier attempt to end his life by jumping into the Rhône only to be "fished" out of the water by Vladimir. This event could be considered an act of baptism, which symbolises cleansing and renewal. This means that the old is discarded and a new man emerges to a fresh beginning. However, for Estragon these do not happen because he is "fished" put of water and the experience is not at all glorious or exalted in true religious terms. Vladimir asserts that the incident is "dead and buried" and there can be no possibility of restitution. The hopeless situation is accompanied by the cold and dark night that Vladimir complains of.

Pozzo's lyrical tirade about the night concludes on a portentous note. He foresees a deceptive gentle evening that hides a black and ill-omened night that will suddenly burst forth. He ends his speech by regarding the earth a bitch and almost immediately asks Vladimir and Estragon what they think about his speech. Lucky's long speech that appears under the heading DIALOGUE is a crude imitation of common intellectual exchanges. The nonsensical elements in the speech do not obscure the underlying coherent, meaningful statements that are observations about life. The words *aphasia, athambia,* and *apathia* are seneseless as far as the context is considered. The latin term *qua* is a common term in academic discussions on theology, but when it is repeated, it is reduced to a quacking sound that ends with a tinge of sarcasm. Lucky stumbles over the word *academy* and this leads to the repetition of *caca,* the French equivalent for *excrement.* Moreover, the names Fartov, Belcher, Cunard and Testew are fictitious. Though the entire Pozzo-Lucky episode is insignificant for Vladimir and Estragon, their presence has only enabled the time to pass quickly.

It could be inferred by Vladimir's statement that he pretended not to recognise Pozzo and Lucky indicates that he has met them before. This suggests that the incidents of this act may have occurred sometime earlier, which is beyond the reference of the drama. This situation is similar to Vladimir's question to the boy whether he has seen them previously, suggesting that they may have been waiting for Godot in the near past and obviously that Godot has promised to meet them the next day. All this points out that the events have been repeating without a solution.

The end of the act reiterates their hopeless condition. Though they intend to move apart, they end up motionless. Their indecisiveness and the inability to act imply that they are ineffective to determine their life and they heavily depend on some external force else to act on their behalf.

Beckett presents a contrast between Vladimir and Estragon. While Vladimir is dissatisfied with his hat, Estragon is displeased with his boots. This suggests that Vladimir is drawn to things of the mind and Estragon, with the body. The men cannot live without each other, but Estragon is more dependent on Vladimir for almost all the minute, everyday things. Estragon needs Vladimir to help him with his boot. From their exchanges, it is quite clear that the characters are interchangeable and the textual repetition vouchsafes the repetitiveness of life is general as enacted by the two men.

Estragon is more elemental and earthier of the two. He is concerned with mundane aspects such as his feet, his books and his stomach. He is less intelligent because he is unable to follow Vladimir's discussions on religion. Estragon is ignorant about the story of the two thieves on the Cross. He is unable to reason out the innumerable interpretations of the Gospels and disagreements of the Gospels. He dismisses the intellectual discourse as "that's all there is to it".

Estragon is rather impatient and he is continually reminded that they must wait for Godot. His frequent references to part ways only sees him getting closer to Vladimir. He is easily tired of such an existence and Vladimir consoles him throughout. Vladimir, a complete foil to Estragon is more philosophically inclined and initiates serious discussions on God and religion. He is more decisive and has excellent memory. The reference to suffering is significant because the two men suffer contrasting physical disabilities. While Estragon as a sore foot that hurts him, Vladimir suffers prostate.

The reference to the nightmares by Estragon symbolise the innumerable fears latent in their alienated condition and Vladimir's refusal to listen to Estragon's descriptions suggests that he would rather have the undisclosed fears remain covert than suffer once they are revealed.

The reference to the two thieves raises the question of textual uncertainty because out of four interpretations, only one seems to be acceptable. Estragon is bewildered over discussions on the Bible, the Saviour and salvation. The fact that there is nothing to be done is repeated to show how bored they are with life, not that they have no purpose in life, but the person Godot, who they are waiting for doesn't turn up, and the act of waiting for Godot becomes a problem. Nevertheless, the confrontation of this problem is significant in the drama.

The men can neither part ways nor leave each other because they are both tied down to the act of waiting for Godot. The relationship of Vladimir and Estragon with Godot is unclear. They are uncertain about Godot's whereabouts, his personal belongings, and his position in society. To make matters worse, they are unsure whether they are supposed to meet Godot, let alone the time and the place. They are uncertain about the day of the week, and whether they had met him earlier; however, they are confident that they were to meet by a tree, but it could be either a bush or a dead tree. The tree could symbolise the cross, the hanging tree or the renewal of the season, but it is definitely not a sign of hope. Completely frustrated, they resign themselves to waiting.

The men depend on Godot to tell them about their needs. Discussions on finance and monetary benefits question the nature of relationship of God and man. If Godot or God can enter into a business contract with anybody, then why does he not appear. If Godot has to consult with the outside sources before taking a decision for them, then Vladimir and Estragon are in a precarious situation. They represent modern man who maintains a relationship with Godot or God and hence they are in a perilous situation.

Conclusion

People were disillusioned after the World Wars and the mood of anguish was appropriately captured by the Theatre of the Absurd. Beckett presents the conflict of modern man, who is desperate to make sense of his actions in a world that appears unintelligible and precarious in the drama *Waiting for Godot*. The introductory scene is an empty stage with Vladimir and Estragon that represent humanity at large are put in a situation they cannot cope up with or respond meaningfully and there is neither consolation nor amelioration to their pathetic condition. They seem to wait for Godot, who presumably could resolve their predicament, but have neither seen nor met him earlier, and they are unsure about his existence. This is the reason why the wait is agonising. The two men engage in meaningless exchanges either related to their physical deformities or their desire to leave the place; however, they cannot for they are tied down to the act of waiting for Godot. They are left clueless about the visit of Godot and their condition never seems to change. Where they would go or what they would do is unclear.

Though the entrance of the master-slave duo, Pozzo and Lucky seem to momentarily digress the men from their desolateness, the entire action rendered by Pozzo and Lucky caricature life and institutions built by man. Pozzo dons the role of the master that holds the tether of the rope tied around Lucky's neck and carries a whip to announce his status. Lucky is the servant who willingly obeys Pozzo and remains servile; however, he does bring out his unruly nature when he hurts Estragon, who tries to console him when Pozzo says that he intends to sell Lucky at the fair. Pozzo's speech on the dark night that would cast a gloom in the world forebodes a ruthless world given the circumstances.

Lucky's protracted speech is an overt abuse of the existing systems of thought and meaningless utterances that end between pauses and silence foreground how unintelligible the world has become and the insecurity that people all over the world suffer from in the face of the World Wars, financial crises and political instability. On the whole, humanity has plunged into the nadir of despair that is evident in the way Vladimir and Estragon grope about in anguish with nothing to be done except wait for Godot who they are entirely dependent upon to find a solution to their existential crisis. The boy sent by Mr. Godot announces that he would definitely meet them the next day. The two men have no other choice but to continue to wait for Godot.

Glossary from the Text

Nothing to be done: This line is the refrain the play. It is repeated by Vladimir and Estragon several times in their conversation. This line is first uttered by Estragon then repeated twice by Vladimir. First, this line is related to the word "appalled" and second, the inability of the tramps to laugh.

His Highness: An ironic address by Vladimir; as if Estragon were of royal blood.

In a ditch: Estragon has spent the night in a ditch. This could probably be a reference to the Biblical parable of the Good Samaritan, in which the man who has been beaten and robbed is helped by a kind traveler. However, there is nobody to rescue Estragon. This phrase refers to the impoverished condition of the two men, who had seen better days.

And they didn't beat you?: Whenever Estragon gets away from Vladimir, he is beaten up somebody. However, who "they" are is never ascertained.

if you had what I have: Vladimir has prostate trouble.

"Hope deferred maketh the something sick": Vladimir is unable to complete the quotation from the Bible of Proverbs (13:12): "Hope deferred makes the heart sick; but a desire fulfilled is a tree of life." The two men are sick at heart and hope is deferred, since they wait for Godot and there is no promise of fulfilment because Godot does not arrive. **something** refers to the **heart.**

One of the thieves was saved: The passage from St. Augustine, "Do not despair; one of the thieves was saved. Do not presume; one of the thieves was damned." Beckett employed this allusion to suggest that there are equal chances of being "saved" or "damned".

Our being born?: "Man's greatest sin is to have been born." This is a quotation from Pedro Calderón (1600-81), the Spanish dramatist.

Only one speaks of a thief being saved: Only one of the four Gospels in the Bible (Luke 23: 43) mentions the reward for one thief.

The tree: It could be compared to a bush or a shrub; apparently a weak example of a tree. It could symbolize the Cross, which of course is not a very hopeful sign.

Wrong place? Wrong time?: The two men are confused over the time and the place, which suggests their confusion about life itself.

Nightmares: Gogo's nightmares symbolise the discomfort and restive state of mind of the two men. Moreover, they are concerned about the fact that they cannot laugh.

The Englishman in the brothel: An unfinished story that indicates the efforts of the two men to pass the time. Beckett brings in such mundane concerns and does not indulge his characters in poetic rendition for long. The story remains incomplete and when the two men embrace each other, Estragon complains that Vladimir smells of garlic.

The hanging incident: The two friends consider hanging themselves. The decision points to the Vladimir's limitations in using his intelligence and show-cases man's inability to think and rationalise to find a way out of his difficulties. The decision also refers to their state of immobility. They rely on some incident that would change their situation.

Where it falls mandrakes grow: A mandrake is plant with a root that is supposed to resemble the human form. The plant, it is believed grows where the human sperm has fallen.

On our hands and knees: Vladimir and Estragon represent the irrevocable condition of mankind. They are mere beggars that have to crawl on their hands and knees (figuratively) and do not possess any rights.

Your Worship*:* Vladimir addresses Estragon as if he were a very important person.

Tied to Godot: It is ironical that though the two men deny that they are tied to Godot, they are tied down to the act of waiting for Godot, which could be beneficial for them only when Godot arrives. They have no other option, but wait for Godot's arrival.

the clap: a venereal disease.

at his last gasp*:* at his last breath, implying death.

your immediate future: Pozzo understands that the two men depend on Godot.

Why doesn't he put down his bags?*:* a question that is repeated and is answered much later.

to cod me*:* to fool me.

Atlas, son of Jupiter!: In Greek mythology, Atlas is the son of Lapetus, not Jupiter. He was punished to hold up the heavens single-handedly after the Titans revolted. Ironically, Lucky carries sand.

You waagerrim: Vladimir's question gets warped when it is ignored and this is noticed by Pozzo.

I told you he didn't like strangers*:* Pozzo warns Estragon about Lucky's terrible demeanour.

knook: refers to Lucky; probably a word invented by Beckett himself. It has no specific meaning.

all four wear bowlers: the reference to the circus and clowning is made clear with this reference.

What have I done with my pipe: Pozzo's pipe mysteriously disappears from his pockets.

briar*:* a pipe that is made out of briar wood.

dudeen: Irish for a pipe made of clay.

Kapp and Peterson: the name of the manufacturers of a pipe.

Pan: Greek God of the wild, and the mountains. He also related to fertility and the spring season. He has the hindquarters, legs, and horns of a goat.

Time has stopped: Vladimir and Estragon feel that time has stopped, but Pozzo and Lucky do not feel so.

Adam: Estragon takes the name Adam, the first man created by God and mentioned in the Bible. He calls himself Adam because he dons the role of Pozzo's interlocutor at Pozzo's call and requests Pozzo to be seated. He assumes the identity of Pozzo. Moreover, the characters in the drama represent the human species. In Act II, Vladimir mentions about himself and Estragon to the blind Pozzo as "We are men" and calls Pozzo by the names Abel and Cain, the two sons of Adam.

Qua sky: "As sky".

tray bong: a parody of the Englishman's pronunciation of the French phrase très bon, which means very good.

Even five: Pozzo is ignorant of Estragon's financial assistance from him.

The farandole…: traditional dance.

The Hard Stool: constipation.

pulverizer: vaporiser.

My Left lung is very weak!: Estragon complains of a weak left lung and a sore foot.

He can't think without his hat: While three other three men remove their hats to concentrate, Lucy need his to be able to think.

quaquaquaqua: Beckett mentions that it refers to Quaquaquaquaversalis, a word Lucky wants to say, but ends saying quaquaquaqua. In *Theatre Quarterly* (Vol. V, No. 19, p. 22), Beckett mentions that it concerns a God who turns himself in all directions simultaneously.

apathia: apathy; indifference; lack of concern; insensitive to suffering.

athambia: unflustered; calm.

aphasia: loss of speech due to a disease of the brain.

the divine Miranda: reference to Miranda in Shakespeare's *The Tempest.*

Acacacacademy of Anthropopopometry: 'caca' and 'popo' are French for 'excrement' and 'chamberpot' respectively. (Taken from *A Student's Guide to the Plays of Samuel Beckett* by Smith Fletcher and Bachem, Faber, 1972, p. 62).

Essy-in-Possy: esse (Latin), which means to be; posse (Latin), which means to be able.

Testew...Cunard...Fartov...Belcher: 'invented names of vulgar origin' (Taken from *A Student's Guide to the Plays of Samuel Beckett* by Smith Fletcher and Bachem, Faber, 1972, p. 62).

Man...is seen to waste and pine waste and pine: the pivotal declaration in Lucky's speech.

camogie: A game similar to women's hockey played in Ireland.

Feckham Peckham Fulham Clapham: Feckham is an invention; the remaining names are places in London.

Bishop Berkeley (1685-1753): An Irish philosopher admired by Beckett.

Connemara: a coastal region of Galway in Western Ireland.

Steinweg and Peterman: names centred on stone. Steinweg (German, which is translated as Stoneroad). Peterman (Biblical, Rockman). The premise of the third part of Lucky's speech is 'the earth abode of stones'.

There's an end to his thinking!: Lucky cannot think aloud once the hat is removed from his head.

deadbeat escapement: The reference is to Pozzo's watch, in mechanical terms and the choice of words is quite ambiguous.

Only we can't: Nothing changes for the two men, although the arrival of Pozzo and Lucky did bring a momentary relief to their anguished condition.

He minds the sheep: It is seen that Mr. Godot favours the boy who tends the goats than the shepherd, the boy's brother.

This information weakens the assumption that Godot is God because in the Bible, God is described as separating the sheep from the goats, or in other words, sifting the good from the bad.

All my life I've compared myself to him: Initially, Estragon seems to have little knowledge of the New Testament of the Bible.

pale for weariness: Estragon mentions that the moon is "pale for weariness", considering the misery in the world indicating a pessimistic outlook.

nothing is certain: This statement is the most significant one that runs as the common thread of thought in the drama.

They do not move: The inherent contradiction between their words and their action stresses their inability to do anything to ameliorate their condition. They have to wait. The decision to leave is marked by inaction and it is repeated at the end of Act II; the only difference is that the speakers are interchanged.

References

Bair, Deirdre. *Samuel Beckett: A Biography*. Jonathan Cape, 1978.

Bloom, Harold, editor. *Samuel Beckett: Modern Critical Views*. Chelsea, 1985.

Fletcher, John. *Samuel Beckett's Art*. Chatto and Windus, 1967.

Kenner, Hugh. *A Reader's Guide to Samuel Beckett*. Farrar, Straus and Giroux, 1973.

——. *Samuel Beckett: A Critical Study*. John Calder, 1961.

Malick, Javed. *Samuel Becket: Waiting for Godot*. Oxford UP, 1989.

McMullan, Anna. *Theatre on Trial: Samuel Beckett's Later Drama*. Routledge, 1993.

Robinson, Jeremy. *Samuel Beckett goes into the Silence*. Kidderminster. Crescent Moon, 1992.

Waiting for Godot. https://edisciplinas.usp.br/pluginfile.php/2335139/mod_resource/content/1/WAITING%20FOR%20GODOT.pdf

https://books.google.co.in/books/about/Waiting_for_Godot_Samuel_Beckett_New_Edi.html?id=nsHSXV3LWF8C&redir_esc=y

Chapter 22

Waiting for Godot: Act Two

Act Two begins: Next Day. Same Time. Same Place. The tree that is bare in the previous act has now sprouted 'four or five leaves'. Estragon's boots and Vladimir's hat are seen on the stage. Vladimir paces up and down in distress. Vladimir sings a song that repeats the story of a dog that steals a crust of bread. He keeps moving around the stage when Estragon arrives barefoot with his head bowed down. Estragon refuses to be embraced because he finds Vladimir happier when he is alone. Vladimir questions whether Estragon has been beaten. Estragon mentions that he is happier without Vladimir, but he fails to understand why he keeps returning to Vladimir. Vladimir replies that it is because he does not know how to defend himself. The two men embrace and Estragon almost tumbles down when Vladimir releases him.

The two men exchange views on how they have spent time in the other's absence. They concur that they must be delighted in the other's company. Vladimir is the first to point out the change in the tree. However, he observes that there is no substantial change to their present condition. This is similar to what he remarks earlier: "The essential doesn't change". Estragon fails to recall the past, until he is encouraged by Vladimir. Vladimir considers the difficulty of putting up with Estragon, who prefers that they go their separate ways than stay together. They pass the time in conversation and the topic is the human requirement for self-expression even when life comes to an end. Though they express this desire, they fall short of words or rather find language deficient to express themselves sufficiently. Time passes in discussing what should be discussed and whether or not to agree, contradict or question each other. Thoughts are terrifying for them.

They stop conversing for some time before removing their hats to focus. They do not find any new topic, until Vladimir remembers the changes in the tree. He makes efforts to stimulate Estragon to think about the happenings of the previous day. He probes Estragon by pointing to the wound on his leg by Lucky's kick. He points out to the boots, but Estragon denies that they are his. Vladimir offers Estragon a radish, which is he refuses to eat because it is black.

Vladimir urges Estragon to try on his boots. Estragon finds them too large. He sits on the mound adopting "foetal posture" in the hope of going to sleep, while Vladimir sings him a lullaby and covers himself with his coat and paces up and down to keep himself warm. Estragon startles to a nightmare and Vladimir coaxes him in his arms. Vladimir refuses to listen to the nightmare, but helps Estragon to "walk it off". Estragon gets tired and when he complains, Vladimir rebukes him and Estragon decides to leave.

Vladimir remains unperturbed and instantly recognises Lucky's hat, which confirms that they are at the right place. He puts on Lucky's hat and hands over his own to Estragon, but Estragon hands over his to Vladimir, who puts it on. The clowning act of exchanging hats continues for some time and it ends with Lucky's hat on Vladimir, Estragon's on his own, and Vladimir's hat on the ground. Though Vladimir poses with Lucky's hat on, he removes it and peers inside it, as he had done in Act I.

Vladimir pretends he is Lucky by imitating him and asks Estragon to play Pozzo, but Estragon seems to have forgotten him. Vladimir begins to dance, but Estragon goes out impetuously and retunes almost immediately announcing, "I'm accursed!" He mentions, "They're coming!" Vladimir is ecstatic that Godot is coming at last, but Estragon barges to the opposite side of the stage again, and returns no sooner commenting, "I'm in hell!" He goes saying, "They're coming there too!", having absolutely no idea about who "they" are.

Vladimir, thinking that they are surrounded on all the sides, drags Estragon from the back of the stage and probably in the effort to escape, rushes to the auditorium. Estragon, however, tries to hide behind a tree. When Estragon finds that the tree can neither protect him nor camouflage him, he decides to face whatever comes up and takes control of himself. The two men occupy opposite positions, one on the extreme right and the other, extreme left of the stage. They glance over the entire place, but nobody arrives and they see nothing.

Soon they abuse each other and Estragon silences Vladimir insulting him, "Crritic!", and they embrace each other. Once again they are left with nothing to do, and they decide to engage in physical exercise. They hop from one foot to the other, then imitate the tree by trying to stand on one leg "for the balance". Estragon, wobbles and stops imitating and flaunts his fists, howling at the top of his voice, "God have pity on me!"

While Vladimir and Estragon move about the stage concerned about their condition, Pozzo and Lucky enter. Lucky is tethered by a shorter rope because Pozzo is blind. Lucky has another hat on his head. He stops abruptly on seeing Vladimir and Estragon and Pozzo collides with him. Lucky falls down and so does Pozzo under the pull of the rope. They lie down helpless and the luggage is strewn on the stage. Estragon thinks that Godot has finally arrived, but Vladimir considers them entertainers to pass the time. Neither Vladimir nor Estragon heed to Pozzo's pleas for help because each one is completely involved in contemplation.

Estragon is certain that Pozzo is not Godot, but the person who gave him the chicken bones the previous day and tries to secure another before helping Pozzo. Vladimir is concerned whether Lucky will turn violent again and concludes: "Let us do something, while we have the chance! It is not every day that we are needed." However, rather than help Pozzo, he continues to ponder: "What are we doing here, *that* is the question. And we are blessed in this, that we happen to know the answer. Yes, in this immense confusion one thing alone is clear. We are waiting for Godot to come." Pozzo cries out for help again after paying Estragon for help. Almost instantly, Vladimir realises that they have both been wasting time and makes efforts to help Pozzo. Vladimir tumbles down as he finds it difficult to raise Pozzo to his feet.

Now, Vladimir shouts for help, but Estragon does not help him. Rather, he decides to leave Vladimir, but he does not. Later, when Estragon tries to help Vladimir he falls down among the others. They all lie one on the other until Vladimir strikes Pozzo for an offensive remark. Pozzo crawls away from the rest and does not pay attention to Vladimir's call for help. Then Estragon calls out to Pozzo, who responds to the names Abel and Cain, and Estragon concludes: "He's all humanity!"

Vladimir and Estragon pull themselves out of the mess without much difficulty. Vladimir says that is a "simple question of will-power". Together, they manage to help Pozzo to his feet, but he falls down the moment they release their hold on him. They hold him between themselves as they held Lucky in Act I. The blind Pozzo wants to know who is rescuers are and the time of day. They assure him that it is evening and allow him to go, but they eventually hold him when he falls down.

They understand that they cannot leave Pozzo and question him about his blindness. Pozzo replies: "I woke up one day as blind as Fortune." This means that Pozzo considers his blindness due to fate or chance and not any personal quality, just as his early life was marked by destiny. Vladimir, earlier in the play feels that he is controlled by "a cruel fate." Vladimir is sure that Pozzo was not blind the previous day and tries to uncover when he turned blind. Pozzo gets angry and replies that the blind have nothing to do with time.

Pozzo enquires where they are, speculating whether they are at the place called Board. Vladimir replies that the place is "indescribable" and its "like nothing". When Pozzo asks them about Lucky, they tell him about the fall and Pozzo asks them to find out if Lucky is hurt. Pozzo asks Estragon to pull on Lucky's rope and if he fails to rise up, kick him on the face and his private parts. Vladimir assures Estragon that Lucky who is lying down is alive and Estragon kicks him, but hurts himself. He limps to the mound and tries to remove his boot, but gives up when he finds it difficult and goes off to sleep.

Vladimir initiates a conversation with Pozzo about the incidents of the previous day, but Pozzo fails to recall any and calls out to Lucky, who rises up along with his "burdens". Lucky unburdens himself twice in order to hand over the whip first and later the rope to Pozzo. When Vladimir requests Lucky to sing for them, Pozzo refuses because Lucky is dumb.

Dumbfounded, Vladimir asks: "Since when?" Infuriated, Pozzo replies: "One day, is that not enough for you, one day like any other day..." and renders a concise speech on human life pitted against the ravages of time: "They give birth astride of a grave, the light gleams an instant, then it's night once more." Pozzo mentions that life is as transitory as a streak of light that shines for a moment, and vanishes in a split of a second. Having said this, Pozzo and Lucky leave the stage but a noise offstage affirms that they have fallen down.

Vladimir wakes up Estragon, and refuses to listen to his dream. Vladimir is captivated by the fact that Pozzo has figured them out, and Estragon claims that Pozzo is Godot. Estragon snoozes off once more after exhibiting difficulty with his boots. Vladimir ponders over reality as he says: "But in all that what truth will there be?" He wonders if he may too be sleeping and surmises that he does not know anything. After making an assessment, he questions whether he has after all said anything worthwhile.

Vladimir's thoughts are interrupted by the boy, who does not recognise Vladimir and says that this is his first visit. Vladimir speculates the boy's message and declares instead that Mr. Godot would not arrive today, but he would definitely meet them the next day. The boy agrees with Vladimir and says that he has also not seen Pozzo and Lucky previously. When Vladimir enquires about Mr. Godot's occupation, the boy mentions that Godot does not do anything. He describes Godot as sporting a white beard. The boy informs them that his brother is sick. When asked for a message for Godot, Vladimir replies: "Tell him you saw me and that... *(he hesitates)* ...that you saw me." Realising that the boy would return the next day without recalling anything of their meeting at present, Vladimir darts towards him. The boy escapes him and runs out.

The sun sets. The stage is quiet and Vladimir stands absolutely still with his head lowered. Estragon suddenly wakes up, removes his boots and places them at the centre of the stage. Both men consider leaving but Vladimir draws attention to the fact that they cannot go far away because they have to return the following day and recommence their wait for Godot. They look at the tree and once gain the idea of suicide comes up before them, but they do not find a rope. Estragon is reminded of the cord that holds on his trousers and removes it and the trousers fall about his ankles. This piece of circus clowning adds to the absurdity of the situation and the sense of helplessness that there is "nothing to be done" and this perception grows intense as the drama closes in.

The two men pull the string to test its strength, however it breaks and they almost fall down. Estragon decides to bring "a good bit of rope" for their attempt the next day as in Act I. Similar to the previous act, he ruminates parting, but Vladimir persuades Estragon that if Godot does not come to save them, they could hang themselves as intended. Vladimir takes off Lucky's hat, looks into it and replaces it on his head. He asks Estragon to pick up his fallen trousers. Estragon obeys and Vladimir suggest they leave. Estragon agrees, but again in Act I, "They do not move" as the curtain drops down.

Analysis

Vladimir's song in the beginning of the second act about the dog that pilfers a crust of bread recurs itself. The pattern where the two verses succeed and repeat so that the song can be sung incessantly is representative of the cyclical nature of the play as well as lives of Vladimir and Estragon. Similar to verses of the song, the events of their lives ensue repeatedly, obviously without a beginning or an end.

Incidents like the pointless switching of hats illustrate the characteristic feature of the absurd drama that concentrates on the purposelessness and monotony of existence. The clowning gesture of playing with the hats could continue forever, but it ends only when Vladimir takes the initiative. Vladimir and Estragon discuss about the clamour of the "dead voices" that end in silence after each repetition.

Vladimir's interest in protecting Estragon that vouchsafes his kind nature is the reason why Estragon returns to Vladimir every day, and he needs Vladimir's support to defend himself, even though he claims that he is happier alone. Vladimir considers it is his duty to help Estragon and this attitude delineates their association.

An interesting and relevant aspect of the drama is the immobility of Vladimir and Estragon who fail to accomplish their declarations and intents. This is explicitly recognized and stated by Vladimir towards the end of the act when he says, "let us preserve in what we have resolved, before we forget." Vladimir asserts that this consciousness of the problem renders him unable to solve it. To act and to move have become excruciating and indecipherable.

Estragon's failure to comprehend the enormity of the situation is expressed in the stage direction when he assumes "his foetal posture, his head between his knees". This position is relevant for it has a dual significance. Firstly, it denotes an attitude of submission and desolation and secondly it could indicate an effort by a character to decipher the gravity of the situation and retrace the path of life by moving back to the initial stages of life in the womb-like state. However, the second interpretation cannot be realised because it ends only as a dream into which Estragon has imagined to have fallen. The sense of falling is symbolic of the spiritual degradation in his life.

While Pozzo is blind, Lucky has become dumb; their condition has worsened. The master-slave relationship is no longer valid, and Pozzo has lost control over life. Since time no longer matters because he is sightless, he declares that at present, a single day is enough for him to see what life actually is. All he can observe is the misery of existence, which appears like a flashlight between the darkness of the womb and the tomb.

Vladimir understands that they are in a state of inactivity and he calls out to Estragon to help Pozzo who is on the floor. Rather than waste their time on meaningless and "idle discourse", he believes that they have to do something fruitful when they get the opportunity to do so. Vladimir consumes a great amount of time to help Pozzo to his feet. This proves beyond doubt that habitual inaction renders resolutions insignificant.

Vladimir considers the opportunity to help Pozzo to use their time properly but they end up adding to the chaos by proving ineffective helpers. In the end, Vladimir declares that the incident is another "diversion" for their main intention is to wait for Godot's arrival. They are both so confused that they end up on the ground. Vladimir and Estragon also represent mankind at large that hopelessly endeavours to keep up promises, nevertheless when Vladimir tries to distinguish them from the rest of mankind, Estragon establishes that they are all of the same kind. Pozzo responds when he is called Abel and Cain, and Estragon concludes that the characters epitomise the human race.

In addition, Pozzo's response to the names Abel and Cain suggests Pozzo's inability to assert his individuality. The fact that they can neither do anything nor find a solution to their condition is the reality and this plays a crucial role in asserting one's individuality, which is a futile exercise. When Estragon complains about his efforts in carrying Pozzo around, he appears more like a statue, a *caryatid*, a comparison he earlier objects to.

While Vladimir and Pozzo have been talking, Estragon assumes the foetal posture as seen in Act I. He is happy but it points to their degenerate state. Moreover, there are instances when Vladimir requires Estragon's help and this proves that for some time their roles are reversed and Vladimir is rendered weak before Estragon. Ironically, Estragon's efforts to help Vladimir ends in chaos with his falling over. Estragon has realised that despite their best efforts to go, they cannot and he utters a crisp dialogue: "Let's go. We can't. Ah!" The hopeless perseverance has impinged upon Estragon's mind and he is perfectly aware of their situation.

Similarly, when the boy arrives in Act II, Vladimir knows what the boy will communicate about Godot and the boy has nothing to say in response except nod his head in approval. The second act concludes exactly as the first one. The stage directions read: "As in Act I, Vladimir stands motionless and bowed." These suggest that the play is just an exposition of the continuous cycle of events that permeate the lives of Vladimir and Estragon and there is neither escape from this existence nor hope of a new life.

Conclusion

In the second act, the tree has four or five leaves, however, this does not offer any hope to Vladimir and Estragon, but points towards the passage of time. The two men are in a similar state of anguish, since they have nothing to do except wait for Godot's arrival. They engage in frivolous activities like exchanging hats and their conversation is reduced to discussions on how to pass time. However, these acts are important as far as the dramatic effect is concerned because it delves into the consciousness of Vladimir and Estragon who are aware to a certain extent of their deplorable condition.

While Vladimir is more alert, receptive and remembers the happenings previously, Estragon does not recollect anything despite the best efforts made by Vladimir. Estragon struggles with the boots, and sleeps, but the nightmares occur repeatedly. Though Vladimir expresses his concern for Estragon by coaxing him and giving his coat to him to warm him up, he is disinterested in listening to the nightmares of Estragon. When Vladimir and Estragon expectantly await Godot, Pozzo, who has turned blind, and Lucky, who is dumb enter the stage. Pozzo comments that life is miserable that appears like a flicker between birth and death.

Though Vladimir tries to lend a helping hand to Pozzo who has fallen on the ground, the initiative turns out cumbersome because in the end all the four men are on the floor and each one is unable to rise up. Vladimir and Estragon exchange dialogues and they perceive that Godot would not visit them this day too. Though Estragon mistakes Pozzo for Godot, Vladimir recognises Pozzo who had visited them the previous day; however, he is shocked to find Pozzo blind and Lucky, dumb. Estragon goes off to sleep, while waiting for Godot's arrival, but Vladimir understands that their wait is futile. He senses the boy's probable message from Godot and along with Estragon contemplates suicide by hanging to death from the tree with the cord of Estragon's trousers that breaks.

Now, all they can do is wait for the next day and expect Godot. As the curtain is pulled, they stand motionless. The repetition of events and the passage of time along with the cyclical pattern of the play iterate that life is a hopeless journey and the titles and battles won are mere external trappings of a civilisation that gropes in the darkness of ignorance and misery. Godot is an illusion, and it would be an endless wait for salvation just as the hope for a better world is far from realisation.

Glossary from the Text

The tree has four or five leaves: The tree has sprouted leaves, but this does not indicate hope rather it shows repetition of events. Bair quotes Beckett who mentions to Roger Blin that the change takes place "not to show hope or inspiration, but only to record the passage of time" (383). In the drama, life persists because it has to, but the appearance of a few does not indicate that things are getting any better for the two men.

Vladimir's song: Vladimir's song about the dog focuses on death. Just as the structure of the play is repetitive and circular in nature, Vladimir's song has a repetitive pattern.

One is not master of one's moods: This suggests Vladimir's inability to improve his condition, which also indicates the helplessness of the two men to effect a positive change in their lives. Neither are they happy in each other's company nor can they part. Moreover, Estragon has been beaten up for reasons that are uncertain.

That was yesterday?: Estragon is confused about the time, which suggests that awareness of time is insubstantial as far as the two men are concerned. Probably, time is to be consumed only in the act of waiting, which is languishing for them.

What is there to recognise?: Estragon does not find any appreciable change in their condition and he can neither recall a particular place nor an event.

this muckheap: the word refers to their miserable condition.

Puke: Estragon refers to his bitter and contemptuous life. He is aware of his hopeless condition.

Tell me about the worms: Estragon realises that his present condition is absurd and the questions of death and decomposition cannot be thought of.

The Macon county: a place in France.

The Cackon country!: a pun using the word 'caca', the childlike French word for excrement.

for a man called...: Refers to Bonnelly, a farmer at Roussillon, in south-east France, from whom Beckett used to purchase wine.

down there everything is red!: the red soil at Roussillon. Beckett brings in personal details that do not have any contextual relevance.

like the other: Estragon refers to Pozzo's remark about killing Lucky.

All the dead voices: Beckett often makes references to dead voices in his plays.

Yes, but you have to decide: Vladimir and Estragon are not only indecisive and inconclusive but also incapable of executing the decisions they have taken.

A charnel-house: the mind is the storehouse of worn-out thoughts.

Que voulez-vous?: French for What can you expect?

canter: Estragon points out to the conversation at hand.

There's no lack of void: Estragon is pessimistic, while Vladimir is optimistic. Vladimir's comment on the tree with sparse foliage is met with Estragon's comment on the presence of a greater lacuna in the world.

To give us the impression we exist: to make their presence or existence known.

No laces!: Estragon dislikes laces, which could be compared to his apprehension of being 'tied' to Godot.

Gonococcus! Spirochaete!: the organisms that cause gonorrhoea and syphilis respectively.

There's no way out there: there are no ways to escape, be it in space or in time. The foetal posture to lie down would not offer any solace.

Morpion: French for pubic louse.

Crritic!: a word of insult.

Do you think God sees me?: Estragon's question is relevant if the tree implies the cross.

Games: Vladimir and Estragon call each other names and the exercises are nonsensical efforts to pass their time, which is a drab and compelling routine.

ballocksed: slang for 'done for'.

all mankind is us: Vladimir points out to the universal appeal of the text that signifies the general desolate condition of the world, which is irrevocable. Man cannot do anything but accept his anguished existence. As Vladimir rightly says: "At this place, at this moment of time, all mankind is us, whether we like it or not."

pros and cons (Latin): for and against.

congeners: kin.

this immense confusion: the state of perpetual uncertainty that Vladimir and Estragon are thrown into.

to prevent our reason from floundering: the way certain disgusting facts of life are closed down or shut out by habit. Vladimir calls habit "a great deadener".

Pyrenees: mountain ranges between Spain and France.

as blind as fortune: Pozzo considers his blindness due to chance or fate just as his early fortune due to fate and not personal attributes.

saws the air blindly: fumble the air with hands.

I'm afraid he's dying: Beckett equates birth with death because birth definitely leads to death.

Abel!...Cain!: the sons of Adam. Beckett uses the names to imply the fallen state of man when the men who are on the floor find it difficult to rise up.

highwaymen: the parable of the Good Samaritan is intended.

Memoria praeteritorum bonorum (Latin): Memory of past happiness.

The place known as the Board: suggests the stage. The Board could also refer to the governing body of Trinity College, Dublin.

No point in exerting yourself if he's dead: an instance of black comedy.

I don't remember having met anyone yesterday: Vladimir interrogates the soundness of his memory.

Are you sure it wasn't him?: The possibility that Pozzo might be Godot is inferred.

The grave-digger pits on the forceps: Vladimir associates life with birth, death and burial.

Was I sleeping, while others suffered?: Vladimir is agitated when he utters this line. He feels that something significant has to materialise in what has happened. He is conscious of his misery on account of the grave-digger's forceps and life resonates to the agony of the suffering humanity. Habit, for him functions as a reliever of pain, which nevertheless, is inadequate to give vent to his frustration. In the end, he denies his desperateness and asks: "What have I said?". Even in the face of absolute misery, humanity emerges obstinate.

habit is a great deadener: actions performed everyday act as pain-killers that protect man from the painful realities of life.

Off we go again: the circular nature of the drama is reiterated as the events repeat themselves in succession.

tell him you saw me: the need of the hour is to acknowledge that one exists.

And if we dropped him?: not actually being tied down to Godot?

A willow: The willow tree, which is also called a weeping tree.

We'll be saved: In Act I, Vladimir mentions that one of the thieves was saved. In Act II, Vladimir has apprehensions whether God is entirely benevolent because there are chances that they could be punished for not waiting for him.

They do not move: The circular pattern of the play is reiterated because irrespective of the one who takes the initiative, the man who thinks or the other, their condition remains unchanged and the final result is the same. They may discuss about leaving, but they cannot because they are 'tied' to Godot.

References

Bair, Deirdre. *Samuel Beckett: A Biography*. Jonathan Cape, 1978.

Bloom, Harold, editor. *Samuel Beckett: Modern Critical Views*. Chelsea, 1985.

Fletcher, John. *Samuel Beckett's Art*. Chatto and Windus, 1967.

Kenner, Hugh. *A Reader's Guide to Samuel Beckett*. Farrar, Straus and Giroux, 1973.

——. *Samuel Beckett: A Critical Study*. John Calder, 1961.

Malick, Javed. *Samuel Becket: Waiting for Godot*. Oxford UP, 1989.

McMullan, Anna. *Theatre on Trial: Samuel Beckett's Later Drama*. Routledge, 1993.

Robinson, Jeremy. *Samuel Beckett Goes into the Silence*. Kidderminster. Crescent Moon, 1992.

Waiting for Godot. https://edisciplinas.usp.br/pluginfile.php/2335139/mod_resource/content/1/WAITING%20FOR%20GODOT.pdf

https://books.google.co.in/books/about/Waiting_for_Godot_Samuel_Beckett_New_Edi.html?id=nsHSXV3LWF8C&redir_esc=y

Chapter 23

A Critical Study of *Waiting for Godot*

The Publication of *Waiting for Godot*

The original text of the drama was written in French, titled *En attendant Godot* and published in Paris in 1952. In 1953-54, Beckett translated the play into English as *Waiting for Godot: A Tragicomedy in Two Acts*, which was published in New York in 1954 and subsequently in London, in 1956. Since there were several issues related to censoring several passages of the text in Britain, the complete version of the drama was published in London only in 1965.

Critics notice several changes in respect of stage direction, dialogues, personalities that Beckett was associated with and certain crucial explanations related to the emotions of the characters. It cannot be ruled out that several French phrases could not find their English equivalents, let alone the word-play employed in the drama. However, the English version of the text gave Beckett the freedom to explore Irish words in many passages.

Duckworth mentions that Beckett wrote the drama fluently as he did not encounter any issues (*Angels* 17). Regarding the origin of the play, Beckett suggested to Duckworth: "If you want to find the origins of *En attendant Godot*, look at *Murphy*" (*En* xiv). Duckworth notices that in the manuscript version of the text, Mr. Godot exists and as proof he sends a letter to Vladimir and Estragon. Beckett affirms to Duckworth that he had eventually forgotten the note in the manuscript that included the identity of Godot. Some critics consider this aspect relevant to the understanding of the drama that is built on ambiguity and highlights the essential paradox of the incidents depicted.

The Premiere of *Waiting for Godot*

The debut, directed by Roger Blin, was staged on 5 January 1953 at the Théâtre de Babylone in Paris. Directed by Peter Snow, The Arts Theatre, London staged the drama on August 3, 1955. In the United States of America, the drama, directed by Alan Schneider was presented in January 1956.

Waiting for Godot: A Tragicomedy in Two Acts—Aspects of the Drama

The Title of the Drama

The English version of the drama is titled *Waiting for Godot: A Tragicomedy in Two Acts*. The subtitle *A Tragicomedy in Two Acts* does not imply that the play consists of the dual elements of tragedy and comedy, but the concerns are profound. Absurdity relies on incongruity and according to the dramatists of the Theatre of the Absurd, when man ruminates upon his position in the world, the sense of incongruity is manifested.

Man realises the inadequacy of reason, logic, and rationality in describing the real meaning of the universe, making him an isolated being in an unpredictable and incomprehensible world. He seeks out to his own individuality, which in his opinion is the only reality; his freedom, the only certainty. In such an alienated situation within his surroundings, his actions seem futile, or absurd. The absurdity is the outcome of the sense of disharmony concerning his affectations, aspirations and the actual disposition of his environment.

Given such a condition, comic and tragic elements are fused to reveal the inherent dynamism in exposing the ludicrous so that the sense of the appalling can be best expressed through a series of actions and verbal connotations that are in themselves ridiculous or appear nonsensical. The method to expose the gravity of the situation involves the articulation of dialogues and actions that sound playful and yet retain the sense of dread and horror. The balance of humorous elements with expressions of despair reiterates the purposelessness of their attempts at anything definite such as the act of waiting for Godot.

The line "Nothing to be done" recurs in the drama, which echoes their hopeless condition and the inherent intensity of pathos. The humour depicted in the drama does not serve comic relief but it would help the audience indulge in the endless hours of waiting, which forms the essence of the drama. Comic elements reinforce the central theme of the drama, where man faces nullity or a lacuna, and becomes conscious of the intensity of the dreadful circumstances he is thrown into.

The Setting

Both the acts of the drama take place in similar settings. A country road without definite location and a single tree nearby. The entire action of the play is concentrated on a single setting and the audience never experiences change of locales. Similarly, both the acts take place in the evening, an information that is asserted by the words "Same time." Though the second act is supposed to be the next day, there is visibly no change in the actions of the characters. The proclivity to repeat whatever was presented in the first act of the drama in the second, is a conscious break with traditional notions of dramaturgy by refraining to introduce any new line of thought or element within its framework.

Time

Traditional drama gives importance to time, which highlights the development of the plot, traces the growth of the protagonist, accounts for the events that logically lead to the climax and the drama often ends at a certain time frame with appreciable changes in lives of the characters. Absurd drama, however, is a deliberate turn away from the conventional modes of presentation.

To discuss time in *Waiting for Godot* is to accentuate the act of waiting in the drama. Esslin remarks: "it is in the act of waiting that we experience the flow of time in its purest, most evident form" (58). In *Waiting for Godot*, time is consumed in waiting and the characters vacillate between anguish and happiness to make time pass quickly. Nevertheless, the predominant mood is characterised by distress. At one stage, Vladimir murmurs,

"How the time flies when one has fun!" and at other instances they say, "the hours are long under these conditions" and seep into despair. This means that being active, time passes by, but when the wait is a passive one, the actual confrontation with the action of time takes place (Esslin 58).

Vladimir and Estragon understand that they can be free from the pain of existence only when Godot comes, but he never seems to come. Moreover, they are uncertain when they are supposed to meet Godot; they aren't even sure on which day of the week they are. Hence, Godot stands for the purpose of their wait—the attainment of their desire, which is outside their grasp.

Pozzo and Lucky are not recognised by Vladimir and Estragon when they first appear on stage, but Vladimir states that they have changed since their last appearance and Estragon mentions that he doesn't know them. When they arrive in Act II, Pozzo is blind and Lucky, dumb because time has distorted them. Neither Vladimir nor Estragon recognise them and Pozzo too does not recall meeting them.

The fact that change is inevitable as time passes is a delusion. The activity of time in turn is about being static, which is "the terrible stability of the world" (Esslin 59). Each day is like any other day and Vladimir and Estragon continue to wait for Godot as they have been doing. Their perpetual wait will end only when Godot arrives and this day would mark the end of the movement of time. Vladimir and Estragon desire to escape the bondage of time and only Godot can release them.

The Structure

Designated cyclic in structure, the action of the drama recurs in the two acts, and parallels can be drawn between them. Tynan comments: "By all the known criteria, Samuel Beckett's 'Waiting for Godot' is a dramatic vacuum.... It has no plot, no climax, no *dénouement*; no beginning, no middle, and no end. Unavoidably it has a situation..." (101). The course of the play is centered on two men who impatiently wait beneath tree, waiting for a mysterious Mr. Godot to keep his appointment with them, but the situation is never developed and from the series of actions depicted, it could be ascertained that Mr. Godot is not going to arrive. This situation could probably have begun from the past, continues and may probably extend to the future, without an end.

This means that Beckett constantly repeats similar actions or statements to present the reality of the universal predicament that surfaces only when form, structure and the pivotal argument of the drama are harmoniously blended. The repetitions of language, ambiguous content, variations of tone, parallels, and incomprehensible references counterpoise the inherent unpredictability of the situation, and the resultant effect is augmented by silences, pauses, stillness, comic gestures and acts of clowning.

It could be ascertained that the structure of the play is important because it is built with a specific orderly method of arrangement that is balanced. The themes of the play are interspersed within the matrix of its structure and the comic effects are timed with precision. On the whole, the structure of the drama holds together all these aspects and maintains a composite balance of two acts with the characters and incidents contributing to the essence of the drama.

The prominent actors, Vladimir and Estragon wait for Godot at the close of the day at the roadside where a solitary tree stands. They encounter Pozzo and Lucky in each act and they are visited by a boy who informs them that Godot will not come this evening, but the next. It is not only in repetitive action, but also in recurring statements such as "Nothing to be done", "I can't go on", "We're waiting for Godot" that the symmetry of the play is maintained. At the end of each act, Vladimir and Estragon decide to leave, but they are unable to move.

The cyclical nature of existence, which is one of the themes of the play is succinctly brought out by the similar ending of the two acts. The fact that chance alters man's condition is evinced when the tree bears a few leaves overnight and Pozzo turns blind "all of a sudden" and Lucky becomes dumb the next day. Another decisive aspect of the play is the limitations of memory. In Act II, Estragon cannot remember having met Pozzo and Lucky earlier. He even fails to recognise his boots.

Sets of short statements that are used in the drama are amusing because they clarify a certain temperament or convey shared feelings as depicted in the following lines in Act II:

ESTRAGON: I am happy.
VLADIMIR: So am I.
ESTRAGON: So am I.
VLADIMIR: We are happy.
ESTRAGON: We are happy.

Invariably such exchanges are followed by repetitive gestures or silence. Repetitive gestures such as Vladimir's peering into his hat or Estragon's habit of examining his boot add to the felicity of expression. It could be deciphered that the structure of the play creates a definitive pattern, contributes to plausible themes of the play and provides the comic element.

The Action

Several obvious repetitions in the action of the drama contribute to its effectiveness in terms of the purpose of the Absurd Theatre. Hassan notes: "The inaction of the play is cyclical, and its events are endlessly repetitious; its two acts are symmetric, both equal images of an absence. Two acts, as Samuel Beckett knew, are enough to represent a sequence stretching to infinity" (176). The action, in both the acts revolve around a similar situation.

In Act I, Estragon observes "So, there you are again" and in Act II, Vladimir mentions: "You Again!" and a few minutes later repeats what Estragon had earlier mentioned. In both the acts, the physical ailments of Vladimir and Estragon are emphasised. Estragon is beaten by somebody and neither the identity of the persons nor the reason is mentioned. Estragon is constantly bothered about his feet and boots, and he desperately tries to pull his boots out and put them on, repeating the action. Similarly, Vladimir is agitated over his prostate problem and often fumbles with his hat.

Radke mentions: "The actions of these Chaplinesque clowns [in *Waiting for Godot*] are but parodies of action. Taking up one sentiment of endeavour and then quickly abandoning it for another, which is just summarily developed, they are like those circus clowns..." (60). Invariably, the acts involve slapstick comedy or clowning with carrots, radishes and turnips; verbal exchanges with repetition of sentences uttered by each; and interchangeable dialogues. The possibility of suicide by hanging from the solitary tree is discussed and planned, but their attempts are foiled due to their inability to execute whatever they say or think of doing. Lucky, Pozzo and the boy are the only characters that appear on stage in both the acts.

Both the acts end with the line "Yes, let's go", however, if it's Estragon who utters the line in the first act, it's Vladimir in the second, and after the utterance neither moves. Specific repetitions in the action of the play allude to the rejection of the traditional linear structure of the play and the replacement with a circular structure that is conclusive so far as the objective of the Absurd Theatre is concerned.

The Dialogue

The arrangement and content of the dialogue in the drama that consists of repetitions and inconclusive exchanges render a circular pattern to the structure of the play. The intermittent pauses either after differences of opinion or frequent short silences in the play offer the space to comprehend the intentions of the characters who are put in a static situation from where there is no way to escape. Pithy statements, monosyllabic answers, contrite expressions followed by gestures complement the grimness of the situation.

Esslin remarks: "He may have devalued language as an instrument for the communication of ultimate truths, but he has shown himself a great master of language as an artistic medium.... For want of better raw material, he has molded words into a superb instrument for his purpose" (*The Theatre* 46). By a deliberate reduction of language, the dramatist achieves the purpose of showing the ineffectiveness of semantically loaded utterances in situations that demand the force of expression through an amalgamation of gestures, silences, and pauses. For instance, in Act I, after a trite conversation, when boredom settles on them, Vladimir asks: "What do we do now?", Estragon replies: "Wait". Such exchanges repeat several times in both the acts.

Trivial conversations and repartee that are often incoherent fill the void when there is no longer any activity to help them pass the time. They have nothing else to do except wait for Godot. The action thus reduces to anxious waiting and ruminating over what has to be done till the time Godot arrives; however, the action disintegrates into a series of utterances followed by silence, and this reflects the weight of the hours that lingers throughout the drama. Every day is just like any other day "a fruitless repetition and no transition can take place" (*Samuel* 127).

Beckett intended the audience to understand the relevance of the use of cross-talk that contains "crudely physical humour" (Esslin, *Samuel* 47), and balances the elements of drama from the situation, the rendition to the demeanour of the characters. There are a few instances where select speeches made by Lucky, Pozzo and even Vladimir are deliberate musings on the essential absurdity of giving importance to learning, systems of governance and time.

Lucky's prolonged speech in Act I addresses the ludicrousness of rationality, belief in God, theological and philosophical discourses at the time when the world confronts the World Wars and the resulting catastrophe. The speech doubts the existence of God, who is indifferent and a subjective entity. Despite the prevalence of systems of thought and claims of progress, man is seen to 'waste and pine'. There is cosmic petrification and the earth is an ensemble of stones "in the great cold the great dark".

Styan mentions that Lucky's speech brings in several persons of diverse vocations that point to important aspects related to human interaction. Lucky imitates the parson who warns of hell-fire, the lecturer who claims to make an indefinite point, the sportsman who exposes the cult of the body, the Cockney businessman who gives importance to facts and the prophet who predicts doom (232).

Pozzo, who gave importance to time in Act I, loses his watch later and on turning blind in Act II, philosophises on the absurdity of human life that is gauged in terms of clocks and calendars. His blindness has opened his eyes to the features of time and human existence that are evanescent. He understands that life is just a hopeless brief existence between birth and death and associates birth with the grave. When Vladimir disbelieves that Pozzo has turned blind and asks him when this has occurred, Pozzo comments that one day is 'enough' for any appreciable change in the life of man, which echoes Vladimir's and Estragon's comments on the way a tree can change in a single night.

Vladimir's soliloquy in Act II, rendered in the form of questions focuses on sleep, blindness, death, time and waiting, which form the crux of the drama. He wonders whether he is awake or asleep, whether he would be able to recall events of the previous day, and if he could rely on his memory. He realises that habit aids to deaden his habitual perceptions. He imagines he is asleep and someone is watching over him. In the end he ascertains: "I can't go on" and once again probes all that he has stated, asking, "What have I said?" Just as Pozzo lectures on time and death, which are fleeting and instantaneous processes respectively, Vladimir understands that time interferes between the twin processes of birth and death, and provides the space for action.

Dialogue, in the drama, is a painful exercise that is delivered only to fill in the gaps when coherence, logic, thinking, and action break down in the face of a static situation. Just as there is no significant plot or well-defined characters in the drama to project the apathy of the human condition, the dialogue situates itself to succinctly explore the anguish of existence in an unintelligible world.

The Style

Dramatists often employ several techniques to foreground certain features that enhance the artistic quality of a presentation and achieve a desired end. *Waiting for Godot* is characterised by several distinguishing stylistic features such as rapid dialogues, images, symbols, gestures, clowning, repetitions, and the use of sets of sentences to reinforce an aspect or express a line of thought.

Just as Vladimir is preoccupied with his hat, Estragon is with his boot. The characters Pozzo, Lucky, Vladimir and Estragon exchange hats and they engage in clowning. Only Lucky is able to think with his hat on, and the speech that follows is replete with musings on death, decay, impermanence of life and the wastage of academic glory.

The perceptible aspect of the drama is the unique ability of the dramatist to place what is trite and brief alongside elaborate oratory. Lucky's long tirade in Act I could be contrasted with the brief dialogues between characters. Pozzo's philosophical outburst is contrasted with his otherwise monotonous exchange. Flashes of thought on life and death are rendered by Vladimir. Such speeches underscore the inhabitual reflections on realities on man's condition in contrast to the habitual cross-talk that portray nonsensical exchanges to showcase the superficialities of existence in a rather bizarre world.

Exchanges between Vladimir and Estragon are sometimes repetitions of lines, and at other times appear contradictory. Statements are followed by questions to emphasise a particular condition or express concern. In Act I, when Vladimir asks Estragon where he had spent the night, the conversation reads:

ESTRAGON: In a ditch.
VLADIMIR: (admiringly) A ditch! Where?
ESTRAGON: (without gesture): Over there.
VLADIMIR: And they didn't beat you?
ESTRAGON: Beat me? Certainly they beat me.
VLADIMIR: The same lot as usual?
ESTRAGON: The same? I don't know.

The conversation is built on questions and assertions, but it ends indecisively.

Sometimes, the dramatist incorporates pairs of statements that appear similar, immediately followed by 'Pause', 'Silence' or 'Long Silence'. This could also hint at the inability of the characters to think beyond a certain level. Estragon is less capable of thinking when compared to Vladimir. The conversation in Act II reads:

VLADIMIR: Rather they whisper.
ESTRAGON: They rustle.
VLADIMIR: They murmur.
ESTRAGON: They rustle.
Silence.
VLADIMIR: They make a noise like feathers.
ESTRAGON: Like leaves.
VLADIMIR: Like ashes.
ESTRAGON: Like leaves.
Long Silence.

Notice that Estragon repeats the lines, but in other instances lines are repeated by either character. Lines such as "Nothing to be done" and "We're waiting for Godot" are restated by either character as the drama progresses.

Conclusion

Waiting for Godot is a drama that incorporates several distinguishing features that account for its appeal and study within academia. The drama gained universal acceptance because it promulgated a fresh look at life that seemed too complex in a world that was wrecked by the World Wars. Devoid of religious support and pitched into the abyss of despair, modern man finds himself in a hopeless situation from where escape is nearly impossible.

Beckett has presented his characters on a bare stage that is the vast, empty road with only a tree by the side, and they await Godot who is supposed to alleviate them from the burden of existence. This seemingly simple situation is depicted by flouting conventions of drama and adopting a strategy that would best suit its exposition. By employing a definitive style, simplifying language, interspersing the serious with the comic, and presenting the unusual thought with strains of the shallow, Beckett has shattered traditional notions of dramaturgy and ushered a renewed interest in depicting the world as it seems to be.

Glossary

vacillate	:	waver
ruminate	:	ponder; reflect
delusion	:	misconception
accentuate	:	emphasise
incongruity	:	absurdity; strangeness
disposition	:	nature
counterpoise	:	counterbalance
plausible	:	probable; conceivable
amalgam	:	combination
felicity	:	appropriateness
decipher	:	make sense of
symmetric	:	in equilibrium

pithy	:	concise; brief
ossification	:	solidifying
crux	:	core
trite	:	clichéd
promulgate	:	disseminate
alleviate	:	assuage

References

Bair, Deirdre. *Samuel Beckett: A Biography*. Jonathan Cape, 1978.

Bloom, Harold, editor. *Samuel Beckett: Modern Critical Views*. Chelsea, 1985.

Duckworth, Colin. *Angels of Darkness: Dramatic Effect in Samuel Beckett with Special Reference to Eugene Ionesco*. Allen and Unwin, 1972.

——, editor. *Samuel Beckett's En attendant Godot*. Harrap, 1966.

Esslin, Martin. *Samuel Beckett: A Collection of Critical Essays*. Prentice-Hall, 1965.

——. *The Theater of the Absurd*. Doubleday, 1961.

Fletcher, John. *Samuel Beckett's Art*. Chatto and Windus, 1967.

Hassan, Ihab. *The Literature of Silence: Henry Miller and Samuel Beckett*. Peter Smith, 1967.

Hobson, Harold. "Samuel Beckett, Dramatist of the Year." *International Theatre Annual*, No. 1, Calder, 1956.

Kenner, Hugh. *A Reader's Guide to Samuel Beckett*. Farrar, Straus and Giroux, 1973.

Malick, Javed. *Samuel Beckett: Waiting for Godot*. Oxford UP, 1989.

McMullan, Anna. *Theatre on Trial: Samuel Beckett's Later Drama*. Routledge, 1993.

Radke, Judith. *Yale French Studies*. Spring-Summer, 1962, pp. 59-63.

Robinson, Jeremy. *Samuel Beckett Goes into the Silence*. Kidderminster. Crescent Moon, 1992.

Theatre of the Absurd. https://www.britannica.com/art/Theatre-of-the-Absurd

https://www.oxfordreference.com/view/10.1093/oi/authority.20110803095345289

https://www.bl.uk/20th-century-literature/articles/nonsense-talk-theatre-of-the-absurd

https://books.google.co.in/books/about/The_Theatre_of_the_Absurd.html?id=J7iQNBOp7Q4C&redir_esc=y

Chapter 24

An Analytical View of *Waiting for Godot* and Samuel Beckett as a Dramatist

Themes in *Waiting for Godot*

Every dramatist unfolds certain aspects of life they feel that have to be conveyed. Themes in a drama unfold relevant aspects related to the principal propositions that needs to be conveyed. Beckett deviates from the conventional scheme of proposing rational ideas for deliberation. His intention is to explicate how man feels alienated when he is put in a situation where the meaning of life is irrelevant. Man's desperate attempt to cohere his thoughts when incoherence dissuades him from gaining insight into understanding the world and organise the thought experience is brought out in *Waiting for Godot*.

Salvation

Harold Hobson quotes Beckett who mentions the passage in the writing of St. Augustine when asked about the theme of *Waiting for Godot*: "Do not despair: one of the thieves was saved. Do not presume: one of the thieves was damned." The argument of the two thieves on the cross, the theme of improbability of the hope of redemption and the fortuity of grace being conferred on the characters are embedded in the drama. A condition of existence where a person is suspended between two diverse responses of despair and belief, which means he is caught between the present condition of despair and the expectations in the future is brought out by the Beckett. For Vladimir and Estragon, the question of salvation is not a fifty percent chance because only one Gospel narrates the incident and hence the probability of deliverance is rather impossible.

Vladimir and Estragon represent Beckett's man without hope. The person who despairs faces a lacuna and there is no hope of salvation. Though there a faint chance of redemption, even amidst confusion, and despair brought about by the situation where meaninglessness of existence is experienced. However, Godot never comes and nothing happens in the play to break the void so that a new condition can be initiated; the series of events end as they began. This circular structure of the drama articulates modern man's anguished existence.

Man faces a world where he can no longer rely on society, brotherhood or religion for his existence. He hopes and yearns for something new, which is disconsolate and dead. He cannot do anything except indulge in "nothing", wait and pass time. Nonetheless, man is uncertain about who or what he waits for; yet, he feels compelled to wait.

Absurdity

Humorous incidents in the drama *Waiting for Godot* range from senseless activities and clowning to nonsense dialogues and word play. These form part of absurdity because their movements and actions are not in accordance with the expectations of what they articulate. Characters have an acute sense of forgetfulness and they speak incongruously. In desperate situations they contemplate suicide.

Lucky's dance, Estragon's and Vladimir's nonsense exchanges and Pozzo's words are amusing enough but they are equally balanced by Estragon's agony and despondency when he is beaten by somebody whose identity is undisclosed, Lucky is horribly treated and even physically abused on stage and all the characters exhibit physical deformities at one stage or the other. Characters engage in activities that seem frivolous while they intentionally convey the underlying truth about their anguished existence.

The audience is exposed to two extreme sides of life and the resultant effect is absurdity. Therefore, characters' reaction to the meaningless world they inhabit cannot be defined as comic or tragic, good or bad but absurd.

The Act of Waiting

Throughout the drama, Vladimir and Estragon engage in nothing but wait for Godot, a situation between action and inaction. Though Estragon wants to leave, Vladimir insists that they stay because Godot may arrive. Both the men are tied down to the act of waiting and time passes. They struggle to wait because there is nothing to do and nothing can be done about their condition. Their conversation is presented in the form of cross-talks, they often engage in comedy, Estragon sleeps, Vladimir paces up and down, and both are vexed because there is nothing to be done.

The audience too remains waiting for something to happen or someone to change the state of affairs, but they too have to wait. The entire drama is the situation in which man finds himself perpetually waiting and wanting, but he is never going to achieve anything. The audience can only partake of the dark humour, but they cannot be assured of Godot's arrival as the drama does not offer any hint.

The messenger boy is the only hope, but he too is uncertain about Godot's appointment with the two men. All he can say is that Godot would definitely meet them the next day and this message gives them the hope to wait for Godot, who could symbolise deliverance, change, achievement or any positive development in their lives and in turn for humanity to rejoice.

The Conception of Time

Uncertainty about the time of the action of the play and the chronology of events are crucial when the theme of the drama is considered. Vladimir and Estragon are uncertain about the day when Godot has promised to arrive. The repetition of events guarantees the passage of time, but the confusion whether they have seen the same boy the previous day or whether the boy has seen the same men the next day remains a question. In Act I, Vladimir says: "Time has stopped". In Act II, the tree has borne leaves, but this does not indicate a new life, promise or regeneration; it simply shows that they have been waiting and the tree is proof that they have been there before. The drama ends where it began and the two men have been waiting for Godot and engaging in conversation for several days. They are trapped in the infinite present time that neither moves forward nor builds on the past.

Suffering

Vladimir, Estragon, Pozzo and Lucky suffer physically, mentally and emotionally throughout the drama. Estragon is beaten up by unknown persons, Lucky is held by the rope around his neck and controlled by Pozzo. Though Lucky turns violent in between and kicks at Lucky's legs causing pain, Pozzo urges Estragon to repeatedly kick Lucky. Lucky is called "a pig" and treated like an animal. Lucky is made a source of entertainment for all and he is ordered to dance. Lucky's unhappiness is attributed to such demeaning activities.

Vladimir and Estragon seek solace in each other's company, though they think of parting ways several times, but they do not leave each other. Estragon returns to Vladimir every time he is beaten up and Vladimir consoles him. Vladimir panics when Estragon momentarily leaves him. In Act II, Vladimir sings a lullaby for Estragon who falls asleep. Their consolation lies in discussing about their suffering, suicide, waiting and engaging in nonsense activities. This also shows the extent to which they are frustrated.

Vladimir seeks recognition when the boy asks him what has to be conveyed to Godot. He seeks to be identified as a person while he is often mistaken or not identified at all. Pozzo and Lucky too suffer but they remain in their own worlds. They do not get involved in lives of others and it could be ascertained that their preoccupation with themselves would land them in greater trouble.

Character-sketch

The drama comprises seven characters—Godot, Vladimir, Estragon, Pozzo, Lucky, the boy and his brother, the shepherd. Vladimir, Estragon, Pozzo and Lucky represent mankind. The names suggest their nationalities. Vladimir is Russian; Estragon, French; Pozzo, Italian; and Lucky, English. On the whole, they stand for the entire human race. Vladimir and Estragon appear in the dress of a tramp, wearing ill-fitting clothes, big boots and bowler hats.

Godot

Not much is revealed about the identity of Godot. The Boy thinks that he has a white beard and mentions that he does nothing for a living. Godot is kind to the boy, but he beats the boy's brother who "minds the sheep". Vladimir and Estragon await Godot for salvation, but he claims that they are not "tied" to Godot "for the moment", Vladimir is scared that they would be punished if they ignore Godot. He tells Estragon that Godot has never promised to come and that they have requested for anything "definite" from him.

Since Godot never arrives, he remains an indistinct character. Esslin quotes Alan Schneider, the American director who asked Beckett who or what was meant by Godot, and received the answer, "If I knew I would have said so in the play" (48). The drama is ingenious because it conveys how anxious and bewildered the dramatist feels in the face of a deplorable human condition and the desperateness in being unable to find a meaning in existence. Any attempt to define or determine who or what Godot is respectively would end in disappointment because the drama rests on this uncertainty.

In the world of *Waiting for Godot*, "Nothing happens, nobody comes, nobody goes, it's awful!" Godot represents every hope for a better future where somebody or some different event would invigorate his existence. Godot is a figure that holds the drama together because his presence is felt in his absence. The drama rests on waiting for this unknown entity. Godot does not give them the appointment and their wait goes in vain. They can neither do anything nor have anything to do but remain entangled in the wearying and continual process of waiting.

Vladimir

Vladimir is the character that reflects and contemplates, and therefore he is the person who thinks. He puts forth serious questions such as "What are we doing here, *that* is the question" and "Tomorrow, when I awake, or think I do, what shall I say for today?... But in all that what truth will there be?" These questions reinforce the fact that Vladimir asks valid questions pertaining to the absurdity of their existence.

Nevertheless, he is more optimistic compared to Estragon. Though Vladimir finds life too much for one man, he realises it is futile to worry about it. He finds that since one of the thieves who was crucified with Christ was saved, it's a reasonable percentage to cheer. While life for Estragon is "worse", Vladimir learns that is better to get used to life as it happens and take things as they come.

Vladimir's soft corner for Estragon is evident when he had once "fished" Estragon out of the river Rhône. His responds to Pozzo's pleas for help in Act II. However, he cannot stand Estragon's "mental torments" of the nightmares and refuses to listen about them. Vladimir is aware of Estragon's physical ailments and offers to help Estragon when Lucky kicks him. He sings a lullaby when Estragon goes to sleep in Act II, and takes his coat off to blanket him.

He too suffers from an enlarged prostate gland and walks in an awkward manner, and occasionally does get irritated with the problem. Though Estragon complains of his "stinking breath", he finds solace in the company of Vladimir.

Estragon

Estragon who was once a poet, feels more and thinks less. Even though he sleeps frequently in the drama to find peace, he is rudely awakened by nightmares that remind him of the "horror of his situation" and he plunges into a state of mental distress. This anguish makes him unhappy, "accursed" and "in hell!" Life is so sordid for him and he often complains to Vladimir about his "puke of a life" and Vladimir expresses his disgust about listening to his railings.

Estragon resonates the poet Shelley and invents the insult "Crritic", but finds it difficult to express himself in words. He uses gestures to compensate for the loss of words. He refers to himself as "gesture towards his rags" and the world, "gesture towards the universe". As the play closes in, he finds that he cannot communicate definitely with words or gestures, and uses "wild gestures, incoherent words" that probably suggest that he can only feel his thoughts and not express them verbally as effectively as Vladimir.

He suffers from a swollen foot that always hurts, his feet stink and his boots are painful. Moreover, one of his lungs is weak. He prefers to sleep than ruminate or philosophise.

Pozzo

Pozzo announces himself proudly on stage in Act I and says "I am Pozzo!". Esslin remarks that Pozzo is "naively over-confident and self-centred" (60). Pozzo asks: "Do I look like the man who is made to suffer?" This boastful nature could be contrasted with his helplessness as he turns blind in Act II. While Vladimir and Estragon languish in an absurd world, Pozzo asserts he is a landowner. He says that they are on his land. He commands a social position that is best expressed in terms of his physical stature.

Pozzo owns Lucky, who he is fed up with and about to sell at a fair. He holds Lucky by a rope and makes him carry a heavy baggage. He uses a pipe, a pulveriser and a watch. Pozzo is attracted to materialistic aspects of life. He is preoccupied with time in Act I, but he loses his watch by the end of the act and turns blind in Act II, and eventually mentions about the advent of darkness and the ridiculousness of being preoccupied with time.

Pozzo dons the role of the master and Lucky is his servant. However, this relationship is not validated because Pozzo asserts that his fortune to fate or chance than his personal abilities. He mentions: "I might just as well have been in his shoes and he in mine". In Act II, he affirms that his blindness is also due to chance and Pozzo reiterates that he is as "as blind as Fortune", which means that fate has played a crucial role in his life. Similarly, Vladimir too says that he is controlled by fate.

Pozzo is clear that actions and decisions taken by man do not influence man's conditions in life as chance or fate does. He remarks: "Night...will burst upon us (snaps his fingers) pop! like that!...just when we least expect it" and concludes, "That's how it is on this bitch of an earth" Pozzo declares that all that that has to take place is predestined. Perhaps the most significant statement made by him is the ephemeral nature of human life that "gleams an instant".

Pozzo reiterates the need for friendship. He seeks the approval of Vladimir and Estragon for the short speech he has rendered. However, his relationship with Lucky is quite ambiguous because at one time he confides that Lucky used to be kind to him once, but now Pozzo is fed up with Lucky's irritable manners and intends to sell him at the fair. He calls Lucky "pig" and "hog" and urges Estragon to "give him a taste of his boot, in the face and the privates as far as possible". In Act I, he requires Lucky's help to shoulder his luggage and to carry out his orders, and in Act II, the blind Pozzo depends on Lucky's sight to be led on and off the stage. He is in fact tied down to Lucky.

Lucky

Lucky enters the stage with a "terrible cry" that petrifies Vladimir and Estragon who huddle at a corner of the stage curious to know where the sound has come from. The entrance of the proud and domineering Pozzo with a whip in his hand and holding a rope tied around his servant Lucky for controlling him is a deviation for Vladimir and Estragon who are anxiously waiting for Godot. Pozzo is initially mistaken for Godot.

Lucky first appears to be sleeping on the stage, standing. He is so weighed down by the luggage he has to carry that he sags down until the baggage touches the floor and startles and sags down again. He assumes the role of Pozzo's servant and expects little from his master. However, Lucky cries when his master says that he is fed up of him and intends to sell him at the fair.

Though Pozzo mentions that Lucky taught him about beauty, grace and truth and was kind to him at one time, but now he is "killing" him, he does not provide more information to prove his statements, hence these claims are dubitable. Pozzo adds that Lucky used to dance for joy, but now he dances to depict how he is trapped "in a net". Lucky is in fact, tied by a rope and held by Pozzo. Lucky exhibits the qualities of a thinker when the hat is on his head. Lucky's lengthy diatribe expresses his difficulty in expressing himself in words.

The speech also presents the noticeable themes in the play—no hope of salvation because of "divine apathia", the insignificance of man because he is "seen to waste and pine" and the hard, indifferent and cold quality of existence as exemplified by the earth being an "abode of stones". Lucky becomes dumb in Act II, and he clings on to Pozzo or rather Pozzo is tied down to him, which means that they are mutually dependent on each other.

The Boy

The boy is Godot's messenger who conveys the message that Godot will not visit Vladimir and Estragon on the appointed day, but the next. He fails to recall seeing them the previous day and addresses Vladimir as Mr. Albert. He says that Godot is kind to him, but beats his brother, who minds the sheep. Godot has a white beard and he does not do anything.

The Revelation of *Waiting for Godot*

The drama maintains a balance of optimism and pessimism, albeit the sense of pessimism pervades the drama. Vladimir's observation that one of the two thieves that was crucified with Christ was saved while the other was damned does instill the sense of hope of salvation; however, none of the characters is said to have been saved, and there is no improvement in their physical conditions. While Vladimir and Estragon have their afflictions, Pozzo turns blind, Lucky becomes dumb and the shepherd boy is sick in Act II. Their salvation from pain, anguish, and the boredom of existence depends on the arrival of Godot, who never comes.

The characters show concern for the other, but they are also cruel at times. They are all distressed and in spite of desperate cries for God's mercy, and pity on their condition, the signs of pity are not manifested in the drama. The drama is open-ended, which means that it maintains a cyclic structure and obviously the wait for Godot will continue ceaselessly. However, Vladimir's observation that nothing is certain cannot be ruled out. The ingenuity of the dramatist lies in the fact the ambiguity of the situation is artistically rendered through dramatic devices and the juxtaposition of contrasting pairs of characters that not only account for the inherent plurality of thematic concerns but also the universal uncertainty in man's condition.

Waiting for Godot as a Universal Tragedy

The starting point of an analysis of tragedy and its dimensions dates back to Aristotle whose *Poetics* provides a comprehensive view of the prerequisites of a tragedy. He delineates characteristics of a hero, who is noble by birth, good or evil by nature, portrays his suffering to show changes in his fortune that culminates in his downfall and the essential suffering being caused by the tragic flaw in his character. For Shakespeare, character is destiny and not entirely "divinity shapes our ends" of things that happen in life. Down the ages, tragedy has taken many forms, but *Waiting for Godot* is pre-eminently the tragedy of mankind. Man's existence is tragic because he lacks a clear vision of the nature of the existence he is put into.

The prominent problems that characterise the age are the ramifications of the social, economic and political conditions that plagued the society. The World Wars, and the internal strife in several countries from the early twentieth century onwards witnessed drastic changes in the perception of art. The contribution of science and the development of technology instilled a new faith in scientific pursuits than religion. Man was considered the epitome of perfection and his ambition was nurtured by conquests and imperialistic notions.

War, destruction of mankind, craze for technological advancements, lust, thirst for domination and economic power in the world exposed the worst side of human civilisation during and after the wars. Irreverence for religion for its seemingly irrelevance at the time, the futility of intellectual pursuits, people's inability to effectively communicate with each other, the anguish felt at being isolated and living in dread resulted in the perception of the absurdity of human existence.

Man's sense of tragic existence is expressed in *Waiting for Godot* through the experiences of Vladimir and Estragon who are desperately waiting for Godot for their ultimate release from mental, physical, and emotional anguish that are now a part of their existence. Vladimir and Estragon are not human beings of any social stature but they are human beings who share their joys and sorrows with the common man.

Life is an incomprehensible nullity and complete disenchantment is at the core of the drama. Vladimir and Estragon engage in the fundamentally absurd and futile activities throughout the drama and they also get involved with Pozzo and Lucky and it becomes evident that their "existence has been a quest ending in nothing" (Le Sage 47). Even in the face of defeat, they show the defiance to give up and continue to wait for better times. Their dignity lies in their stubbornness to endure and this is their tragedy.

Beckett's Ingenuity as a Dramatist

Granville Hicks mentions: "Reading Beckett is an enigmatic experience and often an unpleasant one, but it is an experience" (14). Beckett's works concentrate on several aspects of human life that are beyond materialistic and other superfluous concerns. An analyses of the themes in his works would show his preference for delving into several aspects related to death, destruction, decay, futility of existence, nihilism, solitude, insecurity and the reduced status of man. The world that is occupied by the characters is static because it is devoid of dynamism and motion. If at all they move, they crawl like Molloy and if they are still, they are either glued to the wheelchair like Hamm or reside in bins like Nag and Nell, and Murphy sits on his rocking chair.

The characters in his plays do not uphold positions nor are they entitled to fortune, but they are individuals who experience the anguish of existence is a world that is predestined to end without hope of redemption of mankind. The futility of existence is at the core of Beckett's works who probes into man's discussion with his intimate self, questioning his action, purpose and relevance. The apparent differences in the personalities of his characters in no way emulate his stature, for these are immaterial so far as the dramatic concerns are explicated. Friedman mentions:

> His characters are in a more advanced state of despair than Camus's "absurd" men or *révoltés,* than Colin Wilson's "outsiders". They are physically maimed as

> well as psychologically at disproportion with their society.... They have in common an acute lack of awareness, an inability to cope with the exterior world. Their only concrete wrong, in the moral sense, seems to be that they exist. (281)

Deformed and crippled characters or those with physical ailments figure in Beckett's plays. Watt is a dwarf with a hunchback, and walks awkwardly; Molloy is an old bed-ridden man; the old couple Nag and Nell are legless and Hamm is blind who moves about in a wheel chair. Vladimir suffers from an enlarged prostate gland and Estragon has a swollen foot.

Characters are cast into a bleak landscape, a void, an emptiness that also fills the minds of the characters. Their search for meaning is futile because they do not know what they are searching for. Molloy searches for his mother's room, Malone searches for Pim who lies in the mud for reasons unknown, and Vladimir and Estragon are engaged in waiting for Godot, who never arrives. All the characters in Beckett's plays are curiously agitated, which makes them search helplessly, but the search itself is a tedious activity because the reasons are unknown to them.

A pertinent question related to the search is connected to the central concerns of plays, which are not on an ordinary level, but metaphysical, in that they extend beyond the predictable plane of comprehensibility. Le Sage comments: "The work of Beckett is one long cry of metaphysical despair, and in its utterance nothing is left of the novel we refer to as conventional" (47). Though characters inevitably search for a clue to locate reason in an absurd world, they eventually fail. Murphy, Watt, Vladimir, Estragon, Nag, Nell and Hamm are preoccupied with the inward journey of looking at the self and perceiving it in relation to the world outside.

Beckett's work is characterised by a strong sense of pathos. Physically incapacitated, they wait helplessly. Their helplessness is revealed through the employment of dark humour that intrudes their world. Though the audience may find their actions ludicrous, it is in this capacity that Beckett reveals the essence of living in a world that renders not only them but also the others they come into contact with, as helpless.

Time is a crucial factor because where there is only a grave situation presented, there cannot be fixity of time, and the locales never change. The journey is in the mind of the protagonists, and invariably the stream-of-consciousness technique is applied in the dramas. Formal dialogues are replaced by words, phrases and crisp sentences. Precision of dialogue is replaced by incoherent babbling that delves into the characters' thoughts. Beckett's works are difficult to understand because they do not intend to say something about the character or develop a plot but they convey the sense of experiencing the situation by allowing the situation to speak for itself through the characters.

When a situation is explored in diverse works of an artist, often the theme that recurs assumes greater relevance and that connection appears more significant. Nakedness or the state of semi-nakedness assumes symbolic value in Beckett's works. Murphy sits naked in his rocking chair; Malone, who is bed-ridden crawls naked through the mud in search of Pim, and Estragon's trousers are pulled down to his ankles. These actions disturb the audience than provide comic relief. They indicate man's condition—impoverished, isolated, agitated with his self, suffering ailments, and want of clothing and a few possessions indicate the artist's intention to strip man of the external trappings and expose his real battle with the metaphysical problem of being or existing.

Confinement is one of the most pertinent images that recurs in Beckett's plays. Just as the characters live in constructed environs, they occupy restricted spaces and their world is sealed too. Their lives are examined closely within the narrow confines of a room, an empty space, or a lone road without many companions. The characters are roped into the space from where they cannot escape. Beckett confines space and the other external features of drama to penetrate workings of the human mind and take the investigation to the metaphysical level of understanding human plight.

Beckett has effectively involved the audience into a situation where he confronts a void, remains within the lacuna, and faces nothingness. Beckett's achievement is the creation of the situation that involves human beings as characters and the universal condition is presented with stark reality.

Conclusion

Beckett deserves special mention because he has presented the quest for nothing on stage by defying conventional standards of presentation and does not describe such a situation but creates it on stage with artistic precision, albeit using techniques that depict the condition perfectly. In other words, Beckett has shown how man is alienated by his circumstances being created by himself intentionally and then suffers isolation and moves on to record his sensations in a depraved world to ruminate over possible salvation and culminates in disappointment.

The irony in the world is that man is the cause of distress in the world that cries out in despair against the practices of the world and ends up lamenting on his own downfall. Beckett has used the stage to ponder over such questions rather than discuss contemporary social issues. His dramatic prowess is the outcome of his associations with dramatic inventiveness of an age that witnessed two World Wars that shook the entire world.

The dexterity with which he handled absurd situations by using minimal language and incorporating other dramatic devises supplements his intentions and the audience is swayed by the gradual movement from one emotion to the other without any interruption in the thought pattern. The most impressive part of Beckett's contribution to drama is the felicity of expression by disrupting traditional modes of dramatic presentation and making the world his stage and the people of the world the audience that comments on its own fate.

Glossary

proposition : suggestion
fortuity : chance; good luck
vexed : displeased; upset
yearn : desire
accursed : ill-fated; doomed
resonates : resounds; echoes
petrified : terrified

invigorate : rejuvenate
ephemeral : transient; short-lived
dubitable : uncertain; open to doubt
diatribe : tirade; lecture

References

Bair, Deirdre. *Samuel Beckett: A Biography*. Jonathan Cape, 1978.

Bloom, Harold, editor. *Samuel Beckett: Modern Critical Views*. Chelsea, 1985.

Duckworth, Colin. *Angels of Darkness: Dramatic Effect in Samuel Beckett with Special Reference to Eugene Ionesco*. Allen and Unwin, 1972.

——, editor. *Samuel Beckett's En attendant Godot*. Harrap, 1966.

Esslin, Martin. *Samuel Beckett: A Collection of Critical Essays*. Prentice-Hall, 1965.

——. *The Theater of the Absurd*. Doubleday, 1961.

Fletcher, John. *Samuel Beckett's Art*. Chatto and Windus, 1967.

Hassan, Ihab. *The Literature of Silence: Henry Miller and Samuel Beckett*. Peter Smith, 1967.

Hobson, Harold. "Samuel Beckett, Dramatist of the Year." *International Theatre Annual*, No. 1, Calder, 1956.

Kenner, Hugh. *A Reader's Guide to Samuel Beckett*. Farrar, Straus and Giroux, 1973.

Malick, Javed. *Samuel Becket: Waiting for Godot*. Oxford UP, 1989.

McMullan, Anna. *Theatre on Trial: Samuel Beckett's Later Drama*. Routledge, 1993.

Radke, Judith. *Yale French Studies*. Spring-Summer, 1962, pp. 59-63.

Robinson, Jeremy. *Samuel Beckett Goes into the Silence*. Kidderminster. Crescent Moon, 1992.

Theatre of the Absurd. https://www.britannica.com/art/Theatre-of-the-Absurd

https://www.oxfordreference.com/view/10.1093/oi/authority.20110803095345289

https://www.bl.uk/20th-century-literature/articles/nonsense-talk-theatre-of-the-absurd

https://books.google.co.in/books/about/The_Theatre_of_the_Absurd.html?id=J7iQNBOp7Q4C&redir_esc=y

Chapter 25

Eugene Ionesco and the Theatre of the Absurd

Introduction

The Theatre of the Absurd gained popularity within a short span of time, and though devoid of any stage paraphernalia that the conventional theatre boasted of, this theatre was able to revolutionise the stage because of its ingenuity of perception. The desire to capture the futility of existence in a world of political, social and economic unrest prevailed, and made dramatists of the Theater of the Absurd frame their unique modes of expression. The theatre spread its influence to countries such as Finland, Norway, Argentina and Japan, which means that the theatre was successful in influencing theatrical presentations in every part of the world with their unique mode of presentation.

Eugene Ionesco (1909-94) completed his secondary education in Romania and attended Saint Sava National College. He specialised in French from the University of Bucharest between 1928 and 1933 and qualified as a teacher of French. With a grant from the French government to study in France, he wrote his thesis *Sin and Death in French Poetry since Baudelaire*. He worked as a proofreader during World War II for a publishing house in Paris.

He disliked theatre though he read fiction, listened to music and visited art galleries. He expressed his dislike for theatre actors who were "making a spectacle for themselves" and delineated two trajectories of reality—the concrete that included the movements of characters on stage, limited by the realities they faced; and the imagination, which could never reconcile with the concrete (qtd. in Esslin 82).

The Development of Eugene Ionesco as a Dramatist

It is believed that using the *Assimil* method, he began to study English. He meticulously copied down sentences and memorised them. After reading the sentences several times over, he realised that he was in fact not learning English but discerning several true facts related to common life from the expressions used in English. His encounter with lessons in English only deepened his interest in elements of truth depicted.

For instance, mundane activities of Mrs. and Mr. Smith in several lessons enabled him to realise the methodical approach of Mrs. Smith in her search for truth. This perhaps was responsible for Ionesco's use of parody, disjointed fragments of words and caricatures in his plays instead of clichés of conversation in conventional drama. He described the process of writing a play, which he called *anti-play,* to be "a parody of a play", which during the process of composition, sank into "nothingness" taking him along with it.

Against his will, he wrote his first play (*La Cantatrice chauve*) in 1948 that was first performed in 1950 with the English title *The Bald Soprano,* directed by Nicolas Bataille. The play was not quite successful until it received critical acclaim from the French dramatist Jean Anouilh (1910-87) and the French novelist Raymond Queneau (1903-76). His wrote the other one-act absurd plays such as *The Lesson* (La *Lecon*, 1951), *The Chairs* (Les *Chaises*, 1952), and *Jack, or the Submission* (*Jacques ou la Soumission*, 1955).

These absurd plays, characterised as anti-play (anti-pièce in French) conveyed the modern expressions of alienation and the inability and ineffectiveness of communication by employing the force of comedy and using parody to instigate the conformist tendencies of the bourgeois and traditional forms of theatre. In all his plays, Ionesco disregarded the conventional plot and used cyclical repetition of events to reveal certain situations in lives of characters. Replete with incoherent dialogue, he disregarded exploring mental states of characters and depicted the mechanistic world inhabited by characters who resembled puppets and spoke in illogical patterns. Moreover, the sense of menace pervaded his plays.

His full-length plays are Amédée, *or How to Get Rid of It (Amédée, ou Comment s'en débarrasser*, 1954); *The Killer* (*Tueur sans gages*, 1959) and *Air and Matter* (*Le Piéton de l'air*). The pivotal character in *The Killer* is Berenger who expresses his wonder and anguish at the strangeness of reality. Berenger faces death in the figure of a serial-killer. In *Rhinoceros*, Berenger watches his friends turn into rhinos and he stands alone in his fight against conformism. Ionesco expresses his disgust and horror at the insensible conformist stand of the people and the uselessness of rational thinking in a world dominated by the fascist Iron Guard in Romania in the 1930's.

The King is Dying (*Le Roi se meurt*, 1962) projects King Berenger I, who represents a figure trying to come to terms with his own death. *The Killer without Reason* or *The Killer without Cause* (*Tueur sans gages*) is a play written by Eugène Ionesco in 1958. It is the first of Ionesco's Berenger plays, the others being *Rhinocéros* (1959), *Exit the King* (1962), and *A Stroll in the Air* (1963).

Hunger and Thirst (*La Soif et la faim*, 1966), *Killing Game* (*Jeux de massacre*, 1971), *Macbett*, an adaptation of William Shakespeare's *Macbeth* (1972) and *This Wonderful Mess* (*Ce formidable bordel*, 1973) are other major works of Ionesco. "Notes and Counternotes" is a collection of writings by Ionesco that explain the reasons why he decided to write for the theatre and elicit the responses of his critics. In the first section of the collection titled "Experience of the Theatre", Ionesco details his displeasure with the theatre as a child because "no pleasure or feeling of participation" (Ionesco Marie-France 15) was provided. He seems to have expressed his disregard for realistic theatre, which is not interesting in comparison with the theatre that appeals to an "imaginative truth," which he finds to be more motivating and liberating than the "narrow" truth represented by strict realism (15). Ionesco adds that "drama that relies on simple effects is not necessarily drama simplified" (28).

Ionesco's Perception of Drama

Ionesco's first drama *The Bald Soprano* (1950) did not receive any acclaim, and to his dismay, he found the people more interested in plays that he considered fit only to nurture bourgeois enterprises. Moreover, he disliked the Brechtian stage where the actor functioned like a pawn in a chess game. He intended to enlarge the dimensions of theatre to effect a change in the portrayal of characters. He projected crude caricatures that moved beyond petty drawing-room amusement and intercepted violence with comedy in dramatic presentations.

In the article "The Avant-Garde Theatre," Ionesco observes: "...the new dramatist is one...who tries to link up with what is most ancient: new language and subject matter in a dramatic structure which aims at being clearer, more stripped of inessentials and more purely theatrical; the rejection of traditionalism to rediscover tradition, a synthesis of knowledge and invention, of the real and imaginary, of the particular and the universal...." Through the employment of the grotesque, Ionesco wishes to expose the ludicrousness and artifice innate in language and drama by shattering their constructs. He does not wish to annihilate the language and drama; instead he calls for a new birth and new ordering of literature when he says, "I hope this is just a temporary end, that literature—like the phoenix—will be reborn from its ashes."

He conceived the notion of employing shock tactics with a purposeful negation of language to arrive at a new perception of reality. He went beyond Brecht's notion of the alienation effect and stretched the simulation of reality to a different level. Ionesco firmly denounced developing any new ideas for his plays, but explained his ideas after conceiving them. He explored the static situation of his characters that ended where it had begun. He was more interested in portraying the mystery of life by relying on the surreal experience that captured the absurdity of the common and the usual everyday experiences.

Brief Analyses of Select Plays of Eugene Ionesco

The Bald Soprano (1950) is about the Smith couple from London and another family, the Martins who come over for a visit. Their discussion is meaningless chatter with stories and nonsensical clichés and poems. Mary, the Smiths' maid and the local fire chief who is also Mary's lover join the banter. Later the Smiths and the Martins engage in senseless arguments. As the play ends, the Martins repeat the lines spoken by the Smiths at the beginning of the drama. The characters are dispassionate and they assume the identity of others because they were devoid of an identity themselves. The play is considered an attack against the "universal petty bourgeoise...the personification of accepted ideas and slogans, the ubiquitous conformist" (qtd. in Esslin 28).

The Lesson (1951), a one-act play begins at the office of a professor, who in his fifties or sixties and expecting a new student. At the sound of the doorbell, the maid announces the arrival of a young, cheerful woman in school uniform. The professor introduces himself to the student before beginning the lesson. He writes several maths equations on an imaginary blackboard and tries to make the student understand them. The lesson progresses in an absurd manner, the professor gets frustrated and accuses the student for her ignorance. The student becomes quiet but complains of a toothache. The professor wields a knife under her nose and tries to have her pronounce the word "knife". The professor ultimately stabs the student to death. The scene ends with the maid welcoming another student to the house.

Labelled a "tragic farce" by Ionesco, the drama *The Chairs* (1952) is about an elderly couple who live in a circular tower on an island that sets up chairs and greets invisible guests who have come to their house to listen to the old man's message to the world. The old couple commits suicide by jumping into the sea and the message is left in the hands of an orator who is deaf and mute and cannot communicate the contents of the message to anybody. He writes something on the blackboard, which is a muddle of meaningless letters. Ionesco mentions that the Theatre of the Absurd considers human existence futile and the drama highlights isolation and the purposelessness of human existence.

In the programme for the original production of the drama, Ionesco mentions: "As the world is incomprehensible to me, I am waiting for someone to explain it." The inability to communicate is the predominant theme of the drama; nevertheless, the audience consists of rows of empty chairs, which indicates the absence of people. The theme of the drama is nothingness that is made clear when the impossibility to reason out transgresses the limits.

Amédée or How to Get Rid of It (1954) is a comedy in three acts, where Amédée and his wife Madeleine, who is a switchboard operator discuss what to do about a growing corpse in the other room. The corpse causes mushrooms to sprout all over the apartment and the neighbours get suspicious. The reason why the corpse is in the house is not explained. Towards the end of the play, Amédée makes efforts to drag the corpse away to dump it in the river and many including a person named Eugene, who is apparently the dramatist himself watch the corpse float away with Amédée attached to it because his legs get tangled. The perfunctory actions of the characters and their inability to think logically reinforces the element of the grotesque.

In *The New Tenant* (1955), a new tenant, a caretaker and two movers are seen on stage. The tenant moves into the house and the two movers continuously bring pieces of furniture. Many pieces of furniture accumulate and finally, there is a complete wall of furniture around the tenant. When the last piece is shoved in, the tenant is seen happy in his new room and from somewhere within the room, he asks someone to turn out the lights.

Victims of Duty (1953) is about an investigation, where the detective intends to find out whether the former tenant of Mr. Choubert spelled his name Mallot with a "t" or Mallod with a "d". Choubert does not know Mallot, but the detective convinces himself and Choubert that Mallot is Choubert's pal by bullying him. Choubert gets mentally agitated and he is left dazed at times, sometimes half-dead and ecstatic at other times. The detective and Madeleine force him to track down Mallot. Several images float in Choubert's mind and at one stage, he finds himself conversing with his dead father, apparently they cannot hear each other.

The detective turns into a psychoanalyst and the drama is a sort of psychological drama which Ionesco called a "pseudo-drama" because characters should find a solution to the riddle presented at the beginning of the play. The detective feeds Choubert with bread so that he can recall Mallot and Choubert's wife Madeleine brings cups of coffee; however, Choubert is tortured and nothing is revealed. Esslin notices that the entire drama could be considered the search into the subconscious mind where no solution can be found and only a gaping hole of nothingness remains. The subconscious mind is an endless pit, a complete void (103).

The drama *Rhinoceros* (1959) is about the people of a town who are infected by a strange disease called rhinoceritis, which transforms them into rhinos and makes them strong and aggressive. The protagonist Berenger is the only person who does not change into a rhino because only he possesses faith in humanity and only he can resist the natural tendency to follow the masses. The drama bears historical overtones, where the people of Germany could not resist the enticement of Hitler. The drama is as much an indictment of defiance as it projects how absurd it is to conform.

The individual is caught between the inability to join the masses and concomitantly feels at a loss because he feels an outcast. The drama also points out to the futility of rationality in a world that is largely unintelligible. The logician's explanation of syllogisms and the idea of engaging in rational explanations is also absolutely unnecessary in a world that is torn by the World Wars and existence is painful.

Some of the Selected Works of Eugene Ionesco

Poetry

- Elegii pentru fiinte mici (*Elegies for Minuscule Creatures*, 1931)

Plays

- *La Cantatrice chauve* (1950, *The Bald Soprano* in the United States and *The Bald Prima Donna* in Britain)
- *La Leçon* (1951, *The Lesson*)

- *Les Chaises* (1952, *The Chairs*)
- *Le Maître* (*The Leader*, 1953)
- *Victimes du devoir* (*Victims of Duty*, 1953)
- *La Jeune Fille à marier* (*Maid to Marry*, 1953)
- *Amédée ou comment s'en débarrasser* (*Amédée, or How to Get Rid of It*, 1954)
- *Jacques ou la soumission* (1955, *Jack, or the Submission* in the United States and *Jacques, or Obedience* in Britain)
- *Le Nouveau Locataire* (*The New Tenant*, 1955)
- *Le Tableau* (*The Picture*, 1955)
- *L'Impromptu de l'Alma* (*Alma's Impromptu*, 1956)
- *L'avenir est dans les œufs au Il fot de tout pour fair un monde* (*The Future is in Eggs or it Takes All Sorts to Make a World*, 1957)
- *Tueur sans gages* (1958, *The Killer*)
- *Scène à quatre* (*Foursome*, 1959)
- *Rhinocéros* (1959, *Rhinoceros*)
- *Le Roi se meurt* (1962, *Exit the King*)
- *Le Piéton de l'air* (1963, *A Stroll in the Air*)
- *La Soif et la faim* (1964, *Hunger and Thirst*)
- *La Lacune* (*The Gap*, 1966)
- *Jeux de massacre* (*Massacre Games*, 1970)
- *Macbett* (1972)
- *This Wonderful Mess* (*Ce formidable bordel*, 1973)
- *Productions, 1972 to present* (in French)
- *L'Homme aux valises* (*The Man with the Suitcases*, 1975)
- *Voyage chez les morts* (1980, *Journeys among the Dead*)

Essays and theoretical writings

- Nu (Naked, 1934)
- Hugoliades (Hugoliades, 1935)
- La Tragédie du langage (The Tragedy of Language, 1958)
- Expérience du théâtre (Theatre Experience, 1958)
- Discours sur l'avant-garde (Speech on the Avant-garde, 1959)

- Notes et contre-notes (Notes and Counternotes, 1962)
- Fragments of a Journal (1966)
- Découvertes (Discoveries, 1969)
- Antidotes (1977)

Novels and Stories

- *La Vase* (*The Vase*, 1956)
- *Le Piéton de l'air* (*The Air Pedestrian*, 1961)
- *La Photo du colonel* (1962, *The Colonel's Photograph and Other Stories*)
- *Le Solitaire* (1973, *The Hermit*)

Operatic Adaptations and Libretti

- Le Maître (The Master, 1962) Music by Germaine Tailleferre of Les Six
- Maximilien Kolbe (1988) Music by Dominique Probst

Brief Summary of the drama *Rhinoceros*

Character List

- Berenger
- Jean
- Logician
- Daisy
- Mr. Papillon
- Dudard
- Botard
- Mrs. and Mr. Boeuf
- The people of the Town—the old gentleman, the grocer, the grocer's wife, the housewife, the café proprietor, and the waitress

A Brief Summary of the play *Rhinoceros*

Berenger and Jean are friends, who meet in a small town square. While Jean is refined and looks elegant, Berenger is an alcoholic. Jean reprimands Berenger for his drinking habits and his lousy appearance. Suddenly, a rhinoceros runs through the square and all the people except Berenger are shocked. The logician explains the concept of syllogism to an old gentleman, and the entire conversation is absolutely illogical. Berenger discloses to Jean his love for Daisy, the typist in his office. Jean asks him to change his demeanour and appear more presentable.

Their conversation is interrupted when another rhino rushes by and tramples the housewife's cat. The people of the town discuss about the species of the animal rather than find out the cause for the sudden appearance of the rhino. Berenger and Jean quarrel over the physical details of the rhino and Jean scurries off after calling Berenger a drunkard. Though the people ask the logician for a solution to clear up the confusion, his tirade leads nowhere. Though Berenger decides to change his ways, he is certain that he would not be able to compromise his individuality.

In Berenger's office, his co-workers argue with Botard, and Berenger and Daisy confirm that they have seen the animal. Botard says that the appearance of the rhino is an instance of "collective psychosis" and they carry on with their work. Mrs. Boeuf rushes in and says that her husband is sick and he will resume work soon. She tells them that she was chased by a rhino, which now waits downstairs. The rhino destroys the staircase to ascend, but Mrs. Boeuf recognises the rhino to be her husband. Though Daisy hurries to call the fire station to rescue them, Mrs. Boeuf decides to stay with her husband without caring for the insurance she could claim, and rides off on the back of the rhinoceros. Many rhinos are reported in the town and Berenger decides to meet Jean.

Berenger visits Jean who is sick. His voice becomes hoarser, a bump on his nose grows and his shin gets greener. He becomes cynical about the human species and speaks in favour of rhinos. His visits to the bathroom confirms that he sounds and resembles a rhino. He declares that humanism is dead and sheds his itchy clothes. In the bathroom off-stage, he grows into a full-blown rhino and tries to break free. Berenger rushes out but sees a herd of rhinos galloping.

Berenger has nightmares and struggles not to drink, but eventually he does. Dudard visits him and discusses Jean's transformation. They regard the metamorphosis as an epidemic. Dudard urges Berenger not to feel guilty about Jean's transformation. Dudard reveals that their boss Papillon has turned into a rhinoceros. While Dudard considers the transformation natural, Berenger continues to feel them abnormal. A herd of rhinos pass by and Berenger spots the Logician's hat on a rhinoceros. He vows not to become one.

Daisy visits Berenger, which makes Dudard jealous. She informs them that Botard has metamorphosed. Daisy and Dudard reiterate that it would be better to move along with rhinos, but Berenger refuses. They understand that firemen have turned into rhinos. Dudard leaves them because he wants to experience the transformation in person, and joins the herd of rhinos. Berenger claims his love for Daisy, and vows to protect her. He blames himself and Daisy for the transformations of Jean and Palillon, but Daisy asks him to shrug off the guilt. They turn on the radio, but the sound of the animal is heard. The phone rings, but they hear the rhino trumpeting. The rhinos have taken over every office.

When Berenger proposes to reinvigorate the human race, Daisy finds the rhinos seductive. Berenger slaps her, but Daisy remains firm in her loyalty to the rhinos. Daisy breaks up with him and leaves. Berenger doubts his own humanity. He inspects the photographs and does not recognise any of his former friends. He feels the rhino heads are more elegant and they are more grotesque. He becomes desperate, but vows not to surrender to rhinos.

Conclusion

Eugene Ionesco is one of the absurd dramatists who has projected the world in a novel manner because he has included the imaginative domain in his plays. Similar to the other dramatists of the Theatre of the Absurd, he has endeavoured to present a rather dismal picture of the world shredded into pieces by the World Wars. In his plays, he has brought out the inherent notion of the vacuity of the universe that is devoured by power and greed. His works disparage the world that is replete with designs that forever cause animosity among the people.

The plays are a way of exposing the ridiculousness of language and meaningful communication that is devoid of any purpose.

Each dramatist of the Theatre of the Absurd has delineated several causes for the disintegration of humane values and Ionesco has deftly exposed the same through his distinctive perception.

Glossary

ingenuity	:	creativity
perception	:	insight
menace	:	threat
conformist	:	traditionalist
caricature	:	travesty
artifice	:	pretense
innate	:	inborn
ubiquitous	:	pervasive
void	:	vacuum

References

Brockett, G. Oscar, and Franklin J. Hildy. *History of the Theatre.* 10th edition. Pearson Education Limited, 2013.

Crawford, Jerry L., Catherine Hurst and Michael Lugering. *Acting in Person and in Style.* 5th edition. Waveland Press, 2010.

Esslin, Martin. *The Theatre of the Absurd.* 3rd edition. Penguin, 1991.

France Peter. *The New Oxford Companion to Literature in French.* Oxford UP, 1995.

Ionesco, Eugene. "The World of Ionesco." *International Theatre Annual*, No. 2, London, 1957.

Ionesco, Marie-France. *Portrait de l'écrivain dans le siècle: Eugène Ionesco, 1909-1994.* Gallimard-Arcades, 2004.

Styan, J.L. *Modern Drama in Theory and Practice:* Volume 2, *Symbolism, Surrealism and the Absurd.* Cambridge UP, 2013.

Rhinoceros. http://www.kkoworld.com/kitablar/ejen-ionesko-kergedan-eng.pdf

Rhinoceros. Audio Book. https://learningally.org/BookDetails/BookID/HR537#

Esslin, Martin. *The Theatre of the Absurd*. Doubleday, 1961. https://edisciplinas.usp.br/pluginfile.php/4892127/mod_resource/content/2/THEATRE%20OF%20THE%20ABSURD%20BY%20MARTIN%20ESSLIN.pdf

Chapter 26

Rhinoceros

Act–I

It is summer and the sky is clear blue on a Sunday afternoon as the drama opens at the square of a small, provincial town. There is a house up-stage that comprises a ground floor and one storey. The window of the grocer's shop is seen on the ground floor. Above the window of the shop, the word EPICERIE is written in bold letters. The grocer and his wife stay in their quarters on the first floor of the house. Atop the grocer's house, the spire of the church is visible. A street is visible between the shop and the left of the stage. To the right of the grocer's shop, slightly at an angle the front part of a café is visible. Several chairs and tables occupy the stage and a dusty tree is seen near chairs at the terrace.

The sound of church bells is heard before the curtain rises, and a woman carrying a basket of provisions under one arm and a cat under the other, as the curtain opens crosses the stage noiselessly from right to left and exits. The grocer's wife opens her shop just then and remarks that she does not like the woman because she is too conceited to buy any provisions from her. Jean and Berenger enter the stage at the same time from the right and the left respectively. Jean is immaculately dressed with tidy clothes, polished shoes and wears a clean shaven look. Berenger, however looks shabby with wrinkled clothes, untucked shirt, and disheveled hair.

They sit at the café and Jean criticises Berenger for being late. When Berenger enquires when he arrived, Jean admits that he came at the same time as Berenger, but he does not prefer to wait. Jean provokes Berenger about his scruffy looks and his heavy drinking, and says, "You reek of alcohol". Berenger does not refute Jean's claims. He says that nothing interesting happens in town, and he doesn't enjoy his work. Berenger describes the previous night he has spent drinking, while celebrating their friend Auguste's birthday and as he orders his drink for the day, when a strange noise is heard far off. It appears like the sound of the panting of a beast and it grows louder and reaches a feverish pitch. The two men have to shout to resume their conversation.

Their conversation is interrupted by a rhinoceros dashing off stage and in panic, all those who are at the town square react differently, simultaneously. They all say, "Oh! A rhinoceros! The grocer's wife calls out to her husband to see the animal. The woman with her basket of provisions and cat, drops only the basket in alarm. The proprietor of the café demands an explanation to the noise and confusion outside. The logician wearing a straw hat and an eyeglass notices: "A rhinoceros going full-tilt on the opposite pavement". They cannot believe that they have actually seen a rhinoceros charging past them. The animal disappears as strangely as it appears and the noise subsides.

Except Berenger, they all say at once, "Well, of all things!" and try to resume what they have been doing. Berenger mentions that the animal that went past them looked like a rhinoceros that raised a lot of dust. The grocer, an old gentleman dressed elegantly help her gather the littered grocery and the logician holds her cat. The proprietor mentions that the animal went past like a "comet". Jean and Berenger order their drink, "two pastis" from the waitress and Jean tells Berenger that he cannot believe that a rhinoceros has just galloped past them.

The logician who joins the conversation explains what syllogism is. He says that it "consists of a main proposition, a secondary one, and a conclusion." Jean interrupts saying that animals should not be allowed within the town, and a protest should be made against the Town Council and initiates to fret about the animal. Berenger tries to persuade him that the animal might probably have escaped from the zoo. Jean accuses Berenger of dreaming and he is not convinced because the town does not have a zoo, animals being destroyed by the plague "ages ago". Berenger replies that he has not been dreaming, and dreaming while sleeping and while being awake are the same. He adds that the animal could have come from some "travelling circus". Jean says that the Council has banned travelling performers and there haven't been any since their childhood, to which Berenger responds that it must have been hiding in the swamps.

Jean retorts that his friend lives in "a thick haze of alcohol" and hence he blabbers not knowing that their district is known as "little Castille" because the land is parched. They continue to accuse each other until Jean retorts that Berenger never tries to understand the intensity of the situation where a rhinoceros runs amok on a Sunday afternoon when the streets are full of children and people of all ages. Berenger gives in to Jean's argument and considers their quarrel over a "wretched perissodactyle", a "stupid quadruped" worthless because the animal, which "has already disappeared,...doesn't exist any longer."

Berenger changes the conversation and orders for more drinks even though Jean disagrees. Just then Daisy, the pretty typist who works with Jean and Berenger passes by. Berenger gets nervous and spills Jean's drink on him, which angers Jean. Berenger asks him not to shout so that he can hide from Daisy. He would feel embarrassed if she sees him in this condition. After Daisy moves away from them, Jean enquires why Berenger drinks heavily because he is destroying himself and digging his grave. Berenger answers that he feels more himself and the world otherwise is boring. Jean replies that he suffers from "alcoholic neurasthenia, the drinker's gloom." Berenger says that he feels he has to carry his body that seems as heavy as lead and he doesn't even know who he is. He understands himself only after the drink enters his body.

Jean accidentally knocks the logician, who has returned. The logician resumes his conversation with the old gentleman about syllogisms while taking their places on the chairs at the terrace right behind Jean and Berenger. Jean tells Berenger that he is not only physically strong but also mentally because he does not drink. He says that Isidore and Fricot have four paws, and anything with four paws is a cat and so Isidore and Fricot are cats. When the old gentleman mentions that his dog has four paws, the logician concludes that the dog is a cat.

Berenger continues to express disgust over his solitude and the company of people does not offer solace. He comments that he does not have the strength to continue living. Jean says that Berenger's statements are contradictory and he is "devoid of logic". The logician says that logic is good as long as it is not abused. Berenger observes: "There are more dead people than living. And their numbers are increasing. The living are getting rarer." When Jean questions how Berenger could be oppressed by something that does not exist, Berenger reveals his particular state of mind and wonders whether he himself exists. Jean replies that only thinking confirms existence and Berenger has to sharpen his mind and become a cultured person.

Their conversation is taken over by the logician's bizarre syllogism that all cats die and Socrates is dead, therefore Socrates is a cat. While the logician continues to talk about some weird mathematics on the number of paws that the cats have, the conversation between Berenger and Jean centre on Daisy. The exchange between the two pairs of men is depicted by Ionesco in succession. Jean assesses that Berenger is not indifferent to Daisy, but he cannot expect Daisy to be attracted to a drunkard. Berenger reveals that Dudard, his colleague, qualified in law is just as much attracted to Daisy as he is. Dudard is more qualified than Berenger is, and so he has a great future, therefore he has a better chance to win Daisy's affection.

Jean tells Berenger: "Life is a struggle, it's cowardly not to put up a fight". He could use the "weapons" of "patience and culture, the weapons of the mind" and turn sharpen his intellect. Jean advises Berenger to dress well, "cut down on drinking", and keep himself updated about the "cultural and literary events of the times." Jean says that Berenger could give himself time to nurture his talent with "a little method". He also suggests that Berenger could use time constructively by visiting museums, reading literary periodicals and attending lectures.

These activities would solve his troubles and improve his awareness of facts. In four weeks, he would turn out a cultured man. Jean even suggests purchasing a ticket for an avant-garde play by Ionesco instead of squandering money over drinks. The drama would be an excellent portrayal of the artistic developments of the times. Berenger promises to book two seats for the theatre, but Jean declines saying that he has to accompany his friends for a drink and asks him to keep up his promise. In the meantime, the logician's discussions with the old man continue with the number of paws of the cats and at one stage, their conversation intercepts with Berenger's and Jean's. It seems the logician is answering Berenger's questions.

Suddenly, the sound of rapid galloping hooves, trumpeting and panting is heard from the opposite direction, from the backstage to the front. Though Berenger argues over Jean's party with friends, Jean explains why it is all right for him and not for Berenger. Jean becomes agitated by the noise and everybody, one after the other shout: "Oh, a Rhinoceros". The chairs in the café are upturned and the glasses break. There is commotion as people flee for their lives. When the rhinoceros departs, the housewife laments because the beast has run over her cat. The proprietor tries to calm her down with brandy, which she refuses and the old gentleman consoles her saying that death is natural.

Jean notices that that the rhinoceros looks different from the one that earlier went past them. Though the grocer's wife and the proprietor disagree, Jean affirms that the first rhinoceros with two horns was an Asiatic rhinoceros and the other with a single horn, an African. Berenger refutes Jean's claims because nobody could see the rhinoceros as it dashed past them swiftly; moreover, it was running with its head down. The housewife expresses her anguish at the cat's death and she is inconsolable. Berenger and Jean quarrel over the rhinoceros and Berenger calls Jean a pedant. He claims that the Asiatic rhinoceros has only one horn and the African, two. The argument over rhinoceroses becomes very complex and they continue to argue without any solution. To settle matters, they turn to the logician, who speaks with confidence but does not arrive at any conclusion. Nothing substantial turns out, and Berenger accuses himself for arguing with Jean over the animal.

Analysis

The action of the drama takes place at the centre of a town where people usually gather. Characters such as the grocer, the waitress, and the housewife are typical representations and generic individuals, not individually etched out. Each character is allegorical in nature for they characterise diverse philosophical tendencies.

The act brings forth the theme of persuasive reasoning against deceptive logic. The logician appropriately contradicted the illogical conversation between Berenger and Jean, but his reasoning is absolutely misleading and defective. Though he explicates syllogism, he is unable to distinguish the major premise and the minor one when he has to apply them to real-life situations. His argument that anything with four legs is a cat and for this reason even a dog could logically be called a cat is defective logical reasoning. Mathematical calculations on the number of paws of a pair of cats and otherwise are ludicrous so far as the technique of logical analysis is concerned. Though he exerts considerable confidence when he is asked about the number of rhinoceroses that arrive, his answer is definitely nonsensical. His reasoning does not resonate with the premise framed.

Logic and truth are questionable in the play because the logician is given the upper hand in such discussions and his folly is accepted by the people of the town. Nonetheless, the townspeople blindly accept his faulty reasoning because of their inability to rationalise the situation for themselves. They are not gullible but they depend on the claims of the logician for the simplest and superficial discussions too.

The arrival of the charging rhinoceros from nowhere, twice in the first act forms the basis of the drama that prepares the audience for Ionesco's use of the animal for purely absurdist themes. The animal could be envisaged as the manifestation of a ruthless power that is diabolical and megalomaniac. The sudden appearance of the rhinoceros terrorises the characters and they are completely taken unawares.

An unsettling feeling, foreboding danger lurks round the corner. The people are defenceless against the charge of the rhinoceros and though the first time there is no destruction to property or loss of life, the second charge of the rhinoceros kills the housewife's cat and the proprietor of the café loses some glasses and chairs. The people of the town are not in favour of the rampage of any animal.

Certain critics comment that Ionesco was interested in the theme of futility and this often surfaces in his dramas. Ionesco fervently demonstrated the irrational side of human nature and questioned the importance of everyday life. This could probably be the reason why Berenger drinks to drown his sorrows and seems disinterested in life. He does not care about being socially or personally responsible. His attitude questions the meaning of ordinary and everyday actions that govern human lives.

Jean and Berenger are foils. Berenger is shabby, but Jean maintains himself. Jean is definite about his concerns and his opinions, while Berenger maintains a defeatist attitude. He is not sure about his existence or rather the purpose of his existence. When Jean realises that Berenger's affection for Daisy could bring him about to experience life, his advice to Berenger to maintain himself and become intellectually and culturally well-informed attracts him; however, there are doubts whether he would follow the advice.

Act–II

Scene–1

The act opens in a government office that is a large firm of law publications. Above the double door, a notice reads: *Chef du Service*. Near the door of the Head of the Department at the up-stage is the typist Daisy's little table with a typewriter. There is another table where the employees' register book to mark their presence is kept. Berenger sits on the left and Botard on the right of the room at the up-stage. The tables of Dudard, the Deputy-Head and Mr. Boeuf are also placed. The Head of the Department is Mr. Papillon, about forty years of age, immaculately dressed in dark blue suit with a rosette of the Legion of Honour, starched collar, black tie and wearing a large brown moustache.

Dudard is a promising young man, tall and thirty-five years old, dressed in a grey suit with black lustrine sleeves to protect his coat. He could wear spectacles. He would become the Department Head if Mr. Papillon gets promoted as Assistant Director. Botard is short, and sixty years of age with a little white moustache. He knows, understands and judges everything. He wears a Basque beret, and during working hours he wears a long grey blouse. His spectacles are on his long nose, a pencil behind his ear and he also wears protective sleeves at work. Botard, a former school teacher does not like Dudard.

Botard mentions a strange incident in the town square that has driven the town panic-stricken from the newspaper, which he does not intend to believe. The office discusses the episode involving the rhinoceros. Daisy says that she has seen the animal run across the road and Mr. Papillon reads the news that a pachyderm has trampled a cat to death. Botard enquires about the colour and gender of the animal, which is too insignificant.

Daisy is surprised that the conversation has shifted to the "colour bar", which obviously has nothing to do with the incident being reported, but Botard does not give up. He says that Southerners imagine too much and "People make mountains out of molehills". Mr. Papillon asks Daisy about the incident and affirms that the rhinoceros did not stroll but it ran through the streets. The conversation regarding race, colour of the cat and the rhinoceros resumes in a rather ludicrous manner.

Berenger arrives late to the office and when he is asked about the story of the rhinoceros, he supports Daisy's story and mentions being in town with his friend Jean at the time of the incident. Botard retorts: "Your rhinoceros is a myth", but Berenger affirms that he has seen the rhinoceros. Botard continues to refute Berenger's claims, and says that he is unreliable in being able to recall the incident because he is always drunk. He calls the incident of the rhinoceros "a hoax" that is meant for propaganda. Botard ridicules the so-called "rhinoceritis" movement and says that the people of the town are not gullible to be swayed by empty rhetoric.

Mr. Papillon is curious to know where Mr. Boeuf is because he has not turned up. Just then, Mrs. Boeuf arrives, panting. She says that her husband has contracted flu and he hopes to be back on Wednesday. She mentions that she was chased from her house by a rhinoceros, and now the beast is waiting beneath to come upstairs.

Just then a noise is heard and the staircase steps crumble under the formidable weight of the animal. An anguished trumpet is heard and everybody panics. Botard accepts the reality and determines that there is an "infamous plot" stirring. Berenger says that it has two horns, and it could probably be the Asian species or the African one. Mr. Papillon declares that the appearance of the rhinos is the fault of the management. Suddenly, Mrs. Boeuf cries out because she realises that the rhinoceros is her husband.

Mr. Papillon says that Mr. Boeuf has been fired. The others inform Mrs. Boeuf that she could collect the insurance and file for divorce. Daisy wonders how Mrs. Boeuf would collect insurance if this is the situation in the town. Botard exclaims: "It's the sheerest madness! What a society!" and decides to lodge a complaint with his union. Nobody believes that a man could turn into a rhinoceros.

Mrs. Boeuf is too devoted to her husband to abandon him in such a condition. Though Daisy calls the firemen for help, Mrs. Boeuf jumps out of the window and lands on her husband's back. The rhino trumpets tenderly and they ride away. Daisy reports that she cannot contact the firemen because there are reports of rhinoceros' incidents all over the town. Initially, there were seven but now there are seventeen and thirty-two rhinoceros' incidents have been unofficially reported. Botard declares that he never thought the stories related to the rhinoceros were false. He claims to understand the entire rhinoceros issue, but he will not explain it to anyone.

The firemen arrive and usher everyone out of the window to safety. Mr. Papillon declares that everybody should be back in the office for work by noon. Berenger decides to find Jean and settle the dispute with him. Berenger and Dudard move out of the window together and the curtains are drawn.

Analysis

A group of people in the office read the newspaper and the incident regarding the rhinoceros gathers everyone's attention.

Mr. Papillon, Botard and Dudard find it difficult to believe that a rhinoceros has actually entered the town. Botard criticises Berenger, who he says is always drunk and he cannot be believed. The issues of race and the colour of the cat that are discussed are illogical. His baseless arguments are similar to the logician's false reasoning in Act I.

Botard believes that he is a critical thinker and so he does not believe the news in the papers because he trusts his reasoning power and his false logic. He claims to have a "methodical mind", which is ironical because he is far from being rational, hence he could be considered an absurd figure. He is unaware that the people are turning into rhinos. Botard could be associated with the Germans who refused to believe that the Nazis would exterminate the Jews.

Daisy and Berenger claim to have seen the animal, but nobody believes them until Mrs. Boeuf barges in saying that her husband is sick and she has been chased by a rhinoceros that is waiting to come upstairs. To everybody's shock, Mrs. Boeuf realises that her husband has been transformed into a rhinoceros. The baseless arguments of the people as they talk about the insurance, the species and even the carelessness of the people of the town suggest the fundamental absurdity of the situation that the people do not wish to perceive. The people do not discuss the reasons for such a transformation but engage in discussions related to the species of the animal. They fail to realise that they live in a place where people could be transformed into rhinos!

The intensity of the absurd situation deepens because the element of absurdity seeps through the mind of the audience who surmise the intention of the dramatist. Ionesco adds a tinge of humour at the end of the act, when Berenger and Dudard exit the window together because both of them are too polite to leave first. Just as strange events take place, strange are actions of the people. In this scene, Ionesco portrays how the society and the workplace are disrupted and disturbed. Ionesco leaves the audience to decide why he would have introduced such an inexplicable event as the transformation of people into rhinos.

The drama is Ionesco's denunciation of man's basic savage instincts or his capacity for cruelty. Mr. Papillon and the others who compel Mrs. Boeuf to be pragmatic under the circumstances are more savage than Mr. Boeuf who is tender to his wife even after the transformation. Botard tries to accuse Dudard for the existence of the Rhino. Hence, the question of savagery of the animal is disputed. Botard's claim that the appearance of the rhinos is a matter of "collective psychosis" is to be considered. Moreover, his claims of a conspiracy that those who join the herd are traitors and the others renegades cannot be ruled out. Those who resist are a minority that are bad, the others who are for progress are categorised good. His inconsistency is evident when he first denies rhinos and then contradicts his previous denial.

Act–II

Scene–2

The scene is Jean's house. Berenger visits Jean in his apartment. The door is locked and the neighbour, the old Mr. Jean opens his door. A brief talk, and Berenger understands that his friend Jean was seen last night, apparently grumpy and he has not been around since morning. A disheveled Jean finally opens the door and Berenger notices that Jean has been in bed all the while, he looks sick and his voice has turned hoarse too. Both the men do not seem to recognise each other's voices. Berenger apologises for the indecorous behaviour the previous day, but Jean does not recall the incident in the café or the incident with the rhinoceros.

Jean complains of a sore throat and a pain on his forehead and he does not know how he developed the ache. When Berenger says that he would have developed the ache rather unconsciously, Jean denies the claim and says that he is the "master" of his thoughts, which suggests that he is always clear about what he thinks. Berenger then says that the bump above Jean's nose could have occurred because he would have knocked himself somewhere, but Jean refutes the statement.

Jean continues to behave in an odd manner and mentions that he does not believe in their friendship. As he converses, his breathing becomes heavier, his voice gets hoarser, and he develops fever and headache. He mentions that his forehead hurts and Berenger notices a bump above his nose and other odd signs.

Jean's skin becomes hard and its turns green in colour, while his veins become swollen. Though Berenger suggests consulting a doctor, Jean refuses saying that he distrusts doctors because they are quacks and he prefers veterinarians.

When Berenger mentions that the wretched rhinos are all over the town and the havoc they have created, and admits that it was his fault to start the quarrel, Jean says that he doesn't remember the incident. He becomes increasingly misanthropic, which is evident when he comments: "It's not that I hate people. I'm just indifferent to them—or rather, they disgust me; and they'd better keep out of my way, or I'll run them down." Berenger thinks Jean is passing through a "moral crisis", because the morality of such a change is questionable, but Jean is not bothered. He becomes restive, gets irritated with his clothes and his skin gets greener.

Jean paces the room like an animal in distress. Berenger informs Jean that Boeuf has turned into a rhino and Jean says that it "obviously gave him great pleasure to turn into a rhinoceros". Jean tells Berenger that rhinos are living creatures that have equal right to life as human beings do. Berenger argues that the animals have no right to destroy human life to which, Jean retorts that human life is in no way superior to other lives. When Berenger tells that moral standards have to be maintained, Jean argues that "Nature" should replace moral standards because nature maintains its unique rules, and morality is against nature. As the discussions continue, Jean moves swiftly in and out of the bathroom, loses his human voice and begins to resemble a rhino each time he goes in and comes out.

When Berenger enquires whether moral laws should be replaced by the laws of the wild, Jean consents and says: "We've got to build our life on new foundations. We must get back to primeval integrity." Berenger says that Jean must accept the fact that human beings do not share similar inimitable philosophical values with animals, which has taken several centuries to build. Jean trumpets, and asks not to talk about mankind because "humanism is all washed up", which means humanism is dead and Berenger is a "ridiculous old sentimentalist". When Berenger asks Jean whether it would make a difference if he turns into a rhinoceros, Jean replies, "I'm all for change" and affirms that there is nothing wrong in being a rhinoceros.

Just then Jean's body turns completely green, the bump on his forehead is his horn, and he makes weird sounds. He says that he feels hot, his clothes itch, and he needs the swamp. With his head down, he darts to the bathroom. Berenger notices the longer horn and Jean transforms into a rhinoceros. Though he feels that he cannot leave his friend in such a condition and should seek medical help, Jean shouts out that he would trample Berenger and a fight ensues. Berenger, realising he does not stand a chance in the fight, tries to escape and closes the bathroom door behind him, but Jean, now a full-grown rhino pierces the door with his horn to break free.

Terrified, Berenger shouts: "He's a rhinoceros, he's a rhinoceros!" and goes to the old man and his wife for help. They don't understand what the fuss is about and in a moment they too turn into rhinos. Out of the window, Berenger is horrified to see "an army of rhinoceroses, surging up the avenue", charging. He flees in terror as he declares that rhinos are not isolated animals, and yells, "Rhinoceros!"

Analysis

This scene is quite disturbing because Ionesco presents the actual process of transformation of human beings into rhinos and traces the plausible reasons for such a depiction. Berenger and Jean do not recognise each other's voices. It is strange that Jean forgets the incident of the rhinoceros the previous day. Berenger witnesses the human transformation into the rhinoceroses, and the probable reasons being unkindness to humanity and getting desperate. As people in larger numbers get transformed Berenger gets more terrified and he feels isolated. The central question is whether all the characters would get transformed in a similar manner and if so, what would be in store for mankind.

Jean is like the other people, normal, in the sense that his transformation like others is attributed to the way people are generally unconcerned about others, hostile, mean, insensitive, callous and unsympathetic. It remains to be seen whether

Berenger too would turn out like others. Berenger's individuality is distinct and he seems to act differently from the people around him. It remains to be seen if this difference would in any way contribute to the central question of the transformation of human beings into animals.

Ionesco stages the curious transformation of human beings into animals on stage and the gravity of the situation coincides with the absurdity projected on stage. However, the pivotal argument is that human behaviour is absurd or rather ludicrous so that the theatre is completely justified in presenting such a situation that calls for a precise and better understanding of human experience.

Act–III

Berenger is asleep in his room and he is having a nightmare. Dudard visits him, but Berenger is unable to recognise his voice. Berenger is obsessed that his voice may be changing and that he may be transforming into a rhinoceros, but Dudard convinces him that he is normal so far and there is nothing to worry. Berenger is dismayed about Jean but Dudard reproaches Berenger and says that he must neither dramatise the situation nor think about Jean's transformation.

Dudard comprehends the situation of humans turning into rhinos to be like contracting influenza or developing madness. Though Dudard endeavours to reason out the inexplicable happenings related to the rhinoceros, Berenger rejects any logical or rational explanation offered. When Dudard asks him to accept the situation, Berenger simply refuses. Dudrad discloses the news that Mr. Papillon has turned into a rhinoceros as well, Berenger is unable to believe that Mr. Papillon could turn into the animal. Dudard claims that he neither supports the rhinos nor defends Papillon's choice to become one. They argue as if they are involved in politics of the transformation, which is rather unfortunate. Dudard and Berenger make their political stand clear.

Dudard considers himself logical, objective and scientific in making observations and deducing inferences. Berenger responds that he understands things intuitively. When they take a look down at the window to see the rhinos racing madly, Berenger recognises the logician who has turned into a rhinoceros because of the red hat on its head. Berenger uses the opportunity the prove that Dudard's concept of logic is of little importance. Dudard claims that there should be a substantial reason to turn into a rhinoceros.

Daisy enters Berenger's apartment and conveys the news that Botard has turned into a rhinoceros. Botard's view that it would be better to move with the times is probably true because he is one among the rhinos. Daisy observes: "Nobody seems surprised any more to see herds of rhinoceroses galloping through the streets. They just stand aside, and then carry on as if nothing had happened." This means that people no longer seem to be concerned or anxious about the transformation into the animal. Daisy prepares lunch for all, but the sound of the rhinos become irresistible. They look out of the window to see herds of rhinos galloping, but not a single human being.

Dudard mentions that he is not hungry and prefers to eat outside on the grass. He declares that he chooses "the great universal family to the little domestic one," which means he has decided to be a part of the family of rhinos. He prefers to be a part of the large and thriving family of rhinos rather than human beings whose numbers are dwindling. Though Berenger argues that man is superior to the rhinos, and it is man's duty to oppose the animals firmly and lucidly, Dudard does not listen, but joins the herd of animals. He turns into a rhinoceros that cannot be differentiated from the herds passing by.

Left alone, Berenger and Daisy are at peace and Berenger finds the right moment to declare his love for her. Though Daisy does not sound as passionate as Berenger, she looks forward to a blissful life with Berenger. Later, they imagine their life together, reading books and talking long walks and involve in philosophical discussions and Daisy declares that are mutually compatible, probably better than most couples, and Berenger falls in love with her. The phone rings and though they choose not to answer it, they eventually pick up the phone and hear the rhinoceroses trumpeting on the other line. They turn on the radio and again only hear the sound of trumpeting. It becomes evident that the authorities have also turned into rhinoceroses and they may be the only humans left in the locality.

When Berenger expresses his love for Daisy, she takes on an unsympathetic stand to allow things take on their course rather than force things to happen. She says that nothing can be done in such a condition. Berenger asserts that the rhinos are mad but Daisy reiterates: "We must try to understand the way their minds work, and learn their language." Berenger mentions that they could have children and allow the family to grow, and pleads with Daisy to "save the world," but Daisy replies rather unapologetically, "Why bother to save it?" Daisy is enamoured by the rhinoceroses outside. She compares the sound of trumpeting to singing and their movements to dancing. She extols them as Gods and exits abruptly.

Isolated, Berenger delivers a lengthy monologue. Depressed that Daisy has left him, he poses several questions: "What is my language? Am I talking French?" and "What do I look like? What?" At last he finds the rhinos beautiful and exclaims: "Oh how I wish I looked like them.... Their song is charming." He even tries to turn into a rhinoceros by imitating their trumpeting sound and asking for a horn to grow; however, he remains human. Then he realises the futility of the attempt and as the curtains draw, he declares that he will "put up a fight against the lot of them. I'm the last man left, and I'm staying that way until the end. I'm not capitulating!"

Analysis

Berenger's room resembles Jean's, and when Dudard enters, Berenger does not recognise him. Their dialogue is similar to the exchanges between Berenger and Jean in the previous act. Berenger is the only character that is anxious about turning into a rhinoceros. He says: "I'm frightened of becoming someone else." He cannot ignore the situation at hand, but he does not seem to reconcile with the situation. He confesses, "I can't get over it," but he cannot agree with Dudard's comment that nothing can be done about the situation for he is not prepared to accept defeat.

When Dudard decides to join the animals, he feels he is obliged to join his peers, unlike Berenger who argues against the move and oppose the rhinos. Dudard cannot refrain from joining the majority. Ionesco points out that it is illogical and absurd to fit in and trust an authority like the logician as well as the supposed authority of the majority. Daisy too gradually changes sides by showing her affiliation for the rhinos. Despite the initial reluctance of the people to shift their perspectives, the way the rhinos are swift and effective to attract larger numbers of foregrounds how difficult it is to resist the multitude. Though Dudard is intelligent, focused and career-oriented, and Daisy, beautiful and caring, they could not resist the desire to fit in with the multitude.

The ultimate transformations of Dudard and Daisy have historical implications. Dudard's false perspective represents the covert danger that comes with political or cultural apathy, when he tells Berenger, "You must learn to be more detached." People accept totalitarianism or fascism for several absurd reasons. People are easily taken in by false promises and hopes. They do not train themselves to see through falsehood and adopt good ones. Similarly, democracy is healthy for the society so far as it does not turn out to be tyrannical and the people passively subject themselves to the uncontrollable, dark forces of human nature.

Berenger is different from all the other characters in the drama. He not only resists the influence of the majority but also considers resistance the best weapon to defy the beast. Though he tries to imitate certain features of the animal, his individuality cannot be persecuted, exchanged or transformed. His victory lies in his effort to remain himself in the face of all sorts of pulls and appeals.

Berenger's final monologue testifies to the strength of character and commitment to a moral code. He resolves to wage a battle and stage his resistance to join the helpless crowd that conform to whims and fancies of dictatorship. To claim political and personal responsibility and not be taken in by trivialities and false assumptions or reasoning makes a person active, creative and intelligent, otherwise man would end up dangerous and irresponsible like the animal.

Berenger, who was a drunkard who found little meaning in life discussed ways by which he could refrain from drinking.

He felt hopeless and was left clueless about the necessity of following everyday actions that left him isolated in an absurd world. Towards the end of the drama, he makes a comeback, being strong and resilient enough to defend the human race. The effort to find worth in one's actions is to believe in a cause and fight to achieve it.

Conclusion

Berenger visits his friend Jean, who he finds is sick. Jean has fever, headache and his voice has turned hoarse. Jean behaves oddly and he is twitchy. He is disinterested in Berenger's request to forgive him for his rude behaviour the previous night because he fails to recall the instance. Moreover, he is cynical about human beings and civilisation, which is dead. Principles, morals and values no longer exist. He prefers the law of the jungle and says that the world must be governed by the rule of nature where all the living beings are equal before the law.

Berenger does not accept Jean's claims, but he is unable to argue further because Jean's skin turns green and leathery, his horn protrudes, his clothes itch, and he starts to growl like an animal. His visit to the bathroom each time makes him restless and his transformation into a rhino is complete. When Berenger tries to lock the door, the rhino pierces the door with its horn to run free. Berenger is aghast because the old couple next door has also transformed into a pair of rhinos and the entire street is full of these animals running helter-skelter. Berenger rushes out of the house, crying aloud "Rhinoceros!"

The drama opens on a Sunday noon, where the people carry about their daily chores. The grocer and his wife, the housewife, the waitress, the logician, an old gentleman and the colleagues Jean and Berenger are seen on stage. While each person is involved in one discussion or the other, the sudden arrival of a charging rhinoceros unnerves each one of them. However, Berenger seems the least affected of all. He is dejected with life, which is partly due to his indifference to the importance of routine. His inability to gain the attention of Daisy, the young woman in his office seems to disturb him. Jean advises him to become more presentable by maintaining his looks, being aware of cultural and intellectual pursuits and showing interest in theatre.

The discussion on syllogism by the logician is absurd because it defies the notion of rational thought and valid statements. However, the people of the town approach him to deduce their notions. The arrival of the rhinoceros the second time causes the death of the cat that is trampled on and the proprietor of the café suffers breakage of glass. Though they are all upset about the animal, their discussion about the species of the animal ends in unnecessary argument without any outcome.

Mr. Papillon is the department head of a law firm. The others are Dudard, the Deputy-Head; Mr. Boeuf; Mr. Botard; Berenger; Jean and Ms. Daisy. Barring Jean, the others discuss the situation in the town where the rhinos were seen the previous day. Mr. Botard thinks the incident is a conspiracy, but Daisy and Berenger affirm that they have seen the animal rushing past them. However, the discussion takes a ludicrous turn when the species of the animal and race issues are given more importance.

The scenario changes when Mrs. Boeuf hurries in to inform them that Mr. Boeuf will not attend office because he is down with flu. She says that she is chased by a rhinoceros to the office and it is waiting downstairs. To everybody's shock, Mrs. Boeuf recognises the animal to be her husband, and though she is induced to file for divorce and collect the insurance amount, she rides away on her husband's back because she does not want to desert him. The instance of humans transforming into rhinos becomes a matter of concern and alarm. Daisy reports that the number of rhinos is increasing at an alarming rate and everybody is frantic to move to safety.

Berenger and Dudard disagree on several grounds, especially with regard to their observations on the transformation of human beings into rhinos. While Dudard claims to be more logical, Berenger says he is intuitive. Berenger is aghast that Mr. Papillon has turned into a rhino. Daisy brings the news that even Botard has transformed. Dudard considers it better to move along with the animals than follow human beings because people flow with the times and it would be wise not to go against the tide. Since more number of people are transforming into rhinos it would be unwise to remain different and he transforms into a rhino. Daisy loves Berenger but she too decides not to save the human species from the diabolic forces and joins the herd of rhinos. Berenger is too determined to give up. He is ready to defend the human race from further annihilation.

Glossary from the Text

Steeple	: spire; turret
perspective	: in view
Stuck-up	: conceited; snobbish; arrogant
Cirrhosis	: cirrhosis of the liver due to excessive drinking
wretched perissodactyle	: mammals which constitute the taxonomic order Perissodactyla, are hoofed animals. Here, the reference is to the rhinoceros
a stupid quadruped	: an animal which has for feet. Here, the reference is to the rhinoceros
pastis	: sour whiskey
Chef du Service (French)	: department head
Papillon (French)	: butterfly
Boeuf (French)	: beef
unicorned	: having a single horn
myth	: fable
opiate	: to dull the senses
hoax	: deception
propaganda	: publicity
formidable	: impressive; awesome
illusion	: delusion; false impression
wherefores	: reason to know why
hallucination	: delirium
provocation	: incitement
infallible	: dependable
décor	: interior design
banister	: handrail
quinsy	: inflammation of the throat
virility	: quality of having strength and string sex desire
mauling	: criticising
debauches	: demeaning behaviour

Brrrr... : initial stages of a growling sound, animal like
primeval : primordial
divan : couch
apprehensive : anxious; worried
barricaded : obstructed; blocked
migraine : severe headache accompanied by nausea and disturbed vision
dramatise : exaggerate; overstate
freak : fanatic
caprice : whim; fancy
plausible : reasonable; probable
influenza : virus infection; cold
blue-stockings : women having intellectual or literary interests. The word is derived from the blue worsted stockings worn by members of a C18 literary society.
insomnia : sleeplessness
masochist : a person who takes pleasure in pain and suffering
fatalism : defeatism; acceptance
Don Quixote : A Spanish novel by Miguel de Cervantes, published in two parts, in 1605 and 1615. The eponymous protagonist is a middle-aged gentleman from the region of La Mancha in central Spain, who is obsessed with the chivalrous ideals hyped in books he has read. Here, the reference is to Berenger, who acts like Quixote mentions Dudard.
incensed : enraged
extenuating : mitigating
inquisitors : investigators; cross-examiners
'E pur si muove' (Italian)
: And yet it moves. A phrase associated with the Italian physicist and philosopher Galileo Galilei (1564-

	1642) in 1633 after being forced to retract his claims that the earth moves around the sun.
dogmatism	: rigidity
vestige	: remnant
anarchic	: antigovernment; rebellious
Cardinal de Retz (1613-79)	: He is one of the leaders of the aristocratic rebellion known as the Fronde (1648-53), whose memoirs remain a classic of 17th century French literature.
Prelate	: an ecclesiastical dignitary of high rank
Mazarin	: Original name Giulio Mazarini (1602-61). French cardinal and statesman, born in Italy
The Duke of St. Simon	: Louis de Rouvroy, duke de Saint-Simon (1675-1755). He is a soldier and writer known as one of the great memoirists of France. His Mémoires is a significant historic document of his time.
polyglot	: multi-lingual
capitulating	: surrendering; submitting

References

Brockett, G. Oscar, and Franklin J. Hildy. *History of the Theatre*. 10th edition. Pearson Education Limited, 2013.

Crawford, Jerry L., Catherine Hurst, and Michael Lugering. *Acting in Person and in Style*. 5th edition. Waveland Press, 2010.

Esslin, Martin. *The Theatre of the Absurd*. 3rd edition. Penguin, 1991.

Ionesco, Eugene. "The World of Ionesco." *International Theatre Annual*, No. 2, London, 1957.

Styan, J.L. *Modern Drama in Theory and Practice: Volume 2, Symbolism, Surrealism and the Absurd*. Cambridge UP, 2013.

Rhinoceros. http://www.kkoworld.com/kitablar/ejen-ionesko-kergedan-eng.pdf

Rhinoceros. Audio Book. https://learningally.org/BookDetails/BookID/HR537#

Chapter 27

A Critical Study of *Rhinoceros* and Eugene Ionesco as a Dramatist

Background of the Drama *Rhinoceros*

Ionesco's experience of World War II, Adolf Hitler's rise to power, the formation of the Nazi Party in Germany as well as the Iron Guard in Romania were the immediate causes for the production of *Rhinoceros*. The Iron Guard was a fascist organisation that specifically targeted the universities, while Nazis persecuted Jews. The Iron Guard practiced anti-Semitism. The rather ludicrous argument among the people of the town and officers regarding the species of the animal—Asian or African reflects the Nazi observation that Jews were intruders from Asia.

The rhinos represent the Aryan race that is superior, powerful and violent. Ionesco disagreed with several political agendas that were aimed at destroying humanity. The play *Rhinoceros* goes on to take larger resonances so that its meaning is not confined to the Nazi experience in Europe but moves on to stand for the herd behaviour of people in any kind of totalitarian experience whether of the rightist or the leftist varieties.

Themes

Absurdity

The play presents the situation where a town is first visited by a rhinoceros that creates panic among the people and later, probably another rhino tramples a cat. It is believed that a queer illness called "rhinoceritis" has gripped the entire town and the characters engage in ludicrous arguments that do not lead to the reason for the appearance of the animal, but questions on the number of horns of the animal that decides its species and colour! These strange events followed by the ludicrous arguments of characters to make sense of their situation add to the difficulty in trying to understand what the play posits. Hence, the use of rationale, logic and language fail to explicate the strange incidents of the play.

The logician defines a syllogism as an argument that has two sets of propositions, which help to reach a conclusion. However, his example that if cats have four paws then Fricot and Isidore are both cats because they have four paws is illogical. This conclusion is absurd, the identity of Fricot and Isidore is vague and their existence is doubtful. The logician distorts logic when the old gentleman's dog is actually a cat because it has four paws. The distinction between the categories of dogs and cats is not taken into account and this is sheer irrationality.

The logician carries forward with logic by introducing a math problem. He asks the old gentleman what would happen if two legs are taken away from Isidore and Fricot. He adds that an animal with more or fewer than four paws and the corresponding four legs is not a cat. The old gentleman concludes that they could have cats with six legs and a few with no legs at all. Their discussion entails that any attempt to rationalise and make sense of the world is insufficient and ridiculous and logic, and if distorted can lead to erroneous and inaccurate conclusions. The logician tells the old gentleman that logic is good so far as it is not manipulated as they have been engaging in.

The arrival of the second rhinoceros on the stage, which tramples and kills a cat and causes havoc is more serious. The old gentleman, the logician, Jean, Berenger, the proprietor and the grocer get into an absurd conversation about the number of horns of the rhinoceros that would decide whether it is Asian or African. This discussion apparently surfaces even in Mr. Papillon's office after Mr. Boeuf turns into a rhinoceros and destroys the staircase of the office. Daisy is alarmed that nobody gives importance to the fact that there are rhinos running around and they fail to explain the reason for the rhinos all over and consequences.

Though all the characters except Berenger are well-educated, cultured and intelligent, they eventually turn into rhinos and none of their attributes save them from "rhinoceritis". Berenger is shocked to see his friend Jean turn into a rhinoceros in front of his eyes, and at its readiness to attack him. He is helpless before Dudard and Daisy. He stands alone amidst the raging animals. He concludes that language is meaningless.

He can neither comprehend the situation nor critically comment on the condition of the people around him. He is unsure whether he speaks French because he fails to convince his friends and lover. Now, his question is whether speaking any language would in any way better his lot because there is nobody left to converse with. Berenger is unable to make sense of the world and his own inability to join the rhinos. This indicates that logic and rationality could be futile if the world is essentially illogical, senseless and ridiculous.

Fascism

The play is an overt denouncement of the fascist Iron Guard in Romania and Nazism in Germany. "Rhinoceritis" is a metaphor for fascist regimes and totalitarian concerns. The play alludes to the peculiar effect of coming under the control of such authoritarian rules that gradually infect larger multitudes and spread wide to involve as many people as possible. Their objective to inject their propaganda into innocent minds can have disastrous effects. The fascist organisations destroy independent thinking, step up surveillance, provides no room for escape and command servitude. The dehumanising effects of fascist movements are a threat to individuality and humanity, and they are deftly shown by Ionesco in the play.

Insensible decisions, unhealthy relations, false ideologies, and political propaganda for power overrule democratic ideals and sensitiveness to concerns of social, political and economic importance. All the characters except Berenger are carried away by the rhinos that metaphorically represent fascist ideologies. Irrespective of a good educational background, social stature or sex, all the characters are susceptible to harmful ideology. Dudard, Mr. Papillon, Mr. Boeuf and Botard are not only well-educated but also responsible individuals. It is unfortunate, according to Berenger that they have turned into rhinos, the reason being they are not strong enough to resist the false ideology that the rhinos metaphorically represent.

Berenger and Daisy understand that the rhinos have taken over the radio and the telephone lines, and firefighters have become rhinos. The forces of fascism have taken over all the important spheres of society and it would be impossible to curtail their influence if something is not immediately done to resist their advance. Daisy's turning into the rhino is attributed to her disbelief in humanity. She realises that she would be alone with Berenger and even if she does marry him, there is no assurance of a better world unless more number of people join Berenger, which does not happen.

Violence

There is a direct correspondence between the theme of fascism and the destruction to life and property by the rhinos. The play foregrounds fascism in all its dimensions. Though the play begins with a rhinoceros that just runs through the town and creates panic, the second rhinoceros tramples a cat and causes destruction to property. It is this aspect that Berenger points out to, which others do not foresee. Berenger's drawbacks are pointed out every time, and efforts are made to change him, but nobody realises that violence would affect not only a town but it would spread its viciousness in the entire world.

Berenger shows his animosity for the rhinos because they are violent but he does not realise that he is unable to control his temper and slaps Daisy when she sympathises with the rhinos and for a moment turns violent. This tempestuous act makes

Daisy desert him forever because she does not get assurance of his ability to look after her. This situation becomes too complex for Berenger to resolve and he is left alone.

Individuality

This aspect is perhaps the most relevant part of the play because Berenger is able to resist the rhinos only because he maintains his individuality. Berenger is not ambitious and he gives in to alcoholism. Though he is ready to transform himself for his love for Daisy, he is not ready to sacrifice his individualism or change his ideals for anybody's sake. He expresses his inclination to change but not at the expense of his will to oppose anything he disagrees with. He opposes Jean, who he feels is trying to make him conform with the society.

While Berenger's colleagues and his friend Jean turn into rhinos, their exemplary qualities fail before an ideology that crushes their individuality. These people cannot save themselves from the onslaught of the evil forces who gives them false promises. However, Berenger resists the rhinos from the beginning and he does not spare any occasion to speak against them. Nonetheless, he tries to persuade Jean, Dudard and Daisy to remain steadfast with their humanitarian concerns, but he is isolated in the end. Berenger's victory lies in his resolve to fight the rhinos against all odds because he decides not to "capitulate".

Symbols

Rhinoceros

Though the rhinos were initially watched with dread, later on everybody was transformed into the noisy and destructive animals. Berenger is the first person to think about the causes for the transformation, albeit he is the only surviving human being by the end of the play. From Berenger's responses it becomes vivid that the rhinos stand for conformity. He explains that to turn into the rhino is a matter of choice rather than force. The animals not only represent fascism but also the way people submit to violence and power that turn them into creatures devoid of humanity and individuality, which are lucidly explicated by Jean, Dudard and Daisy.

The Cat

Just as the rhinos symbolise diabolic forces, the cat represents the innocent victims of violence. The Housewife's pet's death is not grieved in the true sense of the term, but it is only seen as one that could be replaced by another. The death of the cat is only an ordinary event that is not worthy of respect. The cat symbolises the vulnerable group of people that cannot openly raise their concerns.

Character Analyses

Berenger

The protagonist who is depressed with life and gives in to alcohol to compensate for his disinterest in life. He is in love with Daisy and understands that he has to mend his ways if he has to win her affection. He believes he may not win over her because his colleague Dudard is much better than him in every way. He is unwilling to fit into the normal world and decides to change his habits only to please his best friend Jean and impress Daisy. Each day is a new experience for him because he is not tied down by the anxiety to perform, keep appointments or be punctual for these are habits of conformity. It is this nature of resistance to flow with the times that makes him withstand the pressures of change and join the multitudes.

The initial incidents involving the rhinos do not influence him and he becomes a part of the conversation that discusses the number of horns rather than the reason for the transformation of people into rhinos. Later, he starts contemplating and affirms that the rhinos are dangerous. He trusts his intuitions rather than logic or reason. The news of Mr. Boeuf's transformation into the rhino is his first experience of the change that he sees in human beings. His attempts to change Jean's attitude to humanity prove futile. He witnesses Jean's transformation and gets shocked because he finds that his accomplished friend cannot resist conformity.

The news that Mr. Papillon, Botard and the logician have turned into rhinos makes him disbelieve rationality and logic. Towards the end, his final arguments with Dudard and Daisy to preserve mankind and save the world ends in desperation.

Though he pleads with Daisy to have children with him so that they can regenerate the human race, Daisy's sympathy for the rhinos, however, leads Berenger to slap her and this complicates his superior position. Daisy leaves him for the rhinos and he remains the only human left, but he declares that he will never give up his individuality or his humanitarian concerns.

Jean

Berenger's best friend who advises him to stop drinking, dress well, look cultured and wear a polished look to impress Daisy. He is an intellectual who is the "master" of his thoughts, which means nobody can influence him. Though Berenger agrees to follow his advice, he realises that Jean is more thoughtful about outward appearances and adapting to the world than maintaining his personality or individuality. He takes interest in pointing out Berenger's drawbacks and insults him whenever they go out. He would never accept his mistakes and makes Berenger believe that anything that goes wrong in their relationship is Berenger's fault.

He exposes his desire to prove that he is right always by talking about the number of horns the rhinos have and the species to which they belong. When Berenger later goes to apologise to Jean, he has already contracted rhinoceritis. Jean is assured that rhinos are good and despite Berenger's best efforts to change Jean's way of thinking, share his belief in humanity and fight for the human cause, he cannot do much except helplessly watch Jean transform into a rhinoceros. This incident later preoccupies his thoughts.

Dudard

A successful, young man who has a great future in his law firm, he is Berenger's friend and colleague. He too loves Daisy and Berenger feels inferior to him because of his accomplishments. Though Dudard earlier reiterates that Rhinos do not exist, later he changes his stand. Dudard claims that these animals are as respectable as humans and they are admirable. He believes that it is important to argue whether rhinos are righteous or evil using logic, and reasoning, and being rationale. He disagrees with Berenger's instinctive reaction that rhinos are evil. This probably indicates that Berenger is sensitive and he has little sense of humour. Despite the best efforts of Berenger, Dudard sympathises with rhinos and joins them.

Botard

A former school teacher, Botard is in his sixties. He believes that he is superior to his colleagues and hence he has the right to contradict their opinions. He is of the opinion that he needs to see and interpret things directly because he was a school teacher who possessed a "methodical mind". An active member of the union, he criticises Mr. Papillon who decides to fire Mr. Boeuf from office because he had turned into a rhinoceros. He observes that journalists lie and the newspaper report regarding the trampling of the cat by the rhinoceros is a fake one because the report does not mention the colour or breed of either animal.

He alleges that Dudard is a part of a malicious plot to set up the rhinos all over the town. Eventually, he turns into a rhinoceros and it is understood that he was interested in attaining power by any of the three means—through the union, in the workplace by bossing over his colleagues or by joining the mass movement. His words that it is important to keep up with changing times echo his belief that rhinos are certainly going to overcome and devastate humans and become the dominant faction.

Daisy

The young and attractive receptionist at Berenger's office is loved by Berenger and Dudard. Berenger agrees to give up alcohol and become cultured only to win her affection. She overtly turns against Botard by reiterating that the rhinos are a fake. However, she becomes sympathetic to rhinos and does not prevent Dudard from turning into a rhinoceros. She realises that the number of rhinos is increasing manifold and becoming powerful. This could probably be the reason why she decides not to have children from Berenger in an attempt to resuscitate the human race and join the rhinos. When she decides to change Berenger's attitude to the rhinos and disregards his proposal to share life with him, he slaps her. However, she deserts him for the rhinos thereby accepting the reality of the situation.

Logician

Wearing a boater hat, he visits the café just like others and engages in discussions about logic with an old gentleman. He is considered superior to the others because of his authoritarian demeanour. He teaches the old gentleman about syllogisms and uses a weird syllogism to prove that the old gentleman's dog is actually a cat because it has four paws. He manipulates logic to his whims and fancy. He uses logic to divert the attention of the people from the havoc created by the animal to delve into petty issues such as the species and colour of the animal. He fails to answer the question whether there is justice in trampling one's pet. The logician eventually turns into a rhinoceros but he is identified among the others in the herd because he wears his boater hat on his horn.

Mr. Papillon

Immaculately dressed, in his forties, Mr. Papillon is the head of the department of a law firm. His badge from the French Legion of Honour suggests that he has been in the military. He is far more interested in ensuring that the work in the office is done rather than engage in discussions about rhinos. Even though the staircase to his office is destroyed by Mr. Boeuf who turns into a rhino, he is not bothered about the destruction caused, but he is concerned about the safety of the officers so that work could continue. He turns into a rhino a few days after the office shuts down. Berenger cannot accept the fact that an authoritative figure like Mr. Papillon could join the multitude, instead he should actually have resisted the rhinos.

The Achievement of Eugene Ionesco as a Dramatist

Esslin notices that Ionesco is a "highly imaginative writer" (187), who gives importance to naturalness of expression as much as he considers spontaneous imagination to involve the working of the mind. Ionesco believes that imagination rests on the expression of reality because the artist is a person who experiences reality first-hand. Creativity depends on the ability to explore and discover. To be able to express directly is to be an expert who possesses the ability to apply his art without consciously being a part of the process of creation.

Ionesco considers avant-garde to be the means to experience and not formulate theatre. To break free from the hold of traditional assumptions of a play and "rediscover the one true and living tradition". Ionesco attempts to show progressive movement in the text to express the state of mind of individuals, a feeling, a situation or an anxious moment. Esslin points out the difference between plays of Beckett and Adamov from those of Ionesco that exhibit "condensation and intensification of the action" (189). The plays of Beckett and the Adamov "have a circular shape, returning to the initial situation or to its equivalent, a zero point from which the preceding action is seen to be futile so that it would have made no difference if it had ever happened" (189).

The principal themes in Ionesco's plays range from isolation of the individual, the difficulty a person faces in communicating with others, the helplessness when the individual feels the weight of degrading pressures to the perfunctory conformism of society. The humiliating internal pressures of his own personality wherein issues of sex, guilt and anxieties when he faces dual problems of uncertainty of his identity and certainty of death are also vividly expressed by Ionesco (Esslin 197).

Ionesco mentions in *Pages de Journal*: "I do not write plays to tell a story. The Theatre cannot be epic...because it is dramatic.... A play is a structure that consists of a series of states of consciousness, or situations" that intensify and get knotted and freed to end in a complex manner (qtd. in Esslin 190). Language, for Ionesco, could disintegrate because it expresses a situation where the meaning of the word is stretched to such an extent that it ultimately contradicts itself to mean nothing.

Ionesco finds comedy to be an effective mode to convey despair. Humour possesses the innate capacity to heighten the effect of a dreadful situation. Logic reveals itself in the irrationality of the absurd, which is significant. The intensity of the tragedy of existence is heightened when it is presented through comedy because it imparts the strength to cope with the tragic situation.

Ionesco considers the ability to convey the basic experiences of humanity crucial because this feature contributes to all other forms of artistic expression. Ionesco is adept at technical inventiveness that would facilitate him to achieve his end in the best possible manner. Esslin quotes Alan Bosquet who identifies thirty-six "recipes of the comic" such as "loss of identity of characters, negation of action, the misleading title, mechanical surprise, repetition...abolition of chronological sequence... doubles, discontinuity of dialogue...use of foreign languages... degeneration of language" in the dramas of Ionesco (196).

Certain other distinguishing features of Ionesco's plays include "animation and proliferation of objects, the loss of homogeneity of individual characters who change their names in front of the audience,...the use of offstage dialogue to suggest the isolation of the individual in a sea of irrelevant small talk...the use of onstage metamorphosis" and several others (Esslin 196). The use of all these features serve several purposes and his theatre has two vital themes: protest against the mechanical, bourgeois culture and the loss of values that ends in the degradation of life. Moreover, he feels that human beings no longer express a revered dread of facing their own existence (Esslin 196).

Ionesco is a dramatist who has imbibed the spirit of the age, wherein he stands as an eminent figure, who shows the extent to which an individual finds himself in a world that seems unreasonable not because of his faults but because of the ability to seep into the world of indecisiveness. The hallmark of the dramatist is not so much to depict an ordinary struggling individual within his circumstances but a person who faces the tragedy of existence realising the desperate and harsh realities of the human condition and tries to find a way out of his anguished existence.

Conclusion

Eugene Ionesco is one of the most effective dramatists to have expressed the anguish of modern man on stage in a unique manner. His depiction of the situation of man is not to point out the essential absurdity of the human condition from where there is no escape and is forever caught in the continuous repetitiveness of his actions, but a person who seeks a solution to his fundamental isolated condition.

Themes in his dramas reflect the inherent anguish of existence, however the situation presents several options from which the protagonist could choose to ameliorate his situation. Characters in his dramas are isolated but they engage in discussions with others to find out whether a suitable explanation could be given to what they experience on stage. Ionesco does not stand outside the mainstream society to announce his avant-garde precepts, but he is the exceptional dramatist who permeates impediments of communication and pronounces more than could actually be said through language.

Glossary

Iron Guard	:	The foremost Romanian fascist organisation formed by the Romanian political agitator Corneliu Zelea Codreanu between 1930 and 1941 that advocated anti-Communism and anti-Semitism.
ludicrous	:	ridiculous
servitude	:	enslavement
deftly	:	skillfully
susceptible	:	prone to
whims	:	eccentricity
boater hat	:	a summer hat for men
perfunctory	:	mechanical

References

Brockett, G. Oscar, and Franklin J. Hildy. *History of the Theatre.* 10th edition. Pearson Education Limited, 2013.

Crawford, Jerry L., Catherine Hurst and Michael Lugering. *Acting in Person and in Style.* 5th edition. Waveland Press, 2010.

Esslin, Martin. *The Theatre of the Absurd.* 3rd edition. Penguin, 1991.

Ionesco, Eugene. "The World of Ionesco." *International Theatre Annual*, No. 2, London, 1957.

Styan, J.L. *Modern Drama in Theory and Practice: Volume 2, Symbolism, Surrealism and the Absurd.* Cambridge UP, 2013.

Rhinoceros. http://www.kkoworld.com/kitablar/ejen-ionesko-kergedan-eng.pdf

Rhinoceros. Audio Book. https://learningally.org/BookDetails/BookID/HR537#

Chapter 28

Significance of the Theatre of the Absurd

The Absurd Situation

The two World Wars, annihilation of an entire race of people, totalitarianism, disbelief in value systems, the negation of religion and God marked the age of disillusionment and the necessity of expressing the anguish became significant during the twentieth century. People learnt the bitter truth that evil and falsity broke down the inherent organising principle that governed social systems. Certain concepts lost their value and the absurd situation expressed the need to search for the validity of those lost values and the purpose of man's existence.

The disappearance of the absoluteness of concepts coupled with the ultimate realities of man's existence in a world that was mechanical and unpredictable made the people aware of their deplorable condition. The disharmonious condition was marked by a sense of loss of faith in religion and hence the desolation was intensely tragic. The impending disastrous situation in the world necessitated the development of a medium of expression, and the Theater of the Absurd exposed this inevitable condition. The modus operandi to delve into the consciousness of the individual to create awareness of the doomed existence and disregard meaning or articulation shocked the audience out of the complacency of the earlier modes of presentation.

The Endeavour of the Theatre of the Absurd

This theatre reproofs the ignorance of the individual to the ultimate reality of the absurd situation they are in and satirises his rather senselessness in grasping the actuality of the incidents happening around him. The theatre is a social criticism of the endeavours of the individual to come to terms with his situation or try to comprehend his condition.

The theatre exposes the waning of religious faith and showed the individual confronting his basic choices within the basic situation that lays bare an existence stripped of every historical, political and other extraneous trappings of civilization. Man is seen wailing, imploring, groaning and crying to come out of the imbroglio of the futility of existence in the universe that is precarious and mysterious. His dreams, fantasies and nightmares arise out of the depths of his personality that gropes in the darkness of impending doom.

The dramatist of this theatre is acutely aware of his sense of being and his plays project his subjective vision of the world. The subject matter of the plays is different from the depictions of the realistic theater and does not intend to look into or resolve the problems of bearings or ethics. The dramatist refrains from telling a story but by providing a comprehensive vision of a bleak and static situation, he explores how man confronts the situation and the responses of the characters that represent the human race draws in universal appeal.

This theatre of situation rather than the theatre of events breaks down the conventional use of language and instead uses series of images to communicate. Rather than employing well-defined characters, using elaborate stage settings, and a linear progression of thought and action, the absurd theatre probes a complex, and static situation, rendering it through poetic imagery. The endeavour of the theatre is not so much to study the conflict in the play as to expose the workings of the human mind.

The theater does not convey a social message as the Brechtian theatre but project how "nothing ever happens in man's existence" (Esslin 295). The effort is to drive home the point that human life is a ceaseless repetition of activities that makes life static and this could only be presented through a web of images and associations that project the situation effectively. Conventions of dramaturgy are conveniently broken down and the emergent presentation is no more than a pattern of impressions and reflections.

The Theatre of the Absurd does not show the progress of time, but portrays that the element of time is purely an accompanying factor that does not play a significant role, which is in contrast to its function in conventional theater. The fact that the presentation of a complex situation does not necessitate a particular time frame is the reason why the structure of the play only projects a complete situation or condition of man's life that is unrestricted by the element of time. Time is only one of those interacting elements that intercepts with the presentation of the complex situation without taking control over the presentation of the play or restricting the action of the characters. The objective is to present a picture of reality as understood by the individual.

The Greek philosopher Plato (428/427 BCE-348/347 BCE) believed in the ideal form and considered that the duty of the artist is to present the absolute essence is its pure form. The British philosopher John Locke (1632-1704) and the German philosopher Emmanuel Kant (1724-1804) based reality on perception and the inner structure of the human mind, and art was explained as a mere imitation of the external nature. Henrik Ibsen and August Strindberg explored the reality of the mind, which was carried on by playwrights of the Theatre of the Absurd.

Dramatists of the Theatre of the Absurd pondered over questions such as the nature of the feelings in an individual when confronted with the human situation; the basic mood with which he would face the world; and how would one feel to be like the other (Esslin 295). Each dramatist provided a unique succession of images that answered the questions in varied complex forms.

There are innumerable ways in which several theatres project their diverse perceptions into discernible thoughts and render them effectively through dialogue while involving characters that act out their parts within stipulations of language and time.

The Theatre of the Absurd projected poetic images that created ambiguous and intricate patterns of denunciation that evoked a kaleidoscope of sense perceptions through which the individual perceived the reality of the world in various dimensions.

The reduction and devaluation of language, and logical and temporal breakdown of intangible thoughts are the natural outcome of the need to communicate this intuition of being. Esslin observes that the Theatre of the Absurd is poetic, ambiguous and associative and goes beyond prose rendering because it "dispenses with logic, discursive thought and language" (296), but the efforts of the theatre cannot be restricted to such findings because the stage is infused with visual elements such as light and movement along with the peculiar use of language. The result is the amalgamation of all these elements that brings forth ideas, concepts and experiences and draws meaning from the association.

The use of comedy, gestures and language in its varied reducible forms as well as the purposeful turn away from grammaticality and acceptability to explain a situation is the hallmark of this theatre that foregrounded the apparent ineffectiveness of language to wholly present the stark reality of the situation of the characters. As man becomes more cynical about the language he is accustomed to and ways in which language is used to manipulate meaning, he finds that the wide lacuna provided by language and reality is the space where the actual meaning of his existence can be found.

To see the self as it really is in the world is to break down language and the barriers erected by language. Limitations of rationality and language have to be accepted just as the prowess of poetic language has to be acknowledged. This theatre advocated presentation of the harsh reality of life through grotesque images and pictures that neither sensationalise nor evoke harsh responses from the audience but shocked them because they were not supposed to learn a message or understand a situation but they were made to witness their own situation in the theatre.

Through the deployment of incoherent dialogue, unintentional motives, purposeless actions, unspecified aims and unidentifiable characters, this theater presented a rather rude and comic vision of the world. Embarrassment, shame, sorrow, violence and bitter incidents portrayed reveal a theatre that goes beyond the normal categorisation into a tragedy but it combines laughter and horror, a crude mix of the real situation of mankind devoid of any artificial entanglements of drama. The audience is glued to a universe that is disintegrating because it is devoid of a central principle or a set of values that could clearly define it and its components.

The world that is filled with purposeless action, unexplainable motives, insensible communication, ludicrous movements and desolation is definitely hostile and uncanny. Repressed fears, anguish, nightmares invade the thought processes of the audience in contrast to the Brechtian theatre that invited a critical and intellectual approach of the audience. While the Brechtian theatre gave importance to the thinking faculty, the Theatre of the Absurd provided no room for thought or logic because one cannot think in an absurd world. The disjointed patterns of thought are interwoven with the dire need to come to terms with the reality of man's situation.

Man sees a world that is grim, and his fears are true. He can no longer be satiated by optimistic illusions, but the anxiety of being in such a universe needs a liberating force that is set in the laughter provoked by the absurd actions of the characters. The states of mind of individuals, innate fears, decapitated bodies, and internal conflicts are shown and the audience identifies them in their own ways. There cannot be an answer to what is happening on stage, the future or the outcome of the play but the central question is the action of the play and its function. Rather than inviting a series of responses, the absurd drama poses questions to each individual in the audience thereby eliciting an individual response to a single question.

The inherent complexity and perplexity of the condition of the world is portrayed through a series of poetic images that are intense and universal and reveal the psychological truth of state of the human mind. It does not mask the anguish of the characters or develop any truth from the situation. The condition is to experience a living reality in its utmost bareness. The ultimate aim of this theater is to make man face the situation and free him from the illusory perceptions of the world he has formulated. The dignity of man lies in his capability to face and accept the reality of the senselessness, and purposelessness of existence, shirk illusions of life and laugh at the attempt to rationalise anything in the world.

Conclusion

The Theatre of the Absurd differs as much as in form as in its mode of presentation because its objective is not limited to the superfluous changes in man due to circumstances related to associations with social and political structures but with the inner consciousness of man in respect of his connection with his irreplaceable condition as he has to face an absurd world. Since chances of revoking the situation is impossible, man can do nothing except face the situation and not be carried away by the falsity of life and its appendages. To effect such a stage is to do away with conversation, language, associations, identity, characterisation, plot and action.

This theatre makes the world the stage and human beings the characters that try to grope in the dark, trying to make meaning of the world without knowing that it is futile to search for something which is not there at all. Man's existence is itself an illusion for whatever he claims to have achieved is nothing but a supplement that has no value in the face of questions related to existence. Time, social stature and identity are mere externalities that cast man into the illusion of living. The endeavour of the Theatre of the Absurd is to make man conscious of his existence in a universe that is devoid of meaning and purpose. Man's dignity lies in laughing at his condition, accepting the situation and facing the reality fearlessly.

Glossary

reproof: admonish

prowess: ability

Plato (428/427 BCE-348/347BCE): He is an ancient Greek philosopher. A student of Socrates (c. 470-399 BCE) and teacher of Aristotle (384-322 BCE), he was the founder of the Academy, and is best known as the author of philosophical works of unparalleled influence that has invited critical attention.

John Locke (1632-1704): British philosopher and academic, Locke's monumental *An Essay Concerning Human Understanding* (1689) is one of the foremost and great defenses of modern empiricism. It is concerned with the explication of limits of human understanding in respect of an extensive range of topics. It thus tells us in some detail what one can legitimately claim to know and what one cannot.

Immanuel Kant (1724-1804): He is a German philosopher whose comprehensive and systematic work in epistemology, which deals with the theory of knowledge, ethics, and aesthetics greatly influenced all consequent philosophy, especially several schools of Kantianism and idealism.

References

Brockett, G. Oscar, and Franklin J. Hildy. *History of the Theatre.* 10th edition. Pearson Education Limited, 2013.

Crawford, Jerry L., Catherine Hurst, and Michael Lugering. *Acting in Person and in Style.* 5th edition. Waveland Press, 2010.

Esslin, Martin. *The Theatre of the Absurd.* 3rd edition. Penguin, 1991.

Ionesco, Eugene. "The World of Ionesco." *International Theatre Annual*, No. 2, London, 1957.

Styan, J.L. *Modern Drama in Theory and Practice: Volume 2, Symbolism, Surrealism and the Absurd.* Cambridge UP, 2013.

https://edisciplinas.usp.br/pluginfile.php/4892127/mod_resource/content/2/THEATRE%20OF%20THE%20ABSURD%20BY%20MARTIN%20ESSLIN.pdf

https://www.britannica.com/

https://plato.stanford.edu/about.html

Suggested Reading

Albert, Edward. *History of English Literature*. 5th ed. Oxford UP, 1979.

Banham, Martin. *The Cambridge Guide to World Theatre*. Cambridge UP, 1995.

Brown, Russel, editor. *Modern British Dramatists: A Collection of Critical Essays*. Prentice Hall, 1980.

Drabble, Margaret. *Samuel Beckett: The Oxford Companion to English Literature*. Oxford UP, 1985.

——. editor. *Oxford Companion to English Literature*. Oxford UP, 2000.

Herman, William. *Understanding Contemporary Drama*. U of South Carolina P, 1987.

Fischer-Lichte, Erika. *History of European Drama and Theatre*. Translated by Jo Riley. Routledge, 2002.

Krasner David, editor. *Theatre in Theory. 1900-2000: An Anthology.* Wiley-Blackwell, 2007.

——. *A History of Modern Drama*. Vol. 1. Wiley-Blackwell, 2012.

——. *An Actor's Craft: The Art and Technique of Acting*. Macmillan International Higher Education, 2011.

——, editor. *Theatre in Theory. 1900-2000: An Anthology.* Wiley-Blackwell, 2007.

Kuritz, Paul. *The Making of Theatre History.* Prentice Hall, 1988.

Morley, Michael, editor. *The Continuum Companion to Twentieth Century Theatre*. Colin Chambers, 2002.

Index

D

Q

R